Fascist Italy in the Spanish Civil War, 1936–1939

In this highly important book, Javier Rodrigo examines the role of Fascist Italy in the Spanish Civil War from 1936 to 1939.

Fascist Italy's intervention in the Spanish Civil War to provide material, strategic, and diplomatic assistance led to Italy becoming a belligerent in the conflict. Following the unsuccessful military coup of July 1936 and the insurgents' subsequent failure to take Madrid, the Corps of Voluntary Troops (CTV, *Corpo Truppe Volontarie*) was created—in the words of an Italian fascist anthem—to 'liberate Spain', usher in a 'new History', 'make the peoples oppressed by the Reds smile again', and 'build a fascist Europe'. Far from being insignificant or trivial, the intervention of Fascist Italy and Italian fascists on Spanish soil must be seen as one of the key aspects which contribute to the Spanish conflict's status as an epitome of the twentieth century. Drawing on sources ranging from ministerial orders to soldiers' diaries, this book reconstructs the evangelisation of fascism in Spain.

This book is the first important study on Fascist Italy's role in the conflict to appear in English in over 45 years. It examines Italian intervention from angles unfamiliar to English-speaking readers and will be useful to students of history and scholars interested in twentieth-century Europe, fascism, and the international dimension of the Spanish Civil War.

Javier Rodrigo is ICREA-Acadèmia Researcher and Professor of History at the Autonomous University of Barcelona, Spain. He holds a PhD from the European University Institute in Florence and currently coordinates a H2020 European Project on forced displacements in Europe.

Routledge/Cañada Blanch Studies on Contemporary Spain
Edited by Paul Preston and Sebastian Balfour
Cañada Blanch Centre for Contemporary Spanish Studies,
London School of Economics, UK

24 **Nineteenth Century Spain**
A New History
Mark Lawrence

25 **Falangist And National Catholic Women In the Spanish Civil War (1936–1939)**
Angela Flynn

26 **War in Spain**
Appeasement, Collective Insecurity, and the Failure of European Democracies Against Fascism
David Jorge

27 **Monarchy and Liberalism in Spain**
The Building of the Nation-State, 1780–1931
Edited by David San Narciso, Margarita Barral-Martínez and Carolina Armenteros

28 **Fascist Italy in the Spanish Civil War, 1936–1939**
Javier Rodrigo

Also published in association with the Cañada Blanch Centre:

Spain and the Great Powers in the Twentieth Century
Edited by Sebastian Balfour and Paul Preston

The Politics of Contemporary Spain
Edited by Sebastian Balfour

For more information about this series, please visit: www.routledge.com/
RoutledgeCanada-Blanch-Studies-on-Contemporary-Spain/book-series/
PAULPRESTON

Fascist Italy in the Spanish Civil War, 1936–1939

Javier Rodrigo

LONDON AND NEW YORK

First published 2021
by Routledge
2 Park Square, Milton Park, Abingdon, Oxon OX14 4RN

and by Routledge
52 Vanderbilt Avenue, New York, NY 10017

Routledge is an imprint of the Taylor & Francis Group, an informa business

© 2021 Javier Rodrigo

The right of Javier Rodrigo to be identified as author of this work has been asserted by him in accordance with sections 77 and 78 of the Copyright, Designs and Patents Act 1988.

All rights reserved. No part of this book may be reprinted or reproduced or utilised in any form or by any electronic, mechanical, or other means, now known or hereafter invented, including photocopying and recording, or in any information storage or retrieval system, without permission in writing from the publishers.

Trademark notice: Product or corporate names may be trademarks or registered trademarks, and are used only for identification and explanation without intent to infringe.

British Library Cataloguing-in-Publication Data
A catalogue record for this book is available from the British Library

Library of Congress Cataloging-in-Publication Data
Names: Rodrigo, Javier, 1977– author.
Title: Fascist Italy in the Spanish Civil War, 1936–1939 / Javier Rodrigo.
Other titles: Guerra Fascista. English
Description: Abingdon, Oxon ; New York, NY : Routledge, 2021. |
  Series: [Routledge/Cañada Blanch studies on contemporary Spain] |
  Includes bibliographical references and index.
Subjects: LCSH: Spain—History—Civil War, 1936–1939—Participation,
  Italian. | Spain—Foreign relations—Italy. | Italy—Foreign relations—
  Spain. | Italians—Spain—History—20th century. | Spain. Ejército
  Nacional. Cuerpo de Tropas Voluntarias—History.
Classification: LCC DP269.47.I8 R6313 2021 (print) |
  LCC DP269.47.I8 (ebook) | DDC 946.081/345—dc23
LC record available at https://lccn.loc.gov/2020057729
LC ebook record available at https://lccn.loc.gov/2020057730

ISBN: 978-0-367-69178-3 (hbk)
ISBN: 978-0-367-76237-7 (pbk)
ISBN: 978-1-003-16605-4 (ebk)

Typeset in Garamond
by Apex CoVantage, LLC

Printed in the United Kingdom
by Henry Ling Limited

Contents

Acknowledgements	vi
List of abbreviations	vii

Introduction: Fascist Italy and the Spanish Civil War		1
1	**Fascist intervention in the coup d'état of 1936**	15
	Blind faith 16	
	No turning back 37	
2	**Fascist Italy at war, 1937**	59
	From guerra celere *to 'Guadalahara' 60*	
	A war in the North 81	
3	**Italy, the CTV, and politics on the *National* side**	102
	Fascistisation 103	
	Evangelise by deed 120	
4	**Identity, combat, rearguard**	133
	He wrote, Viva il Duce!, *and then he died 135*	
	The clean and the dirty 149	
5	**A European war in Spain, 1938–1939**	169
	Without inhibitions 171	
	Sacred testament 186	
Conclusion		202

Bibliography	215
Index	227

Acknowledgements

This book exists, thanks to the financial support received since 2019 from the Catalan Institution for Research and Advanced Studies ICREA-Acadèmia programme.

I am grateful to my wife Alessandra, my daughter Melania, and my son Carlos, for the last twenty, ten, and two years of my life. Some parts of this book, originally published in Spanish by Alianza Editorial, were read and improved by Francisco Morente, Ferran Gallego, Luca Baldissara, Miguel Ángel Ruiz Carnicer, Alan Kramer, David Alegre, Miguel Alonso, Xosé Manoel Núñez Seixas, José Luis Ledesma, Javier Muñoz, and Maxi Fuentes. Robert Langham from Routledge and Valeria Ciompi from Alianza made this book possible. Thanks to Richard Carswell and Ariela House for their excellent work translating and revising the manuscript. Parts of this book have been discussed at the Centre for War Studies (University College, Dublin), Università Ca' Foscari (Venice), University of Santiago de Compostela, Complutense University of Madrid, University of Strathclyde (Glasgow), Institute of History (University of Bern), University of Konstanz, the New School for Social Research (New York), Uppsala University, and the Colegio de México (Mexico City). Thanks to Robert Gerwarth, Laura Cerasi, Daniel Lanero, José María Faraldo, Gutmaro Gómez, Marco Maria Aterrano, Christian Gerlach, Christian Büschges, Sven Reichardt, Federico Finchelstein, David Jorge, and Constantin Iordachi for their kind invitations to share my work. I am grateful for all the comments and criticism received.

Above all, this book is the result of my friendship with Marco Carrubba and his generosity.

I spent the early years of my life in the shadow of the Italian Military Sacrarium at Zaragoza, the tomb of the Italian fascists fallen in Spain. I like to think that my walks there, hand in hand with my parents, put the first interrogation point in the question I have tried to answer in these pages.

Abbreviations

AB	Archivo de Burgos
ACS	Archivio Centrale dello Stato
AGMAV	Archivo General Militar de Ávila
AMAE	Archivo del Ministerio de Asuntos Exteriores
AP	Affari Politici
ASMAE	Archivio Storico Ministero degli Affari Esteri
B	Busta
C	Carpeta
CAUR	Comitati d'Azione per l'Universalità di Roma
CIAUS	Corso Italiani Adestramento Ufficiali Spagnoli
CR	Carteggio Riservato
CTV	Corpo Truppe Volontarie
E	Expediente
EIAR	Ente Italiano per le Audizioni Radiofoniche
F	Fascicolo
GAB	Gabinetto
L	Legajo
MAS	Motoscafo Armato Silurante
MI	Ministero degli Interni
MinCulPop	Ministero della Cultura Popolare
MMIS	Missione Militare Italiana in Spagna
MNI	Missione Navale Italiana
MVSN	Milizia Volontaria per la Sicurezza Nazionale
PNF	Partito Nazionale Fascista
PolPol	Polizia Politica
RSI	Repubblica Sociale Italiana
SIAI	Società Idrovolanti Alta Italia
SIM	Servizio Informazioni Militare
SPD	Segreteria Particolare del Duce
UC	Ufficio de Collegamento
US	Ufficio Spagna
USSME	Ufficio Storico dello Stato Maggiore dell'Esercito

Introduction
Fascist Italy and the Spanish Civil War

Fascists. And, what's more, fighters, soldiers, volunteers, adventurers, legionnaires, *ragazzi del '36*. But above all, first and foremost, and as Italians, fascists. They were the more than 78,000 men who, on Benito Mussolini's decision, took part in the Spanish Civil War, the Anti-Bolshevik Crusade for National Liberation fought on Spanish soil between 1936 and 1939. They were fascists who embarked from Italy and took up arms in Spain not only for diverse reasons—surely each Aldo, Giovanni, Marco, Giuseppe, and Enrico had his own individual motive(s)—but also for ideas which they had in common, for shared desires, which were inevitably linked to the identity, both personal and collective, of being fascists. They believed in a cause which required the eradication of the enemy in order to unite the national community. Naturally, they obeyed the Duce's dictates, but, as men raised in the values of fascism, they also obeyed the call of a fascist faith, which grew by spreading beyond its geographical and identitarian frontiers to converge with other counter-revolutionary experiences in Europe. They fought in a foreign land against Bolshevism, Marxism, anarchy, against those without faith and fatherland, the Red horde, and communism. They believed, they obeyed, and they fought; at the end of the day, that was what it meant to be a fascist and that was what their motto said: *Credere, Obbedire, Combattere* (Believe, Obey, Fight).

Of the different interlocking wars that made up what we know today as the Spanish Civil War, perhaps none has been the object of so much analysis as the international war.[1] Italian Fascism's participation is among the topics which have consumed the most tons of cellulose. From military, diplomatic, political, and cultural perspectives, denunciations and justifications, the presence of the Italian legionary air force, navy, and infantry in the Spanish war has lost none of its historiographic importance in the decades since John Coverdale laid the historical and documentary foundations for evaluating it, nor in the years since Morten Heiberg introduced a novel conceptual framework for interpreting it. Judging by the limited opposition that this framework has encountered, it can be considered sufficiently accepted today by the historiography devoted to the internationalisation of the war.[2] There are, in fact, a wide range of sources and analysis, from Ismael Saz's first works to the more

2 *Introduction*

or less official histories published, with their respective documentary contributions, by the *Ufficio Storico dello Stato Maggiore dell'Esercito* (the Historical Office of the Italian Army's General Staff), the trilogy by José Luis Infiesta (under the pseudonym Alcofar Nassaes), various regional studies, sectoral analyses, and even photographic collections.[3] There is a clear tendency to analyse the beginning of the Italian intervention much more than later developments. Nevertheless, it is perfectly feasible to construct a narrative of Italian participation using published archival sources and the writings of some of its main protagonists (Mussolini's *Opera Omnia*, Ciano's diaries, the copiously published Italian diplomatic documents, Renzo de Felice's monumental biography of the Duce, and Paul Preston's of Franco).[4]

Thus, at least in the academic account, the history of the intervention is generally assumed to include, firstly, Mussolini's conspiracies against the Spanish Republic and the diplomatic moves which led to Italian help for the uprising of 1936; and, secondly, the *Corpo Truppe Volontarie* (CTV, Corps of Voluntary Troops), heir to the *Missione Militare Italiana in Spagna* (MMIS, Italian Military Mission in Spain), the largest military contingent from a single foreign country to participate in the Spanish Civil War.[5] There is general consensus on the number of Italians involved. Their numbers peaked in February 1937, when there were 44,263 Italian soldiers in Spain, of whom 18,477 belonged to the Army (which I will generally refer to as the *Regio Esercito*) and 25,856 to the *Milizia Volontaria per la Sicurezza Nazionale* (MVSN, Voluntary Militia for National Security, although I will mainly call it the *Milizia*).[6] A further 5,699 men of the *Aviazione Legionaria* must be added. In line with the figures given by Coverdale, Infiesta, and the *Ufficio Storico*, the total number of Italian combatants who participated in the war was around 79,000, or 78,846 according to my sources—of whom about 45,000 belonged to the regular army and 29,000 to the fascist militias. Approximately 3,700 died and 11,763 were wounded.[7] These figures align with those found in nearly all books published since the mid-1970s.

There has not been much debate about the motives for the intervention. Most general or analytical syntheses of the Spanish Civil War's international dimension, and particularly those which predate Heiberg's work, hardly move beyond the parameters established by Coverdale in the 1970s, namely that Mussolini's motives for taking action to control the western Mediterranean were essentially geostrategic and anti-French. Consequently, the *Italian*—not (or not always) the *Fascist*—intervention had nothing to do with Spain itself, Franco, politics, nor fascism. Its objective was control of the common sea. It reached its high point with the intervention in the coup d'état of 1936. And further developments amounted to no more than the well-known list of Italian military successes and failures, inseparably linked to places such as Málaga, Alacant, Santander, and, most of all, Guadalajara. According to this version of history, there is little of consequence left to discuss, and we can merely analyse the war's weapons and uniforms, some maps, and documents produced by officers or the ministries in charge of them, because the main

Introduction 3

issues of importance have already been studied and, furthermore, there is consensus on how to interpret them. What remains to be said concerns, well, only details.

This combination of elements and interpretations reduces the Italian intervention in the Spanish Civil War to a rather inconsequential fact of history. It was inconsequential as a territorial-strategic move, because Mussolini did not succeed in taking control of the western Mediterranean, and as a diplomatic policy, because it was Germany's involvement in the war that had a real impact, whereas Italy's was a mere pretext for countering French interests. It was politically inconsequential because, accounting to this account, there was no fascism in Spain but rather, at most, a clerical and military authoritarian regime that was parafascist, fascistised, fascistoid, or whichever derivation of the word fascist with the requisite prefixes and suffixes. It was militarily inconsequential, because Italian fighting incompetence in Spain turned Italian combatants into rearguard personnel. With things as they are, it might seem that there are no questions whatsoever to discuss, that the history of Italian intervention in the war is a closed book, an account settled, a matter exhausted. Consequently, a book like this one would serve little purpose. However, that is far from being the case. Furthermore, the existence of an unquestioned historical account is in itself evidence that there is a problem.

In fact, the results of this sort of consensus could not be more unsatisfactory. On the one hand, there are authors who analyse the CTV in exclusively military terms and out of context, ignoring all other historical dimensions and reproducing, for the most part, a conceptually blinkered perspective that is descriptively repetitive, full of prejudices, and occasionally lacking in factual and interpretive originality.[8] On the other, there are those who reduce Mussolini's intervention to issues of geostrategy, foreign policy, and diplomacy. While such an approach might have appeared innovative in the works of Italian historiography and in the first of those published by Spanish-speaking academic historians,[9] today it is repetitive and hardly original. Indeed, much of the literature, both academic and non-academic, considers the Italian intervention in the Spanish war fundamentally and even exclusively as just another element within Italian foreign policy.[10] Foreign policy was undoubtedly an important dimension in decision-making, not only at the beginning of the intervention but also—and, I would say, most of all—at the times when it had to be sustained, supported, and shored up. This international geostrategic dimension is key to answering the questions generated by the Fascist intervention in Spain. Imperial, aggressive, wide-ranging, and crowned by the alliance with a Nazi Germany to which it would tie its final destiny, Fascist foreign policy had, according to the majority of analysts, a particular Mediterranean vocation aimed at countering French and British territorial interests that contributed to the decision to enter the Civil War on Franco's side. Hence, the intervention in Spain is added to the arguments about the construction of an area of Italian influence and contributed to the varied balances, imbalances, or rebalancing of the great powers' military, economic, and

4 *Introduction*

political forces in inter-war Europe. It is thus a fundamental issue. A different matter is to turn it into a central explanatory argument with enough force to swing the entire interpretation of the Fascist intervention in Spain.

Analyses based on geostrategic and diplomatic perspectives are usually problematic when it comes to identifying historical subjects, which they reduce hypostatically to cities, chancelleries, countries or buildings ('France's opposition', 'Moscow replied', 'the Palazzo Chigi's reply', etc.), or, even more commonly, prominent individuals, in what I have called elsewhere the 'great men theory'.[11] According to this way of thinking, the past is the result of individual decisions by leaders anointed with an almost absolute power and a metaphoric character. I consider this strongly personalist perspective to be highly simplistic. It tends to construct actors with a capacity that is more evocative than descriptive who have nearly complete influence over historical processes and events in which they are almost omnipresent. In the case at hand, the identification between actors (Mussolini), policies (anti-French in the Mediterranean), and stereotypes has hindered a more complete analysis of fascist foreign policy. In my view, excessive attention has been paid to the year 1936, to the beginnings of Mussolini's intervention in Spain and support for the coup d'état, leaving the war's central years, 1937 and 1938, void of content—as if the important issue were the taking of the decision but not its consequences, and as if future events had already been decided from the start. To put it clearly, everything was not preordained in 1936. Initially, the intervention was strategic and concerned aid in acquiring armament. It was the failure of the planned coup—as a result of the rebels' failure to take the capital, Madrid, as originally planned—that opened the door to the Civil War. Consequently, Fascist Italy's subsequent massive intervention was not a mere continuation of the original strategy but the result of its failure. Moreover, contrary to conventional opinion, the real internationalisation of the conflict took place between November 1936 and early 1937. It was, in fact, the large-scale Fascist intervention that drove this process. The central factor in the internationalisation of the Spanish Civil War was the despatch of the mass of Italian soldiers. To prove this point, it is enough to note that they were more numerous and, according to some estimates, more than doubled the total of the International Brigades.

A number of stereotypes and methodological and historiographical problems surround this intervention. There are always subtle differences, of course. Examining geostrategy and sovereignty on an international scale in the era of Fascist expansion and the fascistisation of Europe is not the same as believing that Mussolini's objective was to 'stand on a par' with Hitler and 'impress him by his conquests', satisfy his vanity, and become drunk on pride because, despite the mythologising, his aims 'were worldly'.[12] Indeed, a certain stereotypical depiction of fascism and fascists persists, focusing on their theatricality, gestures, vibrancy, and spectacle. The Duce's 'menacing arm'; the dramatic character, 'as befits a good Italian fascist' of Bonaccorsi (the famous Count Rossi, who will be discussed further on); the populism, 'full of courage, generous, unthinking, sentimental, theatrical', of the consular agent in Málaga, Tranquillo Bianchi, 'another Italian Schindler in Spain'—such are the elements which, according to a very widespread interpretation, are identified with the committed and consistent fascist. Daring, outspoken, and bold, he came to Spain to fight for his Duce and, in a mixture of well-intentioned stereotypes and self-justifying propaganda, to save the endangered Spanish nation. On the other hand, the majority of rank-and-file combatants did not feel this 'spiritual' connection to the war and could not relate to this identification, and one must therefore question—if not openly contradict—their fascist identity.[13]

In my judgement, such stereotyping corresponds to a *flabby* way of thinking about the historical nature of fascism. In the case at issue here, it has created at least three derivatives that mutually feed one another, discernible in everything from the most banal pamphlets to the loftiest historiographical treatises: exaltation, on the one hand; temporisation, on the other; and, in contrast, trivialisation. As will be seen, my analysis of Italy and the CTV's intervention in Spain deals with this sloppy way of thinking by examining its members' motives using their own words and their stories. However, great care must be taken to not turn these narratives into an explanatory axis, thus reaffirming the myth of the Italians as heroes in the Spanish war. A concrete bibliographic example that glorifies the CTV as a faithful reflection of fascist identity clearly illustrates my point. José Luis Jerez Riesco, in his prologue to the 2011 edition of Sandro Piazzoni's important book, writes of 'jubilant' fighters, 'with the anthem and songs on their lips', who displayed 'their irrepressible desire to take part in the trenches where a duel over supreme values was being decided, in the face of the Fatherland in flames' and in danger 'of succumbing to the slavery of the Marxist scourge'. Thus, they carried 'the fascist mystique and sense of epic' in their rucksacks, returning to the 'age-old encounter with the Roman roads and imperial cities which their ancestors designed and established'. They came prepared, returning to assist the eternal Spain with their blazing swords, as honorary brothers on the happy road of a Roman and Spanish peace, sacrificed for continental European civilisation.[14] To manage to assemble so many clichés in such a short text is quite the achievement. Yet, despite his exaggerated use of stereotypes, Jerez Riesco's basic argument is one shared by a significant part of the historiography and para-historiography devoted to the Fascist intervention in Spain—that the epopee of the CTV was that of anti-communism.

As is well known, anti-communism was one of the primary elements used by Franco's dictatorship to construct its own political mythology beginning in 1936.[15] Many of these narrative threads have resurfaced in a number of books published since 1989, a reflection of a view of the past strongly influenced by the present and its political prejudices. This is clearly a problem for historical analysis, which ends up owing far too much to the self-justifying narratives of the actors and subjects of the past. This indebtedness then becomes central to the interpretation. Such is the temporisation that derives from the flabby

6 *Introduction*

analysis of fascism. A book like *Dossier Spagna*, which brings together a significant amount of original documentation and excellent sources, is rendered useless the moment it opens with a warning to fight against the communist plague, which, the authors claim, would have spread throughout the world, had the *nazionalisti* not triumphed. In 1936 and in the 2000s, yesterday and today, it was imperative to say 'no pasaran [*sic*]' to communism, as good Spaniards did, guided by Franco—a man, in the words of Pierluigi Romeo di Colloredo, of incredible coolness and ability and extraordinary intelligence, probably the greatest politician in 12 centuries of Spanish history.[16]

In contrast to this fierce anti-communism—which was the source and matrix of the CTV's legitimacy and historical importance—other interpretations have tended towards trivialisation. According to one common line of argument, based on the anti-fascist propaganda of 1937–1939, Mussolini sent troops, technicians, arms, ammunition, and money to Spain in an attempt to become a new emperor of the Mediterranean, including the Balearic Islands. But, because the Fascist troops made terrible fools of themselves at Guadalajara, they were withdrawn from major military operations or placed discreetly in the second line due to Franco's direct intervention. Add to all this a sizeable handful of clichés about the Italians' lack of skills, incompetence, and even cowardice in war, from the defeat at Caporetto to the *Afrika Korps* coming to their rescue in North Africa during the Second World War. Add, too, the hackneyed image of Italian men as sensual and prone to amorous adventures. Finally, add a good dose of a Mussolini portrayed not really as a fascist but more as a geostrategist in the Italian national style, overwhelmed by the circumstances, swallowed by the quicksand of an intervention on which he had embarked with little conviction and which—according to his ambassador, Roberto Cantalupo—he should have put an end to in the first week, making decisions unwittingly and, hence, feckless as to their consequences. The result is a stereotypical depiction of a disastrous, disorganised, and discredited military intervention, of arrogant, perfumed combatants, hated by the Spanish, whose greatest achievement was procreation and dissemination of the Italian race via their genitals.

As will be seen, the Franco regime's propagandists contributed substantially to this image, because only Franco—never Mussolini—could be seen as Spain's saviour, particularly after 1945. Indeed, the dictatorship and its methods of narrative control may have done the most to deflate the importance of the Italian intervention. It is interesting to observe how the same official historiography of what we can now call early Francoism wipes the slate clean of the Italians or encourages doubts about their intervention, and particularly the defeat at Guadalajara.[17] Nevertheless, this derision on the one hand and trivialisation on the other can also be found on the other side of the Mediterranean. There, the story of the '*brava gente*' persists. Italian fighters are portrayed as mainly good-natured, empathetic, and close-knit, and their military interventions and territorial occupations as free of the horrific brutality committed by their allies, be they the Germans in Greece, Yugoslavia, and southern Italy or the (violent, bloodthirsty) Spanish themselves in the Spanish Civil War. In fact, Mussolini's Italy was extremely violent in its colonial operations. While this violence was limited to political killings in peacetime (as seen in most violent regimes when not in a state of war, including Spain from 1949), Mussolini's Italy acted brutally in times of world war and occupation (in the Mediterranean, in the Balkans, in Russia) and of civil war—first in Spain, and later in the four-sided domestic war (partisans, the fascists of Salò, Nazi, and Allied occupying forces) between 1943 and 1945. Nevertheless, it is unusual to encounter a history of this wartime behaviour which links it to the nature of the Italian regime, to its militarised foreign policy, to fascism as a key praxis in inter-war Europe, and to fascism's violent drift which, in its most extreme expression, meant extermination. According to the myth of the '*bravo italiano*', the transalpine combatants, the Italian fascists did not commit war crimes, did not carry out deportations, and did not practise collective violence, not in Ethiopia, Spain, Albania, nor Greece[18]—nor, of course, in Italy; German occupying forces bore sole responsibility for the violence against civilians in the war of 1943–1945.[19] This polishing of the truth is accompanied by a kind of nationalising and de-fascistising of the wars fought during the 20 years of Fascist rule (the *Ventennio*)—they were Italian wars, not fascist wars.[20] I take a competing stance, as seen in the title of this book.

The military and political intervention in the Spanish Civil War can be read in exclusively national terms, as many authors have done. It can also be read in diplomatic and military terms, removing the fascist variable from the equation and turning the intervention into a participation by Italy in the Spanish war, without adjectives, without subordinate clauses, without nuances. It is my dissatisfaction with these readings which leads me to propose other hypotheses. My argument is that the Italian armed intervention in July 1936 on the side of the military men and civilians in revolt against the government of the Second Republic was consistent with the process of constructing a fascist Europe in the context of the continent's progressively authoritarian and fascistising drift, particularly in the 1930s. But the intervention also looked to the future. As Ramón Serrano Suñer was to say after the Spanish war, a 'powerful alliance of Latin and Catholic countries' in Europe was possibly in the making.[21]

This was how the Italian intervention was received within the complex setting of rebel territory, initially when there was no rearguard to speak of and subsequently at a time when political power was being established, of reciprocal political permeation, and—it must not be forgotten—of all-out total war against and from the enemy. Consequently, in Italy, Mussolini and the political hierarchy of fascism were thinking not only about supporting a friend (or the enemy of an enemy) but also of safeguarding their own territorial space and increasing their capacity to wield influence on Spanish territory, in Europe, and in opposition to the League of Nations. To send 78,000 soldiers to Spain to die and kill, to squander billions of lire on the campaign— Mussolini spent the equivalent of a whole year's budget for the armed forces,

8   *Introduction*

about 8.5 trillion lire[22]—and, in a way, to put the kingdom's prestige on the international political stage was also to pursue the building of a new continent, a new Fascist Era. In fact, 1936 represented a radical turning point in European fascisms' policies and aspirations to converge. This was for two reasons. Firstly, the embargo against Italy and its international isolation due to the occupation of Ethiopia ended up drawing Mussolini's government closer to Hitler's Germany, which had decided in protest to reject membership of the League of Nations. Secondly, the end of the Ethiopian crisis was followed, in March of that year, by the Rhineland crisis, when the German government remilitarised the zone in violation of the Versailles and Locarno treaties, thus testing the limits of the policy of appeasement towards National Socialist Germany's irredentist and expansionary interests.

The third big event of 1936, which for many historians made the Second World War inevitable, was Spain. It was there that the first grand international fascist alliance was sealed. The year 1936 was like the first chapter of 1941; common to both cases was the European crusade against the Bolshevik enemy,[23] which would provide a strong narrative for both the fascisms that were defeated in the Second World War and those that survived. The Italian ambassador said as much, in rather explicit terms, at the ceremony to lay the first stone of the *Sacrario Militare* at Zaragoza in 1941—those who had fallen in the Crusade had handed the baton over to the 'heroes of the Blue Division who, alongside the same comrades-in-arms of yesterday, are fighting today against the same enemy'.[24] The Spanish Crusade was the first assault in the new anti-Bolshevik Crusade, in which Spain stood side by side with its friendly nations on the Eastern Front, the *Ostfront*, in order to 'repay the services and sacrifices made' in the Civil War.[25] However, the fact that a story has been widely used in propaganda, by the historiography whose purpose is to legitimise power, and by memoirists does not invalidate it in its entirety; rather, it adds further layers to the ensemble of overlapping narratives which we call the 'past'.

Thus, the intervention in Spain was much deeper and much more substantial than has generally been described by both the Spanish (which treats it as a rather unimportant aspect of the Civil War) and the Italian (in which it is just another element in the analysis of Mussolini's foreign policy) historiography. Perhaps it is not an enigma, perhaps there are few questions left to resolve. But existing interpretations are undoubtedly far from satisfactory. In my view, an intervention which involved so much military, economic, and human effort, spilt so much blood, and shattered so many lives cannot simply have been the result of the Duce's desire to control the western Mediterranean. It cannot have been merely defensive. And it cannot simply be extricated from the political, ideological, and identitarian elements which sustained fascist power.[26] The Italian intervention was vital for the rebels' victory. The sending of troops and supplies and the fascist armed forces' open participation in the conquest of territory, the bombing of military and civilian targets, and the naval war had a significant impact in determining the main features of the Civil War, from both a Spanish and an Italian perspective. Moreover, the experience of war clearly marked a new chapter in the use of diplomacy and propaganda within the framework of the fascistisation of Europe and the expansion of fascism by way of total war.[27] The Spanish war was thus the war which did the most to advance Italian Fascism's ambitions in Europe, in the Mediterranean, in Spain, and in relation to its neighbours' foreign policies, at least before the Second World War. Furthermore, it definitively cemented the inseparable relationship between fascism and war; between expansion, saturation, and violence; between obedience, combat, and belief.[28]

To the extent that the work we do as historians is nearly always a history-problem—that is to say, a way of approaching the past from perspectives which differ from those adopted by other authors, in order to question a particular facet, process, or event—we must be explicit when identifying exactly which problems we are referring to, which landscape we are looking at, and from which window of which building. The history-problem of this book is fascism. And, possible considerations aside, I think it is important to underline how fascism, far from being the object of interpretative consensus, is a problematic issue for historiography. No less problematic is its relation to the other central theme of this book, war. The Italian war in Spain brings together both phenomena as few other examples can. This book thus starts off with at least two advantages. The first is that it examines a power, Fascist Italy, which was explicit in its military, political, and identitarian intentions and, insofar as was possible, was coherent with these intentions. The second is that it does so from the perspective of a disparate but recognisable group of soldiers and fascists, using definable military, political, and diplomatic sources and a rich and complex body of memoirs. Using these sources, I have been able to address questions that include the international dimension of the Spanish war, the relationship between propaganda and the penetration of political ideas behind the front lines, and the Italian combat experience—what is called, in somewhat pompous terms, the social history of war. As my friend Sergio de Molino says, the social history of war is simply an attempt to tell a story in which soldiers—in addition to posing nicely in photos, parading, and fraternising with comrades—kill and are killed, rape and loot, hate and avenge, march under the sun or through the snow, accumulate hours of sleep and fear, and spend weeks reeking of faeces and blood.

In the light of recent studies, and with so much information at hand, writing this book has been a tiring and exciting game of hypotheses and discoveries. I have tried to focus my attention on aspects of the subject which are different and which have been neglected by the predominantly diplomatic and military historiography. I argue that the Italian intervention in Spain was part of a political logic of supremacy over not only the Mediterranean but also Europe. The Fascists knew of the planned uprising of July 1936 down to the minutest detail and acted accordingly (Chapter 1). It was the failure of the uprising—rather than the continuation of the initial plan to support the rebellion—that led Mussolini to despatch an expeditionary army in 1937,

10 *Introduction*

capable of waging a total war of annihilation and transform it into a fascist enterprise (Chapter 2). This is why so much importance was given to political influence, to the extent that Italian fascists could consider themselves to be the inspiration for the structure of the New State and fascism's evangelists— even though the experiences of fighting and the life behind the lines of the more than 78,000 Italians who made up the fascist divisions in Spain clearly demonstrate the variety of interests, aspirations, stories, and memories which every historical process generates, and even more so when we are talking about a civil war and a framework such as that of fascism (Chapters 3 and 4). The changes made to the mechanisms of Italian military and political assistance from 1938 until the end of the war were essentially aimed at bringing about the rebels' victory, because Franco's side was fascism's natural side (Chapter 5) in the context of a Europe heading towards a continental war.

The date of 27 July 1936 marked the beginning of the Italian intervention in the Spanish Crusade, the National Liberation, and the Civil War. A 'new race' was being born for Europe and for the world, the race of 'Mussolini's boys', of a 'heroic and hard' life and of 'extraordinary faith', fighting for a flag not of their own country. They were 'real men' who had understood that by fighting against Bolshevism in Spain they were fighting for fascism and for Italy.[29] Thus began what was undoubtedly the most fascist of all the wars that had been fought up until that point, an intervention beyond Italian soil which unmistakably fits the definition of what Alan Kramer designates as 'fascist warfare'.[30] Kramer's phrase encapsulates fascism's specific way of waging war, characterised by a war of rapid movement, *la guerra celere*; by aggression dressed in intentional, positive, protective, and revolutionary rhetoric; and by a fascination with air power as a violent and lethal means of combat against the armed enemy and of wholesale political cleansing behind the lines. Fascist warfare is further characterised by the convergence of arms and ideas in a political process of fascistisation which accompanied the making of a blood-brotherhood and by the identification among powers of a unity of geostrategic, ideological, cultural, identitarian, and political interests, in the service of which they were prepared to make whatever sacrifices were necessary. As Mussolini's son-in-law and Minister of Foreign Affairs Galeazzo Ciano wrote on 22 February 1939, those who had laughed at the Italian intervention in Spain would one day understand that the true foundations of Rome's Mediterranean empire had been laid on the Ebro, in Barcelona, and in Málaga.[31] Far from being insignificant or trivial, the participation by what we might call the 'Fascist International' on Spanish soil must be seen, in European and global contexts, as one of the key aspects of the events of 1936–1939 in Spain which contribute to the conflict's status as an epitome of the twentieth century.

My main hypotheses are based on the aforementioned and can be summarised in a single one: to more fully understand the Fascist intervention in the war in Spain is to more fully understand war and fascism.

Notes

1 The list of works would be endless; they will appear, to a large extent, in this book's endnotes. There are various articles summarising the Italian literature, such as Marco Puppini, 'Las difíciles cuentas con el pasado. Bibliografía italiana reciente sobre la Guerra Civil española', *Studia Storica. Historia Contemporánea*, no. 32 (2014): 385–399; and Miguel I. Campos, 'La historiografía en torno a la internacionalización de la Guerra Civil española (1936–1939): el caso italiano', *Ab Initio*, no. 3 (2011): 119–141. An excellent review of some of the big debates stirred up in the 1970s by the books which were forerunners to the studies on Fascist imperial policy and the Spanish war is Denis Smyth, 'Duce Diplomatico', *The Historical Journal*, no. 21/4 (1978): 981–1000. For an introduction to fascist memoirs and several of the official books on the war, see Marco Carrubba, 'La memoria del Cuerpo de Tropas Voluntarias en las publicaciones del régimen fascista y en las biografías de los voluntarios', in *I Encuentro de Jóvenes Investigadores en Historia Contemporánea da la Asociación de Historia Contemporánea*, eds. Óscar Aldunate León and Iván Heredia Urzáiz (Zaragoza: Prensas Universitarias de Zaragoza, 2008) (electronic resource). Nadia Torcellan, *Gli italiani in Spagna. Bibliografia della guerra civile spagnola* (Milan: Franco Angeli, 1988) is the most complete review of the literature up until its 1988 publication date.

2 John Coverdale, *La intervención fascista en la Guerra Civil española* (Madrid: Alianza Editorial, 1979). Morten Heiberg, *Emperadores del Mediterráneo. Franco, Mussolini y la guerra civil española* (Barcelona: Crítica, 2004).

3 José Luis Alcofar Nassaes [José Luis Infiesta], *CTV. Los legionarios italianos en la Guerra Civil Española* (Barcelona: Dopesa, 1972); by the same author, *La aviación legionaria en la guerra española* (Barcelona: Euros, 1976) and *La marina italiana en la guerra de España* (Barcelona: Euros, 1975). The volumes by Alberto Rovighi and Filippo Stefani are essential, more for the narrative reconstructions they contain than as interpretive guides: *La partecipazione italiana alla guerra civile spagnola* (Rome: USSME, 1992). Nevertheless, several works published by the same Historical Office of the Italian Army fail to include the Spanish war, such as *L'esercito italiano: dal primo tricolore al primo centenario* (Rome: USSME, 1961). An excellent photographic collection can be found in *Francone: La Mirada de Mussolini en la guerra de España* (Zaragoza: Gobierno de Aragón, Departamento de Educación, Cultura y Deporte, 2009).

4 Of the nine volumes of the Duce's biography I have mainly used Renzo de Felice, *Mussolini il Duce. II. Lo Stato totalitario (1936–1940)* (Turin: Einaudi, [1981] 1996). Paul Preston devotes considerable attention to Mussolini's participation in the war in his biography of Franco, *Franco, 'Caudillo de España'* (Barcelona: Grijalbo, 1994). Generally speaking, the most convenient (and also the most laborious) way of knowing the Duce's thinking is to turn to his collected works: Duilio Susmel and Edoardo Susmel, eds., *Opera Omnia di Benito Mussolini*, 44 volumes (Florence/Rome: La Fenice, 1951–1963 and 1978–1981).

5 Christopher Othen, *Franco's International Brigades: Adventurers, Fascists and Christian Crusaders in the Spanish Civil War* (New York: Columbia University Press, 2013); Enrique Moradiellos, *El reñidero de Europa. Las dimensiones internacionales de la Guerra Civil española* (Barcelona: Península, 2001).

6 A first approach to this topic can be found in Camilla Poesio, *Reprimere le idee, abusare del potere. La Milizia e l'instaurazione del regime fascista* (Rome: Quaderni della Fondazione Luigi Salvatorelli, 2010).

7 As will be seen, there is no agreement on the exact figure, though it varies little, from the 3,189 given by Coverdale to the 4,000 indicated by Alcofar Nassaes in *Los legionarios italianos* and by Francesco Belforte in *La guerra civile di Spagna* (Milan: ISPI, 1938). The official figures on burials speak of some 3,400, to whom the missing and those who died of their wounds in Spain should be added—3,796 casualties, according to Dimas Vaquero, *Credere, Obbedire, Combattere. Fascistas italianos en la Guerra Civil española* (Zaragoza: Mira, 2009), 180. A summary can be found in a short synthesis without notes and primary

12 Introduction

sources by José Miguel Campo Rizo, *La ayuda de Mussolini a Franco en la Guerra Civil española* (Madrid: Arco Libros, 2009), 28.

8 An example is Carlos Muria, Carlos Castañón, and José María Manrique, *Militares italianos en la Guerra Civil española. Italia, el fascismo y los voluntarios en el conflicto español* (Madrid: La Esfera de los Libros, 2010). It is a tendentious book with almost no references, no notes, a conceptual vocabulary characteristic of propaganda (specifically, that of the insurgent side), and a bibliography that is brazenly disdainful of professional historiography.

9 See, above all, the doctoral thesis by Ismael Saz, published as *Mussolini contra la Segunda República: Hostilidad, conspiraciones, intervención* (Valencia: Alfons de Magnànim, 1986). The same line of investigation led to the collective volume of conference proceedings entitled *Italia y la Guerra Civil Española: Simposio celebrado en la Escuela Española de Historia y Arqueología de Roma* (Madrid: CSIC, 1986). More recent are Ismael Saz, 'Fascism and Empire: Fascist Italy against Republican Spain', *Mediterranean Historical Review* 13, nos. 1–2 (1998): 116–134; and, by the same author, the chapter 'El fascismo y la Guerra Civil española', in *Las caras del franquismo* (Granada: Comares, 2013).

10 Among others, see Angelo Panebianco, *La politica estera italiana: un modello interpretativo* (Bologna: Il Mulino, 1977); and Carlo María Santoro, *La politica estera di una media potenza. L'Italia dall'Unità ad oggi* (Bologna: Il Mulino, 1991).

11 Javier Rodrigo, 'Su Majestad la Guerra. Debates sobre la Primera Guerra Mundial en el siglo XXI', *Historia y Política*, no. 32 (2014): 17–45.

12 Vaquero, *Credere, Obbedire, Combattere*, 19, 12, and 24. Without disparaging an amenable and at times very useful study, it must be said that Vaquero's work is hampered by a sometimes stereotypical vision of fascist politics and, most importantly, constant mistakes in transcriptions from the Italian.

13 Ibid., 14, 44, 143, 144, and 137, respectively.

14 José Luis Jerez Riesco, 'Prólogo', in Sandro Piazzoni, *Las Flechas Negras en la guerra de España (1937–1939)* (Molins de Rei: Ediciones Nueva República, 2011), 8 and 12. I will refer further on to the original 1939 edition of Piazzoni's book, quoted in chapter 3, which was unenriched by such a moving prologue.

15 Hugo García, 'Historia de un mito político: el *peligro comunista* en el discurso de las derechas españolas (1918–1936)', *Historia Social*, no. 51 (2005): 3–20; and Rafael Cruz, '¡Luzbel vuelve al mundo! Las imágenes de la Rusia soviética y la acción colectiva en España', in *Cultura y movilización en la España contemporánea*, eds. Rafael Cruz and Manuel Pérez Ledesma (Madrid: Alianza, 1997), 273–304.

16 Licio Gelli and Antonio Lenoci, *Dossier Spagna. Gli italiani nella guerra civile (1936–1939)* (Bari: Giuseppe Laterza, 1995), 7, a book so tendentious that it does not even mention the participation of Italian planes in the bombing of Gernika. No less tendentious is Pierluigi Romeo di Colloredo, *Frecce Nere! Le camicie nere in Spagna 1936–1939* (Genoa: Clu, 2012), a book riddled with inaccuracies, value judgements, and apologias disguised as objective facts. Also highly biased and limited is Massimiliano Griner, *I ragazzi del '36. L'avventura dei fascisti italiani nella Guerra Civile Spagnola* (Milan: Rizzoli, 2006); according to the author, there was nothing but Bolshevisation, revolutionary violence, and Red terror in the civil conflict in Spain, and these were some of the main reasons behind the Italian intervention.

17 I have analysed this in Javier Rodrigo, *Cruzada. Paz. Memoria. La Guerra Civil en sus relatos* (Granada: Comares, 2013).

18 David Bidussa, 'Il mito del bravo italiano', in *Crimini di guerra. Il mito del bravo italiano tra repressione del ribellismo e guerra ai civili nei territori occupati*, ed. Luigi Borgomaneri (Milan: Guerini e Associati, 2006), 113–132.

19 Familiarity with the literature which has contributed the most to redefining the debate on violence in Italy at war (civil war, in my view) is essential: Claudio Pavone, *Una guerra civile. Saggio storico sulla moralità nella Resistenza* (Turin: Bollati Boringhieri, 1991); Lutz Klinkhammer, *Stragi naziste in Italia, 1943–1944* (Rome: Donzelli, 2006); Paolo Pezzino, *Anatomia di un massacro. Controversia sopra una strage nazista* (Bologna: Il Mulino, 2007);

Introduction 13

Michele Battini and Paolo Pezzino, *Guerra ai civili. Occupazione tedesca e politica del massacro. Toscano 1944* (Venice: Marsilio, 1997); Gianluca Fulvetti and Francesca Pelini, eds., *La politica del massacro. Per un atlante delle stragi naziste in Toscana* (Naples: L'ancora del Mediterraneo, 2006); Toni Rovatti, *Leoni vegetariani. La violenza fascista durante la RSI* (Bologna: CLUEB, 2011); and, above all, Luca Baldissara and Paolo Pezzino, *Il massacro. Guerra ai civili a Monte Sole* (Bologna: Il Mulino, 2009). In Spanish, see Camilla Poesio, 'La violencia en la Italia fascista: un instrumento de transformación política', in *Políticas de la violencia. Europa, siglo XX*, ed. Javier Rodrigo (Zaragoza: Prensas Universitarias de Zaragoza, 2014), 81–115.

20 The best vaccine against this syndrome is Giorgio Rochat, *Le guerre italiane 1935–1943. Dall'impero d'Etiopia alla disfatta* (Turin: Einaudi, 2005); along with Davide Rodogno, *Fascism's European Empire: Italian Occupation during the Second World War* (Cambridge: Cambridge University Press, 2006).

21 Archivio Storico Ministero degli Affari Esteri (hereafter ASMAE), AP, b58.

22 Brian Sullivan, 'Fascist Italy's involvement in the Spanish Civil War', *Journal of Modern History*, no. 59 (1995): 697–727.

23 Judith Keene, *Fighting for Franco: International Volunteers in Nationalist Spain during the Spanish Civil War, 1936–1939* (London: Hambledon Continuum, 2007), 2: 'Just as outside Spain the Republic appealed to the Left, so Franco and the Nationalists were a powerful symbol for pious Catholics, crypto-Nazis, aspiring fascists, old-style conservatives and anti-Semites of every stripe.' I have mainly consulted the Spanish edition, *Luchando por Franco. Voluntarios europeos al servicio de la España fascista, 1936–1939* (Barcelona: Salvat, 2002).

24 Archivio Storico Ministero degli Affari Esteri, AP, b61.

25 Juan Manuel de la Aldea, 'La escuadrilla azul', quoted in Archivo del Ministerio de Asuntos Exteriores, AB, L5162, C2 (hereafter AMAE).

26 This is one of the major components of comparison between fascisms, as emphasised by Ferran Gallego in *El evangelio fascista. La formación de la cultura política del franquismo (1930–1950)* (Barcelona: Crítica, 2014); and as Giulia Albanese reminds us in 'Comparare i fascismi. Una riflessione storiografica', *Storica*, nos. 43–44–45 (2009): 313–343.

27 For the concept of fascistization and its application to Spain, I draw on Ferran Gallego, 'Fascismo, antifascismo y fascistización. La crisis de 1934 y la definición política del periodo de entreguerras', in *De un Octubre a otro. Revolución y fascismo en el periodo de entreguerras, 1917–1934*, eds. José Luis Martín Ramos and Alejandro Andreassi (Barcelona: El Viejo Topo, 2010), 281–354. See also, by the same author, *Ramiro Ledesma Ramos y el fascismo español* (Madrid: Síntesis, 2005); 'Ángeles con espadas: algunas observaciones sobre la estrategia falangista entre la Revolución de Octubre y el triunfo del Frente Popular' and 'La realidad y el deseo: Ramiro Ledesma en la genealogía del franquismo', both in *Fascismo en España. Ensayos sobre los orígenes sociales y culturales del franquismo*, eds. Ferran Gallego and Francisco Morente (Barcelona: El Viejo Topo, 2005), 179–209 and 253–447, respectively. From a different perspective, which categorises Spain as not a fascist regime but a fascistised one, see Ismael Saz, 'El franquismo: ¿régimen autoritario o dictadura fascista?', *El Régimen de Franco (1936–1975). Política y relaciones exteriores*, eds. Javier Tusell et al. (Madrid: UNED, 1993), vol. 1, 189–201. For a general perspective, but one which misses the opportunity to understand the case of Spain, see Aristotle Kallis, '"Fascism", "Para-Fascism" and "Fascistization": on the similarities of three conceptual categories', *European History Quarterly* 33, no. 2 (2003): 219–249. See also Eduardo González Calleja, 'La violencia y sus discursos: los límites de la "fascistización" de la derecha española durante el régimen de la Segunda República', *Ayer*, no. 71 (2008): 85–116; Miguel Ángel del Arco Blanco, 'El secreto del consenso en el régimen franquista: cultura de la victoria, represión y hambre', *Ayer*, no. 76 (2009): 245–268, in which the author defends the use of the term 'parafascism' for Spain. For the intense debate between these authors, see the website of the 'Seminario Interuniversitario de Investigadores del Fascismo', http://seminariofascismo.wordpress.com.

14   *Introduction*

28 On this point, as on nearly every other, Enzo Collotti's intuitions stand out. See his *Fascismo, fascismi* (Florence: Sansoni, 1989), 56.

29 *Frecce Nere. Epopea Fascista nella Spagna insanguinata*, supplement to *Excelsior*, no. 28, 7 July 1938, 4.

30 Alan Kramer, *Dynamic of Destruction: Culture and Mass Killing in the First World War* (Oxford: Oxford University Press, 2007), 329. It is also clear that the Spanish war was a fascist war from the Italian perspective, according to Ismael Saz, *Las caras del franquismo*, 47.

31 Galeazzo Ciano, *Diario 1937–1943*, unabridged edition ed. Renzo de Felice (Milan: Rizzoli, 2004); also 257–258 in the Spanish edition (Barcelona: Crítica, 2004).

1 Fascist intervention in the coup d'état of 1936

It was the seventh month of 1936, the fourteenth year of the Fascist Era, when the coup d'état in Spain erupted. In the days beforehand, Mussolini was travelling around Italy. And, if we follow his declarations on the dates when the first news arrived from North Africa and the Iberian Peninsula, it would seem that the coup was something totally alien to his concern.[1] However, although it remains within the realm of conjecture, there are signs that point to what he was doing. Curiously, for a man with so full and intense a schedule, based on the activity recorded by the compilers of his *Opera Omnia* (complete works), the Duce had no public engagements between 15 July, when he delivered his famous speech on the '*bandera bianca*' (white flag) raised by '*sanzionismo mondiale*' (global sanctioning), and his first trips in August, which began on the fourth. In all that time, he made no reference whatsoever to Spain, but he referred repeatedly to the Italian Empire in Africa. And, from that, an interpretative inference can be made. In Mussolini's speech in Avellino on 30 August, Africa appears as the context for rejecting 'perpetual peace' as an absurdity; for describing the Geneva Disarmament Conference as a catastrophic failure; for emphasising that the Empire had not been born out of compromise or diplomacy but out of the glorious and victorious battles against an 'almost universal' coalition of states; and for reminding his audience that the Italian maxim of the Fascist Era was to be strong, always stronger, strong enough to face any circumstances and look the future in the eye.

He did not mention Spain, but Mussolini could not claim ignorance. Firstly, he was promptly informed of what was happening on the Iberian Peninsula and in Africa by his consular network, Ciano's ministry, and the *Servizio Informazioni Militare* (SIM, Military Information Service). Moreover, he had full access to the European media and its day-by-day reporting on the events in Spain and their repercussions for the political situations in other countries. Above all, however, Mussolini could not claim ignorance because he was aware that preparations for the July coup had been going on for some time. Indeed, he himself and his government's services helped bring it to fruition. It may not have acquired its final shape until 1936, but it is increasingly evident that, in order to understand the complexity of what happened that summer, one must look back at least two years to the summer of 1934. Agreements

16 *Fascist intervention in coup d'état of 1936*

and contracts existed from that time to help the anti-Republican political forces with their plans to overthrow the regime. We should bear in mind that much more was possibly known than was said about the conspiracies against the Second Republic. Without claiming an excessively teleological correlation of cause and effect, it seems clear that, at the very least, there was a connection of interests, preparation, and prior orientation—although, of course, this does not imply that the manner, timing, and results of the July coup were already decided. The Fascist intervention in Spain was the result of a complex—though not pre-determined—sequence and juxtaposition of contexts, processes, circumstances, and decisions.

Some of these decisions, and the situations that preceded them, have been the subject of numerous publications. The literature was already abundant during the Civil War and the post-war years.[2] It has continued to fill shelves and bookshops to such an extent that there is a sort of bibliographic excess regarding the period that begins with those first weeks in the summer of 1936 and extends, arguably, until the Italian defeat at Guadalajara. This contrasts with the little attention that has been paid to the ensuing long months of Fascist military, political, and cultural intervention in Spain. In most works, coverage is as extensive for the first eight months as it is scarce for the following 24.[3] In all this, perhaps the only advantage is that the chronology of the beginning of the intervention has become very familiar, despite the fact that, as Morten Heiberg has pointed out somewhat tartly, much of the historiography, especially the Italian, is limited to 'recycling the viewpoints of Coverdale and De Felice'.[4] Thanks to the punctilious reconstructions available to us, we can be more than sufficiently certain as to the line of reasoning that led to the final decision to send the initial aid and arms, followed by large numbers of troops. However, the overall interpretation of the events is far from a settled matter. Moreover, I lean towards a hypothesis opposed to that of the majority. What took place subsequently in 1937 is usually projected onto July 1936, as if everything was foreshadowed from the beginning, namely the massive intervention in Spain by Mussolini's Italy. However, I argue—and attempt to demonstrate—that this massive intervention was not the continuation of the original plan of 1936 but the result of its failure, or, rather, the failure of the entire plan of rebellion that the fascist powers supported from July onwards. Though by no means exhaustive, this chapter seeks to examine the *what*, the *how*, the *when*, and, above all, the *why* of the Fascist intervention in the coup d'état, specifically from July to November of 1936, by examining its antecedents and objectives.

Blind faith

An imperial, wise, strong, and disciplined Rome; a Rome revived by fascism; a Roman Mediterranean. This was what the hierarchy of the Fascist *Ventennio* aspired to, beginning with Mussolini himself. He dreamed in 1928 of a Roman Italy, wise, strong, disciplined, and imperial, in which the history of tomorrow, which the fascists wanted to create, was neither in contrast to nor a parody of 'the history of yesterday'.[5] For all the hollow rhetoric that it incorporated—common in newly established and year-zero regimes—the Duce's quote leads us to reflect not so much on the imagery that it contains as on how this imagery served as the framework for political strategies, set the coordinates for international action, and established his regime's hierarchy of values.[6] Fascism, the political movement which best took advantage of the governance of an Italy in crisis following its troubled path in the Great War,[7] established a tremendously aggressive foreign policy and made political use of the myth of Ancient Rome and the Empire. This myth would serve to accommodate, in symbolic and metaphorical terms, fascism's place in Italian history.[8] In his first speech before the Chamber of Deputies on 16 November 1922, Mussolini reminded his audience that treaties—referring to Versailles—were neither eternal nor irreversible; they were chapters, not epilogues, in history.[9] Consequently, for almost 20 years, Italian diplomacy and military action pursued the declared objective of carving a niche for Italy on the international stage as a great power, not subservient to the interests of other countries.

Even Renzo De Felice, so inclined to believe that fascism lacked its own foreign agenda, attributes the features of Mussolini's international policy to an ensemble of states of mind, convictions, and cultural motivations specific to fascism and directed towards action. As Mussolini said in a speech during his famous rabble-rousing tour of Florence, Livorno, and Milan in May 1930, 'words are beautiful things, but carbines, machine guns, ships, aeroplanes, and cannons are more beautiful still'.[10] Italy's repositioning on the international chessboard after the Great War, its Mediterranean vocation, and the palingenetic myth of Rome combined in the Duce's words with social Darwinism to form an understanding of the development of societies—conceived in organic and vital terms—that explained fascism's continental presence. If history was an aggressive struggle between peoples—young and old, dynamic and decadent, revolutionary and conservative, anti-democratic and liberal-democratic[11]—then international politics had to grant Italy the new place it had won through the dynamism of its national revolution. Dino Grandi, renowned as one of the most violent leaders of early fascism and Minister of Foreign Affairs in 1926, formulated strategies of rapprochement with the western European powers using the hallmarks of anti-communism and disarmament.[12] Thereafter, in 1932, Mussolini himself took up the reins of foreign policy. From that moment onwards, Mussolini would set out the ancient claim to Empire.

The first area subject to claim was indeed East Africa, an objective of Italian expansionism since the end of the nineteenth century, under the governments of Agostino De Pretis and Francesco Crispi. The Italian Minister of Colonial Affairs, Emilio De Bono, had maintained liberal policies and signed a friendship treaty with Ethiopia in 1928, but, as early as 1932, he put together an aggressive campaign against Abyssinia. The international context

18 *Fascist intervention in coup d'état of 1936*

was favourable at the time. As De Felice reminds us, the formation of an anti-German front in January 1935, prompted by the Nazi putsch attempt of July 1934 in Austria and crystallised in the conversations between Mussolini and the French minister Pierre Laval, brought with it the question of expanding Italy's possessions and giving it a 'free hand' in Africa.[13] At that moment, and in spite of British attempts at mediation, Mussolini began the tremendously one-sided campaign to occupy Ethiopia. A small skirmish in Wal-Wal in the Ogaden Desert, at the border between Haile Selassie's Abyssinia and Italian Somalia, served as the excuse for the attack. Though Ethiopia belonged to the League of Nations, the first Italian troops set foot on Ethiopian territory on 3 October 1935, initiating a policy of *faits accomplis*.

Thus, the Empire was born and, with it, the institutional order of Fascist supremacy, which was to determine Italy's entry into the Spanish Civil War. Four days later, Italy was condemned as an aggressor nation by the League of Nations. In May 1936, after the conquest of Addis Ababa, and in the face of the British and French governments' incapacity to broker an agreement between Mussolini and Emperor Selassie, Vittorio Emanuele III was declared Emperor. The Italian armed forces, which totalled some 600,000, had enormous superiority in weapons and few scruples in using mustard gas against African troops, despite Mussolini's vigorous denials. As has been investigated in recent decades, this rebirth of Imperial Rome, incarnated by the Duce and Fascist Italy, had more than a few negative aspects, particularly in relation to the violence used in the conquered territories.[14] Italian colonial power inflicted many forms of violence on indigenous people, from expropriation to deportation, from racial segregation to summary justice.[15] Both the territorial conquest itself and the repression of guerrilla fighting against the Italian Army were characterised by the use of poisonous gases, a real and deadly practice that has been denied until very recently.[16] Between December 1935 and March 1936, Italian aircraft deployed on the northern Ethiopian front dropped almost 1,000 bombs, with a total of 272 tonnes of mustard gas. Moreover, on the southern front, they dropped 44 tonnes of phosgene gas, the same type of gas that was used in the trenches during the Great War due to its effect of paralysing the respiratory system. Angelo Del Boca recounts that, during the battle of Amba Aradam in February, more than 1,300 missiles were fired containing arsine, which is extremely lethal if inhaled.[17]

This was the immediate, 'marvellous' background to participation in the coup d'état against the Spanish Second Republic. Until 1996, the Italian Parliament refused to acknowledge the violence and use of gases in the war to occupy Ethiopia. Until then, despite the sources and evidence found by Giorgio Rochat and Del Boca, it had been a taboo subject surrounded by denial and wishful thinking.[18] The catalogue of judgements and valuations stemming from the trivialisation of Italian colonialism extends to the analysis of Fascist foreign policy and, therefore, to the intervention in Spain and is difficult to reconcile with the complexity of historical contingency. It created the metaphorically perfect narrative. Spain was the war which, due to the alliance with

Germany, served as the turning point between the pleasant dream of empire and the nightmare of the world war. This narrative contrasts 'good' colonialism in Libya and Ethiopia with a misguided policy of expansion in Europe marked by the alignment with the Third Reich, onto which Italian Fascism's most sinister inclinations are projected.[19] It was the classic account—Africa was an adventure, Spain a war which would diminish Mussolini's popularity, and Hitler the epitome of all evils. One man's testimony speaks explicitly of how:

> The war in Africa was a marvellous adventure. The Spanish one was a war. The widespread enthusiasm in Italy then began to wane. Then came the contacts with Hitler, who did not appeal to many Italians. And so that Fascist spirit began to decline, until we reached the outbreak of the war, which was the biggest mistake made by Mussolini. The first was the war in Spain: people began to change their mind . . . with the war in Spain, people began not to think about fascism and the Duce in a uniform way.[20]

In fact, against this whole background, intervention in the Spanish Civil War was what served as the link between foreign colonial aggressiveness and military interventionism in Europe. Thus, just a few months after the African triumph, the same month the League of Nations lifted the boycott against Italy, Spain represented an opportunity for Mussolini to introduce a new fascist politics in foreign diplomacy, not dependent on the great powers but founded on Italian power, which would gain, at a low cost, an ally of prime importance in the Mediterranean that would replace a potential enemy, the openly anti-fascist Popular Front of the Republic.[21] Spain represented the link between colonialism and fascistisation.

The chain of command was short and consisted essentially of the Duce and Ciano, with barely any input from the monarch, Victor Emmanuel III, who was kept out of the major decisions of 1935 and 1936. Although it had been born of a collective spirit, as the jurist and journalist Giuseppe Bottai (a heavyweight in the regime, director of *Critica Fascista*, Minister of Education, Mayor of Rome, and member of the Fascist Grand Council) would say, Fascism's personalist drift in the 1930s brought with it decisions that affected the regime and its policy. For example, Mussolini did not inform the Fascist Grand Council of the decision to intervene in Spain until after he had concluded the agreement with the insurgents of July 1936. (The Grand Council applauded the decision nevertheless.) Like the exaltation of the myth of the Roman Empire and the pageantry of the Emperor Augustus, his recent successful run in foreign policy accelerated the concentration of power in the person of Mussolini. In 1933, he convened his Council of Ministers 72 times; in 1936, only four times.[22] This was the result of relegating the influence of military officials, politicians, and diplomats to a merely functional role.

20 *Fascist intervention in coup d'état of 1936*

As the minister Ciano would say, thanks to the Duce, Italy had broken out of its age-old isolation and, thanks to its alignment with the Spanish insurgents, found itself at the heart of the most formidable political–military combination that had ever existed. Nevertheless, this intervention was far from merely geostrategic. In a period of stellar philosophy concerning Italian foreign policy initiatives, especially between 1935 and 1943, involvement against the Spanish Second Republic fits well with the logic of fascism—the fusing of myth and reality, identity and geostrategy, assimilation and violence. There are, however, important nuances here as well. Following the successful African campaign, not all opinions in Mussolini's Italy favoured intervention in Spain. The military leadership, headed by Marshal Pietro Badoglio, considered it necessary to refrain from further intervention overseas for a while. Meanwhile, Ciano was promoting aggressive interventionism in line with the Duce's Mediterranean and universal ambitions, aspirations which left colonialism behind and depended on exporting Italian Fascism to the world—the 'fascistisation of the world'. This was the central aim of Italian Fascism, as can be seen in a map of the *Servizio Storico-Diplomatico* (Historic-Diplomatic Service) entitled '*Fascistizzazione del mondo!*' (Fascistisation of the World!), which was included among the working documents of the *Movimenti Fascisti Esteri* (Fascist Foreign Movements).[23] To turn the world fascist was the task of a foreign policy in keeping with a movement that, while Italian in spirit, idea, doctrine, and execution, had to be, according to its followers, universal.

As the great executor of his father-in-law's (interventionist, aggressive, imperialist, supremacist) decisions in matters of foreign policy, Ciano tended to make rash decisions, according to Paul Preston. As the guardian of the idea of Italy as a great power, he advocated using the diplomatic network to inject momentum into these aspirations, in contrast to the position taken by Dino Grandi. Ciano made use of the ministry for this purpose, especially the *gabinetto*, his closest group of collaborators, led by Ottavio De Peppo. Against this background, support for, and recognition of, Franco's government—implicit from July 1936 and explicit in November 1936—and direct intervention in the war confirmed a logical identity based on the recognition of a common enemy, leaving aside differences of content, development, and success for the moment. However, which enemy was it exactly? Some of the historiography chooses to depict Italian Fascism's intervention in Spain as the 'fruit of the anti-communist duty to stop the Soviet Union from gaining a foothold in the Mediterranean'.[24] But, perhaps more than Soviet influence, it aimed to block that of the anti-fascist Popular Front. More than the risk, in almost propagandistic terms, of communist expansion, the Duce may have feared the loss of political hegemony in the face of a potential common front between the French and Spanish Popular Fronts in the western Mediterranean and of potential territorial hegemony in the east, threatened by the presence of British fleets to ensure the 'guarantees' of support for Greece, Turkey, and Yugoslavia. For Aristotle Kallis, behind all this was a further aim to expel British power, beginning with its control of the Straits of Gibraltar.[25] In any

Fascist intervention in coup d'état of 1936 21

case, the fascist war involved the bringing together of different factors.[26] Moreover, it had an explicit and preventive defensive interest. In fact, in the secret protocol between Italy and Franco's Spain, signed on 28 November 1936, the Italian government and army agreed to respect Spain's territorial integrity in the event of a continental conflict, in exchange for which French colonial troops would not be allowed to cross Spanish territory. Thus, as Mussolini would say, no black soldier could use this route to come to the defence of metropolitan France. And this view ended up becoming canonical. In fact, for De Felice—the progenitor of a large part of the interpretations accepted by Italian historiography in this area (and mentor of many of its members)— Italy played no role in the conception and preparation of the military uprising. Its intervention had no ideological character, nor did it aim to install a fascist-style regime in Spain. It was motivated, essentially, by traditional politico-strategic reasons, namely to prevent Spain from allying itself with France and allowing the Balearic Islands to be used as a bridge for transporting African troops to metropolitan France.[27] It was all about ensuring Franco's victory, so as to gain greater control of the western Mediterranean and prevent any French influence on Spain.

Whether or not one agrees with De Felice, it is clear that the destruction of an enemy, the anti-fascist Popular Front, and support for a potential subordinate ally, the New Spain, had the purpose of protecting and defending fascism itself. The first head of the Italian Naval Mission in Spain, Admiral Giovanni Ferretti, said as much when he acknowledged that the idea behind intervention in the Spanish Mediterranean was, above all, to lay the material, spiritual, and informational groundwork for Italy's future naval influence in Spain, based on Fascist 'supremacy'. 'Today', he said, the 'famous Mare Nostrum' was for Italy and its expansion a prison to which they did not have the keys. Collaborating with insurgent Spain would not give them the keys but would force open an exit through Gibraltar and the door to control of the western Mediterranean from the Balearic Islands. Despite the insufferable, quixotic yet impressionable character of the Spaniards, he said, it was important to continue maritime operations even after the war, in order to maintain influence and penetration.[28] It was a question of attacking in order to defend, as propounded by Francesco Belforte. Among his supremacist allegories of a united Mediterranean as a single bloc—held together by the iron grip of two 'sister' nations on the same path to greatness, stability, peace, and a common civilisation—he did not fail to recall how the affinity between Italian Fascism, *National* Spain, and German National Socialism should 'logically' lead to a common political platform, which would include 'healthy autarky'.[29] And its great objective would be the aggressive defence of their common interests, in keeping with their collaboration in arms in the military field and the proud shedding of blood.

All of this had its own origins. Motives in international politics must almost always be understood as part of a bigger picture that goes beyond diplomatic questions and enters the realm of politics, culture, and identity.[30] And here

22 *Fascist intervention in coup d'état of 1936*

the picture included the Fascist conspiracies against the Second Republic. Thus, Ismael Saz, whose work has been corroborated by many other authors, has studied how the history of Italian support for anti-Republican forces was almost as old as the Republic itself. In April 1932, only a year after the proclamation of the new political system, José Antonio Ansaldo met Italo Balbo, the Fascist air minister, to ask him for 200 machine guns to help with General José Sanjurjo's coup. (They were never delivered.) On 30 March 1934, Balbo and Antonio Goicoechea signed another secret pact, by which Spain would receive weapons and money in exchange for rejecting—in the event that the monarchists' conspiracy managed to seize power—any agreement between Spain and France.[31] Though neither of these pacts materialised, other types of political support did, such as the 50,000 lire per month (soon reduced by half, then cancelled in April 1936) paid to José Antonio Primo de Rivera's party, the *Falange*. During the Republic, it seems that Mussolini lent support to the *Comunión Tradicionalista* (Traditionalist Communion), the *Falange*, and *Renovación Española* (Spanish Renovation).

By February 1936, the Italian ambassador to Spain, Orazio Pedrazzi, reported rumours of conspiracies following the Popular Front's victory in the elections to the *Cortes*, though it would not be until the early summer that events would take an accelerating and unstoppable turn towards the coup d'état.[32] Goicoechea himself recognised, in mid-June, that the gravity of the situation, 'the importance of negotiation, and the urgency of the circumstances' prevented him from leaving Spain to continue his negotiations. However, this did not prevent him from asking the Italian government for considerable economic assistance on behalf of his party and also, on a formal basis, for the Falange and the *Bloque Nacional* (National Bloc) in a message to Ernesto Carpi. The one million pesetas he requested were not granted. What is of interest here is that Goicoechea included a detailed report of the situation with his request. The fact that the Italian government had knowledge of the contents of this report, in addition to other information, in itself gives the lie to the idea that nothing was known in Rome about the conspiracy prior to 18 July. The report included an explanation of how the electoral defeat in February had given power to 'the revolution' and how the 'anarchic situation' left 'no other path save that of a takeover by force or a violent insurrection'. For the moment, he said, the 'atmosphere of violence and the inescapable need to organise' the insurrection had given birth, 'within the national parties, to small groups which favour direct action and which have acted against the revolution by attacking people, assaulting buildings, and so on'. Many of these groups called themselves 'fascists, and the big increase in young people joining the Falange Española is noteworthy'. However, given the lack of vehicles to mobilise them, and the absence of ex-combatant groups such as those found in Italy, in the end, the key had to be with the Army. For that reason, they were turning to Italy to ask for a million pesetas to finance troops 'of an anti-democratic political orientation' in their 'move to regain the nation through violence', to 'stage an urgent coup d'état' that would bring Sanjurjo to power.[33]

Fascist intervention in coup d'état of 1936   23

Thus, the matter was more than a rumour. The preparation of the coup d'état was already common knowledge in Rome in June. The Fascist government knew of its final form at least a day before the uprising,[34] although the SIM had obtained information earlier in June about the 'imminent' character of the 'military and Falangist movement'.[35] And it certainly knew of its precise and definitive form on 18 July. The archives of the Ministry of Foreign Affairs in Rome house the complete series of telegrams that reached Rome relaying the different pieces of information about the uprising. These telegrams begin on 18 July 1936 itself,[36] when the Italian consulate transmitted Franco's first proclamations: 'Glory to the heroic Army of Africa. Spain above all else. . . . Blind faith in victory. Long live Spain with honour.' Blind faith, Spain with honour, above all else—this was the language that persisted in the following days in a series of coded telegrams from Tétouan or from the embassy in Madrid on the 'Situation in Spain'. More than a few readings can be deduced regarding the unfolding of the events, how the Fascist regime perceived them, the chain of command that was revealed by the coup d'état, and, last but not least, the language used for the occasion.

It was a situation that was marked, naturally, by a movement said to have 'both a military and a civilian character' and to be sponsored by all the united forces of the Right and by many commanders of military garrisons in provincial towns. Led by General Sanjurjo (who resided in Lisbon but, according to the telegram, had already left for Spain, which we know was not true), and with the full agreement of the command of the Foreign Legion—already in rebellion on Moroccan territory—the movement gathered together the heads of the monarchist parties, who, it was said, had been joined by José María Gil Robles after a meeting with the Carlist leader Manuel Fal Conde in Saint-Jean-de-Luz. They made up a disparate group, to which the Italian ambassador (on summer holiday with part of his staff in Donostia) gave a name that, when seen in perspective, was highly peculiar—'*i rivoluzionari*', 'the revolutionaries'.

Their plans were clear by 18 July, according to the information in the ambassador's possession:

> The Revolutionaries' plan is as follows: uprising of the 'Foreign Legion' in Morocco (already happened); passage of the Legion to Málaga on warships, which were due to have left two days ago to take them and transport them to Spain. March by the rebels on Madrid and, at the same time, uprisings by the garrisons in Burgos, Valladolid, and Pamplona under the command of General Mola, Sanjurjo's deputy. If the government yields and [if] it would be desirable that control of the country [missing text], the movement would limit itself to this programme; otherwise, action would be taken by numerous civilian elements and above all traditionalist military formations, who have the training and disposition to fight in order to take Madrid by force.

Pedrazzi had a great deal of highly precise information, especially if we consider that the formal request for help addressed to Mussolini's Italy was very much concerned with ferrying the Foreign Legion to Andalusia. The conventional account of the Fascist intervention in Spain has almost always been based on the idea that either nothing was known of what was going on and the rebellion forced immediate decisions to be taken, or, if anything was known, it amounted to very little. This telegram, which Ismael Saz also cites, but to which little importance has been attached,[37] refutes both ideas. Pedrazzi knew of the strength of the uprising and the powerful civilian plot. He knew of the capability of the Carlist militiamen (*Requetés*) to attack Madrid if the coup failed as a whole. He knew that the uprising would occur in the North the following day, in order to direct the government's attention towards the events in the South and thus, in theory, facilitate the taking of the capital, which had some 5,000 assault guards (*guardias de asalto*), but in the taking of which the insurgents were prepared to 'overcome any resistance'. He knew that the military chiefs were in agreement, as he understood it, in the event of victory, on forming an 'authoritarian provisional military government' with an appropriate 'corporative and anti-subversive' character. And he knew that, whether the insurgents were victorious or not, Spain would enter a serious and 'violent period of convulsion'.

There was little doubt about this last point, especially when it came to violence. On the other hand, the point was surprisingly explicit and obvious to Pedrazzi; as he pointed out, the repression against elements of the Left, who had governed the past two months with 'terror and blood', would be relentless if the movement triumphed. Pedrazzi said that the insurgents' thoughts were focused, if not exclusively centred, on avenging the numerous political assassinations committed by government elements, the most recent being the killing of José Calvo Sotelo. The ambassador expanded on this topic and sent a copy of the photo of Calvo Sotelo's dead body to Umberto Grazzi, Director General of the Foreign Press Service of the Ministry of Press and Propaganda. The photo (unpublished, as far as I know, although there are others from the same period taken from different angles) was taken of the opposition leader's dead body in La Almudena. Calvo Sotelo had been a 'reliable and fervent' friend of fascism. The photo could not be published in Spain, but Pedrazzi asked for it to appear in an Italian newspaper.[38] He went on to indicate that, if the movement was unsuccessful, the repression would be equally relentless from the 'opposite side, which has shown itself to be merciless against the enemies of the current regime'. It could not be forgotten that what was at stake were not only the armed forces but also the masses, which had been 'fanaticised by the Left' and, in areas such as Asturias, were already prepared for revolution. There was no doubt, he concluded, that the Spanish democracy was suffocating on its inexorable path towards a civil war and would give way either to a military reaction or to 'an increasingly Bolshevised socialist radicalisation'.

This telegram of 18 July shows that the degree of knowledge about the coup d'état, with its variables, actors, and immediate consequences, was very high.[39] It was detailed, very precise, and reached Italy on the same day as the uprising through the embassy in Madrid. The embassy was a place where a lot of information was exchanged and filtered, although until now its significance has not been fully appreciated. In that same month of July, the military attaché, Lieutenant Colonel Manlio Gabrielli, also received from a trusted source (and passed on to the SIM) the putative programme of the 'revolutionary' movement. And, though it reads almost like science fiction, what it said was not without interest. The document was typed, unsigned, and undated, and therefore highly dubious; moreover, it was annotated with a phrase, '*non mi pare proprio aderente*', which translates roughly as 'this doesn't seem relevant to me'. The remark begs the question as to whether it was not considered relevant to the situation as it really was, to Italian policy, to fascist intentions, or to something else. But it is not a forged document. It is a highly detailed and surprisingly peaceful plan of action for the insurgents in the event of the coup d'état's rapid success. It may have been given to the military attaché Gabrielli in order to influence the SIM—that is to say, Roatta and, by extension, Ciano.

In his memoirs of the period, Gabrielli does not give many clues as to when, how, or from whom he obtained the operational plan. He does indicate that it was before the coup and that Pedrazzi discredited it, inviting him to modify the report that he would send to the SIM and Ciano because, in his judgement, there was no reason to think that there would be any serious incidents in Spain. Thus, it may have been Pedrazzi who wrote the remark about the document's irrelevance. The ambassador was constantly insisting that they should stop sending news about conspiracies, either because he did not believe in them or because he wanted to avoid giving them publicity. At all events, there are reasons not to give too much weight to the speculations by the military attaché staying at the Palace Hotel; his account of the young man who approached him in a bar in Madrid on 15 July to tell him that a coup d'état with Franco at its head was on the verge of starting reads like something out of a novel.[40] In those July days, before and after the 17th–19th, all sorts of reports of civil and military plots were doing the rounds. What is interesting is that, to a large extent, they conveyed the opposite of Mola's confidential instructions. According to the reports, after the declaration of a state of war in the military divisions, the Army would remain in 'a position of passive anticipation', keeping watch 'with extreme rigour over the maintenance of public order'. Provincial civil governments would be taken over by their secretaries. Catalonia's autonomy would be respected 'in its current state of affairs and persons, as long as this region recognises and immediately complies with the new legal order to be established in Spain'. All this was to be done 'with great speed and surprise, to avoid at all cost having to fire a single shot or spill a single drop of blood'.

In Madrid, the same 'general lines' indicated that Manuel Azaña, President of the Republic; Diego Martínez Barrio, President of the Council of Ministers; the Government; the Director General of Security; the Civil Governor of Madrid; and the Under-Secretary of the Interior would be 'taken by a plane of the LAPE [*Líneas Aéreas Postales Españolas*] to the Portuguese border with complete guarantees and respect for their persons, their families, their property and assets'. None of them would be allowed to return to Spain for 90 days, and, if they did, the new government 'would continue to guarantee their lives, as those of all Spaniards, without subjecting them to any persecution or trial or in any way infringing their civil and political rights'. With the government out of the country, 'the office of the President of the Republic will be filled *ad interim* by the first Citizen of Honour named by the Republic in strict order of seniority'—that is to say, Francisco Cossío, already deceased. Consequently, 'Don Miguel de Unamuno will provisionally assume the functions of President of the Spanish Republic *ad interim*' until the holding of 'free and fair elections, first municipal, then provincial, then general elections for a constituent *Cortes*'. The new *Cortes* would reform the constitution and designate the new president. The new government would 'uphold the most recent Amnesty granted to political and common prisoners in February', expand it, and implement 'a rigorous observance of the 40-hour working week and an increase of two pesetas per day for all workers and employees'. It would proclaim 'the freedom to work, worship, education, press, speech, and thought' and recognise 'the right of free association, assembly, and the right to strike'. Lastly, after '48 hours', 'those persons failing to comply with Spain's new legal order will be deemed incompatible with it and will leave the national territory without suffering the slightest persecution or harassment'.[41]

Respect for Catalan autonomy, persons, and the government; no bloodshed; Unamuno as President of the Republic—the contents of this document leave little doubt as to why the plan of action was considered in Rome to be unrealistic. Not knowing who wrote it nor when does not help us to identify its place within the intrigues of the rebellion. But it does reveal that at least some of the rebels were planning a swift coup that, within the limits of what was possible, would not use violence. It also reveals that this faction sought constitutional reform based on continuity rather than on monarchist or corporatist lines. It was open-minded on social issues (the workweek, salaries), though probably as a way of neutralising similar demands by forces within the Popular Front. We know that the key points of this plan were sent to the Italian embassy, but we do not know if the intention was to inform or to facilitate Italian intervention, however much the ambassador refused to associate himself with the contents of some of the reports. Though it cannot be considered more than speculation, it seems to me, at least, that Fascist Italy's embassy in Madrid wielded more weight than has been recognised—if not in actual decision-making, then at least in the circulation of information that led to those decisions.

Naturally, this was obviously not the only information channel to Ciano and Mussolini, just as it would be rather naïve to believe that such a large-scale intervention as the Italian one was the work of a single person or group of persons. However, from the protagonists' memoirs to the most recent research, it is rare to find a study that does not discuss whether it was Luis Bolín, Goicoechea, or Franco himself who secured Mussolini's support. And the question is certainly important in helping us to understand the *when* and the *how*. As early as 18 July, the Italian Consul and Minister Plenipotentiary in Tangiers, Pier Filippo De Rossi del Lion Nero, ordered the consulate's military attaché and SIM agent, Giuseppe Luccardi, to go to Tétouan to gather information about what was happening there. The following day, 19 July, the consul wrote to Ciano that the reports were contradictory, insofar as the forces in Morocco were said to have rebelled, whereas government communiqués denied that the movement had spread to the Peninsula. Other reports indicated that the Foreign Legion's expeditionary corps had already disembarked in Cádiz and that the uprising was spreading in Andalusia. The same day, Franco signed the written request for air support which Bolín took to Rome. A day later, 20 July, Pedrazzi confirmed from St-Jean-de-Luz that the uprising was underway, and the outcome was unforeseeable. In his opinion, this was not a simple military coup like previous ones. Rather, Spain was heading towards a period of 'partisan tyranny', a dark time of blood and persecution from which it would not emerge for a long time.[42] It is not clear from his papers whether he thought that all this violence would stem from the 'Revolutionary' insurgents or from the Bolshevik enemy. But it is clear that either the Italian ambassador was in possession of a lot of information, as we have just seen, or he was a magnificent clairvoyant.

Thanks to General Emilio Faldella's personal archive, examined by De Felice, we know more details of the matter.[43] On 20 July, Franco asked Luccardi for ships to transport troops. This telegram reached the SIM on 21 July, and Roatta asked for his opinion. '*La Spagna è come una sabbia mobile*' (Spain is like quicksand), Luccardi purportedly replied, using what has now become a famous phrase. Italy had much to lose in Spain and little to gain. Defeat would bring infamy and victory a pittance. The formulaic wording of the phrase raises doubts about its authenticity. In any case, it did not stop contacts from continuing. On 21 July, the consul De Rossi indicated that it was increasingly difficult to assess the situation in Spain and in Tangiers amidst contradictory reports about Cádiz, Almería, and Málaga, about government ships firing shells at the population of Ceuta, and about Italians fleeing from a Málaga 'plundered, set alight, and in the middle of a revolution' on board the steamer *Silvia Tripcovich*, following mediation by the Italian consulate.[44] However, on Roatta's instructions, Luccardi (whom Roatta had apparently already asked to stand aside and avoid appearing as the link between the Italian government and the insurgents) relayed to Franco the difficulties of providing him with the air support he had personally requested. (Bolín had

28 *Fascist intervention in coup d'état of 1936*

conveyed this request to Ciano the following day.) Luccardi offered vague and misleading excuses about the 'international political situation' and the 'air service in Ethiopia' during the rainy season. For Franco, as the Italians learned the following day, this lack of support seemed short-sighted on the part of the Italian government, which stood to gain a position of influence in Spain that would otherwise be held by Germany.

That same day, Ciano received Franco's first envoy sent to Rome, Bolín. A correspondent for the newspaper *ABC*, Bolín made sure that his role in securing Italian assistance was given top billing and praised. As is widely known, it was he who received from Franco's hands the famous note signed on 19 July in Tétouan: 'I authorise Don Luis A. Bolín to arrange in England, Germany, or Italy the urgent purchase of planes and materiel for the non-Marxist Spanish Army . . . General in Chief, Francisco Franco.' The note, which underlined the existence of a Marxist army on the side of the uprising's enemies, added under the signature: '12 bombers, 3 fighter planes with bombs (and bomb releases) from 50 to 100 kilos, 1,000 of 50 kilos, and 100 of 500 kilos'. From that moment onwards, all reference books agree on the factual order of events, despite the scant documentary record. After leaving Franco in Tétouan, Bolín flew to Lisbon to obtain Sanjurjo's signature and authorisation of the request for planes and supplies for the insurgents. He took the request to Rome on 21 July, after stopping in Biarritz for a meeting with the Marquess of Luca de Tena. Meanwhile, Franco was able to put pressure on the Italian attachés in Tangiers, particularly Luccardi and De Rossi. On 22 July, Bolín was joined by the Marquess of Viana, sent by Alfonso XIII. Together, they had a meeting with Ciano the same day. Bolín's account is important, although of dubious veracity; he wrote in 1967 that Ciano had proclaimed to them, 'We have to put an end to the communist threat in the Mediterranean!'[45] The next day, however, they were met by a high-ranking official, Ciano's personal secretary and head of the Ministry of Foreign Affairs, Filippo Anfuso. He received them and relayed Mussolini's refusal to provide the help requested. Ciano promised to keep trying and telegraphed De Rossi on 24 July to enquire as to the chances of Franco being victorious. Meanwhile, following a decision taken the previous day (and therefore not the result of Mussolini's first negative response), Mola sent Goicoechea, Pedro Sainz Rodriguez, and Luis María Zunzunegui to Rome.

Goicoechea knew Mussolini. He had met him before, in 1934, together with the Carlist traditionalists Rafael Olázabal and Antonio Lizarza and General Emilio Barrera, when Goicoechea was the leader of *Renovación Española*. This time, judging by the dates, it would appear that Goicoechea brought with him another persuasive factor, a letter from the Modelo Prison in Madrid written on 20 May 1936 and signed by José Antonio Primo de Rivera:[46]

> I see, as you do, Spain's tragic situation and believe that thought has to be given urgently to extraordinary counter-measures. My situation as a prisoner prevents me from taking many steps but not from leading the

Movement, which is growing daily and fully effectively. If, in these steps before persons who are unable to come and visit me, you would be willing to represent me, I would be very grateful, as I have much constant evidence of your loyal conduct as a friend.

Thus, the founder of the Falange made the representative of the monarchist party his personal representative in all political negotiations. The presence of this letter, together with 'photographic copies of the testament' of José Antonio, among the papers of Mussolini's personal secretary, can only indicate that Goicoechea used them to press for Italian intervention, possibly in the interests of restoring the monarchy. No one knows if this was what determined the Duce's view. The problem is that, contrary to how he normally acted on nearly any issue he considered important, Mussolini did not record the ultimate reason for his decision.

In the meantime, information continued to arrive from Tétouan. As the future *Generalissimo*, Franco, indicated to Luccardi, his problems had begun to acquire dramatic overtones. Franco was unable to transport his troops to the mainland. As he revealed to Luccardi (initiating a chain of requests for help that would pass through De Rossi, Ciano, and finally reach Mussolini), this problem risked causing the entire uprising to fail. In order to finally convince the Duce and his son-in-law, De Rossi pointed out that German influence on insurgent Spain would grow if Italian assistance was not provided. That is to say, he indicated clearly how the Third Reich would become the power of reference in the attack on an anti-fascist regime, a role which ought to fall to Italy. In fact, he believed the difficulties were enormous. But they were nothing compared to what they would be, should the conflict, which was 'still confined today within Spain's borders', take on, 'under the pressure of a global revolution', the 'character of a struggle for the supremacy of social disorder over the order that we represent with our Regime'.[47] In other words, he showed how the failure of the coup d'état would radicalise the Left and, with it, European anti-fascism.

Whether it was luck, chance, or Franco's persuasive abilities that acted as the final lever can only be informed speculation. The language of the telegrams sent to Italy from North Africa left little doubt as to whom they were dealing with. Italy's decision to support Franco in July would be a decisive factor in his eventually becoming the highest authority in insurgent Spain.[48] In a revealing example, when Franco moved on to the Peninsula, he left Jaime Parlade as his representative in Tétouan, but the Italian government preferred to send Luccardi with him. On 20 July, he was already described as '*Generale Franco, capo movimento spagnolo*', the leader of the Spanish movement. A day later, Franco intimated his intention to establish (opportunistically, according to Heiberg; sincerely, I am inclined to think) a 'fascist-style republican [government] adapted to the Spanish people', following the 'hard but necessary struggle to avoid [a] Soviet state'. This would lead, in exchange for Italian assistance, to more than friendly relations between the two countries. It

30 *Fascist intervention in coup d'état of 1936*

was a struggle that, in these early days, was beginning to go off the rails. The telegram of 23 July said as much: 'For Franco to succeed, urgent intervention is needed.'[49]

On 21 July, Franco spoke of a fascist-style government; on 23 July, the need for intervention was urgent; on 25 July, the situation was dramatic. Mussolini held the key to removing the obstacles, a key which amounted to little more than a handful of planes. It is difficult not to see the real reason for sending the initial military assistance in the desperation of a Franco who found himself cornered. According to Angel Viñas, the reason was Goicoechea's arrival, which would tie 1936 to the document of 1934, in which Mussolini had promised to help to overthrow the Second Republic. According to Paul Preston, however, Goicoechea had little to do with it, given that the centre of gravity lay in Tétouan with Franco. I am inclined to think these movements are not mutually exclusive. Rather, they overlap and corroborate one another. The first point of a memorandum presented in Rome on 25 July by Goicoechea's group confirmed the 'requests made by General Franco'. It did not make new requests, nor did it refer to previous contracts; it confirmed what Franco had requested through Luccardi and Bolín. It went on to ask for belligerency, recognition of a future provisional government, and military materiel, as Bolín had also requested. It stressed the need for a loan of two radio stations, one to cover the entire national territory and the other with enough power to drown out Radio Madrid. Lastly, he requested a plane to return his whole group to Spain.[50] The similarity between the requests cannot lead us to think that they were opposing missions, even if one was sent by Franco and the other by Emilio Mola. The importance of the reports sent from the embassy in Madrid remains to be determined, but, in my opinion, they were fundamental.

Ultimately, the decisions taken had to do with a complex analysis of how Europe was to be governed, with the calculation of fascism's chances, and with the information coming from the Peninsula and Africa, which spoke of a blocked army and a failed uprising in Madrid. Mussolini was only sure of the situation once, having confirmed that the insurgency was viable and that 'the Kremlin did not intend to favour a Republican victory', he learnt that the French government would not assist the Spanish militarily, thus allowing the Duce to intervene without provoking a direct confrontation with Léon Blum. At all events, the debate about when the decision was taken is above all a debate about the relative weight of the different reasons for the final decision to intervene in Spain, initially by sending material assistance and later by becoming a belligerent in an internal war. In that sense, Enrique Moradiellos rightly points to two main lines of interpretation. One is that the fascist powers' intervention was immediate, in advance of the assistance provided by France, Mexico, and the Soviet Union; that it had 'very defined strategic and political' motives; that it was on a much larger scale than the assistance received by the Republic; and that, in short, it was decisive in the insurgents' victory. The other line of interpretation is that the fascist powers' intervention was a response to the French assistance, which provoked Italy's entry to the same extent as the Soviet's subsequent intervention intensified it; that it was of an exclusively anti-communist character and was not linked to fascism's supremacist ambitions in Europe; that it was not more substantial than the assistance received by the Republic; and that it was not so important, 'given that the external assistance provided by both sides cancelled itself out by virtue of being practically equal'.[51] Here I obviously opt for the first line of interpretation. Nevertheless, the second interpretation has left a deep imprint on the historiography. Indeed, it is generally accepted—as shown by Joaquín Arrarás, De Felice, and Coverdale—that the Italian commitment is due to the knowledge of French weapons and planes being sent to the Republic, as well as to its 'anti-communist duty', both factors being intrinsically united. But, while the second point is factual, the first is not. Ramón Serrano Suñer himself would later claim in his memoirs, in a way that openly contradicted the documentary record, that the fascist assistance was reactive, even though the 'National Movement did not need material assistance of a military character' and that those who were 'well informed' knew that 'the assistance that the Axis gave us was pretty sparse in the grand scheme of things; it was barely enough to counteract the military and material help lavished on the Reds'. Nevertheless, he also said that the insurgents needed it for other reasons, 'to secure diplomatic protection and friendly powers that could limit the assistance which other countries—most of all, France and Russia—were giving to the other side'.[52] For Franco's brother-in-law, their side, 'the millions of Spaniards fighting for order and freedom in National Spain', did not have any 'less of a right to obtain help from the world and relations with it . . . than those who, through the most implacable terror, maintained themselves in arms in Red Spain', even if they had the same right to receive the requisite moral assistance. 'But nobody will believe that this truly mattered at the time to decide the regime.'

Nobody believes him, even if nobody underestimates him. To do so would be not to understand the reality of Fascist Italy's intervention, as well as its record of anti-Republican conspiracy. In fact, Mussolini's involvement was consistent from the Republic's establishment onwards and contributes strongly to explaining July 1936, when the insurgency counted on 'substantial collusion' with the fascist power 'closest to the radicalised Right of the period'. It was a movement that was, in Viñas' words, 'operatively and massively supported by Italian Fascism' in the shape of four contracts to buy war materiel from the *Società Idrovolanti Alta Italia* (SIAI); the most important, dated 1 July, was for 16,246,750.55 lire, mainly for the 12 SM-81 (Savoia-Marchetti) aircraft, together with explosives, fuel, lubricants, and other items. Together with the three other contracts, all signed by Pedro Sainz Rodriguez, they totalled 39.3 million lire, spent on a 'combination of bombers/transport, fighter planes (33 CR-32s), and seaplanes'. The first were for taking the Army of Africa to the Peninsula; the second, fighter biplanes, for strafing enemy lines and destroying the government's obsolete air force; and the third for

32 *Fascist intervention in coup d'état of 1936*

supporting operations in the Balearic Islands.[53] It is impossible to underestimate such a contribution.

Payments for all this materiel were basically handled by the Mallorcan banker Juan March's business. In August 1936, March signed an agreement with Gómez Jordana, president of the *Junta Técnica del Estado* (State Technical Committee), which extended the credit of 50,000 pounds sterling granted to March by Kleinwort Sons & Company of London on 6 April 1936 to 80,000 pounds, which would function as a current account on credit for the Junta to use. On the other hand, on 3 and 9 September, he deposited 25 and 37 gold ingots, respectively, with the Bank of Italy, which together with various deposits of coins amounted to about 178.6 kilograms.[54] Thus, Mussolini's first intervention relied on March's credits and deposits, all based on the negotiations prior to the coup d'état that continued in the form of payments during and after the war. None of this is unknown—the Mallorcan was the economic facilitator of the coup d'état.

That was how things stood, when, on 25 July, Hitler decided to take part in helping the insurgents, and two days later, on 27–28 July, Mussolini did the same. The Republic's international isolation became plain in the face of the British government's refusal of assistance and the French government's subsequent backtracking on its plan to support the Spanish government.[55] It was a magnificent opportunity and, furthermore, came with a perfect alibi, anti-communism, handed to them on a plate by the requests for help which the Republic had to make to the Soviet Union. But this would not be the only alibi. For example, the news reaching Rome from Barcelona could not be worse. On 23 July, the embassy in Madrid signalled to Ciano that, according to newspaper reports and information gathered from staff disembarking at Marseille from Barcelona, the Italian consulate had been set alight and destroyed. The consul, Carlo Bossi, had been forced to take refuge in the French consulate and was incommunicado. All cars of Italian make had been destroyed or seized and, more seriously, many Italians had been killed on 'Monjuic [*sic*]' by armed gangs.[56] Although he had no confirmation from the Quai d'Orsay and was suspicious of the accounts by the staff landing at Marseille, Pedrazzi put forward an issue which hitherto has not been assessed by the historiography on the internationalisation of the Civil War: the protection of fellow nationals.

Whatever the case and, as mentioned previously, after a request for more information, on 25 July Ciano received the telegram from Tangiers which specified the insurgents' requirements and gave assurance that, if the materiel were supplied, Franco was certain to be successful, even if the French were allegedly continuing to send help to the insurgents' enemies.[57] In this overlapping game of delegations, telegrams, and urgent meetings, Franco assured De Rossi that five of the eight military divisions, as well as Melilla airport, were under his control and that what he urgently required was transport, fighter and reconnaissance planes, and a ship, all to ferry the African troops to the Peninsula. Strictly speaking, it was true.[58] The minister responded on 27

Fascist intervention in coup d'état of 1936 33

July that 12 appropriately camouflaged planes and a steamer loaded with war materiel were ready to leave for Melilla. However, there were a few matters left to resolve. Before making any commitments or promises, Ciano required assurance regarding Franco's situation. De Rossi's answer was immediate and the most persuasive of all that he sent to Rome. The supreme struggle between order and Bolshevism posited by Franco required the fresh blood of the Moroccan troops stranded in Africa by government naval forces. Only the breaking of that blockade could prevent the collapse of Franco's movement and guarantee his success. And, consequently, only Fascist Italy's assistance could extract the '*capo movimento*' (movement's head) from the African trap.[59] The few doubts still lingering were dispelled. Thus, the effective date of the decision was 27 July 1936, and came after Hitler's decision to act and Blum's not to.

From that moment on, everything accelerated. On Tuesday, 28 July, Lieutenant Colonel Ruggero Bonomi was summoned to the Air Ministry, where he was received by the sub-secretary and Chief of Staff of the *Regia Aeronautica* (Royal Air Force), Giuseppe Valli (we will see him again bombing Barcelona on New Year's Day 1938). Valli gave Bonomi the job of taking charge of flying a squadron of 12 Savoia-Marchetti S-81 bombers from Elmas aerodrome in Sardinia to Morocco. Two days later, the first despatch of Italian aeronautical materiel left the island for Spanish territory: two trimotor transport planes; a ship; the vessel *Morandi*, carrying fuel and munitions; and the famous S-81s.[60] Travelling in one of them was Ettore Muti, a pilot, *Milizia* official, and personal friend of Ciano's, whose name will appear regularly in this story. The initial objective was to help the insurgent forces to maintain their initiative and the Army of Africa to cross the Straits. In order to do so, Bonomi and his men enlisted in the *Tercio Extranjero* (Foreign Legion) under Franco's command. However, only nine planes arrived, because two crashed and a third had to make an emergency landing in French Morocco. The strong headwinds had exhausted their fuel. On 31 July, a telegram arrived in Rome addressed to Ciano, which indicated that 'Router [*sic*]' (the news agency Reuters) had reported that three aircraft of a group of six which had taken off from Sardinia for Morocco had been forced to land on French territory. According to the teletype, one carrying five machine guns had come down nearly 25 miles from Saïdia, in Algeria. Two pilots had died and a third had been injured. Two more planes had landed, injuring the crew of three, one of whom was flying without identity papers. One of the injured had claimed they were on a mission to Nador, to the south of Melilla.[61] The intervention had remained a secret for exactly four days.

Nevertheless, none of this stopped the despatch of arms and assistance. Ciano reportedly told Roberto Cantalupo, Fascist Italy's first ambassador to Spain following the recognition of Franco's government in November, that at the beginning they had considered sending only aircraft to help transport troops but that, as a result of 'pressure from all sides', 'we are now well and truly involved'. At first, it was simply a matter of supporting a plan, by which

34 *Fascist intervention in coup d'état of 1936*

Franco would take Madrid from across the Jarama river; the Foreign Legion would attack Valencia and then, from Guadalajara, support the liberation of the capital; the North would fall as a result; and, finally, the war would be reduced to the siege of Barcelona, 'a matter of weeks'.[62] But one has to doubt such certainty, as well as the relationship of cause (pressures) and effect (being involved up to their necks) purportedly suggested by Ciano, particularly given the strength and speed with which the Fascist government took the insurgents' side and, above all, Franco's. On 7 August, they despatched 27 Fiat fighter planes, five Fiat-Ansaldo light tanks, 40 machine guns, and 12 cannons to Spain. Furthermore, they sent three seaplanes to Mallorca on 13 August and six fighter planes on the 19th of the same month. In the same period, Germany sent 46 aircraft. In fact, confidence did not match reality, and it was actually a question of help to resolve an almost desperate situation. Ciano is said to have mentioned this plan of rapid attack again to Cantalupo in January 1937, showing him, on a military map of Spain festooned with little Italian, Spanish, and Red flags, how Roatta was to have captured Málaga and Valencia; Orgaz, the Jarama and Madrid; Roatta, again, the Sierra de Guadarrama and Guadalajara, followed by the march from Donostia to the Catalan capital. In no time at all, a 'general peace and the end of the game' was to have followed, as in board game. But the game would not end for many more months.

Until now, all the clues about the decision to help rebel Spain have focused on Spanish territory. Therefore, it is also interesting to observe this process from a different perspective, one centred not only on Tétouan and Ciano's ministry. Both the Italian state archives (*Archivio Centrale dello Stato*) and those of the Spanish foreign ministry (as it will be possible to verify once it finally reopens its collections) house information about how the Fascist support for the insurrection may also have been determined by the conspirators' own activities in Italy.[63] Though it remains a matter of conjecture, it is conceivable that the steps decided upon at the Spanish embassy in Rome at the end of July and in August 1936 influenced the direction of decision-making by reinforcing the idea that the rebels' victory could be a matter of time and by proving that the Fascist government's effective support against the Republican cause was yielding the results hoped for. The first message along these lines arrived at the General Directorate of Public Safety (*Direzione Generale di Pubblica Sicurezza*) on 26 July. It indicated, in the words of a group of Spaniards living in Rome, that the military attaché at the embassy in Italy had decided to resign in protest against 'the massacres in Spain committed by people armed by the Popular Front government, and in complete support of the insurgents'—that is to say, in support of Franco and against the 'murderous' Popular Front. On the morning of 31 July, José Maria Aguinaga, hitherto the Spanish ambassador in Berne, arrived in Rome to replace Manuel Aguirre de Cárcer, who had resigned. He was received with open and growing hostility by the embassy's local staff, and the embassy premises were occupied.[64] Commander Rafael Estrada, the naval attaché, had received a telegram from

Franco asking him to persuade the new ambassador to make a gesture of solidarity with the rebels, which Aguinaga refused to do.[65] The next day, Estrada, the commercial attaché, and others who supported the insurgents entered the ambassador's office to make another attempt and received the same response. But his stance would not last long.

In order to exert pressure, Aguinaga met Ciano, who was apparently more worried about whether the insurgency looked likely to succeed than ensuring decent working conditions for diplomats. Shortly thereafter, the same situation cropped up again. On 11 August, the embassy rebels invited all the Falangists in Rome to meet there at ten o'clock in the morning. They had been informed that the new ambassador had tried to take up his appointment. The welcome was discourteous, weapons in hand, and, despite the presence of an Italian policeman who appeared to be there to protect the ambassador, a shocking scene ensued. As the story is told, a representative of Franco wanted to introduce him to the Spanish community in Rome. Then, Admiral Antonio Magaz, a diplomat, former member of General Primo de Rivera's directorate, fervent Falangist, 'great friend of Italy', great admirer of the Duce, and the rebels' unofficial representative in Rome, inflicted the following invective on the ambassador, according to an account that is too verbatim to be considered reliable:

> You are the most repulsive riff-raff to walk on the face of the earth. You come here to represent a gang of assassins who have murdered the best that we had, our mothers, our brothers. You have first raped and then murdered our wives and sisters. You should leave here as a corpse, but we have too much respect for our Italian brothers and do not wish to create problems for them.

At that moment,

> Estrada and his colleagues, pistols in hand, forced the Ambassador to surrender the embassy safe and hand over the offices. Faced with this situation, the ambassador gave way and handed over what was requested to Estrada and, that evening, left Rome for Paris.

That is to say, Estrada imposed his will, gun in hand, using what Magaz called 'arguments of great persuasive force'. While all this was happening, Rafael Villegas, former military attaché, threatened the diplomatic staff with a gun and demanded the embassy's meagre funds: nothing in the safe, 1000 lire in the bank. With the key to the office safe, the rebel embassy in Rome soon broke with the Madrid government and became part of the external network of those who called themselves 'Spanish nationalist republicans', supported by Portugal (which the United Kingdom was said to accept), Italy, and Germany, in opposition to the government's supporters, 'the French, the Russians, and powerful North American Jewish capitalist groups'. Luis de

36 *Fascist intervention in coup d'état of 1936*

Zulueta, ambassador to the Holy See, also resigned, both for Madrid and for the Ministry of Foreign Affairs, authorising the transfer of the current account to the bank, thus allowing it to be used by the embassy's new occupants in the Quirinale. According to an official document, 'he would sign any document, even his own death sentence'.

Another attaché, Suárez (who hurled insults at fascism, for which he was arrested), was also forced to hand over the keys to the commercial section's safe. With the ambassadors having been replaced and the consul and the vice-consul, Serra, removed from their posts, the Falangists had usurped the power of the Spanish representation in Italy in order to use it as a recruitment office for the rebel army. Immediately afterwards, they ordered the monarchist flag to be retrieved from its hiding place and repaired so that it would be ready for the capture of Madrid, which Franco had told Estrada would take place on 15 August. They also ordered Falangist uniforms to be made for a parade through the capital. As a result of this whole succession of resignations, office closures, and violent occupation of the official Spanish representations in Rome, as well as the consulates in Genoa, Palermo, Naples, and Milan, the connection between Italian and rebel power became much more fluid. The economic representative, expelled at gunpoint, considered that the police's attitude and the lack of official support clearly demonstrated that all this had happened with the Italian government's consent and cooperation, so as to force the Republican government to break off diplomatic relations. Magaz confirmed this in communication with the Junta: 'they [the Italian authorities] completely disregarded procedures and created all manner of difficulties'. As he wrote very clearly to Francisco Montaner, spokesman for the *Junta de Defensa Nacional*, 'the Duce, as you know, has decided to lend all types of help, so that we find here the very best conditions for everything'. With the (state-controlled) press and public opinion favouring the insurgents,[66] from 26 August (when Magaz took complete control), the Spanish embassy in Rome worked as a branch of the rebels of the *National* zone.

The embassy's first concern was the problem of deserters, as it was calculated that about 1,000 men might be sent to the front. A committee was set up to question the Spaniards in Rome, man to man, and find out if they wanted to return to their country. Those who refused were deemed Reds camouflaged as Whites, who would be put 'on a blacklist'. By their own account, they were overwhelmed with requests to enlist in the '*Esercito Franco*' (Franco's Army), the characteristics of which will be described in Chapter 5. 'With the last group that left for the front yesterday, there are no more young Spaniards left in Rome.' All of this, and the fact that the committee's work was carried out with the utmost impunity and non-intervention by the Italian authorities, provided 'empirical [proof] of Italy's support for the Spanish nationalists'. Indeed, Franco lost no time in communicating his appreciation and complete gratitude to the naval and military attachés of the Spanish embassy in Rome, Rafael Estrada and Manuel Villegas, for their 'energetic and patriotic attitude' in standing their ground against the ambassador. 'Everything is going very well, and the road to victory is becoming clearer all the time.'[67]

As we know, not everything was going well, and the road to victory was not becoming increasingly clear. And Franco's requests for help and weapons from Italy had only continued and increased, particularly from the end of August, when the heads of the Reich's and Italy's intelligence services, Wilhelm Canaris and Mario Roatta, settled on the steps for sending their military missions to Spain. Roatta would direct the Italian mission, the MMIS, assisted by Emilio Faldella as his chief of staff. In my opinion, this further reinforces the idea that the first intervention—weapons and intelligence—was intended to be of limited risk and was accordingly confined to the SIM's field of activity. Roatta himself probably wrote a very interesting note in the margin of one of the telegrams of late August 1936 in which Luccardi relayed the need for more air support to neutralise the attacks sustained by Franco's columns during their advance on Madrid. The note warned of the need for gas masks to defend against chlorine, which he had been told (incorrectly, however) was being prepared in Valencia to be dropped on their armies. It also spoke of the need for more resources in general to counter what the Republic was receiving from the governments of France, Russia, and England, via Portugal—a flagrant falsehood. Roatta (or somebody else; the note was not signed) commented that General Franco had not organised things sufficiently. Thus began a long list of Italian complaints about the Spanish command, the Spanish way of waging war, Spanish methods, and Spain in general. Paraphrasing the Italian saying 'we have 30; make it 31', which usually referred to excess (a little more does no harm), the note declared that for Franco it was unfailingly a case of 'he always needs 30 more to make it 31'.[68]

No turning back

The game was being played out on multiple playing boards simultaneously and resulted in Fascist Italy's massive and almost unconditional entry into the war. One of the playing boards was obviously the League of Nations, which had just lifted the sanctions imposed on Italy because of its invasion of Ethiopia. Its Non-Intervention Committee served as a cover for double diplomacy, half-truths, and the construction of a narrative in which Fascist Italy was not taking part in any Spanish war; rather, those taking part were Italian volunteers who were opposed to Soviet expansion in southern Europe. The complaints raised by Julio Álvarez del Vayo, the Republic's representative in the Assembly, on 26 September 1936 about Italian ships docking at Tétouan, Palma de Mallorca, and Melilla made no difference, nor did his notes of 'vigorous protest' to the Italian Embassy's chargé d'affaires on 15 September, which indicated:

> From the beginning of the military uprising the Spanish government has amassed information proving that the rebels in revolt against the Spanish

38 Fascist intervention in coup d'état of 1936

government enjoy constant help consisting of arms, munitions and men sent from Italy.

He was referring to the forced landing in Algeria of the Savoia-Marchetti seaplanes, which, despite being painted white, had Italian 'outer markings' that could not be hidden. He was also referring to the statement by Vicente Sartriarca, the pilot of a Fiat CR-32 shot down between Talavera and Santa Olalla; the pilot had confessed, in detention, that 'I fought for 18 months in Abyssinia. . . . We left Genoa on 14 August for Melilla, on a ship that did not have a Spanish name but flew a Republican flag when it left the port.'[69] Such protests made no difference, in part because they were redundant. First was because Mussolini clearly had no intention of submitting to the League of Nations' sanctions. Second was, regarding the planes, because neither the insurgents (who obviously were not members of the League) nor the Italians (their unofficial representatives) could deny the shipments—the Spanish air force had no Savoia-type planes.

The beginning of the Fascist intervention in the Civil War took shape essentially with the sending of armaments to support the insurgents. In fact, the arrival of foreign help allowed the rebels to undertake two campaigns which improved their situation to a large extent, thanks to the transport in ten days of 15,000 men from Africa to the Peninsula.[70] However, more help was needed if they were to go beyond the Sierra de Guadarrama and take Madrid, even if (as De Rossi said to Ciano) it meant calling into question the insurgent command's autonomy and, possibly, even territorial integrity. The agreement between Roatta and Canaris in August 1936 clearly stipulated that Franco was obliged to accept their military advice, in view of the substantial military assistance received from both countries—in Ciano's words, materiel worth 55 million lire, for which payment in exchange had not been requested, and the loss of 12 pilots in what he saw as a 'conflict . . . of direct concern to the anti-communist states'.[71] In practice, this conflict was primarily being pursued in the air at the time. On 18 August, as bomber and fighter planes continued to be sent to Melilla to complete a fleet of eight S-81s and seven CR-32s, the despatch of the air force group to Sevilla was arranged. Just a day later, it went into action over Antequera by attacking an enemy column, an attack similar to the one it would carry out on 20 August over Córdoba. On 21 August, it destroyed the petrol tanks and an enemy column at Málaga, while an air patrol headed for Salamanca to provide cover in the North. Its first action would have been to attack the arsenal at Toledo, but one of the aircraft exploded, killing three technicians. This plan of attack foreshadowed another of the *Aviazione Legionaria*'s central theatres, Madrid.[72]

All this was meant to serve as a guarantee of German and Italian political, military, and economic interests. In this regard, the relevance of the Balearic Islands increased exponentially. The fear of losing them to the Republicans, whose government might use them as a bargaining chip in exchange for French support, contributed to the prompt establishment of a stable Italian force on

Mallorca. Thus, starting in August, when the first air base was established on the island, and especially from December of the same year, when the *Aviazione Legionaria* became answerable—at least nominally—to the MMIS, Italian fighter and bomber aircraft based on the Balearics would be fundamental to controlling Spanish airspace during the war. In 1936, the Legionary Air Force was key to controlling the Straits of Gibraltar and to the subsequent bombings of Cartagena, Alacant, and Almería. Used to control the ports of Barcelona and Valencia, taking the coast and inland territory from the French border to the Cape of Sant Antoni as their point of reference, flights from the Balearic Islands were also used to experiment with new military techniques. In Spain, the *Aviazione Legionaria* was able to show that bombing the water within ports was very useful, given that, although it might not hit ships, it caused a large amount of damage.[73] As we will see further on, this was only the beginning of an intense series of experiments in the use of air power—the most fascist of weapons—throughout the whole of the Civil War.

Control of the Balearics, and especially Mallorca, was thus fundamental. Clearly, a key element at stake in Mussolini's decision to enter the war was control of maritime traffic in the western Mediterranean. The islands were so important and weighed so heavily in official opinion that Mussolini felt obliged to tell the *Daily Mail*, as early as 9 September 1936, that he had no intention of taking control of them. In December, Eden confirmed before the House of Commons that the British government had received verbal assurance from Ciano that no change would be made to the status quo of the Balearics. On this occasion, as on so many others, outward appearances did not tally with Fascist Italy's real intentions. As Mussolini himself acknowledged to Ribbentrop in November 1937, it was fundamental that Franco understand the need to maintain a stable Italian base in Mallorca, even after the end of the war. Use of it, along with the base at Pantelleria and others already in existence, would ensure, that in the event of war, 'not a single black [soldier] will be able to reach France from Africa across the Mediterranean'.[74]

There was, however, a distorting element, the presence of a fascist mission in Mallorca, headed by the consul (equivalent to a colonel) of the *Milizia*, Arconovaldo Bonaccorsi, the famous 'Count Aldo Rossi'.[75] Prior to his arrival, Carlo Margottini, commander of the Italian Royal Navy's vessel *Lanzerotto Marocello*, stationed in Palma, was already on the island. A man who dedicated 'heart and soul to our cause', he was the main liaison between Rome and Bonaccorsi.[76] Margottini brought the military materiel needed to repel a Republican invasion attempt under Alberto Bayo in August. But, in a first attempt at political blackmail, he made it known that he would not unload armaments of such importance until the political situation was clarified, by which he meant until the *Confederación Española de Derechas Autónomas* (CEDA, Spanish Confederation of Autonomous Right-wing Groups) and its militias were dissolved and until Juan March's power on the island was limited. Accordingly, the local Falange leader asked, via Sainz Rodríguez, for Italian help in organising the island's defence. Sent by the Italian government

40 *Fascist intervention in coup d'état of 1936*

in response to the request by local authorities, the impetuous, bad-mannered, and popular Count Rossi began his work.

Bonnacorsi was the subject of all kinds of opinions, considered a bloody assassin and organiser of political cleansing by some and an energetic fascist and hero of the capture of Eivissa by others. Even judging by the documentation which he himself produced, he turned out to be a problematic factor in Mallorca, to say the least. He arrived in Palma by seaplane on 25 August and single-handedly managed—without speaking the language—to take control of the tactical situation, instil confidence and bravery, and, with his bold courage, take over the direction of operations from the military command, according to Margottini's account. All this led, in less than a week, to the island—low in morale, disorganised in its defence, and run by inept military authorities—being 'liberated'. The withdrawal of Republican forces on 3 September is sometimes attributed to their poor defence, although it could equally have been the result of 'orders from Madrid'.[77] However, it was Bonaccorsi who reaped the symbolic capital of the Republican retreat, and on 19 September he took charge of the operations to capture Eivissa. 'General Count Aldo Rossi' himself told the story of both the defence of Palma and the occupation of Eivissa in epic and personal terms. It was he who led the attacks, he who was the first to jump off the ships, he who risked his life, he who organised the 50 Falangists known as the Dragoons of Death, and he who asked to be shot if the operations—which he had ordered against the wishes of the military and civil authorities—failed. They did not shoot him. But, in return, he ordered the execution—according to his interpreter, a priest named Adrover—of most of the prisoners, 'dreadful elements' who were illiterate, including five women who had come to Mallorca from Barcelona to work as nurses.[78]

Bonaccorsi and the summer expeditions aside (which is where they should be left, because, though they will appear again in these pages, the Balearics had little connection with the ups and downs of the uprising on the Peninsula), the real Fascist military escalation in Spain took place in the autumn of 1936. Everything points to the escalation being considered and calculated in parallel with the coup d'état, anticipating the possibility (which became the reality) that it would not be as successful as claimed by rebel propaganda. One of the cases which anticipated the massive sending of troops was Italian naval control from the summer onwards. As early as 10 August, there were ten Italian submarines operating in the Mediterranean.[79] Two days later, Italian planes bombed and sank a Danish cargo ship off Barcelona, and the following day they hit a Spanish cargo ship, the *Conde de Albasola*.[80] In November 1936, the Italian submarine *Torricelli*, with help from the air force, put the light cruiser *Miguel de Cervantes*, anchored in the port of Cartagena, out of action until 1938. Indeed, submarine warfare was crucial at the beginning of the hostilities. The French vessel *Parame*, the Panamanian petrol tanker *MacKnight*, the Russian vessels *Timiryasev* and *Blagoiev*, and the British vessel *Havock* were attacked by Italian forces assisting the rebellion, preventing

Spain's legal government from receiving any help, in a flagrant case of piracy. In fact, Italian participation was key to all aspects of the war at sea. According to his own testimony, Admiral Giovanni Ferretti, the military delegate responsible for the *Missione Navale Italiana* (MNI, Italian Naval Mission) from 3 October 1936 to 22 November 1938, had been charged with putting the sea at the service of the rebels.

Intended not only as a liaison mechanism between the Italian and Spanish navies but more as a body for active collaboration, the MNI had to meet the Italian expeditionary force's naval requirements but, most importantly, remedy the 'catastrophic' situation of a navy whose command centre was still, even at the end of 1936, semi-buried in Franco's headquarters at the archbishopric of Salamanca. With only one high-ranking officer and a voluntary typist, no wireless telegraphic posts, no repair offices, no staff, and no organisation, it was a time when 'everything' had to be created 'out of nothing'. To this end, Ferretti, who enjoyed good relations with the German admiralty, decided to move the MNI's offices to Cádiz, bridgehead for the Italian transport ships; to Burgos, the general command centre and observation post for watching the 'complex and turbulent' world of Spanish politics; and to Palma de Mallorca, the command centre of the forces blockading the Mediterranean, in addition to its office at the CTV's headquarters.[81] All this reorganisation allowed the MNI to collaborate with the nascent insurgent navy, for instance in the mission of escorting the merchant ships bringing supplies to rebel Spain, as well as supplying it with armaments: the machine guns of the *Baleares* and *Canarias* heavy cruisers, the medium-calibre weapons of the *Baleares*, anti-aircraft batteries for the naval bases, reserve munitions, telemetric, and underwater instruments. So important was the MNI's work that it turned into the liaison point and coordinating centre for joint land-sea operations, like the capture of Málaga, and assumed control of port traffic at Cádiz, Huelva, and Sevilla. In fact, the vessel *Verazzano*, flying the Italian flag, took part in the capture of Málaga. A delicate balance had to be struck between the need not to compromise official Italian neutrality and the need to provide effective support to the *Motoscafo Armato Silurante* (MAS, Torpedo-Armed Motorboat) and the Italian legionary submarines (*Onice, Iride, Ferraris, Galileo*) which carried out 13 naval operations on the 'Red' coast.

In fact, it was the international situation which limited and ultimately postponed, *sine die*, large-scale action in the Mediterranean, like the planned and approved sinking of enemy ships in Mediterranean waters. It was to have been a combined air and submarine attack, which Ciano supported with 'enthusiasm and determination'. There was no lack of enthusiasm, but rather of opportuneness. Within naval control, a plan of operation was prepared that, had it been implemented, would have involved the transport of 20,000 men to Spain in October 1936, the so-called Operation Garibaldi. Led by General Ezio Garibaldi, grandson of the Giuseppe Garibaldi, the plan did not come to fruition. However, that did not stop it from becoming the reason for long deliberations by the rebel military command and by Ciano and

42 *Fascist intervention in coup d'état of 1936*

Mussolini, with the important and problematic participation of Ottavio De Peppo, head of the Diplomatic Cabinet at the Ministry of Foreign Affairs and the Ministry of the Navy. Franco's envoy to negotiate the transfer of this contingent of troops and materiel, Antonio Magaz, indicated that his relations with the Italian government were 'extremely easy, since the Duce and . . . Count Ciano consider the war in Spain as their own war, for which they spare no moral or material aid'. However, when it came to specifying the assistance, he always ran into a tangled administrative and governmental web, full of difficulties, headed by De Peppo. Having served as an attaché at the Italian embassy in Madrid, De Peppo believed that 'he knew our country intimately'. He thought of himself as 'Machiavellian' but was, in reality, 'something of a snob, boasting of his friendships with the most distinguished and aristocratic members of Madrid society'. Perhaps because he 'has not known us in a brilliant period of our history, he does not have the best opinion of us' and lacked confidence in 'our worth and our reliability'. In Magaz's opinion, it was De Peppo who was responsible for the cancellation of Operation Garibaldi. When all sides were in agreement, the Ministry of the Navy paralysed the operation, 'though no new cloud had appeared in the international sky, already quite dark'. For Magaz, the truly fascist impetus with which the Duce and Count Ciano embraced even the 'most daring conceptions' was significantly damaged by those whose reluctance had 'squandered opportunities to destroy the fleet under the Madrid government's command. With control of the sea and the blockade of the enemy coast, the campaign would have been easier and less bloody.'[82]

However, no one could allege that Mussolini lacked commitment. As Faldella later recalled, in late September, 15 tanks, 38 anti-aircraft pieces of 65 mm calibre, and radio and telegraph equipment had arrived in Spain, along with a group of 160 volunteer instructors, who were integrated directly into the *Tercio* and engaged in combat in the outskirts of Navalcarnero.[83] Thus, with the completion of the first phase of aid in the form of armaments, the phase of tactical and combat intervention was to begin. To prepare for this intervention, Roatta boarded the *Leone Pancaldo* for Spain on 1 September, accompanied by Emilio Faldella, Carlo Sirombo, and the Germans Walter Warlimont and Lucan, who entered the country with Italian passports. Their purpose was to meet Franco and present their credentials, which they did on 6 September. Meanwhile, on 4 September, the section of the SIM dedicated to the Civil War, the famous *Sezione S*, was constituted under the command of Filippo Guarini, with Vittorio Bonardi as its officer and with the assistance of Marshal Francesco Errico and Sergeant Michelangelo Fedele. The *Sezione S* was to handle all questions related to the Spanish political and military situation and act as a liaison with the operational and advisory groups in Spain, Tangiers, and the Balearic Islands. All this was intended to convince Franco that, by now, his fate was linked to the support of the fascist powers. A mere five days later, the future *Generalísimo* explicitly enunciated some of his main requirements. As he declared in Cáceres to an Italo-German delegation, the possibility of a return to the 'old Spain' was totally out of the question. The new government would adopt a programme of reconciliation with the masses, which the parties of the Right that had supported the coup 'practically' seemed to accept. Any disagreement between factions, he said, would be ironed out after the victory; what united them, that is, the concern with eradicating communist activity in Spain, was greater than any internal differences. And in the military field, there was the ever-present bait of the capital, which the fascist powers would nibble at until March 1937, at least, by which point the point of no return was months behind. 'Good overall situation', he said, predicting that Madrid would be occupied by the end of September.

The impressions of the Italian delegation during its journey to meet Franco are not to be missed, useful, and help explain what Roatta saw and the impression it had on him. Firstly, as in the first telegrams from Africa, it was clear that Franco was the leader of the rebels, that Queipo de Llano was a secondary figure, and that Mola was a traditionalist and a little rigid. Franco, on the other hand, appeared to them to be sympathetic to fascism, the leader best qualified to reconcile the different political tendencies (including the volunteer militias that occupied the rearguard but, in the Italians' view, were not very active at the fronts). Of great importance was the fact that Franco was the commander of the best troops, namely the *Tercio* and the *Regulares*, who occupied areas efficiently, nearly always with bloodshed. This same report, which the Duce read (and sent to his private secretariat, as well as to the SIM), indicated that, though they were more cohesive and disciplined than the 'Reds', the insurgent troops characteristically fought in a disorderly and confused way, using primitive tactical methods and having virtually no information or knowledge of the enemy. They did not form patrols to control the areas between the front and the occupied areas. As a result, nothing short of an extremely limited military capacity could explain why the 'Reds' did not penetrate behind the lines, which did not really exist. Most houses did not fly the flag of the *National* side, the report went on, only white flags, and the inhabitants did not give the Falangist salute but wore white clothes. The civilians wore a belt with the flags of Spain, Italy, Portugal, and Germany, which they 'elegantly' called '*me cago en Francia*' (which might be loosely translated as 'to hell with France'). When a village was occupied, the prisoners were summarily shot, and any member of the population suspected of or believed to be helping, cooperating, or sympathising with the 'Reds' was subject to a 'purge (now commonly called hairdressing)'.[84] In Fuente de Cantos it had been confirmed that the repression in retaliation against 'Red atrocities' was exemplary. Up to 800 persons were said to have been disarmed. To the Italians' questions as to why he had ordered non-combatants to be shot, the mayor, who belonged to the *Requetés*, replied, '*¿Desarmados? ¡Desalmados!*' (Disarmed? Heartless!).

Against the heartless Reds, Spanish fighting tactics were primitive, slow, and extremely violent, which, according to Ciano, could prove counterproductive, not so much for saving lives for fascism and rebuilding the nation,

44   *Fascist intervention in coup d'état of 1936*

but rather because cruelty would increase the enemy's will to resist.[85] However, when pondering the heartless Red, Mussolinian fascism's position cannot be downplayed. Nor is it possible to dismiss, among the primary motives which led to the Fascist intervention in Spain and the enlistment by the first volunteers, the communion of interests and political identities that would forever unite, by blood (and *through* blood), the destinies of the two nations. Only in this way is it possible to understand the 'extraordinary confidential bulletin' sent by the ambassador in Madrid to Ciano and Mussolini in late August, which described Calvo Sotelo's assassination as inspired by freemasonry and carried out with the government's complicity and accused Santiago Casares Quiroga, 'repugnant tubercular vermin', of being ultimately responsible for his death.[86] This is also the only way of explaining the early references to Red barbarity, atheistic terror, and godless Spain in the personal documents of some of the first Italian combatants. A recruitment mechanism was quickly established in Roma and Genoa 'to take advantage of the favourable environment surrounding our struggle against Marxism'; the recruitment outlet was discreet and located away from the embassy and consular buildings, under the direction of Colonel Estrada. However, these were men who had chosen to fight in Spain before the *Ufficio Spagna* (Office for Spain) even existed. At that early stage, the options consisted of enlisting in the *Tercio*, presenting themselves at the embassies, or going to Spain at their own risk.[87]

Following the resolve to destroy the Republic, decided in July and settled in September, it was between October and November 1936 that the *how* and *when* of the large-scale intervention in Spain were determined as a result. Up until that point, it had been limited to the sending of materiel, from which all traces of Italian origin were erased, and a small number of specialists, who arrived in September via Cádiz and Vigo to join Italo-Spanish units.[88] Italy became a third belligerent in the conflict, at least in the spring of 1937, but different writers adduce different motives for this escalation. For Gianluca André, it was a reaction to the Republican defence, thanks to the help of the International Brigades. According to De Felice, it was the result of the pressure exerted by the *Milizia* to fight its fascist war. For Coverdale, especially, it was in response to the Bolshevik intervention and due to the conviction that a larger commitment would help Franco to a rapid victory, thus favouring Italy's geostrategic position in Europe enormously. The historiographical quasi-consensus appears to be that the motives were defensive.[89]

However, it does not seem that the Italian moves that contributed to the making of the Civil War can be reduced to defensive actions. Rather, they were a combination of pro-active aggressiveness and reaction to (among other things) the revolutionary radicalisation of the Republican rearguard. As Morten Heiberg has underlined, in the winter of 1936–1937, Mussolini sent 'an expeditionary army of 45,000 soldiers to Spain, officially composed of volunteers to avoid entering into conflict with the norms of the recently created Non-Intervention Committee'.[90] An entire army is not created, in my opinion, in order to defend a geostrategic position. It was fielded to attack, conquer, and vanquish, whether in pursuit of the annihilation of the enemy or in pre-emptive defence of its own political system and its own Fascist regime. As Ciano put it, Italy was at war to defend civilisation and the fascist revolution.[91] For this reason, the summer and autumn months of 1936 saw the Italians redouble their efforts to influence and even determine the evolution of insurgent Spain. Their efforts ranged from the unsuccessful task of mediation in Alacant to free José Antonio, Miguel, and Carmen Primo de Rivera to the meetings with Olazábal to strengthen the already existing ideological ties between fascism and Carlism;[92] and from the rescue of Queipo de Llano's family in Málaga, for which he personally thanked the Italian consul, to Mussolini's statements welcoming Franco's statements about seeking a popular base for his power. Another example was Ciano's suggestions to strive for a social slant to the rebel government and make gestures from Burgos that would encourage 'the feeling abroad that the nationalist movement is not one of the customary *pronunciamientos* but a revolution originating with the Spanish people and being carried out for the good of the same people'. Efforts went as far as the Duce's pressure on Spain to leave the League of Nations when Italy did. In the course of those months, Italian intervention was not being gestated. It was unfolding de facto.[93]

Many declarations and initiatives support this view, such as the sending of volunteers within the framework of the Foreign Legion. Franco was able to inspect some of these units in person, at least judging by a telegram, dated 19 October, received by the SIM. It detailed how the Caudillo had gained an 'ideal impression', despite the clear difference in comparison to the more up-to-date war materiel provided by the Germans, and even despite the fact that the Italians had, on more than one occasion, transported scrap materiel, which was 'unforgiveable' and very serious.[94] That the intervention was already being developed and would be deployed between November 1936 and early 1937 is in fact the most coherent vision of the Spanish conflict's development and progressive transformation into a civil war. It is no coincidence that many of the initiatives intended to deal with a long war were taken in November. The out-and-out fascist military escalation took place in that month, from the recognition of General Franco's government at Burgos by Italy and the Third Reich. It was, as Mussolini reminded Roatta on 22 November, so that he would point it out to Franco, a step that would oblige him to continue operations with the utmost energy. In Mussolini's words, it was absolutely essential to prevent '*codesta gente si metta sull'imbraca*'—that is, to make sure the Spanish did not, in counting too much on Italo-German materiel and moral solidarity, rest on their laurels and evade their obligations and responsibilities. It was an undoubtedly aggressive admonition, even if the Duce did not make it in public, but rather to his right-hand man in Spain. Behind it were both the offer of a massive entry into the war, made in the favourable context of September, and the follow-up to that help under the same precepts (sending volunteers under the Italian flag and with Fascist

46 *Fascist intervention in coup d'état of 1936*

commanders) but at an extremely more complex moment—the onset of a civil war which would last a long time.

The origin of this recognition lay in the meeting between Ciano and Baron von Neurath on 21–22 October, out of which a nine-point bilateral pact emerged. These points included the strengthening of relations between the two powers; mutual assistance in the League of Nations (especially if Italy withdrew from it); recognition of communism as the great danger threatening Europe's security and peace; and, above all, de facto recognition of the Spanish insurgent government, pending recognition de jure, along with confirmation of the principle of non-intervention and respect for Spain's territorial integrity and sovereignty. Accordingly, they laid the diplomatic foundations for the subsequent military escalation. While the meeting between Ciano and Hitler has received more attention, it was November 1936 that was truly the critical moment in every sense. In fact, this was the moment when the insurgent army was closest to taking the capital, as all the reports transmitted between Italy and Spain indicated. As in Toledo, the attack on Madrid, planned by Mola and approved by Franco, was to be used to make a quick entry into the capital from the west. The Falange even had a detailed plan as to which of the capital's radio stations and newspapers to occupy immediately.[95] But not everybody was so optimistic. In one of his reports, Roatta revealed his doubts about the overall military situation. He was highly critical of the rebel troops' military abilities. Their poor organisation, shortage of weapons, and lack of coordination above battalion level prevented integrated operations. Even worse was his opinion of the commanders. Varela, in particular, gave orders like an old Napoleonic general; he had only one telephone line linking him to the outside world and, at his command centre in Leganés, he was surrounded by rubbish, sherry bottles, and coffee. Roatta's criticism extended to all the generals from the Army of Africa, except Franco. They had scarce means (the best had been provided by the Italians and Germans but were not always used correctly) and were cruel in combat; the mass shooting of prisoners taken alive was their hallmark. There were enormous doubts about the ability of the 'revolutionaries' to finish what they had started. Therefore, he said, the Italians' efforts to help them had to be redoubled.[96]

The thinking was that the war would be brief, lasting until the end of the month at most. However, this was not the impression of the pilot Muti: 'Our flights wreak more and more destruction daily in Madrid. But for weeks now, nothing is happening on the ground.' At that rate, 'we will manage to take Madrid sometime in the first half of the twenty-first century'.[97] Even that, in his opinion, would not mean the end of the war or the Republic. As the Italian command itself acknowledged, the reorganisation and reinforcement of the Republican Army, its greater capacity for resistance, and the insurgents' own combat experience (which was slow and diametrically opposed to the *guerra celere* advocated by the fascists) made it difficult to foresee an immediate victory with the occupation of Madrid. According to Roatta, the Spanish military considered the capital to be their final destination, as though the enemy would then simply dissolve. He thought that, in the best of cases, if they were lucky, it would be an intermediate stage in a long war.[98] The tactical and strategic differences were already becoming evident between the Spanish and Italian generals; the latter advocated the very fascist idea of *guerra celere*, swift, motorised warfare accompanied by the equally fascist weapon of air power. These differences would fill Italian military reports for the next two and a half years.

In fact, the plan to take Madrid was soon frustrated. Thus, the coup d'état and its by-product of a war of infantry columns immediately came to an end, and a long and exhausting war until the total destruction of the enemy began. In this situation, Mussolini took his own decisions. Instead of withdrawing from the 'quicksand', he recognised Franco's government on 8 November. He sent a chargé d'affaires to Spain as the recognised head of the Italian diplomatic mission.[99] He signed the Spanish-Italian Secret Protocol, based on solidarity in the fight against communism, the development of reciprocal relations, and Italian help to preserve the integrity and re-establishment of political and social order. The mission to ratify the protocol fell to the diplomat Filippo Anfuso.[100] And it gave final shape to the massive despatch of soldiers. Mussolini clearly did not share the unease with and rejection of Franco's *modus operandi* when he gave the order that

> since General Franco's government has taken possession of the greater part of Spain and the evolution of the situation has shown it to be increasingly evident that in the rest of Spain there is no functioning governmental power to speak of, the Fascist government has decided to recognise General Franco's government and to send him a chargé d'affaires [De Ciutiis] to initiate diplomatic relations.

The declaration made official what had been the de facto reality for months. According to the rebel government's first envoy—unofficial but soon to be official—in Rome, Antonio Magaz, this move had not come earlier because, in anticipation that the Francoist troops would take Madrid, recognition would have been considered premature and could have 'exposed Italy's play in our favour'. However, in his opinion, the 'advance of our troops and perhaps Russia's blatant support of the Madrid government' had changed the 'signs' and favoured the new situation.[101] Magaz was mistaken, however. Without a single insurgent soldier setting foot on the Paseo de la Castellana, and within the space of a month, Mussolini had gone from projecting a public image of caution and limited risk to unconditional involvement in the war, a genuine military escalation which would soon bring 10,000 men to the Peninsula. They embarked at night, dressed as civilians and carrying false passports.[102] It was a journey of no return from the birth of the Axis in October and the recognition of the Burgos government, which continued with the meeting on 6 December in the Palazzo Venezia between Mussolini, Roatta, Ciano, the under-secretaries of the armed services ministries, and Canaris, the head of

48   *Fascist intervention in coup d'état of 1936*

German military intelligence, to discuss increasing the amount of the support for Franco and setting up the *Ufficio Spagna*. The latter was to be under the command of Count Luca Pietromachi and comprise officers of the *Milizia* and the three armed forces but exist outside the armed services ministries. Between 6 and 18 November, Hitler sent 92 combat aircraft to Spain, with more than 3,800 pilots and technicians. Soon afterwards, the air unit comprised 140 aircraft, with a support battalion of 48 tanks, 60 anti-aircraft guns, and 5,600 men. On 7 November, Mussolini appointed Brigade-General Roatta (promoted to divisional general, thanks to the capture of Málaga) to take command of 50,000 men in four divisions. Roatta himself requested that no reserve officers and troops be sent. It was essential to show, right from the start, Italy's absolute supremacy in the war and in Spain.[103] Now was not the time for urgent and timely missions of little importance, but rather a 'direct and intense intervention'.[104]

Might Mussolini have felt any obligation to do so? The ultimate reasons for the military escalation may yet remain nebulous, but the interpretations based on geostrategic calculations for control of the Mediterranean do much to cloud the analysis. One aspect that is not usually considered is that the Italian recognition of the rebel government may have been due to the pressures of German high-ranking military circles on Hitler. They told the Führer at a meeting on 17 November that they considered it necessary, as they put it, to 'define' and 'legalise' the context of the military and diplomatic intervention.[105] In fact, at the same time, Ciano asked his diplomatic agents in Germany what the German government's confidential opinion was of Franco and the war and what action it was thinking of undertaking to support him. And, despite the slowness of Franco's progress, there was no obvious pessimism in Berlin. For Goering, even though time was running out for maintaining appearances in the international arena, and despite openly expressed doubts about the insurgents' military capability—which had led him to propose sending 10,000 SS men to Spain in early November—the Germans had to continue clearly supporting the Caudillo.[106]

I am inclined to think that Mussolini took ownership, first of the coup d'état against the Republic and then of the process of a large-scale open war, which, although its force was implicit in July–August 1936, did not unfold in all its dimensions until October–November of that year. The Duce saw no contradiction between the 'gentlemen's agreement' with the British government concerning the western Mediterranean in November 1936 and going to war. There was no contradiction, even if, in order to pacify Eden, he had to withdraw the head of the *Milizia* from Mallorca, the 'general' of the 'anticommunist army', Bonaccorsi, no matter that he did not represent his government's official policy. It was preferable to maintain appearances on the international stage if this allowed Mussolini to increase his actual presence in Spain. Thus, on 14 December, after Mussolini had read various reports about the difficulty of 'our definitive occupation of the Balearics', Count Rossi, 'the best of fascists, a man of action', received Ciano's order (sent by telegram

Fascist intervention in coup d'état of 1936   49

via the Royal Navy vessel *Zeno*) to conclude his tour of Mallorca proselytising fascism and to leave the island. The presumed enthusiasm about Italian influence had evaporated, according to official documents. Despite the prestige achieved by Bonaccorsi, who claimed to have understood the Spanish mentality perfectly and imprinted the movement with an exquisitely fascist character, the local authorities wanted nothing more than to be rid of him. From that moment, Italy withdrew its enormous political influence and, in exchange, ensured for itself a decisive military presence and the significant opportunity to 'monopolise the internal market' by taking over the trade in almonds, wool, tobacco, and medicinal products. Given this situation, as Bonaccorsi was informed, 'the mission entrusted to him in Palma' could 'be considered completed to total satisfaction'.[107]

There was no satisfaction, of course, for the excitable 'Count Rossi'. Only days earlier, he had complained that the air force on the islands was being left in 'incompetent' Spanish hands—those of Franco's brother, Nicolás, whom Bonaccorsi considered an immoral, harmful man, a communist, and a bitter enemy of the Duce and fascism. He complained that the military authorities were working against Italian prestige (by diminishing his own prestige, even though, he said, he enjoyed the esteem and confidence of the *whole* Mallorcan population). He complained that nobody was taking into account Mussolini's revolutionary and popular fascism, for which he himself was an evangelist. Indeed, for some time now, insurgent officers—and, he claimed, Italians as well—had been telling him that the MMIS had only one general, 'Mancini' (that is to say, Roatta), and that the other one (that is to say, he himself) was one only as 'a manner of speaking'. He thus had to leave the island so that Mussolini could demonstrate that his decision to intervene in Spain was, above all, a question of supporting an ally, a friend. Bonaccorsi never managed to understand. Only a few weeks earlier, he had organised a fascist parade in Palma, exceeding all expectations (according to him)—30,000 men and women cheering Spain, Italy, fascist doctrines, and their creator, Mussolini. The whole population would have joined up, in his opinion, but for the intercession of old politics and the Army, which, in his opinion, had put an end to his mission on the island. It was a time when he still believed that Franco was fighting against communism and for the triumph of fascism. He certainly did not know that the whole of the Italian administration, from the embassy to the Army, were demanding he leave Mallorca. However, not only did Bonaccorsi not leave Spanish territory, he was to become the source of major tensions during the occupation of Málaga, as will be seen in the next chapter.

Thus, as a result of the Italo-German agreements of 6 December, Mussolini transferred the command of all Italian troops to Roatta. At the same time, he asked him to meet the German ambassador, Wilhelm Faupel, and Franco to organise the chiefs of staff that had been decided in the agreements mentioned earlier. Mussolini also informed Roatta of the creation of the *Ufficio Spagna* in the Ministry of Foreign Affairs.[108] The despatch of troops to Spanish soil

50 *Fascist intervention in coup d'état of 1936*

began immediately. On 14 December, Faldella, Roatta's second in command, informed Franco of the despatch of 3,000 soldiers. Franco is said to have replied, as apocryphal as it sounds, 'And who asked for them?'[109] The men were volunteers, many of whom were veterans of Abyssinia, in the charge of the MVSN, which received 'continual applications from volunteers seeking the enlistment bonus of 300 lire and daily pay of 20 lire'.[110] With high moral, he would say, and a resolute state of mind, they were Mussolini's bet on decisive action in Spain, so much so that they supposedly came already entrusted with the mission to conquer Málaga, as the Duce had himself supposedly signalled to Franco. I have not found any evidence of such a statement, which, two months earlier, had ostensibly already indicated the Fascist troops' first military mission in Spain.[111] But in this instance anything is possible.

In the final analysis, Mussolini and Ciano thought that the presence of Italians in Spain did not contradict their promise to respect the status quo. Ciano, in particular, thought that the creation and despatch of the International Brigades made it difficult to prevent volunteers from enlisting.[112] Later, I will return to the issue of motivation in the successive waves of combatants. What I do wish to underline here is that, whether they were Fascist volunteers, soldiers of the Italian Army (also Fascist), or officers seeking pay and promotion, all of their cases were consistent with the aggressive and supremacist policy of a fascist great power struggling against the ontological enemy in defence of Christian civilisation in Spain and, by extension, in Europe. The despatch of troops began in November with the aim of '*innervare*' (innervate), to spur on the Nationalist forces, while a contingent of 1,500 men remained in Italy in preparation for later transfers.[113] Their departure from Gaeta was made in 'absolute secrecy' from a secluded pier far from curious eyes—even if they spent the time while boarding cheering the Duce. They remained unarmed during their voyage on the *Lombardia*. The risky voyage without hoisting the flag and the arrival of the first contingent at Cádiz on 22 December,[114] together with other activities—such as Major De Blasio's implementation of a counter-espionage plan, was not merely the result of supporting a natural ally. It was much more—intervention as a third belligerent. This is the only way to explain the informal request received verbally by Roatta from Franco's cousin that he take part in assessing operational questions regarding the fronts, acting in the shadows as a chief of the General Staff.[115] It was not only aid to a friend; it was, above all, the identification of fascism as a protagonist involved in the front line.

However, Italy was not *officially* at war with Spain. But the war that it was entering de facto generated salaries; accrued rights; and produced widows and orphans, medals for bravery, and sentences for treason and self-mutilation. In 1936 nothing had been prepared to address such issues. The opening of the *Ufficio Spagna*, through which Ciano's ministry was to coordinate everything relating to the intervention in Spain, was precisely the first attempt to move in that direction. It reaffirmed the centralised control of all matters relating to Spain, including the fact that, in 1936, among the different areas involved in the war, the military aspects would remain subordinate to the realms of diplomacy and politics.[116] Certainly nobody thought, at the beginning of 1937, that the massive shipment of an entire army to Spain would not end in a swift and crushing victory by the insurgent troops. In Cantalupo's words, not only did Italy wish to support them, it hoped to use this support in order to secure the triumph of fascism in Spain. This dependence on diplomacy soon changed into a strengthening of the military dimension of the Italian intervention. As in nearly every case, the turning point was the Battle of Guadalajara.

Thus, on 15 December, the MMIS was declared operative, with headquarters in Sevilla. On 22 December, a contingent of 3,000 soldiers disembarked from the *Lombardia* at Cádiz, followed by another on 15 January 1937, making a total of 10,000 men just one month later. According to some authors, applications to join the voluntary Blackshirts exceeded requirements, although as with everything this assertion requires much qualification. Use of the *Milizia* can be explained, according to Rovigho and Stefani, by the difficulty of sending so many men in such a short span of time, as well as by the political demand to involve volunteers and fascists.[117] It is another matter entirely to believe that applications exceeded official demand, a conclusion for which I have found not a shred of documentary evidence. Indeed, Mussolini insisted a great deal (and left written evidence in his extant papers) that the voluntary character of Italy's support should be underlined, both in the fascist *Milizia* specifically and in the military, thus emphasising that officers and troops for Spain would be selected from among those applying as volunteers.[118] Nevertheless, it must not have been simple within the *Regio Esercito*, the Italian Army. Quite often the 'invitations extended to the soldiers to enlist in the army intended for Spain' were received with 'visible signs of unease', conversations *sotto voce*, and all manner of excuses, and only threats achieved the 'desired effect'. Consequently, it appears that a lottery system was put together to fill the places required of each regiment, and those selected were obliged to serve, on pain of arrest or court martial for indiscipline.[119]

Mussolini himself described the process in his usual broad-brush way, projecting responsibility elsewhere. In his article of July 1937, entitled 'The Volunteers and London',[120] he explained how, in his opinion, the international situation regarding the Spanish war was nothing but a masquerade on the part of the French and British governments. When, in August 1936, they proposed non-intervention, they did so without imposing a ban on volunteers going to Spain, on propaganda, or on aid by public subscription, because that would have been at odds with their own political traditions. Thus, they merely vetoed the sending of arms and munitions. In the meantime, he continued, Stalin had already decided to send aid to the Republic, giving the struggle the character of a doctrinal battle, an anti-fascist character, in order to make the war the scene of fascism's destruction. It would have been suicide not to take up the gauntlet. In his words, the Blackshirts could not remain indifferent and, even if Franco did not need it, it was necessary

52 *Fascist intervention in coup d'état of 1936*

to provide proof of their solidarity and fight against anti-fascism. 'A new and great Spain is rising amid the blood and the ruins', and Italy was to be the midwife at this painful birth.

Thus, 1936 was far from being a year in which there was more doubt than certainty in Italy about openly taking part in an outright war. The total Italian contribution during those months was, in the air, 105 aircraft shot down, 150 air raids, and 170,000 kilograms of explosives dropped; at sea, general support and submarine operations; and, on land, direct intervention in the operations at Navalcarnero on 23 October, the occupation of Esquinas and Seseña on 24–25 October, and the operation on Torrejón.[121] All of this incurred an important expenditure of approximately 110,000,000 lire on the air force, 16,575,460 on the navy, 42,000,000 on land fighting, and 85,961 in 'foreign balance (Buonacorsi [*sic*]-Bianci etc.)'—that is to say, 168,661,421 lire, covered only in part by the gold deposited into the foreign ministry's account at the *Banca d'Italia* (5,533,407 lire) and by the deposit, on 20 August, of francs and sterling equivalent in value to 5,750,115 lire into SIAI's account at the *Banca Commerciale*, a total of 11,283,522 lire. The balance of expenditure was, in short, hugely disproportionate in the year when Mussolini decided to embark on a war of the dimensions that the Spanish one could acquire. Thanks to him, Franco was about to order arms and buy them on credit, even without guarantees to back the purchases. Although the commercial agreements guaranteed payment in minerals to the value of nearly four million lire and 30 per cent of imports from Spain were retained, allegedly in order to pay for the military equipment, the balance of the accounts was very negative. Clearly, the Fascists had not joined the war in Spain to get rich.

As was pointed out a month later in the meeting held between Ciano, Goering, and the under-secretaries of the armed services ministries, what the fascist powers were putting on the table was a truly formidable effort towards a war of large-scale proportions that ought to have brought it to a swift end. Mussolini decided on a maximalist programme of materiel and blood in Spain and indicated as much to his son-in-law on 16 January. However, the war was not won in November, when in theory it could have been, nor would it be won later, with the massive transfer of troops and assistance to Franco's army. The Axis powers had promised to recognise the Burgos government once the capital had been taken, but they were obliged to backtrack (a mistake, according to Goering), resulting in the rather extravagant message cited earlier— their recognition of a country without a capital. They said they would comply with the League of Nations' requirements regarding the neutrality of Spanish territory; yet they sent troops and arms, insofar as nothing had supposedly been said about support for sending volunteers to fight Bolshevism in Spain. And, in the meantime, their fears were beginning to be confirmed. Franco would not win the war quickly, nor would he use the support of European fascism to do so. Rather, he would use this support as reassurance in a drawn-out war, convinced that it would enable him fight on indefinitely.

'We want Franco to win',[122] Ciano would say. They wanted victory as soon as possible. Overwhelming. And over Madrid. And they wanted guarantees that the maximum effort would be made to secure it. At the end of the day, the almost 49,000 Italian forces that would arrive in Spain at the end of the winter of 1937 provided a legitimate justification for their demand. That was the logic within which the Italians' progression in the war would be situated in a year that began with strength and success in Málaga and, most off all, when momentum ran out, literally sunk in the mud, snow, and ice of Guadalajara.

Notes

1 Duilio Susmel and Edoardo Susmel, eds., *Opera Omnia di Benito Mussolini*, 44 volumes (Florence and Rome: La Fenice, 1951–1963 and 1978–1981), vol. XXVIII, 28.

2 The earliest literature is that of the protagonists: Roberto Cantalupo, *Fu la Spagna. Ambasciata presso Franco, Febbraio-Aprile 1937* (Milan: Mondadori, 1948); and Emilio Faldella, *Venti mesi di guerra in Spagna (luglio 1936-febbraio 1938)* (Florence: F. Le Mannier, 1939). The latter author had moreover a private archive, which Renzo de Felice was able to consult, as he indicated in *Mussolini il duce, vol. II: Lo stato totalitario (1936– 1940)* (Turin: Einaudi, 1996) and other volumes.

3 A paradigmatic example is that of Fernando Schwartz, *La internacionalización de la guerra civil española: julio de 1936—marzo de 1937* (Barcelona: Ariel, 1971).

4 Morten Heiberg, *Emperadores del Mediterráneo: Franco, Mussolini y la guerra civil española* (Barcelona: Crítica, 2004), 45. The Danish author regrets, as do I, the little weight given to Ismael Saz and Paul Preston's interpretations in the pro-Franco historiography and (as is generally the case with the work of Spanish and Hispanist historians) in the Italian historiography.

5 Benito Mussolini, *La mia vita* (Milan: Biblioteca Universale Rizzoli, 1999).

6 Simonetta Falasca-Zamponi, *Fascist Spectacle: The Aesthetics of Power in Mussolini's Italy* (Berkeley and Los Angeles: University of California Press, 1997), 90ff. Emilio Gentile, *La Grande Italia. Ascesa e declino del mito della nazione nel ventesimo secolo* (Milan: Mondadori, 1997). On the Mediterranean question in Italian foreign policy, Carlo Maria Santoro, *L'Italia e il Mediterraneo. Questioni di politica estera* (Milan: Centro di Studi e Ricerche di Politica Comparata, Università 'L. Bocconi' Angeli, 1988).

7 In concrete terms, a late and little-desired entry into a war of mobilisation and attrition at Isonzo and Carso, followed by defeat at Caporetto and then the recovery of territories with as much dignity as possible at Vittorio Veneto. Antonio Gibelli, *La Grande Guerra degli italiani, 1915–1918* (Milan: Sansoni, 1999); by the same author, *L'ufficina della guerra: La Grande Guerra e le trasformazioni del mondo mentale* (Turin: Bollati Boringhieri, 1991). See also Piero Peli, *L'Italia nella Prima Guerra Mondiale. 1915–1918* (Turin: Einaudi, 1968); Alberto Monticone, *Gli italiani in uniforme, 1915–1918. Intellettuali, borghesi e disertori* (Roma and Bari: Laterza, 1972).

8 Emilio Gentile, *Il culto del Littorio: la sacralizzazione della politica nell'Italia fascista* (Rome and Bari: Laterza, 1993); Claudio Fogu, *The Historic Imaginary: Politics of History in Fascist Italy* (Toronto: University of Toronto Press, 2003).

9 *Opera Omnia*, vol. XIX, 18. See also Ennio Di Nolfo, *Mussolini e la politica estera italiana (1919–1933)* (Padua: CEDAM, 1960).

10 *Opera Omnia*, vol. XXIV, 235.

11 Elena Aga Rossi, 'La politica estera e l'Impero', in *Storia d'Italia, vol. 4, Guerre e Fascismo 1914–1943*, eds. Giovanni Sabbatucci and Vittorio Vidotto (Rome and Bari: Laterza, 1997), 245–303.

54 Fascist intervention in coup d'état of 1936

12 According to Ennio di Nolfo, it was only a 'veil' aimed at democratic and pacifist public opinion. Di Nolfo, *Mussolini*, 305.

13 Giorgio Rochat, *Le guerre italiane 1935–1943: dall'impero d'Etiopia alla disfatta* (Turin: Einaudi, 2005), 29.

14 Among others, Giorgio Rochat, 'La repressione della resistenza cirenaica (1922–1931)', in *Omar Al-Mukhtar et la reconquista fascista della Libia*, eds. Enzo Santarelli, Giorgio Rochat, Rainero Romain, and Luigi Goglia (Milan: Marzorati, 1981); Angelo Del Boca, ed., *Le guerre coloniali del fascismo* (Rome and Bari: Laterza, 1991); Angelo Del Boca, *I gas di Mussolini. Il fascismo et la guerra di Etiopia* (Rome: Editori riuniti, 1996); Nicola Labanca, 'L'internamento coloniale italiano', in *I campi di concentramento in Italia. Dall'internamento alla deportazione (1940–1945)*, ed. Constantino Di Sante (Milan: Franco Angeli, 2001), 40–67; Giorgio Rochat, *Guerre italiane in Libia e in Etiopia. Studi militari 1921–1939* (Paese: Pagus, 1991).

15 Antonella Randazzo, *L'Africa del Duce: I crimini fascisti in Africa* (Varese: Arterigere, 2008).

16 Gianluca Di Feo, *Veleni di Stato* (Milan: BUR, 2009).

17 Angelo Del Boca, 'I crimini del colonialismo fascista', in *Le guerre coloniali*, ed. Del Boca, 239. For general context, see also Gian Luca Podestà, *Il mito dell'impero. Economia, politica e lavoro nelle colonie italiane dell'Africa orientale 1898–1941* (Turin: Giappichelli, 2004); and, by the same author, 'Il colonialismo corporativo. Politiche economiche e amministrazione coloniale nell'Africa italiana', in *Governare l'oltremare. Instituzioni, funzionari e società nel colonialismo italiano*, eds. Gianni Dore et al. (Rome: Carocci, 2013), 59–70. For colonial camps, see Angelo Del Boca, *Gli Italiani in Libia. Dal fascismo a Gheddafi* (Rome and Bari: Laterza, 1988); Nicola Labanca, 'L'internamento coloniale italiano'; Luigi Borgomaneri, ed., *Crimini di guerra: il mito del bravo italiano tra repressione del ribellismo e guerra ai civili nei territori occupati*, (Milan: Guerini, 2006). On Somalia, see Labanca, 'L'internamento coloniale italiano', 57.

18 On the narrative construction of the Ethiopian war, see Nicola Labanca's excellent *Una guerra per l'impero: Memorie della campagna d'Etiopia 1935–36* (Bologna: Il Mulino, 2005). More recently, Giacomo Lichtner, 'Italian Cinema and the Italian Past: Tracing Memory Amnesia', *Fascism*, no. 4 (2015): 25–47; and Robert Mallet, *Mussolini in Ethiopia, 1919–1935: The Origins of Fascist Italy's African War* (Cambridge: Cambridge University Press, 2015).

19 On Libya, see Nicola Labanca, *La guerra italiana per la Libia. 1911–1931* (Bologna: Il Mulino, 2012); on both cases, see, by the same author, *Oltremare: Storia dell'espansione coloniale italiana* (Bologna: Il Mulino, 2002).

20 Atteo Merlo, quoted in Liliana Lanzardo, *Immagine del Fascismo. Fotografie, storia, memoria* (Milan: Franco Angeli, 1991), 86.

21 Gerald Howson, *Arms for Spain: The Untold Story of the Spanish Civil War* (New York: St. Martin's Press, 1999).

22 Stanley Payne, *Historia del fascismo* (Barcelona: Planeta, 1995), 297.

23 ACS, MinCulPop, b9.

24 Paul Preston, 'La aventura española de Mussolini: del riesgo limitado a la guerra abierta', in *La República asediada: Hostilidad internacional y conflictos internos durante la Guerra Civil*, ed. Paul Preston (Barcelona: Península, 1999), 43. The historians to whom Preston refers to are the 'official' historians of Francoism, as well as Renzo De Felice and John F. Coverdale.

25 Pietro Pastorelli, 'La politica estera fascista dalla fine del conflitto etiopico alla seconda guerra mondiale', in *L'Italia fra tedesche e alleati: La politica estera fascista e la seconda guerra mondiale*, ed. Renzo De Felice (Bologna: Il Mulino, 1973), 103–114.

26 As pointed out by Coverdale, but also by Alberto Rovighi and Filippo Stefani, *La partecipazione italiana alla guerra civile spagnola* (Rome: USSME, 1992); and, of course, De Felice, *Mussolini il Duce vol. II.*

27 De Felice, *Mussolini il Duce vol. II*, 359.

Fascist intervention in coup d'état of 1936   55

28 USSME, F6, 280.
29 Francesco Belforte, *La guerra civile in Spagna* (Milan: ISPI, 1938), vol. IV, 237ff.
30 Paola Lo Cascio, *La guerra civile spagnola: Una storia del Novecento* (Rome: Carocci, 2013).
31 Michael Alpert, *Aguas peligrosas: Nueva historia internacional de la Guerra Civil Española 1936–1939* (Madrid: Akal, 1998).
32 Massimo Mazzetti, 'I contatti del governo italiano con i conspiratori militari spagnoli', *Storia Contemporanea*, no. 6 (1979): 1181–1193; Heiberg, *Emperadores del Mediterráneo*, 51.
33 ASMAE, GAB, b786.
34 Ministero degli Affari Esteri, *I Documenti Diplomatici Italiani*, Serie 8, vol. IV, 16 June 1936, 607.
35 Heiberg, *Emperadores del Mediterráneo*, 51.
36 ASMAE, MinCulPop, b230.
37 Ismael Saz, *Mussolini contra la Segunda República: Hostilidad, conspiraciones, intervención* (Valencia: Alfons el Magnànim, 1986), 212.
38 The answer was no, although it was not explained in writing—or, at least, was not archived as a reply to the original message.
39 Morten Heiberg and Manuel Ros Agudo reach the same conclusion in *La trama occulta de la Guerra Civil: los servicios secretos de Franco, 1936–1945* (Barcelona: Crítica, 2006), 34.
40 Manlio Gabrielli, *Una guerra civile per la libertà: La Spagna degli anni 30 alla luce degli anni 60* (Rome: Volpe, 1966), 9ff. Still, from page 30 onwards, this book contains an interesting account of how the failure of the coup was experienced in the embassy in Madrid at a time when the ambassador was in Donostia.
41 USSME, F6, 327.
42 ASMAE, GAB, 785, unnumbered.
43 De Felice, *Mussolini il Duce vol II*, 364. The general himself appears to have made these notes in a sort of private review of Alcofar Nassaes' book on the CTV.
44 Ibid., for Luccardi's telegrams and the replies from Italy.
45 Luis Bolín, *España: los años vitales* (Madrid: Espasa Calpe, 1967), 178. For a detailed account, see Sandro Attanasio, *Gli italiani e la guerra di Spagna* (Milan: Mursia, 1974) 38ff.
46 ACS, MI, PolPol, SPd, CR, f5.
47 ASMAE, GAB, b795.
48 Paul Preston, *Franco, 'Caudillo de España'* (Barcelona: Grijalbo, 1994), 201ff.
49 Ministero degli Affari Esteri, *I Documenti Diplomatici*, Document 584, 'The official in charge of the consulate general in Tangiers, Luccardi, to the Ministry of War', Tangiers, 21 July 1936, 652.
50 ASMAE, US, b12.
51 Enrique Moradiellos, *La guerra de España (1936–1939): Estudios y controversias* (Barcelona: RBA, 2012), 79.
52 'Only in this respect was help that the others gave us was important, since otherwise the only official Spain in the eyes of the whole world would have been Red Spain and only it would have been able to gain access to credit, raw materials, and enough weapons to pursue the war. Without Italy and Germany's veto, with which there was reason to fear a widening of the war, Russian and French help would have given way to open intervention.' Ramón Serrano Suñer, *Entre Hendaya y Gibraltar* (Barcelona: Planeta, [1947] 2011), 40–41. On the issue of the war as one of national independence, in which foreign intervention was irritating and complicated to explain, see Xosé Manuel Núñez Seixas, *¡Fuera el Invasor! Nacionalismos y movilización bélica durante la guerra civil española (1936–1939)* (Madrid: Marcial Pons, 2006).
53 Ángel Viñas, 'La connivencia fascista con la sublevación y otros éxitos de la trama civil', in *Los mitos del 18 de julio*, ed. Francisco Sánchez Pérez (Barcelona: Crítica, 2013), 79–181. On the international dimension of the war and particularly relevant to the subject of this book, see, by the same author, *La soledad de la República. El abandono de las democracias y el viraje hacia la Unión Soviética* (Barcelona: Crítica, 2006); and *El honor de la República. Entre el acoso fascista, la hostilidad británica y la política de Stalin* (Barcelona: Crítica, 2009).

56 *Fascist intervention in coup d'état of 1936*

54 AMAE, AB, L1466, C9.

55 There is little to add to the now canonic account developed by Ismael Saz in *Mussolini contra la Segunda República*, and his earlier, related chapter 'Antecedentes y primera ayuda material de la Italia fascista a los sublevados en España en julio de 1936', in *Italia y la Guerra Civil Española: Simposio celebrado en la Escuela Española de Historia y Arqueología de Roma* (Madrid: CSIC, 1986), 155–169.

56 ASMAE, MinCulPop, b230.

57 Ministero degli Affari Esteri, *I Documenti Diplomatici*, Documento 617, 'The Consul General in Tangiers, De Rossi, to the Minister of Foreign Affairs Ciano', Tangiers, 25 July 1936, 690–691.

58 Saz, *Mussolini contra la Segunda República*, 184.

59 ASMAE, GAB, 796.

60 John Coverdale, *La intervención fascista en la guerra civil española* (Madrid: Alianza, 1979), 21–22; Saz, *Mussolini contra la Segunda República*, 184–186; Moradiellos, *La guerra de España*; Attanasio, *Gli italiani e la guerra de Spagna*, 42.

61 ASMAE, MinCulPop, b230.

62 Cantalupo, *Fu la Spagna*, pp. 63 ff.

63 ACS, MI, PolPol, F168; MAE, AB, C RE101.

64 See the factual account in Marina Casanova, 'El inicio de la guerra civil y sus repercusiones en los diplomáticos españoles acreditados ante el Quirinal y el Vaticano', *Espacio, Tiempo y Forma: Serie V, Historia Contemporánea* IV (1991): 31–40.

65 AMAE, AB, C RE155.

66 Magaz's words in AMAE, AB, L1460, C16.

67 AMAE, AB, L1460, C16.

68 USSME. F6, 327.

69 For the many authors who have dealt with the subject, the reference is a classic work published in Franco's Spain with a foreword by Manuel Fraga, Minister of Information and Tourism and guarantor—in a manner of speaking—of historiographical objectivity about the War of Liberation: Francisco Virgilio Sevillano Carbajal, *La diplomacia mundial ante la guerra española* (Madrid: Editora Nacional, 1969).

70 Paul Preston, *La Guerra Civil Española* (Barcelona: Debate, 2006), 130; originally published in English as *A Concise History of the Spanish Civil War* (London: Fontana Press, 1996).

71 USSME, F6, 327.

72 ASMAE, GAB, b786.

73 ASMAE, US, b23.

74 ASMAE, UC, b46.

75 Josep Massot i Muntaner has devoted several books to Bonaccorsi: *Vida i miracles del 'Conde Rossi'* (Barcelona: Publicacions de l'Abadia de Monserrat, 1988); *El primer franquisme a Mallorca* (Barcelona: Publicacions de l'Abadia de Monserrat, 1996); *Guerra civil i repressió* (Barcelona: Publicacions de l'Abadia de Monserrat, 1997); as well as the updated information available in the chapter 'El *comte Rossi*, un fantasma a la guerra civil', in *De la guerra i de l'exili: Mallorca, Montserrat, França, Mèxic (1936–1975)* (Barcelona: Publicacions de l'Abadia de Monserrat, 2000), 71–92.

76 AMAE, AB, L1460, C6.

77 Coverdale, *La intervención fascista*, 135. For a detailed account of Bonaccorsi's action in defending Palma harbour, including the famous incident of him begging to be killed with his own pistol by García Ruiz, the commander reluctant to attack, see ASMAE, GAB, f794.

78 ASMAE, US, b22.

79 On this point, see José Miguel Campo Rizo, 'El Mediterráneo, campo de batalla de la Guerra Civil Española: la intervención naval italiana. Una primera aproximación documental', *Cuadernos de Historia Contemporánea*, no. 19 (1997): 55–87. On the naval base at Sóller, see Ignacio Recalde Canals, *Les submarinos italianos de Mallorca y el bloqueo clandestino a la República (1936–1938)* (Mallorca: Objeto Perdido, 2011). See also José Luis Alcofar Nassaes, *La marina italiana en la guerra de España* (Barcelona: Euros, 1975).

80 Dimas Vaquero, *Credere, Obbedire, Combattere: fascistas italianos en la Guerra Civil Española* (Zaragoza: Mira, 2009), 22.
81 USSME, F6, b280.
82 MAE, AB, L1459, C3.
83 Faldella, *Venti mesi di guerra*, 122.
84 USSME, F6, 327.
85 Cited in Heiberg, *Emperadores del Mediterráneo*, 102.
86 ASMAE, MinCulPop, b230.
87 USSME, F6, 328. As a test, it was decided to form a contingent of 130 officers and 1,000 men, competent and trained and, where possible, with combat experience and with full knowledge of their service records and history: recruitment for the duration of the campaign, enlistment into the *Tercio*, recognition of their employment in the Italian Army, travel paid by Spain. Soon afterwards, in February 1937, a request was made to send no more officers—firstly, because they were not needed and, secondly, because the recruitment at the embassies was producing questionable results: there were volunteers who falsely claimed to be officers, without invoking the specified salary of six pesetas, of which two were for food and one for clothing.
88 Faldella, *Venti mesi di guerra*.
89 A reasonable middle position is contributed by Marco Puppini, 'Gli italiani alla Guerra Civile Spagnola', in *Congreso Internacional sobre la Batalla del Ebro*, vol. 1, *Ponencias*, eds. Josep Sánchez Cervelló and Sebastián J. Agudo Blanco (Tarragona: Arola, 2011), 171–187. There were moreover economic aims which remain to be explored. See Gennaro Carotenuto, *Franco e Mussolini: La guerra mondiale vista del Mediterraneo: i adversi destini dei due dittatori* (Milan: Sperling & Kupfer, 2005).
90 Heiberg, *Emperadores del Mediterráneo*, IX.
91 From an interpretative point of view, this seems to me the most interesting idea in Coverdale, *La intervención fascista*, 89.
92 For Pilar Primo de Rivera's handwritten petition, which pleaded also for her aunt María and for her sister-in-law Margarita Larios, and in which the presence of Indalecio Prieto's family in Genoa was noted as possible a means of exerting pressure, see ASMAE, GAB, f792, which also contains the documents on Olazábal and fascism.
93 ASMAE, GAB, b796.
94 USSME, F18, b9.
95 Preston, *Franco*, 257.
96 USSME, F18, b5.
97 ASMAE, GAB, f792.
98 USSME, F6, 327.
99 See the Italian Embassy in Madrid's list of past heads of Italy's diplomatic mission to Spain, 'Capi missione italiani in Spagna', last consulted 28 August 2020, https://ambmadrid.esteri.it/ambasciata_madrid/it/i_rapporti_bilaterali/capi-missione-italiani-in-spagna.html.
100 See the analysis by Rossella Ropa, 'L'Italia fascista nel conflitto spagnolo', in *Immagini nemiche: La Guerra Civile spagnola e le sue rappresentazioni 1936–1939*, ed. Luca Alessandrini (Bologna: Editrice Compositori, 1999), 248.
101 MAE, AB, L1459, C3.
102 Mussolini made a veiled reference to the matter in a speech in Milan on 1 November, when he indicated that, among the different issues relating to the agreements with Germany, there were currently several burning ones. *Opera Omnia*, vol. XXVIII, 69.
103 USSME, F18, b9.
104 Ibid.
105 USSME, F18, b2.
106 ASMAE, US, b1.
107 ASMAE, US, b22.
108 ASMAE, US, b1.

58 *Fascist intervention in coup d'état of 1936*

109 Coverdale, *La intervención fascista*, 162. Faldella told Attanasio that the reason for such a reaction was that 'when you send troops to a friendly country, you at least ask for permission'. Sandro Attanasio, *Gli italiani e la guerra di Spagna* (Milan: Mursia, 1974), 107. According to the telegrams from the MMIS, he would ask for 9,000 more, already trained, dissenting from Mussolini's wish that they have complete military autonomy. See Ismael Saz and Javier Tusell, *Fascistas en España: La intervención italiana en la Guerra Civil a través de los telegramas de la 'Missione Militare Italiana in Spagna' (15 diciembre 1936–31 marzo 1937)* (Madrid: CSIC-Escuela Española de Historia y Arqueología en Roma, 1981).

110 Attanasio, *Gli italiani e la guerra*, 167–168.

111 USSME, F18, b9.

112 According to the German ambassador to Italy, in December 1936 'Rome's efforts were undoubtedly directed at obtaining Spain's adaptation to its Mediterranean policy or at least at avoiding political cooperation between Spain and the French-British bloc'. Rome's methods were very clear: support for Franco, encampment in the Balearics, political commitment. *Documents on German Foreign Policy 1918–1945, Series D (1937–1945), volume III* (London: His Majesty's Stationery Office, 1951), document 157.

113 ASMAE, US, v5, final report *Ufficio Spagna*.

114 USSME, F6, 328.

115 USSME, H9, 1. Roatta did not think it useful for Italian interests, as it would have created unease among the lower Spanish ranks, and because this could lead to poor compliance with orders issued, which was common anyway. In short, he would be held responsible for defeats, but he would not be the beneficiary of victories.

116 The date of the first telegram is 15 December, as can be verified in Saz and Tusell, *Fascistas en España*.

117 Rovigho and Stefani, *La partecipazione*, vol. 1, 104 and 171.

118 USSME, H9, 1.

119 AMAE, AB, RE101, C27.

120 *Opera Omnia*, vol. XXVIII, 218–220.

121 ASMAE, US, b1.

122 ASMAE, US, b1207.

2 Fascist Italy at war, 1937

Complaints. Constant, reiterative, repetitive, in all directions, sparing nobody, not even Franco himself. Complaints are what feature most in the documentation housed in the Spanish and Italian military archives. But, contrary to what might have been apparent, and to what might perhaps have been justified after the fiasco of Guadalajara in March 1937, they were not always complaints about the Italian troops' performance, their mistakes in underestimating the enemy, or the attitude of superiority which their commanding officers adopted towards the Spanish troops. There were also disparaging complaints about the manner in which the *Nazionali* (the *National* side) were conducting the war, the mentality of their leaders, and the antiquated way of operating by a command that was in difficulty even when the fronts were long and stable and nearly always lacking in knowledge of the enemy. Franco drove Mussolini to desperation, to the point of predicting his defeat during the Republican offensive on the Ebro. The Duce thought that the *Generalísimo* had missed all the opportunities which had been offered to him to win the war. And he was probably right.

That was in 1938, but the Italian complaints about the insurgents' organisation of the war were as old as the uprising itself. Yet they intensified notably in 1937 and dogged the Fascist journey in Spain until well after the offensive leading to victory. Even before the first large contingents of soldiers were sent from Italy, Colonel Emilio Faldella requested, on 9 December 1936, that time not be wasted on the lengthy training of a 'slow and incompetent' Spanish force, badly led, badly armed with weapons of different calibre types, and with barely any transport. Instead, he preferred to despatch Italian troops alone, already disciplined, trained, and with their own weapons.[1] The lack of confidence in the Spaniards' training and abilities only grew following the Italian success in rapidly taking Málaga. And when the defeat at Guadalajara chilled relations between the two armies and their commands, the mutual recriminations escalated to the level of insults. Few armies have been subject to such a campaign of derision and ridicule as that directed at the Italians in Spain. And, as a result, few armies have felt obliged to bolster their combatants' self-esteem in such an obvious way. All this happened in the year of 1937—three hundred and sixty-five days in which the euphoria of victory

60   *Fascist Italy at war, 1937*

gave way to the humiliation of defeat, and the search for revenge to dissatisfaction with the outcome.

What drove the Italian military escalation, in the final analysis, was the desire to test what Italian troops could do on Spanish soil using reliable people and to bring this face to face with the aspirations behind the intervention in Spain (to fight fascism's existential enemy, eliminate the Republic, guarantee supremacy in the Mediterranean, and encourage the creation of a regime which would be in debt, if not dependent). It was an escalation which resulted, by the end of the winter, in Mussolini having a real expeditionary force in Spain, controlled by his own administration and with a degree of independence that was highly unusual for an army fighting, in theory, in support of another. The year of 1937 was a time of propaganda, display, experimentation with military tactics, and the performative demonstration of power. The Italian expeditionary force was formed, grew, and fought in Spain in pursuit of the fundamental objective of winning not a but *the* fascist victory. During the course of that year, in short, the spiral of victory–defeat–victory contributed in the most potent way to reinforcing the fascist presence in Spain.

From *guerra celere* to 'Guadalahara'

There was to be no type of meddling, including on the economic front, if the Spaniards wanted to count on Italian weapons and assistance. Mussolini was so sure of the importance of his assistance in defeating the Republic that, from the start of the year, he dedicated an enormous amount energy to creating his own army that, most importantly, would be independent of the insurgents' command,[2] with no interference whatsoever, to the extent that, on 4 January 1937, he decided that the Italians serving in Spain would not ask for any salary from the Spanish authorities. The latter would be asked only to provide living quarters, food, fuel, lubricants, and general consumer goods. A proportional amount of money in pesetas would be handed out to the Italian soldiers to cover their living expenses. A censorship service based in Italy would be established to screen correspondence. Mussolini further decided that the units sent to Spain would include a 'large and good band to play music' and a chemical unit with materials to create fog and flamethrowers. And the command of this whole expeditionary army would not fall to the low-profile lieutenants who were the first to be chosen but rather—in an indication of the importance which the Duce attached to the intervention— to 'highly decorated fascist'[3] senior officers.

Thus, in January, Fascist Italy became the only foreign country with a whole army in Spain, wielding influence from the fighting on the ground to the upper echelons of political and military decision-makers. In the same month, in response to criticisms about how he was conducting the war, Franco accepted the establishment of a combined Italian-German high command, which was, at the end of the day, what guaranteed his military pre-eminence. This acceptance allowed form to be given to the pact Franco had signed on 28 November in Salamanca, in which he accepted Italian policy in the Mediterranean, and more assistance to be requested by virtue of the December agreements, ratified once again in January at the meeting between Goering and Mussolini on the 14th. As can be deduced from their conclusions, both fascist powers firmly believed that Franco would win, though they had to continue putting pressure on him so that he would speed up operations and not fall into idleness.[4] A sort of false ultimatum was established—international circumstances and the impossibility of extending adhesion to the non-intervention agreements to send volunteers meant that, as Franco was told, the assistance sent in January would be the last. Mussolini wrote in *Il Popolo d'Italia* that the Fascist regime had scrupulously complied with the Non-Intervention Committee's decisions, given that the Italian volunteers had placed themselves exclusively under Franco's orders and not under any kind of Italian command.[5] We know that both statements were false, but that was nothing new in Mussolini's articles.

Franco, then, in no way turned his nose up at help from the Axis. According to Filippo Anfuso, he appeared initially confused by the requests addressed to him. But soon, and after consulting with his closest collaborators, he proved willing to agree to the joint command and to accelerating, to the extent that it was possible, the operations that would lead to the insurgents' victory. Indeed, he used the urgency expressed by Mussolini and Goering to his advantage. In a note verbale of 24 January, he replied to both their requests, expressing his gratitude for the sympathy and friendship of the two nations towards his struggle to re-establish peace in Spain and the principles of Western civilisation. And, fundamentally, he called for more assistance to cover at least three months of fighting, mainly in the shape of arms, ammunition, and military equipment: 100,000 hand grenades; 800 tons of TNT; 12,000,000 cartridges; 775 tons of gunpowder; 500 kilograms of mercury; 400 tons of zinc; detectors for chemical warfare; masks; and bombs loaded with mustard gas, phosgene, magnesium oxide, and calcium hypochlorite, among a long list of requirements.[6] Essentially, he asked for weapons, raw materials, and tools to win the war. To this end, Mussolini, in his determination to emerge victorious from the war as well, offered Franco a whole army. At a meeting held on 15 January at the Ministry of Foreign Affairs between Ciano, Anfuso, General Giuseppe Valle, and Admiral Luigi Biancheri, among others, a decision was taken on the materiel that the Italian government was ready to supply Franco with as soon as possible: 30 aircraft with Italian crews, nearly 2,000 tons of explosives, and more than 850,000 shells for bombarding the Catalan coast, and personnel according to a programme of minimums or maximums. The minimum was 11,000 men and materiel for two months, while the maximum was the same number of Blackshirts plus a special division of the Army.[7] They obviously chose the second programme.

To centralise and handle the growth of the Italian contingent, an organisation was set up in Rome with total economic independence and, as originally

62 *Fascist Italy at war, 1937*

conceived, under Mussolini's sole command. This led Franco to complain before Cantalupo and Colonel Emilio Faldella, though the animosity would not last long. Mario Roatta, the former head of the intelligence service and future Chief of the Italian General Staff in the Second World War, took command and would remain in the post until March 1937. At the time of the CTV's formation, the *Milizia* contributed 30,000 men and the Army 20,000. It was organised on the basis of four divisions of 6,300 men each (the three divisions of Blackshirt volunteers, *Dio lo Vuole*, *Fiamme Nere*, and *Penne Nere*), plus the Army's *Littorio* Division (7,700); the Francisci Infantry Group (3,600); troops integrated into various mixed brigades, among them the *Frecce Nere* and *Frecce Azzure* (2,500 men each); an artillery group (4,100); a specialised group (600); and the service corps (5,000). In total, there were 1,964 officers, 3,697 non-commissioned officers, and 37,915 ordinary troops—43,567 Italians in March 1937.[8] Indeed, if we review the figures from the first landings in December, we can see that, in 45 days, six wholly equipped battalions of volunteers were mobilised, trained, and assembled in four camps (Noceta Inferiore, Eboli, Naples, and Caserta) and then transported. In addition, the 12,000 men of the *Littorio* Division, organised by the Ministry of War under the command of General Annibale Bergonzoli, were transported from Gaeta. All of this amounted to a massive organisational success that was difficult to keep under wraps (as will be explained more thoroughly in Chapter 5) and for which Ciano, Roatta, Faldella, and Mussolini could feel proud.

The troops' first battle, while they were still at the training stage, was the campaign at Málaga. In order to take this island of Republican territory— which, according to the daily operating orders, would provide Franco with a Mediterranean port[9]—Roatta had at his disposal the *Aviazione Legionaria* and 10,000 militiamen, some of whom had recently landed or had barely been trained after a brief instruction period at the operational base at Almazán. The high command deemed it a relatively simple operation. Roatta knew from Ciano that Mussolini fervently hoped for a fascist victory, above all if it took place on 1 February, because of the symbolic value of this date as the anniversary of the MVSN's founding in 1923. There was no reason to think that it would not be possible. The programme of expeditions was moving forward normally, which, Mussolini hoped, would facilitate the job of taking Málaga.[10] However, in the end, it did not take place on the first day of the month. Between 5 and 8 February, Italian troops of the *Dio lo Vuole* Division fought mainly in the mountains surrounding the city. Once the Republican defences had been broken with the help of the air force (which the defenders lacked almost completely), the Italian troops and the insurgents entered the city without too much difficulty. There they were received, according to Fascist propaganda, with 'praise for Italy and for its liberating Army'.[11] Roatta addressed his troops, telling them that, in three days, they had 'liberated a province from Red barbarism, you have brought back peace, freedom, and life. That is how fascism behaves, and you, its armed vanguard fighting for an ideal, have interpreted its spirit and shown its dynamism.' The occupation of Málaga offered the insurgents a spearhead (though Roatta decided not to advance towards Almería). For the Italians, it was the demonstration of *guerra celere*'s viability: mechanised advance, rapid capture, few casualties. All this confirmed what Mussolini's friend Luigi Barzini, *Il Popolo d'Italia*'s correspondent in Spain, had asserted when he told the Duce that one or two divisions of a modern army like Italy's could cut through the Republican lines like a knife through butter.

Following this spate of successes, Mussolini certainly thought that his troops were unbeatable and that a historic destiny was taking shape, none other than the repetition of the steps taken by the legions of Ancient Rome (as will be seen in the statements collected in Chapter 5). 'The conquest of Málaga is the work of the Italian troops', Cantalupo later wrote. He presented his credentials to Franco in Salamanca on 1 March.[12] The whole of 'White Spain' was aware that the victory at Málaga had been an Italian victory (which had left nine officers and 85 soldiers dead, 26 officers and 250 soldiers wounded, and two soldiers missing) and that the MMIS had been behind the plan of conquest. Prestige was high, he said, and they enjoyed great technical authority. Málaga had given everybody, and perhaps above all the Germans, the sense of Italian military maturity. 'The admiration for our army is widespread.'[13] In Málaga, however, together they were able to test the combined occupation tactics of the Italians' *guerra celere* and the insurgents' war of annihilation. However many attempts have been made to portray a Fascist intervention free of reprisals and violence, there is enough evidence to question this assessment. The first such indication is an appraisal by Cantalupo, according to which the intervention by the 10,000 Italians had been decisive in taking the city, because only 1,500 Spaniards had taken part, undertaking mainly 'cleansing' duties, though they were not the only ones who participated in such practices. Despite his initial orders that prisoners were not to be handed over to the Francoist army—which ended up being reversed—Ciano ordered 'mercenaries', 'naturally, beginning with Italian renegades', to be shot on the spot.[14] Thus, orders arrived from Rome that their own countrymen were to be shot without trial and without delay. Nevertheless, Roatta did not order a continuation of the violence once the area had been occupied. That was, in the opinion of the CTV's commander, the responsibility of the Spanish command, albeit with the necessary cooperation of the Italians. In fact, at the same time, very serious issues were raised at the MMIS's operational base in Sevilla, literally, 'news of atrocious reprisals' in the wake of the occupation of Málaga.

'What happened in Málaga is, Your Excellency, very sad', began the report on this affair, may have been written by the consulate and was presented to the Duce in February 1937. It was very sad because the MMIS, Italy, and fascism had found themselves at the heart of an action to eliminate, cleanse, and annihilate real or potential resistance. In the report, the order of events was assembled to prove the Italians' lack of responsibility for the action. The Italian

64 *Fascist Italy at war, 1937*

troops' entry had, firstly, prevented the 'usual plundering' by the Moroccans and Spaniards and the senseless massacres which had become commonplace in Spain. Nevertheless, once the Italian soldiers left the town, a wave of terror took hold. It was said that the 'Reds' had forced all men aged between 18 and 60 to join the ranks of the Communist Party. These lists were later used to carry out shocking summary mass executions, after Roatta handed over the city to the insurgent troops. His only condition was that they respect, as the Italians had done, the lives of the roughly 2,000 prisoners taken in battle, but this condition was not respected. Once the prisoners were handed over to Spanish authorities, they were liquidated en masse. As he earnestly begged the Duce, Italy should not take part in such slaughter, not even indirectly; similarly, it could not allow its support to be used as a pretext for vengeance and atrocities such as those committed in Málaga against 'people who were trapped and did not even know which saint to pray to'. Mussolini, who was a 'man with a good heart', ought to do something about this lack of respect for human life. His would be a serene voice in the midst of this bloody chaos in which everybody was shooting but nobody was speaking, as the fascists did, 'to people's hearts'. If the firing squads were countered with a campaign of healthy fascist education, Spain would change significantly. If not, 'Franco will hoist his flag over a graveyard'.[15]

It is difficult to bring together so many clichés in a single document. This was, in fact, one of the different channels through which news about the occupiers' repressive practices reached Rome. Tranquillo Bianchi, the Italian consul in Málaga, pointed out how people for whom half the city's inhabitants begged for clemency were eliminated following farcical 'trials consisting of primitive methods and hate' on the sole charge of having been mobilised by the Army of the Republic. He had asked Cantalupo to mediate and had obtained Ciano's authorisation to intervene in the interests of preserving Italy's good reputation.[16] His consular offices were providing shelter to people who asked him for moderation, justice, and clemency. These people (women, priests) waited for him every morning at the door of his hotel. The efforts to stop the executions and have the condemned (some 400 according to his own calculations) placed under Fascist protection were taking up all his time. Carrying the lists of those whom he had decided to protect, he entered and exited the city's prisons, stopped firing squads, and conversed with prison directors. Branded as overly sentimental and dramatic and—in Cantalupo's view—exceeding his authority in his work to provide asylum, Bianchi was, according to Italo Sulliotti (the Minister of Popular Culture Dino Alfieri's envoy in Spain), a 'typical man of [fascist] action'. He tried to save the lives of as many people as he could, without any clear criterion, lives like that of a young man condemned to death for singing 'The Internationale' or those of the 22 prisoners for whom he obtained a partial pardon from Franco by telegram, a pardon which he reportedly extended to all of them by manipulating the text sent by the Caudillo.[17] For Bianchi, 'true fascist justice' should not 'sow death, but rather redeem and construct'. He had carried out similar work in the months when the city was under Republican control (according to some documents, he had saved the lives of General Gonzalo Queipo de Llano's family). Bianchi believed that the excesses of the repression might also affect Italy's image and prestige. But his work was criticised as imprudent by Cantalupo and as demagogic by Ettore Conti (who thought him motivated by '*amour-propre*').[18] He also offended the sensibilities of those in charge of this random system of annihilating the political opposition, and in particular those of Queipo de Llano.

Thus, far from being without problems, Bianchi's intervention forced Cantalupo—who disparaged him as a heavy drinker—to send a subordinate, Livio Gaetani, to inform him about what was happening in the city. And what was happening was nothing other than summary trials, with shoddy defences and conducted in groups, of men and women who had been unable to escape the city. Executions were initially carried out by shooting victims in the back of the head and later by the firing squad (at eight in the evening, midnight, and dawn) against a cemetery wall, which had to be repainted every morning, leaving piles of bodies, which family members could take away to bury. The 'repression carried out by the *Nationals*' was astonishing; while it was 'undoubtedly necessary in depth, perhaps it has been excessive in its extent'. It is important to emphasise this point—for Gaetani, the repression was necessary, even if it was proving excessive. The problem, as would be seen throughout the conflict, was not its nature but its degree. Such violence could, in fact, be moderated. Nationalist Spain, he said, would still be saved if 'some hundred fewer Communists' were shot in Málaga.[19]

At all events, the fact is that Franco had no real problem in admitting to what had occurred in Málaga and, generally, acknowledging the enormous amount of violence involved in establishing his power. In an interview with ambassador Cantalupo (described by telegram to Ciano on 5 March 1937), the 'Generalissimo has stated clearly that the massacres by White militias ended some time ago'; except in 'uncontrolled' cases, the exercise of 'summary justice was being handled by military tribunals'. He admitted that, following the occupation of Málaga, the tribunals had acted severely—about 50 per cent of those accused of being 'leaders and criminals' had been condemned to death, some 20 per cent had been charged and some 25 per cent acquitted, and more than 5 per cent had been pardoned. He indicated, nevertheless, that he had given instructions for 'more mercy [to be shown] to the uncultured masses and the same severity towards leaders and criminals'. Some weeks earlier, he had given orders that prisoners of war were not to be shot and that publicity to that effect should be broadcast by radio. The 'Reds' had to understand that the Fascists' arrival meant 'protection and pacification and not terror and reprisals'. Yet, despite these changes, the number of capital punishments still seemed enormous to Cantalupo.[20] For this reason, and with the prospect of the 'repression' continuing and spreading in an inhumane manner when Madrid was occupied, the ambassador requested nothing less than Mussolini's direct intercession before Franco. Cantalupo's motives were

66 *Fascist Italy at war, 1937*

certainly not humanitarian. What worried him was that, for a long time to come, nobody would be able to remove the stain of violence from the Fascists' record in Spain.

As is well known, the insurgents' military justice continued along the same path signposted by the occupation of the city and the province of Málaga. General Franco's headquarters acknowledged 804 people had been shot in mid-March, far from the 3,000 reported by Bianchi. But, sentimentality and exaggeration apart, the fact is that the estimate made by the consul (who was named freeman of the city a few days later) took into account the killings carried out before the establishment of the military tribunals, whereas the official figure did not. Moreover, the insurgents' own justice administration admitted that, of the total tried, about 25 per cent were acquitted, about 25 per cent were sentenced to prison terms, and about 50 per cent were sentenced to death.[21] This percentage was intended to give the MMIS proof of the Francoists' adherence to the law but, seen from the vantage point of today, amounts to incriminating evidence of intentional political and social cleansing behind the front lines.

In any case, it is rare to find official documents from the insurgent side in the Spanish Civil War that contain as much information about killings, and as much calculated compassion and hypocrisy, as the report sent to Mussolini. Indeed, as these same reports acknowledged, the Italians had also shot unarmed prisoners, but 'only' communists who had allegedly fired at their columns in acts of guerrilla warfare, and especially those who had fired at them from behind or who had stayed behind in the houses of occupied villages to fire their last cartridges at the victorious troops. The Italians' actions were 'logical and healthy' ('*logica e salutare*'). Furthermore, in Málaga, Consul Bonaccorsi had taken an active part. After leaving his assignment in the Balearics, he joined the MMIS as an inspector of the volunteer units, tasked with disseminating propaganda and providing moral support. His role in the taking of the Andalusian city is shrouded in the suspicion, or rather the certainty, that he was responsible for the killing of unarmed prisoners. '*Si non è vero, è ben trovato*' (Even if it is not true, it is well conceived). In view of the rumours that he had ordered the shooting of a prisoner or had done it himself, Count Rossi had to remind Roatta of the great affection with which the Duce had sent him on his mission to serve the fatherland against communism in Spain and that, subsequently, on a proselytising mission, he had visited the places where Italian troops were fighting as combatants for civilisation and representatives of a great empire, in order to spread the fascist idea and the word of Mussolini. And he had encountered nothing but difficulties, starting with the jealousy of the Italian Army's commanders, despite remaining close to Roatta, whom he claimed to have accompanied to the sick bay after the latter was injured by machine-gun fire during the taking of Málaga. None of his explanations refuted the accusations concerning his role in the spur-of-the-moment killings. What he actually submitted as evidence in his defence was a reminder of his intimacy with Mussolini and the commander of the CTV.

Nonetheless, his reputation for violence was already widespread. In a note of February from Italo Balbo about a dinner with various acquaintances—including Senator Vittorio Cini and the director of the periodical *Il Lavoro Fascista*, Luigi Fontanelli—the Fascist air force commander had indicated to him that Bonaccorsi's conduct was a 'despicable matter: he has done nothing but kill prisoners'.[22]

Rejected by the entire Italian military caste, Bonaccorsi was seeking the recognition for which Roatta recriminated him. And Bonaccorsi's words would not carry much weight, other than perhaps to show that, in the timeline of his activities, there are moments that are of great interest when it comes to reconstructing the occupation's violent practices and policies. Perhaps he was not conscious of the significance of his words when writing certain paragraphs, but today we recognise the importance of finding documentation which admits to and justifies killing prisoners of war on the spot, such as the prisoner who, as he wrote, had to be killed during a transfer on the grounds that he was trying to escape. We know well what that normally means. Bonaccorsi admits to having ordered the shooting in situ of a 'communist' for having fired at a Blackshirt while surrendering and to having authorised the shooting of three other prisoners found unarmed the night before entering Málaga.[23] From the two reports—the one on the 'logical and healthy' shootings and Bonaccorsi's—some provisional conclusions can be drawn. The first is the need to, at the very least, suspend the widespread indulgence towards the Italian intervention in Spain and the scandal of the summary executions and mistreatment of prisoners. As will be seen, the Italians also shared the world view regarding the anti-Spain in terms of alarmism, animality, and hatred for 'the other', and they did not abstain from acting in accordance. In addition, it is important to thoroughly examine the reasons for the calls for mercy. As was indicated in the report addressed to the Duce, a bloodbath of this kind 'clearly' generated only rancour among the defeated, exacerbated the problem of revenge in Red territory, and provoked desperate resistance. The result of the terror was hardened resistance, and for that reason alone its indiscriminate use had to be rethought. Generosity, on the other hand, 'would demolish the Spanish anarcho-communist shack at a stroke', given that morale in the rear areas 'was dreadful'.[24]

Violence against prisoners and civilians was not the only reason for the friction between Italians and Spaniards in the wake of the Andalusian city's capture. As Cantalupo admitted, the 'currency of gratitude' was in short supply in Nationalist Spain; indeed, following the capture of Málaga, it was necessary to conceal the Italians' participation due to the 'requirements of diplomacy' and make it appear that it had been the Spanish. Nobody wanted the Fascists to be the victorious troops. The official Italian position in the Non-Intervention Committee required silence; in return, the Spanish authorities were relieved of the debt of gratitude. Faldella met Franco on 13 February in an attempt to guarantee the CTV's freedom and ensure it would receive orders only from the Italian government. Yet Franco neither congratulated

68   *Fascist Italy at war, 1937*

him on the capture of Málaga nor indicated any gratitude (which was odd, to say the least, in Faldella's words) for the delivery of the hand of Saint Theresa de Ávila, a holy relic captured from a convent in the town of Ronda during the offensive. In fact, Franco was considering redistributing Italian troops to make their presence less obvious during large-scale attacks and critical manoeuvres. It is possible that the Italian press correspondents' treatment of the success of Málaga and the resulting propaganda was overkill. In this context, in the words recorded by Olao Conforti (which, as always with exact words attributed to others, are suspiciously literal), Franco blurted out that 'the Italian troops came here without asking me for permission'. At first, they had told him that 'companies of volunteers [would come] to form part of the Spanish battalions'. Then, they asked him for 'Italian battalions to be formed and I agreed'. Later, 'officers and generals began arriving to command them, and finally units already formed began arriving'. Now, in addition to the rapid conquest of Valencia, 'you want to force me to allow these troops to fight together under the orders of General Roatta'.[25] It was very clear to the Caudillo that Valencia had to be taken by the *National* troops, as with any other major attack that could change the course of the war. The military and political fiasco of Guadalajara would end up taking care of the rest of the petitions (for a sole command, etc.).

In all this, however, Franco's reluctance to use the legionary troops sounds more like apocryphal legend: firstly, because the words attributed to him were reported too literally to be believable; but, secondly, and most importantly, because, as the communications with the MMIS command show, and as the facts demonstrate, Franco was far from abandoning their use. Indeed, Roatta began to settle the details of the CTV's plans of action as soon as the operation against Málaga came to an end. He was already planning the capture of Guadalajara in detail; in a note addressed to Franco, he advised him to deploy legionary units around the 'Siguenza [*sic*]-Guadalajara' line, with the objective of descending heavily on the rearguard of Madrid in an operation of rapid movement, at the same time coordinating with the Spanish troops deployed to the south, at Alcalá, and between Somosierra and Guadalajara. Faldella relayed this operational plan to the *Generalísimo*'s headquarters at a meeting on 13 February. Despite maintaining strong reservations about the massive use of the Italian legionary troops, operating 'on their own and independently', so as to avoid problems in the international arena—including further intervention by the anti-fascist powers—Franco considered that the MMIS's proposal for occupying the centre of the country generally aligned with his general staff's plan. Most importantly, this was because the plan was predicated on Spanish troops absorbing the enemy's energy and besieging and then finally taking the capital. For Franco, this last point was fundamental. The key to allowing Italian troops to take part en masse in the operation lay precisely in Roatta's promise that the Spanish would be the first to enter Madrid as victors.[26] The imminence of the final offensive against Madrid, following the failures of the period from July to September 1936, made the

Italians more necessary than ever, and that meant overcoming Franco's initial resistance to the first plan for Guadalajara. The pincer movement against Madrid included the (ultimately futile) Battle of the Jarama, begun by Franco before the Italian troops had returned from Málaga. Everybody was in agreement, yet the result was a fiasco through and through. The maps, reports, recollections, and all the information available—accusations, mutual recriminations, and disavowals of responsibility—basically point to four controversial issues,[27] namely, the date of the offensive's start, the Italian troops' incompetence and lack of preparation, the cowardice and mistakes of their generals, and the cover provided by the Spanish troops.

The issue of the offensive's start date would provoke a long debate afterwards. According to the Italian commanders, Franco wanted it to begin on 25 February, then it was moved to the 27th, then to 2 March, and, eventually, to the day of Roatta's return from Italy; the latter fixed it for 7 March. In the CTV commander's note delivered by Faldella, the end of February was indicated as the target start date, pending approval by Franco's general staff and the MMIS.[28] At that time, the operations on the Jarama front were significantly weakening the enemy and the International Brigades, as the Italian general would acknowledge later (but not at the time). However, something similar was happening to the Francoist forces as well—they had lost some 6,000 soldiers as a result of the heavy attacks by the Republicans. Thus, the subsequent criticism which sought to justify the fiasco at Guadalajara (41 officers and 382 soldiers killed, 120 officers and 1,715 soldiers wounded, and 10 officers and 486 soldiers missing, mostly taken prisoner) by blaming the lack of Francoist support was unfounded. The fighting along the Jarama had made the People's Army's response slower and less effective. In my view, there is no reason to place blame for the defeat anywhere but on the Italians themselves. Yet, drawing on a single source (Conforti) and, indirectly, on Italian military documents, many authors argue that the defeat was something sought by Franco in order to lower Italian aspirations. But this view falls flat on at least three factual grounds. Firstly, General Franco himself thought of the Italian force as part of his own. Secondly, the operational plan for Guadalajara was discussed and approved by the *Generalísimo*, who commanded of all the armies. Lastly, the Italian documents themselves disprove this view. Ambassador Cantalupo made the point in a telegram dated 20 March—the criticism directed at Franco by the Italian command and government, to the effect that he had failed to order a joint attack on the 8th in the Jarama, was groundless. The request had come from Italy that the attacks take place on 25 February and 1 March, which is what happened and which meant losses for Orgaz of about 32 per cent of his army, 6,000 men, according to the same report from Cantalupo. This was why Orgaz opposed a third attack on the 8th. The lack of coordination between the two fronts would end up being decisive.

Roatta did not see things the same way. For him, as the man ultimately responsible for the failure of the military offensive, the criticism directed at

70 *Fascist Italy at war, 1937*

the Spanish high command was not that groundless. The problem, according to Roatta, was that the Italians had not been ready to attack on 27 February and 1 March, for want of men and equipment after the attack on Málaga. In fact, during the worst of days of the fighting along the Jarama at the end of February, he had to turn down the support of his reinforcements stationed at Sigüenza. At all events, there appeared to be a huge lack of coordination. But, most importantly, there was little communication from Roatta, as well as much obstinacy and limited influence on the part of the three Italian officers attached to Franco's general staff during the battle. In the days prior to the attack, the strong Republican response along the Jarama had paralysed the insurgents' thrust and halted their operations, bringing the situation back to square one, with severe losses on both sides. When news reached the Republican Army's headquarters that Italian troops were being sent northwards (Roatta would complain bitterly that 'in this country a secret is an impossibility'), some of the international fighters were, in turn, sent there. All eyes and hopes were fixed on the Fascist troops, which, according to the Italian general, would rely on diversionary attacks in the Somosierra and Guadarrama area, as well as to the southwest of the capital, where a mixed brigade would be sent.

On 5 March, Roatta, who had returned from Italy only two days earlier, announced 'his' operation for seven o'clock in the morning on the 8th, which met with Franco's favour despite the exhaustion of Orgaz's troops and their limited capacity to penetrate. Thus, Franco raised no objection to the start date of the offensive. The original plan anticipated the capture of the entire area and the capital between 8 and 11 March, despite a snowstorm severe enough to block the roads. Roatta telegrammed Ciano and Mussolini the day before to tell them of the hour of the attack and of the presence of International Brigades troops on the Algora–Guadalajara line at Miralbueno. Moreover, other units were moving between Alcalá and Guadalajara, which led him to presume that the enemy would offer positional resistance. He also told them of the importance of reaching Guadalajara quickly, which was why, of the three available divisions, the one in the lead would have the artillery's full support, in order to break through the front rapidly. Thereafter, a second motorised division would overtake the first to head for the capital. Two groups of *Banderas* would protect the left flank of the Tajuña River, while the right flank near Jadarque would be in the hands of a Spanish brigade. The bad weather continued on the 7th, making the air force's preparatory work difficult, but the forecasts predicted that conditions would improve. As Consul Grillo was to indicate in his report, rather than improving, atmospheric conditions were worsening at the time of the attack. Yet, according to Roatta, the barometer was rising, indicating that the weather was improving. A very hard fight was predicted, though they faced it full of faith and confidence.

Too much so, judging by Mussolini's hurried reply to Roatta's telegram, in which he predicted Fascism's second victory in Spain. The Duce was travelling to Libya on the *Pola* at the time, a sign of the overconfidence surrounding the whole operation. Roatta had no maps of the area other than a Michelin guide on a scale of 1:400,000.[29] To put his plan into operation, he had the *Fiamme Nere* Second Division, under General Amerigo Coppi; the *Dio lo Vuole* First Division, under General Edmondo Rossi; the *Littorio* Division, under General Annibale Bergonzoli; and the *Penne Nere* Third Division, under General Luigi Nuvoloni. Apart from the *Littorio* (made up of conscripted men and regular officers), all of them were formed by Fascist militiamen, about 35,000 men in total. An additional 9,000 from Colonel Mazo's brigade, integrated into General José Moscardó's Soria Division, must be added. They were all supported by four squadrons of Fiat-Ansaldo tanks (small three-tonne armoured vehicles with a machine gun but no cannon), 170 field guns, 1,500 lorries, and four squadrons of Fiat CR32 fighter aircraft (some 80 planes, initially unusable due to poor visibility and the muddy airfields in the Soria area).

This last issue turned out to be fundamental. Beyond the clichés, the Fascist troops' misfortune and the factors that made the difference in Guadalajara can be attributed to the shortcomings of the service corps, which forced the soldiers to endure eight days with very basic munitions (12 ammunition clips and four grenades), and to the even more serious infrastructural shortcomings of the airfields used by the insurgent army at Soria, whose muddy landing strips impeded supporting flights. The airport at Albacete, from where the People's Army's aircraft took off, had landing strips made of cement.[30] Equally unhelpful was deficient organisation in a battle excessively reliant on motorisation, which failed in a gigantic traffic jam of lorries, tanks, and artillery pieces when the *Penne Nere* Division tried to relieve the *Fiamme Nere* out in front. The road was blocked with vehicles. There was no air cover. Republican aircraft were taking off. There were no diversionary actions to prevent the People's Army's troops from concentrating in defensive positions. All told, it was the perfect setting for a disaster.

On the 7th, the weather was still described as dreadful, with snow, rain, and gusty winds. It did not improve during the whole of the offensive. '*La pioggia, la neve, il nevischio*' (the rain, the snow, the sleet) feature in all the descriptions. The bad weather persisted from the end of February, exposing the Italian troops to conditions making for considerable physical weakness. Recently arrived from the good Andalusian climate, mostly dressed in colonial uniforms intended for Abyssinia, they found themselves thrust into battle in extremely harsh conditions and with no hot meals for several days. In temperatures several degrees below zero, none of the legionnaires had woollen gloves or balaclavas, not even those who spent several days immobilised in lorries by the side of the road. Roatta was not wrong to point out, in justifying his decisions, that the bad weather was the same for them and for their enemies, and that postponing the attack would have equally meant leaving the troops exposed. Nevertheless, the bad weather had more of an effect on those who were less prepared—the Italians of the CTV.

Snow, fog, and poor supplies were indeed the major problems from 8 March 1937 onwards. The information bulletin of that day reported how,

72 Fascist Italy at war, 1937

sure enough, the fighting had begun at seven o'clock in the morning with the Italian artillery preparing the ground at Miralbueno. When the motorised division of the *Fiamme Nere* and its armoured vehicles launched their own lightning war—the *guerra celere* extolled by Mussolini—they found that, in addition to the Spanish contingent's inability to follow their advance, visibility was less than a hundred metres, it was freezing cold, and the ditches and fields adjacent to the only road forwards were muddy and full of snow, impracticable even for walking.[31] Even so, half an hour after the start of the offensive, the troops managed to take the first places from the enemy, despite their defence, and advance some ten kilometres.

As soon as he was informed, Mussolini wrote a euphoric telegram, praising the legionnaires' tenacity in the face of the enemy's resistance and recalling that the defeat of the international forces would be seen as a success of great political value. However, the offensive, which resulted in the Francisci group occupying Brihuega on foot during the early hours of 10 March, was unsuccessful. They advanced no further. The Italian advance on Torija ran into Republican opposition in the famous wood at Brihuega. At the same time, resistance at Trijuerque slowed the CTV's capture of the town. The *celere* offensive was thus blocked. It reached its furthest point on the 12th at kilometre 77 of the highway to Madrid. The legionnaires were forced to fight in conditions of the utmost severity. From that point onwards, the story has been used for the purpose of reducing the Fascist military intervention to a sort of *opera buffa* and to point to lack of skill (the second major debate among those mentioned previously) as the main cause of the defeat. With the troops immobilised, the famous episodes took place when the Fascist troops seemingly confused a patrol of the Garibaldi Brigade (the Italians of the XII International Brigade) with the troops of the *Littorio* Division. Similarly, the *Garibaldini* made tragic use of the false orders given in Italian by loudspeakers on the orders of Luigi Longo, their political commissar. The messages were used to urge the fascists of the *Bandera 'Indomita'* hiding in the woods of Ibarra Palace to surrender; to question why they had come to Spain to kill those belonging to the same proletarian class; and to accept their shared brotherhood and, of course, the superiority of the just, anti-fascist cause. Despite all this, it does not seem that the question of the orders given over loudspeaker, to which much emphasis has been given in anti-fascist literature, had much effect. Nevertheless, the fascist resistance in the palace took on the characteristics of tragedy, as well as *opera buffa*. The chronicles speak of heroism, of blood flowing down the stairs, of the lack of ammunition and food, of the lack of water to cool down the machine guns and the need to use the soldiers' urine instead, and, lastly, of hand-to-hand fighting in the palace's courtyard, of heroic death. Few of those cornered managed to escape. Italians against Italians in Spain—the echoes of this battle continue to reverberate in the history of Italy, even if the majority of its inhabitants are incapable of pronouncing 'Guadalajara'.

In such conditions, the soldiers' complaints regarding the terrible fighting conditions and, above all, the command's mistakes regarding military tactics and supply are more than understandable. They were thrown into the battle stiff with cold, weary, and asleep on their feet, under Republican aircraft fire, amidst cries of pain, and under a black sky. Still dressed in the cotton clothes brought from Málaga, many of them were without '*capamantas*' (protective clothing), wearing frozen socks, which they were unable to change for days and sometimes weeks.[32] Captain Nanni Devoto would call the hell of the 20 days of fighting a '*bellezza meravigliosa*' (marvellous beauty), the real life dreamed of in the monotony of the garrison, which every young man of the New Italy ought to experience, that of a man on his own, face to face with death and the pain out of which enthusiasm and faith are born.[33] But here it is obvious that propaganda is being constructed after the fact. As Davide Lajolo was to write, when the *Littorio* Division went into battle on the 13th, they found, in the ditches beside the road, corpses, knapsacks, and rifles encrusted in the scarce water which had frozen into ice. It was, at last, the 'face of war. Dead, wounded, screams, grenades exploding, shrapnel coming from the sky'.[34]

Clearly, it was not an experience of trenches, because there were barely any at Guadalajara, although orders were given to dig them and, in some cases, the combination of the stormy weather and the weight of soldiers' bodies lying face down in the mud dragged them down so heavily as to create personal trenches. It was the experience of the enemy's staunch defence and of the fear of friendly fire, shells falling near the terrified legionnaires; of the unbearable cold; of nights in the mud at ten degrees below zero; of hunger. 'They forgot to feed us', Franco Bonezzi would write in his diary, 'but as compensation the devilish cold made our teeth clink together in the same way'.[35] They lacked supplies, orders were wrong or too optimistic—Roatta's decision to commit a third division on the 9th, when the first one had not completed its advance, for example—and most of the soldiers were not ready for what awaited them.[36] Some did not even know what was happening in front of them. Men of the *Littorio* Division, for example, thought they were part of a victorious offensive when, on the 12th, Roatta changed the marching orders and placed them in front of the motorised *Dio lo Vuole* Division, while the hard-hit *Penne Nere* and *Fiamme Nere* Divisions were re-assigned to the reserve. The highest-ranking Italian soldier to die in Spain, Consul General Alberto Liuzzi, was killed that day in battle, in command of the 11th Group of *Banderas*, integrated into the *Penne Nere* Division.[37]

The withdrawal of defeated and demoralised troops and the advance of others along the same road created tremendous chaos, which facilitated the lethal Republican counter-attack combining land and air forces (the latter consisting of fighters and bombers). The CTV's ability to retreat was now reduced by being forced to travel along a single space shared by the advance and the retreat. Moreover, swooping down above the road was 'a storm of

74   *Fascist Italy at war, 1937*

planes, an unbelievable thing . . . they dive, hell erupts, they were Reds, everywhere bombs can be seen falling, the fighter planes on the other hand machine-gun blithely'.[38] Even though Italian fighter planes entered the action from the 13th and shot down ten enemy planes, the Líster Division's counter-attack along the highway to Zaragoza caught the Fascist troops when they had not taken up defensive positions. Much of the CTV's materiel and vehicles were destroyed. Roatta in situ blamed the problems on the lack of support from the Spanish troops, which had also not participated in the fighting on the Jarama, as the telegrams sent to the *Ufficio Spagna* explicitly indicated.[39] Mussolini agreed with him on several occasions. In his telegram dated the 14th, he considered the tactical success achieved to be satisfactory and identified the lack of support as responsible for the failure to make good the initial success. The order was 'regroup in order to attack'.[40] But there was no order, no attack. The most that Roatta could do was defend half of the territory taken, thanks mainly to Bergonzoli.

After several days of relative calm, during which Roatta surprisingly travelled to Salamanca to ask Franco for reinforcements—or, at least, a diversionary operation on the Jarama front—the final Republican offensive began on 18 March. After the first artillery and aerial bombardments of Brihuega, General Rossi (widely identified as the man principally responsible for the defeat) decided to abandon the front, even ignoring Faldella's orders. The *Dio lo Vuole* Division's retreat was chaos. The attacks forced many to withdraw even before they had received orders to do so, with some resorting to climb onto the lorries' bumpers. Sandro Sandri, *La Stampa*'s correspondent, would write, in a censored letter dated 21 March, of a frenzied escape by whole battalions, driven by the machine gun fire of enemy aircraft, free to fly low because nobody was shooting at them. Everybody ran to hide at the first canon shots, abandoning their weapons, even those confronted by less intense attacks. He was, therefore, not surprised that, in the face of the furious attacks of the 18th, the Italians had lost more than ten kilometres of territory. The fighting in the woods terrified the soldiers, who felt surrounded by Russian tanks the whole time. Adding to all this, the lack of hot food, the Arctic cold, and the fatigue, the logical outcome was apathy. Equally logical was the success of the enemy's counter-attack. For Silvo Leoni in the *Littorio* Division, there were 'unforgettable days. No sleep, a lot of work, worn out in every way. A lot of bombing and aerial machine gun fire. Waiting anxiously for change, because we are all exhausted.'[41] The *Littorio* Division managed to endure very violent attacks and even regain territory with the use of flame-throwers. But not even the best prepared Italian division was now in a position to resist. And on Roatta's authority, Bergonzoli gave up defending and ordered the retreat. Only the range of the defensive line prevented a total and unmitigated defeat from becoming a veritable massacre.

Enemy aircraft continued attacking the Italian lines, while the Italians' general asked Franco for his troops to be replaced by Spanish forces, the Navarra brigades, which would arrive on the 23rd. There would be no further change in the fronts. On the 29th, Roatta relinquished command of the area. The Italians had suffered heavy casualties, between 3,000 and 5,000 dead, wounded, and missing. The official figures issued after the battle speak of 340 soldiers and 37 officers killed, 1,871 soldiers and 123 officers wounded, and 574 soldiers and ten officers missing, while the Spanish suffered virtually no casualties. The defeat was overwhelming. Roatta was the first to be sacked by Mussolini, replaced by Ettore Batisco. The Duce's military prestige became the butt of jokes; as a large part of the historiography recounts, even soldiers from the *National* side sang, 'Guadalajara is not Abyssinia/here the Reds throw explosive bombs/the withdrawal was an awful business/some Italians ended up in Badajoz', to the music of the famous Fascist colonial song '*Facetta Nera*' ('Little Black Face'). Oddly, on the 19th, in the middle of the Republican offensive, the first edition of *El Legionario* appeared. According to one of history's longest subtitles, it was the 'newspaper of the workers fighting in Spain in defence of European civilisation against Red barbarism' and carried a famous picture on its front page, that of a pair of pincers on a map of Madrid. Beside it, there was a list of slogans which ordered the volunteers to avenge the fallen, forecast that they would soon enter the capital 'covered in glory at the side of their brothers of *National* Spain', and declaration that 'Italian volunteers . . . victory is near'.[42] In time, those words would become a kind of macabre joke.

With the defeat came the time for explanations. From top to bottom, the first to offer them was Mussolini himself, in an article entitled 'Guadalajara' published in *Il Popolo d'Italia*. From his peculiar perspective, he tackled all the controversial issues, from the start of the offensive to the insurgents' responsibilities, from the character of the soldiers to the command's tactical decisions.[43] And the picture that emerges is one of courageous volunteers whipped by the wind, who, after an approach march of nearly 30 kilometres in the snow, at five degrees below zero, and in uniforms more suitable for the Mediterranean, were unable to count on the 'marvellous' Italian air force—legionnaires, then, who were confronted with a rudimentary and terrible enemy: the elements. They could have waited longer, wrote the Duce, but that would have multiplied the problems. Undeterred, they broke through the enemy's defences in the opening days, achieving a depth of 40 kilometres in the mud and snow, without much food and without the systematic support of the artillery or tanks. Thus, there had been no cowardice, but, rather, soldiers abandoned to their fate and cut off by a 'French-Russian' command in Madrid, which was able to send the International Brigades to counter-attack, thanks to the calm on the southeast front (where Franco had obtained successes of an exclusively tactical nature). The Italians had been subject to the rigours of the toughest battle, full of fluctuations, together with 'violent and inevitable' disorder, in which they went so far as to fight with daggers and other bladed weapons. A battalion lost nearly all of its officers. It was not cowardice but the collapse of technical resources due to slipshod Spanish infrastructure, which caused the only access road to become jammed when the first division was due to be

76 Fascist Italy at war, 1937

replaced, making the legionary units an easy target for the Red air force. The only tactical mistake was the order to withdraw the troops. The legionnaires, who had fought like lions and had demonstrated bravery to the point of rashness, believed that they had won and did not think they had any reason to fall back—so wrote the Duce, revealing a clear loss of perspective. Twenty of the 40 kilometres gained by the advance remained in Italian hands. In this way, Mussolini rejected the campaign of 'lies and slander' by the international press, which portrayed the fall of a battalion as a total defeat, while the 'hyenas with [human] faces' pounced on the 'purest and youngest Italian blood as if it were whiskey'. For the Duce, rather than a failure or non-success, an '*insuccesso*', one ought to speak of a Fascist success, an Italian victory which events had prevented from being used to full advantage. And he finished with a reminder: the fallen of Guadalajara had died for an ideal and, inexorably, like a dogma of faith, they would be avenged.

Mussolini seemed to suggest in this article that the Italians had been abandoned by Franco. Indeed, this was the interpretation that many members of the Royal Army made in order to explain a defeat that, although it did not result in a major victory for the enemy, accounted for around 18 per cent of all Italian casualties in insurgent Spain. A major effort to make the opposite case to Mussolini was undertaken by Roberto Farinacci, former secretary of the PNF and member of the Fascist Grand Council, on a political mission to Spain since February. As the Spanish ambassador to Italy, Pedro García Conde, would later point out, Farinacci was sure that the blame for what had happened at Guadalajara was not to be pinned on Franco and Spanish forces but on Roatta. He had relayed that message to Mussolini and been influential in the decision to dismiss the CTV commander. Although there was no lack of exonerating reports and, in fact, the general was allowed to remain in Spain in a minor role within the CTV,[44] the more widely accepted version was the one adopted by the high command in Rome and circulated in official reports. This version spoke of improvisation and excessive confidence; of mistaken assessments of the enemy's forces; of a lack of liaison and even of information sharing between lines and operative units; of the misuse of military equipment (battalion commanders did not even have maps of the area); of the inefficiency of lorry and tank drivers, some of whom were civilians; and of the dreadful management of supplies, with any available ammunition, hot food, and fuel located more than 30 kilometres from the fronts. All this served to underline the lack of tactical perspective and technical depth caused by Roatta's failure to understand that such a deep territorial offensive without defensive aerial support would leave the troops constantly exposed to bombing and machine gunfire from the enemy, which had clearly been underestimated. In short, it made clear the excessive confidence of those who, like Ciano, thought that the Italians would be able to enter Madrid 'in eight days'. 'They figured that what our forces had not done in several months they were going to manage in a week', as Conde would tell Franco.[45]

Cantalupo was also of the opinion that Roatta had treated the Spanish command with 'arrogance, distance, and coldness'. And, the ambassador said, perhaps he was right in his opinion, because he himself thought that Franco and his generals were the least prepared for the war that was being conducted. But he could not make his opinions known, if he wanted to be respected by the person who was really giving orders. According to the ambassador, neither Franco nor the Germans had wanted the Guadalajara operation because they judged it 'dangerous and of little benefit' at a time when the internal situation was 'fragmentary and provisional' and when it was important to continue fomenting Franco's appreciation of, and dependence on, Mussolini. Following the defeat and the changes of command, 'the Italian troops [would] never again be abandoned'. For that reason, it was necessary to maintain an image of coolness and unity in the eyes of the rest of the bodies dependent on Rome. The MMIS, the embassy, the consulates, and the rest of the political elements, including Farinacci, had to emulate the German mission and its coordinated command and show no signs of disunity. To do otherwise would, in Cantalupo's opinion, only promote 'Spanish ingratitude' and 'coldness towards the Italians' from a 'materialistic and egotistical' people and from a command which took an 'absurd satisfaction in the Italians' lack of success' in a Spain of 'national militarism (it is not possible to speak of Spanish fascism for the moment)' led by a Franco who was 'frigid, feminine, and always non-committal' and who agreed 'with everybody'.[46] As we have invariably seen hitherto, the opinion of the ambassador in Burgos was the result of a mixture of views, ideas, and disjointed propositions, always directed at the same target—the *Generalísimo*, his dubious ability to command, and his alleged femininity, which, he would say, had yet to be disproved.

After the explanations came the search for those responsible. At the end of March, the CTV's command asked Franco's headquarters for a temporary prison in Salamanca for 20 soldiers and two officers due to appear before a military tribunal to explain the defeat at Guadalajara—the reply to which was, curiously, that Franco did not want any military tribunals or prisoners where he lived.[47] This amounted to an implicit recognition of a share of the responsibility, although unfortunately I have not been able to read the conclusions of the cases heard. They would be far from the only accounts to call into question the military abilities of the Italian Army and of its senior and junior officers. Roatta would express the issue in bitter terms—the International Brigades 'were peasants, labourers and workers', but they were well organised and fought with skill and, above all, with 'fanaticism and hate'.[48] Leaving aside the 'dregs', self-mutilators, deserters, and the old and men with families, his soldiers were not bad fighters, but neither did they represent military excellence. At times, they were passive and impressionable due to lack of training, disenchantment, or because they felt that they were simply cannon fodder. But their biggest fault was that they did not hate the enemy. And, according to Bergonzoli (who complained that his division had 2,000

78 *Fascist Italy at war, 1937*

greying men who had never seen a war), in war you had to hate the enemy. To that end, Roatta would recall, those men who had come to Spain on a promise of working the land or of controlling the cities occupied by the *National* side were of no use. They had not come to die for a country that, moreover, was not Italy.

As lessons for the future, the Fascist generals asked Rome for action on four fronts. The first was the removal of the 'opportunists', the 'dregs', and the all too many who had come to Spain in too much of a hurry and with insufficient military training.[49] The second was the despatch of more and better men, ready to fight and conscious of their mission. The third was a much more careful selection of volunteer staff. And the fourth was better training of officers who, given how the Italian mission had been organised, did not know how to lead, abandoned equipment, and did not move their troops correctly. A defeat like Guadalajara could not be repeated. For First Captain Giuseppe Martini, the defeat was indefensible because the CTV had faced no more than a thousand men 'in rags'. However, the defeat was not the only reason for the Italian military increase in the months that followed. The defeat was important because of the repercussions it had in Europe and beyond, its powerful effect in the anti-fascist world, and how it reflected the state of relations between Rome and Burgos and between Spanish and Italian soldiers on the ground. It also tarnished Italy's image. But its impact on the Fascist government's attitude to Spain was limited. It created doubts, but the crisis did not last long: only the time it took for the CTV to achieve success at Santander.

There were those, like Cantalupo, who thought that Franco had engineered the defeat at Guadalajara in order not to agree to the Italian sole command. But nothing in historical or documentary terms substantiates the idea that Franco would have welcomed the defeat of units attached to his own army. Guadalajara provoked doubts about a quick victory and about the means at their disposal to achieve it, as well as doubts about the feasibility of the Fascist war plan in Spain, particularly after the easy capture of Málaga, but it did not cause the Fascists to desist in their effort. Doubts about the Spanish commands existed, though they have perhaps been blown out of proportion. As Conde would write to Franco, the 'disappointment matched the excess of confidence'. The Italian generals' long and discontented faces implied (according to what he knew from Ciano) that they 'had been left on their own' and that the enemy had been able to deploy 'all its forces in the Guadalajara sector', thanks to the 'clearing of the other Madrid fronts' because Orgaz and Varela's troops were inactive. But for Ciano, Franco's reply—that, without a doubt, if there had been defection, 'highly severe and unbending sanctions would be applied'—was sufficient.[50]

Propaganda aside, it was an unmitigated defeat. All divisional heads and officers, except Bergonzoli, were sent back to Italy as a result of their disastrous performance. Roatta, who had become hesitant and insecure following the injury to his arm sustained at Málaga, was replaced as CTV commander. The Italian General Staff accused him of launching an operation without knowing either the terrain or the enemy, using badly trained troops, and with an eye to propaganda. As a report by the *Carabinieri* indicated, he, in turn, blamed the defeat on management failures by the commanders of the First, Second, and Third Divisions. They, in turn, accused the senior officers of the fascist *Milizia* of being incapable of leading units larger than a platoon. No agreement was reached. The different parties to the Italian intervention in Spain (the regular army, the fascist *Milizia*, the political and propaganda section, and, above all, the diplomats) blamed each other for the defeat at Guadalajara, uncorking all manner of tension and internal bickering. Cantalupo could not bear Roatta and accused him of coldness, of lacking the psychological qualities required to charm soldiers, of unnecessary rashness and logistical confusion, of not understanding war's human dimension, and of having a depressive state of mind. He also suggested that he was dominated by Faldella, incapable of waging war, a pessimist, lacking in faith, and annoying and harmful for the troops. Roatta, for his part, ignored the ambassador, whom he saw as distant, stupid, uninterested in the war, and as thinking of himself as Fascist Italy's real and sole representative in Spain. Military men versus the *Milizia*; diplomats versus military men; *e così via* (and so on): all were more or less in agreement about the necessity of achieving the triumph of fascism in Spain, and all more or less identified (with considerable nuances) the insurgent generals as the source of political and military problems for Italy and the CTV. For the rest, they were in open disagreement.

The defeat at Guadalajara signified, in short, the emergence of the serious problems that had been afflicting the Italian intervention as a whole. Mussolini sent Generals Mario Berti and Carlo Favagrossa to work together on restructuring the CTV and General Attilio Terruzzi of the MVSN as inspector and senior commander of the Blackshirts. The CTV's new head, Ettore Bastico, appointed on 15 April to replace Roatta, had to face a difficult situation and try to resolve it, without delay, using the means available. He sent four generals home: Rossi, Nuvolenti, Coppi, and Molinari. He ordered a unit of *Carabinieri* to be brought to Spain as the CTV's police force, adding to the 350 policemen who were already in Spain and had taken part at Guadalajara. In addition to carrying out their normal duties of traffic control and maintaining security behind the lines, they had been used as a means of coercion, inadequate in the end, to prevent a generalised disorderly retreat. Bastico asked that up to eight Italian generals supervise the work of inspecting and restructuring the CTV. And, lastly, he decided to send home those deemed of no use to the war, above all the *Dio lo Vuole* and *Penne Nere* Divisions. Thus, the new CTV commander's first decision was to return to Italy 2,255 wounded men, 2,685 sick men, and, above all, 3,719 men (including 171 officers) on grounds of ill-discipline and poor physical, professional, or moral fitness. This followed several weeks of investigation, pursuing deserters and purging wounded in hospitals. Many of the latter were alleged to be malingerers or self-mutilators, some 930 between the two categories, who would be put into preventative detention.[51] In return, he asked for the

80 *Fascist Italy at war, 1937*

shipment of reinforcements, who would reach 1,500 by June. After training, they would be used to restructure the CTV into three large units: the *Littorio* Division with 7,600 men; the *Fiamme Nere* with 7,700; the *XXIII Marzo* Division with 5,700; plus the mixed *Frecce Nere* Division with 4,300 Italians. He thus kept Bergonzoli's *Littorio* Division and the Blackshirts' Francisci group, the latter repurposed as the *XXIII Marzo* Division, while the three units of the *Milizia* were merged into the *Fiamme Nere* Division, under the command of General Luigi Frusci.

So there would be no going back on the enterprise. On the contrary, as Bastico himself would point out, he came to Spain at a time of chaos and demoralisation, in order to take large-scale action and achieve 'an Italian victory' against the Spanish criteria of using his troops only when contingency and the occasion required them.[52] Italy had transferred a whole army to Spain. On 31 March, it comprised six generals, 22 colonels, 184 senior officers (most of them from the *Milizia*), 2,207 lower-ranking officers (divided equally between the Army and *Milizia*), 3,288 non-commissioned officers (mainly volunteers), 774 men attached to the Army, and 43,714 soldiers, a majority of them (25,872) Blackshirt volunteers. The average daily expenditure was 2,300,000 lire. Following the defeat at Guadalajara, the removal of 3,700 men, the merger of the *Milizia*'s divisions, and the new reorganisation of the CTV[53] were steps taken by the Italian generals, with Bastico at their head (and Berti, his future replacement, second in command), in search of the opportunity to recover lost military prestige, rather than going back on the enterprise. They had 35,832 soldiers under their command[54] following a reorganisation and expansion of services aimed at improving effectiveness. The most noteworthy was the development undergone by the mixed units. In any case, their prestige had been hit following the defeat, as Captain Frederico Garofoli would acknowledge while travelling in Spain two months later. They had to achieve victory, in his words, not 'in spite of Guadalajara, but because of Guadalajara'.[55] They had to do so in order to avenge the Italian dead— 'those dead burn inside us'. The order was revenge, 'and never had an order been received with more enthusiasm'.[56]

Guadalajara had served to purge, to demonstrate publicly Italy's participation as a belligerent in the Spanish war, and to reaffirm the intervention's principles. There would be no place for defeat or withdrawal, as long as the Duce continued to think that, in this great struggle, 'which has pitted two kinds of civilisation and two conceptions of the world against each other', Fascist Italy could not be 'neutral, but has fought and will therefore be part of its victory'.[57] For that reason, they had to carry on fighting against a Republic of 'hate, division, hunger, chaos', bereft of food for the body and for the mind, whose government was no longer legitimate, because since July 1936 it represented nobody but a group of local self-seekers under Moscow's orders— a Republic based on a 'regime of mutual extermination . . . democratic in name only', which would collapse immediately if Franco managed to strike a powerful blow at the right place.[58] Madrid, the Duce would say, in a new show of foresight, would soon fall. Contrary to what the Red literature might say about Madrid being the graveyard of fascism, in fact, Spain would be the graveyard of Bolshevism.

A war in the North

Guadalajara was the last of the offensives against Madrid to fail. Following this defeat of the Nationalists (there is no way of interpreting it other than as a failure of the whole insurgent army), Franco stopped the Italian forces in Spain from operating independently and, as is well known, steered the war towards the north of the Iberian Peninsula.[59] The objective was to eliminate an entire front, which was badly connected with the rest of the Republican territory. Viewed in perspective, it was the first big operation in a total and lengthy war, with all that this entailed, including a system of concentration camps and forced labour for a prison population which, until April 1937, had lived in the most complete anomie.

The Italian intervention in this northern campaign was not straightforward but rather full of tensions between the CTV's new commander, Ettore Bastico, and Franco himself. In fact, the latter successfully manoeuvred to have Bastico dismissed on grounds of disobedience and the Italian general's constant complaints and interference in the decisions taken by the *Generalísimo*'s headquarters. But it was, above all, a time to rethink the Fascist intervention in global terms. Italian troops had fewer military responsibilities, but, precisely because of this, they were more efficient. In fact, after the defeat at Guadalajara, Mussolini demanded operations carrying little risk but a lot of prestige, so as to restore Italy's and the CTV's military honour. It was on this premise that the Francoist command took the decisions to stop the Italians from acting as the initial strike force.

The actual situation after the defeat forced the Francoist command to stabilise a front which had been increased by 20 kilometres. Lacking reserves, Franco transferred the CTV and the *Frecce Nere* Second Mixed Brigade under Piazzoni from Toledo to the North, in order to move closer to the defensive belt around Bilbao along the Urduña-Amurrio-Laudio line. The operation against the Basque capital, decided by Franco in the middle of March, had a high strategic, political, and economic value. Moreover, it was hoped that Italian participation would act as a counterweight to Guadalajara and contribute, in Ciano's words, to 'the Basques' desire to rebel against control by the Reds'.[60] But, despite such lofty desires, the first attacks were repelled starting on 31 March, requiring, in the foreign minister's words, a slow and methodical operation. What was planned was, put simply, the antithesis of *guerra celere*. The defeat had generated distrust of the CTV's military capabilities and, although it had an important air force at its disposal, the role would go to the larger and more decisive participation of the German air force.

The Germans had reaped the prestige of exposing themselves to no risk and capitalising on victories, as Berti would complain, and now it seemed

82 *Fascist Italy at war, 1937*

they were directing the operations in Biscay and taking charge of the operative army. And this was not an agreeable situation for the Italians, as it was Italian blood that was flowing every day in the hard Cantabrian Mountains. And Berti continued, 'We are fighting at full stretch, with and for the Spanish.' The Germans had arrived with a force far larger than the intervention required. They too were fighting, to a certain extent, by and for the Spanish, and, moreover, they sought 'to train and experiment *in corpore vili* with as many of their personnel as possible and with certain types of materiel'.[61] But all this by no means meant that the Italian intervention fell into simple military insignificance. On the contrary, as is well known, the offensive against Bilbao was covered extensively in the air by the *Aviazione Legionaria*. The bombing of the towns of Durango and Elorrio on 31 March by Savoia-Marchetti aircraft of the Italian air fleet, escorted by Fiat CR-32 fighters, caused some 250 victims, most of them civilians. It also heralded the beginnings of a bombing technique which the Italian squadrons would use for the duration of the war: repeated flyovers and sometimes at high altitude in order to evade the anti-aircraft defences and, above all, air attacks with no declared military objectives other than the principal military objective of terrorising the population. It is also well known that the Savoia-Marchetti gave cover and support to the Condor Legion on 26 April during the bombing of the town of Gernika. On entering the town, *Corriere della Sera*'s correspondent, who was accompanying Piazzoni's *Frecce Nere*, wrote categorically that 'Guernica no longer exists'.[62]

However, this was nothing new. This type of bombing had been carried out over Madrid since November and would be carried out over the capital of the Republic, Valencia, because of its status as the capital and because it had an important port. Terror bombings of the Republican cities on the Mediterranean by air and sea were in fact a constant feature of the war. On 14 February, the naval vessel *Duca d'Aosta* fired 125 shells on the centre of Valencia. The city also suffered air attacks. The Italian air force's SM-79s and SM081s based in Mallorca bombed it repeatedly in February, May, July, August, September, and October 1937, leaving hundreds dead and wounded. The same occurred in many other cities along the Valencian coast, including Alacant, Sagunt, Castelló, Peníscola, and Benicarló. Similarly, the port and urban centre were the targets of the Italian bombing of Barcelona; from February, the city was subjected to firing from the sea (70 volleys aimed at the city centre from the *Eugenia di Savoia* on 13 February, causing 'anxiousness and disorganisation'),[63] and, from the end of May, it was subjected to flyovers by the Savoia-Marchetti aircraft. The Catalan capital suffered attacks like the one that destroyed the Barceloneta area on 1 October and established a bloody precedent for the notorious bombing raids of March 1938. An official report by the CTV's *Ufficio Informazioni* on the bombing indicated that the armaments factory, the main target of the attack, had been hit by a single bomb, while the other 12 or 13 had fallen within an arc of 400–500 metres. One fell on a school, causing the majority of the total of 112 victims killed

Fascist Italy at war, 1937 83

and 201 injured. The Catalan government, the *Generalitat*, used a bomb fragment to try and prove Italian involvement in a bombing raid. The attack had impressed the 'French' by its severity, which was apparently what mattered the most to Ciano.[64] It was not the only one in Catalonia. Italian bombs also fell on Reus, Badalona, and Tarragona, striking the city's historic centre, causing numerous civilian victims, and the fuel tanks, which were practically destroyed in September.

The CTV, too, sought to explore new forms of warfare. In this vein, in July 1937, Bergonzoli requested the use of phosphorus bombs, in light of the enemy's alleged use of grenades containing a 'special liquid'. However, Franco informed him that the investigation that had been conducted ruled out the possibility of premeditated use of gas shells by the Republican Army, although on occasions, at the Bricia front, they had fired old shells containing a 'mixture of substances causing tears and sneezing and a little mustard gas in the process of decomposition'. According to the Italian report, they were the remains of shells from the Great War, which had been resold or mixed with some batch by 'unscrupulous dealers'. In any case, it was 'international reasons' and not humanitarian considerations that induced Rome to prohibit the use of this type of bomb. Thus, the shells already in Spain remained in storage and were not distributed.[65] According to a report of mid-September 1937, the CTV had 59,000 shells containing 'special liquid' and 4,000 phosphorous hand grenades, as well as 297,035 gas masks. The fact that gas was not used did not mean that the technology had not been investigated and tested by the Italian army stationed in Spain. The Italians had created the *Corsi Addestramento Ufficiali Spagnoli* (CIAUS), training courses designed to train Spanish officers in military technology (a form of 'hidden propaganda'[66] in competition with the Germans, covering all aspects of Italian military technology, from photo-electrics to hydraulic services). In October 1937, the CIAUS asked its men stationed in Salamanca to help in securing the concealment and defence of aerodromes by means of artificial fog, following a machine-gunning incident in Zaragoza. After the activation time was successfully reduced from five to three minutes, the plan to use artificial fog was established for implementation at all the aerodromes in the North. However, more important was the other big plan for chemical warfare. In 1937, the CIAUS developed a plan for the defensive 'mustardisation' of the Pyrenean border using the Chemical Warfare Service. The plan entailed sowing the Pyrenees with mustard gas, which would be purchased in Italy. The ultimate goal of this plan, and of the possible creation of a factory to produce dangerous chemicals in Spain, was to use the gas if a war broke out between Italy and France.[67]

For all these reasons, it was of paramount importance to gain control of the industrial resources of the North. The CTV's participation in the conquest of Biscay from 27 April onwards took the form of Colonel Piazzoni's *Frecce Nere* Mixed Brigade as the spearhead, which, from Gernika, and despite having received orders from General Mola to the contrary, advanced towards Bermeo. There, they had to resist Republican attacks, forcing the *Frecce Nere*

84 *Fascist Italy at war, 1937*

to fall back and defend themselves in a siege of the Italian troops that some commentators called 'little Guadalajara'.[68] It was obviously an exaggeration. Besides, on this occasion, the support provided by the Navarrese troops tipped the balance in favour of the besieged, such that the Italians never found themselves fighting alone. Nor was it an operation as important as the one at Guadalajara, even if it was relatively significant in the context of the conquest of the Basque capital. However, what turned out to be really fundamental in breaking the Bilbao's defensive belt was not the infantry, which was kept in a secondary position, but rather the artillery commanded by Lieutenant Colonel Enzo Falconi.

'The news of the entry into Bilbao has been received with elation by the Italian people', wrote Mussolini to Franco on 21 June, describing the Basque capital's fall as 'a gigantic step towards the triumph of the *National* cause'.[69] Mussolini was aware of the complex situation which his troops and commanders had gone through and were going through in Spain. Above all, he was aware that the CTV had played little role in the Basque capital's fall, which, by any reckoning, was connected with the defeat at Guadalajara. Franco asked for more Italian troops, and the Francisci group, six brigades, and two escort battalions arrived in Miranda de Ebro on 9 April. But he rejected the use of the *Littorio* Division, which was undergoing a process of reorganisation, and Italian preponderance in general. General Mario Guassardo's First Mixed Brigade was at the Córdoba front and stayed there. But the brigade was not required. The massing of Italian troops suggested—or, at least, led them to believe—that they would be used to take the city, in a repeat of the waging of *guerra celere* against Málaga. Carlo Basile, inspector of the *Fasci Italiani all'Estero* (Italian Fascists Abroad) on assignment in Spain, would write to the *Milizia*'s command that everybody was waiting for an immediate attack, an operation not to erase the memory of Guadalajara but rather so that 'we recover the status which we enjoyed following the capture of Málaga'.[70] Mussolini himself thought that, given the importance which the fall would have to the military and political situation, it was an objective requiring the maximum effort, which meant placing all available legionary forces at Franco's disposal.[71] On the occasion of the Caudillo marking the first anniversary of the founding of the Italian Empire, in the name of the true and eternal Spain in its struggle against communism, the Duce had no difficulty whatsoever in renewing his most fervent wishes for the triumph of the insurgents' cause.[72] All the Italians thought that they would go into battle to take the Basque capital. However, despite being concentrated there, despite Mussolini's fervour, despite the need to erase the memory of the defeat, the CTV was not used for the occupation of Bilbao.

Franco thought, or at least seemed to think (though it sounds implausible), that the position of the Italian sector, between Soncillo and Urduña, could not offer Mussolini a brilliant victory, neither in terms of its impact nor in terms of its effects. Where he believed he could do so and maximise the use of the CTV was to have it operate either above the Amurrio-Laudio communication line or by joining the Fourth Navarre Brigade on its left. Ciano himself wrote of the plan, '*ma così andiamo a rimorchio!*'—that is to say, that they were being towed along by the Spanish leadership when he was demanding they fight in the front line. In fact, Bastico refused the three possible operations offered to him, because he wanted it to be the CTV who broke through Bilbao's defensive belt, rather than having it join the battle later, when the 'demoralised enemy was in a position to be destroyed and pursued'. And he took offence when Franco pointed out that he could not expose the Italians to an operation 'of such severity and difficulty as the breaking' of the city's defensive belt, an operation 'that could fail', with the excuse of wanting to protect Italy's prestige. 'Everything recommends' proceeding with a great deal of caution, the *Generalísimo* noted, so as 'not to be in the absolute impossibility of achieving that Italian success, or at least predominantly Italian' success, which he indicated as the 'principal objective of his mission and which he never forgets'. That was why the complaints were sent to Rome about the failure to use the Italian troops. According to the complaints, when the Francoist command saw that they could enter the city alone, having broken the defensive belt 'without firing a shot', it decided to do without the Italians (who, even so, lost 15 officers and 114 soldiers taking Bilbao, in addition to the 26 officers and 338 soldiers who were wounded and four soldiers who went missing). Roatta was even forbidden to enter the city centre until the Spanish troops had been there for five hours. Without 'an established plan, living from day to day',[73] the CTV was relegated to entering via the coast from the Bermeo sector and going as far as Ontón, in Cantabria. Its irrelevance was considered a grave affront and a punishment.

Whatever the case, from now on the Italians would exaggerate matters as never before. The affront was twofold—Guadalajara and Bilbao. From now on, they would seek only one thing—redress, with the name of Santander. The Battle of Brunete of July 1937, which the CTV did not take part in, acted as a brake, however. It allowed the *Corpo* to carry out reorganisational tasks, purging, and improvement of tactics in anticipation of a battle that would fully engage the Italians, to the extent that all their units would be used in the field. Franco wrote from the Madrid front that the Italian troops were 'excellent in armaments, enthusiasm, and technique, but sometimes they deviate from orders, inasmuch as such orders are considered to be in conflict with those received from Rome'. He had to remind Bastico that not using the Italians troops to take Bilbao, although they had been concentrated there, had been dependent on the 'interests of the war'. His remarks amounted to saying nothing or, better still, to saying that the troops were under his command and that he was the one who decided. In fact, he had no trouble reminding Bastico that the Duce himself had given him complete command of the Italian troops. Nevertheless, 'to the *Generalissimo*'s statement that he had the Duce's permission to use the troops as if they were his own, General Doria [Bastico's codename] countered by invoking his government's opposing orders and saying that he would seek information'.

86 *Fascist Italy at war, 1937*

From then on, the shadow of disobedience hung over the relations between the *Generalísimo*'s headquarters and the CTV. Both commands agreed on the attack to divide Santander from Asturias but not on the method of doing so. In contrast to Franco's invasion plan, the Italians proposed a frontal attack, because they believed the enemy to be in a 'moral depression' due to the lack of food supplies. In the face of the impasse with the CTV's command, let us not forget that, after Bastico rejected a direct order to attack, Franco proposed an operation in the direction of Valmaseda or in the sector of the Escudo Pass and Reinosa. The Italian commander accepted this last option 'with enthusiasm'. He did not give a direct order to attack. However, the following day, Bastico ordered the preparation of an operation, not according to plan, but instead at Ramales, midway between Bilbao and Santander, envisaging a chaotic retreat of the fleeing Republican Army.

Franco's headquarters saw the move as reckless, ineffective, and dangerous. Even so, Bastico ordered its implementation. It was said that he had not correctly understood the orders that he had received. This immediately provoked a direct confrontation with Franco, who forbade the operation (which was already being prepared by the laying of 300 kilometres of telephone wire). He would subsequently rationalise his decision. He did not believe that there would be a chaotic retreat, because Santander and Asturias had their own Republican armies, which were defending territory in staggered formation and making use of the complicated relief of the terrain, unsuitable for rapid motorised warfare. Too far from both Bilbao and Santander, facing terrain difficult to penetrate, and unsure of blocking the enemy's retreat, the ideal move would be for the CTV to strike in the direction of Bilbao or the Escudo Pass and Reinosa. It would be a quick and appropriate operation for the Italian forces, giving them control of the most important pass above Santander, a 'city which would be heavily threatened and surrounded by at least 14 enemy battalions'.[74] It would be a triumph for Mussolini, in the Caudillo's words.

Indeed, the *Generalísimo* had never doubted the Duce's political and moral reasons for asking for quick and decisive use of the Italian troops, including his offer that they take action in Madrid, which had been refused. Nevertheless, according to Bastico, Franco was always insecure. His impression of Franco's 'tergiversations' was that they were not unrelated to political, national, and international worries. However, it was the Republican offensive at Brunete, and not some kind of political trouble, that put a stop to all operations in the North, paralysing the plans of both the *Generalísimo*'s headquarters and Bastico. They had to watch the days pass by in the cantonments, which was wholly improper and pointless from the fascist perspective. On 20 July, Mussolini wrote a tough telegram to Bastico, ordering him to present himself before Franco and 'tell him in my name that the Italian legionary forces must absolutely be used in the shortest amount of time possible'. They were already at the peak of preparation, and the volunteers did not deserve the torment of a long wait. If the situation was not defined, he said, it would soon become 'negative and humiliating'.

Fourteen days later, and with no change in the situation, Mussolini had lost patience; 'the Italian volunteers [will] either fight or come back' ('*i volontari italiani si battono o ritornano*'), he wrote. The Duce had a strong negotiating hand—military equipment—as Franco himself recognised when he asked that 'small details like this' not delay or paralyse the sending of artillery and aircraft, collaborating as they were on finding a quick solution to the war.[75] Apparently, the threat had an effect. Indeed, two days after his telegram of 15 August, the CTV went into battle together with the rest of the Francoist units, breaking through the front at Soncillo and fighting at the foot of Escudo Pass, which they occupied on the 17th, managing to cut off 22 battalions of the People's Army. Then and there, the debates and polemics ended. Franco wrote to Mussolini that the Italian forces had fought a 'most brilliant' fight, demonstrating the 'high quality of the Empire's soldiers and Fascist Italy's elevated spirit'. The Duce replied that the 'blood that was shed in common for a common cause would make of Spain and Italy two peoples united in brotherhood'.[76] General Gastone Gambara's telegram to Ciano read, 'Guadalajara dead more than avenged. Stop. Victory hard but complete and brilliant. Stop. We are very happy. Long live Italy.'[77] It was the eve of victory, and it seemed that all was forgiven. Soon it became clear that this was not the case, as Bastico could confirm on being dismissed at the *Generalísimo*'s request.

In the face of the Francoist advance, the Republican troops positioned themselves to defend Santander and communications with Asturias, while the *Frecce Nere* were penetrating towards Castro Urdiales and the Basque army was beginning its withdrawal towards Santoña, trusting in the surrender negotiations underway with the Italian government. On the 24th, when Ciano ordered the cutting of the drinking water supply, the abandonment of the capital's defence was already official. On the 26th, the soldiers of the *Littorio* Division and of the 4th Navarre Brigade entered the city, reaching the centre by midday. The surrender took place at six o'clock. It was initiated by Lieutenant Francisco Delgado of the *Guardia de Asalto*, accompanied by Captain Ángel Botella of the *Carabineros* and Captain Palmiro Ortiz of the militias (the CTV command interceded for their lives before the occupying army's military justice). It was not 'the beginning of the end, but certainly a hard blow for Red Spain', in Ciano's words.[78] The battle for the North did not end there, but the Italians' participation was over. They had lost the 27 officers and 368 soldiers, and 89 officers and 1,451 soldiers were wounded or missing. Between the end of October 1936 and the closing of the front (and without counting the Italians attached to the *Tercio*), the CTV had lost 98 officers and 963 soldiers, 270 officers and 3,852 had been wounded, and 10 officers and 502 soldiers had gone missing. In the same period, of the members of the *Aviazione Legionaria* (which had shot down 407 enemy planes), 21 officers and 68 soldiers had died, 19 officers and 71 soldiers had been wounded, and six officers and four soldiers had gone missing.

Nevertheless, despite all the Fascist paraphernalia, it was predominantly General Fidel Dávila's troops that had managed to put an end to the Republican resistance, incurring an enormous number of losses. Seen in perspective, the CTV's participation was minor: '90 Spanish battalions, seven mixed [battalions] whose forces are 80 per cent Spanish as well, and 24 Italian [battalions]' took part in the operation. In other words, the weight of the fighting was carried by the Spanish troops, which endured notably severe and far from straightforward fighting. Years later, Davide Lajolo would write that, by the second day, they stopped counting the dead, and by the fifth day, everybody, officers and men, were completely exhausted, unrecognisable, laying siege to a city which seemed beyond reach.[79] Fascist propaganda nevertheless made Santander the subject of the most impassioned rhetoric. The victory over the Cantabrian capital was cast as an anti-Guadalajara of heroism, courage, and daring.[80] So much heroism and overexcitement surrounded the victory that, although it did not fit with 'international policy', Bastico staged a 'display of volunteer troops on parade', tolerated out of respect, despite the distortion of reality that it signified. The world might have deduced that the success had been a solely Italian one and that its force in Spain was much greater than the reality. The Spanish command understood the desire to counter the earlier slander in relation to Guadalajara but considered so much parading and celebration to be a 'sin of excess', because it might provide an excuse to send more men 'to the Reds'.[81]

None of this stopped the propaganda machinery from portraying the combatants as fighting 'like lions', with an enormous spirit of vigour and enthusiasm, arousing everybody's admiration. (See, for example, the front page of *La Domenica del Corriere* of 29 August.) It was a 'well organised, thought out, and managed affair', which had restored Italy's value (meaning after Guadalajara). As a result, Frusci, Bergonzoli, Gambara, and Francisci were elevated as heroes. Santander was an unprecedented success, even greater and riskier than Málaga. In the Andalusian city, there had been only snipers scattered here and there. In Santander, the Italians had confronted whole battalions, defensively organised, with all the means of modern warfare and mounting bloody counter-attacks. The Battle of Santander had been 'a real war, unlike Málaga'. Here they had been machine-gunned and bombed by the Red air force despite the cover of the *National* side's fighter planes. In short, the Italian infantry had had 'the honour' of winning territory, position by position, including closing the pocket where the Basque battalions were positioned; General Attilio Teruzzi spoke to the three representatives of these battalions, imposing an unconditional surrender.[82] The result of all this was that a funerary pyramid was erected at Escudo Pass, in memory of the more than 480 soldiers who had died in the fighting. In the long term, it would become the second most important monument commemorating the Fascist presence in the Spanish war, after the one at Zaragoza.

Franco wanted to communicate the CTV's success to Mussolini personally, conscious of the importance that the latter would give to his gesture. He relayed how the legionary troops had entered Santander in close cooperation with the Nationalists, both in the name of Western civilisation against

Asiatic barbarism and how proud he was to have them under his orders. Mussolini replied, again in a tone suggesting all was forgiven, that 'this now intimate brotherhood of arms is the guarantee of the final victory which will liberate Spain and the Mediterranean of any threat to our common civilisation'. He would tell Bastico afterwards that Italy was proud of its brave fighters on Spanish soil and that the victory crowned the Italian legionnaires' heroism, which was recognised and extolled not only in Italy but in the whole world.[83] They were so proud that, following Santander's capture, and in order to emphasise the 'strong impression' created in Republican Spain, Ciano ordered Bastico to carry out a 'mass aerial attack' on Valencia during the night of 26 August in order 'to demolish the population's morale'[84] using terror. Here, as they would on other occasions, the Fascists did their job with brutality. Everybody had to know of their victory party, not just the civilians in the North.

Nevertheless, one of the main features of the occupation of the North, in which Italian Fascism was the main protagonist, was the surrender by the Basque government and army at the request of the Basque Nationalist Party, a surrender to a victorious Fascist Italy, behind the Republic's back, and with Franco's full knowledge. Documents and Francoist military sources indicate that, despite the veto of the *Generalísimo*, Roatta had briefly initiated contacts and negotiations on his own responsibility with the Basque military advisers, when they could no longer escape following the occupation of Torrelavega. He even invited their senior officers to eat (a major scandal) in order to guarantee their escape. The escape was not made, because Franco ordered the *Frecce Nere* Brigade to stop it. However, the issue is much more complex and, as is often the case, much less straightforward and clear-cut than is normally claimed.

In fact, it was not at all a matter of isolated negotiations, nor did Roatta conduct them without any kind of precedent or political cover. It is enough to bear in mind that, on 8 July, Ciano reminded the CTV command that 'here' (that is to say, in Rome; that is to say, for Mussolini), the Basques' surrender into Italian hands was important and the negotiations needed to be quick.[85] Judging by the tone of the communications between its departments, it is indeed the case that the Italian government attached much importance to the matter. To negotiate on its own responsibility with the Basque government, even while informing Franco, would underscore Fascism's importance and autonomy in national and international political questions and further Italy's military victory and influence in the face of the Germans' ambition. And it would allow Italy to wipe away the trace of complicity in the killings at Málaga with a moral success of great importance in the eyes of the whole world, including Republican Spain. The more prisoners fell into Italian hands, 'the fewer killings there will be, the less difficult the Basques' surrender will be, the less involuntary joint responsibility we ourselves will have in the massacres perpetrated by the *Nationals*'. The Spanish method of shooting prisoners was allegedly the greatest impediment to fascist war.[86]

90 *Fascist Italy at war, 1937*

The first approaches leading to the surrender by the Basque nationalist army were not made in July but started at least as early as May 1937. Thus, they took place in parallel with the Basque Nationalist Party's negotiations with the Vatican requesting the latter to mediate in the situation and to ensure the humane treatment of those Basques who, according to the consul Francesco Cavalletti, were being terrorised by the troops of the *National* side. It is possible that there had been earlier contacts, because he refers to approaches on Franco's behalf between the Basque government and the Jesuit priest Pereda. But it was in May, in fact, that the communication took place between Major Da Cunto and the brother, who had been taken prisoner, of the Basque parliamentary deputy José María Lasarte concerning the possibility of negotiating with the Basque government. (The brother was later transferred to the Italian embassy in Salamanca.) Previously, they had been certain of a Republican victory and there had been no convincing need to consider the possibility of surrender. But when Franco turned his troops towards the North and the situation underwent a radical change, voices in favour of an agreement began to appear. The most appropriate interlocutor to conclude an agreement, Cavalletti continued, would not be the *Lehendakari* (Basque Autonomous government president) José Antonio Aguirre, a 'fatuous man with no sense of responsibility', but rather the Basque government's Minister of Justice and Culture, Jesús María de Leizaola. He would be joined by names such as Telesforo de Monzón, the Basque Interior Minister; the Finance Minister, Heliodoro de la Torre; and important public figures such as Anacleto Ortueta, Eduardo de Landeta, the Capuchin father Altiso, Canon Alberto de Onaindía, and the banker Ramón de la Sota. They were all said to be in favour of surrender, provided that a great power guaranteed their lives. Days later in France, Cavalletti met José Horn, Onaindía, and Doroteo Ciaurriz of the Basque Nationalist Party. They were all 'enthusiasts' for Italian intervention and suspicious of the 'adequate guarantee' of Franco's word to Carlo Bossi on 2 May and of Mola's letter to the Basque government, in which he gave assurances that insurgents' troops 'would not commit the slightest abuse' if the Basque militias in Bilbao cooperated in blockading non-nationalist soldiers and then laid down their arms. These soldiers would be considered as having escaped, not as prisoners of war. They would succeed in saving the Basque capital from the destruction that would be caused by withdrawal and occupation. And, as Onaindía would say in June, they would prevent the 'retreating Red troops' from committing 'all kinds of abuse', such as 'the destruction of the city'.[87] In any event, such negotiations existed, but they did not bear fruit.

In order that these contacts go through Italy, direct communication between *Lehendakari* Aguirre and the Duce was requested, which could be used as an argument before Franco. However, on 17 May, orders were given to suspend the negotiations in view of the turn of events, including the doubts of Aguirre, who was 'depressed and . . . stunned, with a crucifix in his hand', and the burgeoning decision by the Basque troops not to fight outside their own territory. At the beginning of June, Onaindía once again contacted the Italians, specifically Cavalletti, regarding a possible exchange of prisoners between the Basque and Italian governments. It did not come to fruition.[88] Yet, despite its scant success, this renewal of contact was the one that ended up going the furthest. According to consular sources, two 'important Basque persons' landed at Algorta on 26 June, sent by the Basque government (although it is not clear whether authorised by Aguirre) to negotiate the surrender to Italy as the victor, on condition of guaranteeing the return of civilians, the wounded, and soldiers, as well as promising to spare the lives of officers and the members of the government. One of them was Juan de Ajurriaguerra, president of the Basque Nationalist Party's executive committee (in Basque, *Euzkadi Buru Batzar*). His objective involved Italy managing to shorten the war, which would and give it the 'moral advantage of having saved a noble people', a 'non-Bolshevik' people, from 'being decimated'. However, the hesitation on the part of the now so-called 'former Basque government' led to it demanding direct contact with Mussolini via an emissary (Italy, it was said, did not 'wish, or was unable, to take any further interest in this question'). This occurred at the same time as the CTV advanced the technical aspects of the surrender at a meeting in Bayonne. There, the terms of the evacuation were agreed upon. The emissary was Onaindía himself, authorised by Aguirre on 3 July to set out 'the Basque national problem and the current situation in Euzkadi [Basque Country] before the Italian government' and by the Basque Nationalist Party's executive committee, chaired by Doroteo Ciaurriz, to speak of 'the wishes and hopes of a humanitarian kind and relating to people's rights harboured by the people of Euzkadi . . . and the political demands constituting the doctrine and program of Basque nationalism'.

These agreements did not seem very important to anybody. Ciaurriz went to Rome accompanied by Pantaleón Ramírez de Olano to offer the surrender of up to 12,000 Basque soldiers (in the end they totalled about 22,000). At the same time, on the 9th, General Roatta took the reins in the negotiations in Spain. But Franco had direct, first-hand information about everything—Bossi in person read him Mussolini's telegrams, in which he explained his view of the matter, which included his idea that the Basque surrender would be very beneficial for the insurgents in the international arena, given that they were 'fervent Catholics who have made a mistake, but almost all of whom are redeemable for Your Spain'. As reported by Colonel Ferdinando Gelich, head of the Italian delegation to the *Generalísimo*'s general headquarters, Franco attached 'little importance to the matter' because Aguirre was a prisoner of the '*Santanderinos*' and the delegates in Rome were only looking after their personal interests. Nevertheless, contrary to what has been said many times, he was kept informed of the changing terms of the negotiations.

In the final analysis, the negotiations centred on technical questions, the *how*, because the *what* of the military surrender—in fact, there was hardly any diplomatic involvement in the matter—had already been decided on 30 June. The negotiations aimed to ensure that the Basque battalions would not be enrolled into the Francoist army and, at the Basque government's

92 *Fascist Italy at war, 1937*

request, that the surrender take place not as such but as a defeat 'in appearance', 'staged', 'simulated', 'legitimate in the eyes of third parties'—these are all phrases found in the official Italian documents—or a cutting-off move, a local action, or a surrender of arms without fighting into Italian hands. They sought an operation to '*salvare la faccia*' (to save face), 'to make it look like' it was a Fascist victory. It would be complicated to arrange, because it would mean concentrating the Basque battalions before the Italian troops, with little justification for doing so. This was not the only complication. Aguirre did not reply to telegrams, and the Basque representatives feared the reaction of the non-Basque officers and soldiers to a manoeuvre of this nature. And Franco, despite having approved of Mussolini's remarks, did not appear ready to accept the terms of a negotiation which included the evacuation of civilians, the treatment of soldiers, and the management of their officers.

Nevertheless, what prolonged the situation for a month and a half more was the delay in occupying Santander caused by the Republicans' offensive at Brunete. This was enough time to settle the means of evacuation and the military agreements; time to try and reach an agreement with Aguirre from Paris on the final terms of the surrender (even though he did not consider it opportune to meet with the Italian emissaries); time to confirm the delays and evasions, if not obvious belligerence, with which the Basque government responded to the Italian command's vigour; and time to break off the negotiations, firstly with Da Cunto's departure and then with the break on Roatta's part on 19 August, now that the operation against Santander was underway and after various ultimatums that each and every one of the conditions had to be accepted. According to Roatta, the military saw disloyalty in the 'chitchat' and lies of the Basque military delegates—officers Sabin de Egilleor and Raimundo de Puxana—regarding the supposed slowness of the evacuation of civilians, given as an excuse to delay the surrender. Rather, the civilians became hostages of the Republican Army, used to force the *Gudaris* (Basque nationalist soldiers) to fight. The four days of 'generosity' given by Roatta were not put to good use. Bastico commented that there were battalions throwing themselves into battle against the CTV and the Mixed Brigade, which obliged him to point out to the Basque delegates that they could make the most of his humanity, but not abusively so.

Nevertheless, everything came to a head on 22 August. That day, three battalions of *Gudaris* of the 50th Division abandoned their positions on the Basque Nationalist Party's orders and went to Santoña, soon to be joined by another twelve. With the same parliamentary deputy Lasarte and de Ajuriaguerra as intermediaries, the Basque government had to accept all the conditions of the handover. These conditions were settled on the 24th in the Pact of Santoña (as it was dubbed for posterity), by which the CTV ratified what had already been agreed upon. The Basque soldiers would not be forced to fight in the Francoist army; officers would not surrender to the Spanish authorities, unless they expressly wished to; weapons would be given up at the moment of the surrender; and the prisoners in the Santoña prison would be freed. In return, the Basques requested that the occupied Basque territory not be bombed and that the surrender be announced only when it was completed, so as to avoid reprisals against civilians. At that point the negotiation involved serious problems concerning Franco. The Basque soldiers fell back at dawn on the 23rd and surrendered to the *Frecce Nere* Brigade on the 25th, the same day the Italians entered Santander. It was 'too late' for Berti. In his opinion, Italian generosity would end up forcing the CTV command to suffer 'bleak consequences' vis-à-vis General Franco. Indeed, that very day Franco had forbidden any form of agreement with the Basques, in view of his victorious position. Even so, new emissaries arrived from Santoña on the 26th to try and revive the terms of the negotiations, which had lapsed on the 24th at 00.00 hours. By then, the treatment of the Basque battalions depended solely on the legionnaires' 'generosity'.[89]

On the 26th, the *Frecce Nere* Brigade occupied Santoña, where 11 battalions surrendered peacefully. They were joined by three more the following day, their officers at the head. Colonel Farina would state that only the imminence of total defeat led to the gathering in Santoña of soldiers and the 'politically compromised' (the government's former leaders and officials, military chaplains, career officers). They were waiting for an evacuation by the British ships *Bobie* and *Seven Seas Spray*. The evacuation was blockaded by the Francoist navy and forbidden by Dávila. Although he allowed the *Bobie* to set sail with more than 500 wounded on board, he ordered the Italian troops to make the evacuees disembark, some 200 of the 'compromised' out of the roughly 1,000 civilians who remained ashore. This order was not carried out because it was not considered right for Italian troops to board a ship flying a British flag, but the escapees were urged to disembark of their own accord, so that their personal safety could be guaranteed. Bastico, however, offered 'no concession', nor any favourable treatment. Whoever did not surrender would be made a prisoner—but a prisoner of the CTV, in honour of the moral obligation arising from the generosity already obtained and in the light of the troops' surrender as if the agreements reached were in force, even though they were not operative. Thus, they were interned in camps guarded by Italians, kept in isolation without any outside contact, so as, firstly, not to create an image of excessively favourable treatment and, secondly, to safeguard the prisoners, for whom they took responsibility, from 'any action not coming from us'. It is clear that they wanted to protect them from the on-the-spot 'cleansing' of prisoners which characterised the Francoist army's military occupations.

The protection did not last long, however. On the 30th, Fidel Dávila arrived in Santoña to relieve the *Frecce Nere* Mixed Brigade guarding the prisoners. The relief took effect on 4 September with Italian approval, after Colonel Antonio Barroso of Franco's general headquarters had given assurances that there would be no political persecution and that whatever was done would be done in agreement with the CTV. The prisoners were handed over to the Prisoner Concentration Camps Inspectorate (*Inspección de Campos de Concentración de Prisioneros*), which brought four camps into operation

94 *Fascist Italy at war, 1937*

in Santoña, the El Dueso prison (using makeshift barracks), the Institute, the Infantry Headquarters, and El Fuerte de la Plaza.[90] For Franco, the surrender could not confer rights of any kind, because it had not been carried out when it should have been, but rather only when there was no other option. Leizaola is said to have acknowledged as much to his representative at the French border, Major Troncoso—they could not demand rights, nor was there any justification for allowing them to leave the country. The formula would be the one that was already well known—'maximum clemency' for the defeated, fair trials and few death sentences for the politically responsible and common criminals (Franco would say that most of the 510 death sentences had been commuted through pardons), and concentration camps and forced labour for those of military age who did not enlist in the Francoist army—in short, exactly the same treatment given to other prisoners of war.

Histories of the relationship between the CTV command, the Fascist government and the 17,000 prisoners distributed between Santoña, Laredo, and Castro Urdiales usually end at that moment of the handover to the Spanish troops. Nevertheless, the prisoners' relationship with the Italian command continued, insofar as there were a number of death sentences, including those of the prisoners' political representatives, Juan de Ajuriaguerra and Lucio de Artetxe, whose death sentences were commuted by Franco. (Ajuriaguerra later became the president of the Basque Nationalist Party in exile.) Both complained, not unreasonably, that they had 'acted in good faith until the last moment'—good faith, however, towards the enemy—and believed that the CTV was not fulfilling the commitments it had made. They used harsh words, speaking of the dishonour of the Italian people and its methods of gaining 'easy fictitious victories', 'false glory', which, in their opinion, would be punished by God. In fact, many of these commitments were not fulfilled, but by the Francoist occupation forces. The CTV had no representatives on the committee to classify prisoners, nor did it have a say in the tribunal emanating from the occupying army's *Auditoría General* (Office of the Judge Advocate General).[91] Nor could it do anything for the 14 (according to Italian calculations) of the 200 disembarked from the *Bobie* under Italian custody who were executed. On 15 September, to set an example, six Basque nationalists, two socialists, two trade unionists, a communist, and three inhabitants of Santander had been shot. However, the fate of the *Gudari* battalions had not been in Italian hands for some time.

In reality, more than the Santoña affair, what mattered to the CTV in the North was the taking of Santander, carried out, according to Bastico, 'following our way of thinking and acting, as personified by Berti'. The success provided the basis on which to request the reorganisation of the *Corpo* by boosting the artillery and by separating the infantry from its transport units. The thinking behind this request was that, as had been shown—referring to Guadalajara, but also to the difficulties encountered at Escudo Pass—the infantry, although very effective, delayed the progress of the transport units and made them sluggish and more vulnerable to the disastrous effects of interruptions and aerial attacks. However, the success, glorified in the propaganda, was not enough for Bastico to keep his position. Indeed, the power struggle within the military leadership did away with the CTV commander's prestige. His dismissal at Franco's request was a sign of the changes taking place at the heart of the Italian command, of the military and political relations between the two regimes, and of the nature of warfare in the context of a long war. Bastico had systematically opposed the use of his troops, of which Franco had as good an opinion as if they were Spanish troops. Franco thought the CTV was made up of 'good and enthusiastic officers and troops', which he could have made 'better use' of had his own judgement—discussed and rejected time and again by the CTV's commander—prevailed. Bastico's behaviour and character, which was 'violent and impulsive', insubordinate, and uncooperative, did not make things easier. And for that reason, Franco asked Mussolini for Bastico's head.

He was not wrong. In Bilbao, Bastico had refused to obey orders (which was unforgivable for the Caudillo), delaying—according to Franco—the destruction of the 'Basque Army' by two months by allowing its retreat towards Santander and the 'slowing down of the war in the North'. Moreover, he had let the Italians make off with war materiel (armaments and vehicles) in Santander. According to a report of the Ministry of Foreign Affairs, 'the legionnaires tow away cars they find on the way, scrap them, and sell the usable parts'.[92] Their inappropriate behaviour extended to demanding fuel at public petrol stations without handing over vouchers in exchange and while threatening with their weapons, forcibly entering convents (like that of the Sisters of Charity in Sigüenza), stealing from businesses in the places where they were living, and even throwing bombs from trains 'just for fun'.[93] And, following the taking of Santander, when rapid action was required in the Zaragoza sector in the face of the Belchite offensive, Roatta had delayed movements by not making his artillery units available immediately for Franco's use while he waited for authorisation from Bastico, who was issuing orders from 200 kilometres away and without any knowledge of the situation. This was inadmissible, in Franco's view, all the more so given that these troops had by then been under Spanish command for nine months. The *Generalísimo* considered the Italian general's communications addressed to his command to be unacceptable, and he was of the opinion that Bastico's behaviour had been severely detrimental to his side's progress in the war. Thus, in September, he asked for his dismissal, Roatta's return to Italy, and Berti's appointment as commander of the CTV. He even did so in writing, with his recurrent spelling mistakes (such as omitting the accent marks in the words '*Ejército*', '*también*', '*simpatías*', and '*reúne*' and adding one to Bastico's name).[94] 'Relations with the Italian military command in Spain are not being carried out with the required cordiality and understanding, with undoubtable repercussions on the progress of the war', he said.

> Bástico [*sic*], who is undoubtedly a good leader. . . has exercised a direction which has not only an unfavourable influence on the progress of

96 *Fascist Italy at war, 1937*

operations, but also tends to cool the harmony that has existed until now between the Italians and the Spanish.

These anomalies, 'noted and commented upon unfavourably by high-ranking German officers', such as the 'outcry of the civilian population wherever the CTV's troops are billeted' and other cases of indiscipline, could give 'the Reds grounds' for a campaign to smear Italian prestige.[95] If all the Italian's honour was not openly called into question, certainly Batisco's was, and not only by the Francoist military high command. Indeed, what perhaps made him understand that things had changed were the replies received from Rome, which, regarding his complaints, told him very clearly that the Spanish war was a 'war with a strong political character', which had to be settled by arms, but also by *other* arms. And concerning these other means, 'you, soldier, are not always kept up to date by the Spanish command', because 'your mission is not to devise political agreements' but to give the enemy a good whipping (*'buone legnate'*). The Duce's order had been to subordinate everything to the rapid definition of the conflict. While confidence in him was total, he, in turn, had to understand that the CTV's job now was not that of a front-line force but rather that of a reserve for Franco. On the other hand, an internal report of the MVSN portrays him as not very brilliant in military terms and indebted to Berti for the success at Santander. Furthermore, he would also arouse political misgivings (because of his scant sympathy for the Blackshirts) and misgivings about his private life. Bastico was in the habit of letting himself be seen in the company of Victoria Rosado, wife of José Rojas y Moreno, the Count of Rojas, a diplomat who would be posted to Bucharest in 1941. The Italian general was alleged to have a real 'senile passion' for this 'mature and, in truth, not beautiful' woman, who accompanied him to performances, ceremonies, bullfights, and even military inspections. In the view of the report's author, the lady had been placed at Bastico's side by Franco in order to learn more about the Italian mission, with the complicity of her husband. Rojas, who had been removed from the diplomatic service, hoped to be recalled, thanks to this spying job. In fact, thanks to the countess, Bastico had gone from being the 'man who always says no' to serving as an obsequious soldier in Franco's general headquarters. Whatever Mussolini's final motive was, and although the Italian ambassador in Spain who had replaced Cantalupo, Count Viola di Campalto, had warned him that the source sent by Franco to inform him about Bastico, Lieutenant Colonel Villegas, was unreliable and opportunist, the fact is that on 5 October Ciano summoned the commander of the CTV to tell him that he 'would not again return to Spain'. Ambassador Conde was informed, 'You may tell the *Generalissimo* on my behalf that General Bastico is now in Italy and he will never again see him in Spain.' Bastico was replaced by Berti, Franco's favourite, who 'will be under strict instructions to place himself unreservedly and without any exception whatsoever under Your Excellency's orders'.[96]

According to Captain Donato Turrini's report on the *Ufficio Spagna*'s activities from July 1937 to July 1938, Bastico's withdrawal and Roatta's move were due to an 'envious and jealous state of mind', sharpened by the brilliant victory of Santander, which demonstrated 'the legionary corps' strategic and tactical superiority; pride and wounded ego'. Bastico's greatest sin, in my opinion, more than his womanising or his circumstantial opposition to Franco (because he was, after all, interpreting Mussolini's orders regarding the CTV's rapid and decisive intervention) was his refusal, in the first instance, to allow the CTV to be used in Aragon and his decision, alongside Roatta, to opt for Italianising the *Frecce* Mixed Brigades. They both wanted to exercise direct command over them, even though they were responsible to the Spanish command. Roatta wanted to rely on the brigades to make corrections to the vanguard, even though they were, in fact, replacement troops for Franco. They both thought that the *Frecce* should not be simple reserves with an Italian character, because they had been created with Italian commanding officers and weapons, but rather wholly Italian units integrated into the CTV. But neither Franco, who thought they were troops to be pampered and not to be exposed unduly to combat, nor Mussolini, who preferred to go along with the *Generalísimo*'s decisions, supported them.[97] The fundamental explanation is that, during the course of 1937, the Fascist conception of the war in Spain had changed substantially, from thinking of themselves as a belligerent country to placing themselves in Franco's service in order to achieve total victory over the enemy.

The CTV's intervention would actually be more important in future, despite the appearance of insignificance that persisted after the taking of Santander. It would be even more important than it had been in the North, where it played a prominent role, but not as decisive a role as Fascist propaganda claimed. It would have a decisive role, however, in September in Aragon, where it participated in the Francoist counter-offensive, in the *Flechas Negras* Mixed Division, by attacking the north of Zaragoza and occupying Zuera. Similarly, the Italian artillery played a decisive role in the operations to regain Teruel, as did its motorised infantry regiments, supported as they were by the artillery and tanks, used as a kind of spearhead in the Francoist offensive against Aragon in 1938. Franco had indicated to Berti that he would start the campaigns once the Large Units (*Grandes Unidades*) had been assembled in October. As Alberto Pariani of the War Ministry would write to the minister Ciano, some Italian officers in Spain had information that the Nationalist command wanted to leave the resolution of the conflict until the spring of 1938. This would be disastrous, in his opinion, for reasons of international politics, military factors (as it would allow the enemy to increase its strength), and the effect it would have on the voluntary corps' morale. If they were going to send more resources and continue to play the card of the air force, which the Nationalists lacked, they would have to put pressure on Franco to act more decisively.

Nevertheless, Ciano replied emphatically that nothing had changed. The Duce's instructions remained the same and were clear in endorsing the

98 *Fascist Italy at war, 1937*

CTV's use as part of the reserve, which could be utilised to block Republican counter-offensives. If it was used in the front line, it was not to be employed in isolation but as part of larger operations, so as to avoid situations like Guadalajara. During the course of 1937, Italy became a belligerent on Spanish soil, thus converting the Civil War not into an internationalised conflict but rather into an international war. Italy had gone from independent participation 'without meddling' to supporting Franco unconditionally. When, in December 1937, Berti suggested to Mussolini the possibility of withdrawing the infantry from Spain and leaving only aircraft, artillery, tanks, and engineers, the answer was a clear no. They would not be enough to achieve the principal objective—winning great victories, insofar that was possible, and, above all, supporting Franco's complete success with all their might. This difficult balance between pride in being different and unconditional support despite being different would be settled in a more convincing way from 1938 onwards. Ciano recorded in his diary in October 1937 that 'the Spanish problem is becoming an international crisis: either a break or clarity'. Beginning in 1938, Mussolini, Ciano and, in fact, all the political, diplomatic, and insurgent actors came to understand that the Civil War was a European war fought on Spanish soil, as I will argue in the last chapter of this book.

Notes

1 USSME, F6, 328.
2 USSME, F6, 327.
3 USSME, F18, b9.
4 ASMAE, US, b12.
5 Duilio Sumsel and Edoardo Sumsel, eds., *Opera Omnia di Benito Mussolini*, vol. XXVIII (Florence: La Fenice, 1959), 218–220.
6 ASMAE, US, b1.
7 Ibid.
8 Alberto Rovighi and Filippo Stefani, *La partecipazione italiana alla guerra civile spagnola* (Rome: USSME, 1992), vol. 2, 582. See also Sandro Piazzoni, *Le Frecce Nere nella guerra di Spagna* (Rome: Edizioni della Rivista Nazione Militare, 1939).
9 USSME, F7, b1.
10 USSME, F18, b4 (copy).
11 ASMAE, US, b22.
12 The function of presenting credentials turned out to be a 'solemn and grandiose ceremony'—never had an Italian representative been received 'abroad with such happiness and participation by the people'. ASMAE, AP, b21.
13 USSME, F18, b2.
14 Rovighi and Stefani, *La partecipazione italiana*, vol. 1, 215–216.
15 USSME, F18, b2.
16 USSME, F6, b334.
17 ACS, MinCulPop, Gab, b75.
18 ASMAE, AP, b14.
19 Gaetani in ASMAE, US, b11.
20 USSME, F6, b334.
21 USSME, F7, b1.

Fascist Italy at war, 1937   99

22 ACS, MI, DirPolPol, SPD, CR, b44.
23 ASMAE. US, b22. 'Count Rossi' was accused of many more infractions: shipping alcoholic spirits from Málaga to Italy, socialising with all sorts of women in his office, commandeering cars, and ordering the shooting of prisoners simply in order to assert his authority.
24 USSME, F18, b2.
25 Olao Conforti, *Guadalajara: la prima sconfitta del fascismo* (Milan: Mursia, 1967).
26 USSME, F18, b2.
27 The ostensibly complete series of communications between the commands and the explanations subsequently gathered on the ground are collected in the Archivio Centrale dello Stato, although the best guide to the events is the CTV's own report, entitled *Azione su Guadalajara*, ACS, MI, DirPolPol, SPD, CR, b72. The report can be found in ASMAE, US, b2.
28 ACS, PolPol, SPD, CR, b72, F1.
29 Luis Urteaga, Francesc Nadal, and José Ignacio Marcos, 'La cartografía del Corpo di Truppe Volontarie, 1937–1939', *Hispania*, LXII/1, no. 210 (2002): 283–298. Until its reorganisation, the CTV lacked a topographical service, as did the Francoist Army, since the cartographic sections stayed in Madrid in July 1936.
30 On this matter, a publication by the USSME reports the different tactical views which, according to the experts of the time, explained the defeat. For Canevari, it was the failure to use the vehicles to support the infantry and not the other way around, as well as the lack of continuity between the infantry and artillery due to motorisation. In brief, it was the failure of *guerra celere*. Ferruccio Botti and Virgilio, *Il pensiero militare italiano dal primo al secondo dopoguerra 1919–1949* (Rome: Stato Maggiore dell'Esercito, 1985), 235ff.
31 ACS, MI, DirPolPol, SPD, CR, b72, F1; ASMAE, US, b2.
32 Tullio Rispoli, *La Spagna dei Legionari* (Rome: Cremonese, 1942), 73.
33 Quoted in Dimas Vaquero, *Credere, Obbedire, Combattere: Fascistas Italianos en la Guerra Civil Española* (Zaragoza: Mira, 2009), 142.
34 David Lajolo, *Il 'voltagabbana'* (Milan: Rizzoli, 1981), 55.
35 Alessandro Bonezzi, *Il diario del nonno fascista* (Rome: Robin, 2006) includes the unpublished diary of his grandfather Francesco, a Blackshirt in Spain. The quotation about food can be found on page 22; the muddy holes in the wood at Brihuega on page 23; and the firing by friendly artillery on page 25.
36 Lajolo, *Il 'voltagabbana'*, 54ff. Regarding the temperature, see Sandro Attanasio, *Gli italiani e la guerra di Spagna* (Milan: Mursia, 1974), 127.
37 The feathers in the division's name referred to the background of many of the men and officers in Alpine units. The division tends to be seen as braver than the *Dio lo Vuole* Division, which was the first to give way to the Republican attack at Brihuega.
38 Luigi Angelo Tonelli's diary in Gabriele Ranzato, Camillo Zadra, and Davide Zendri, *'In Spagna per l'idea fascista': legionari trentini nella guerra civile spagnola 1936–1939* (Rovereto: Museo Storico della Guerra, 2008), 51–54; quotation on page 53.
39 Ismael Saz and Javier Tusell, *Fascistas en España: la intervención italiana en la guerra civil a través de los telegramas de la 'Missione Militare Italiana in Spagna' (15 diciembre 1936–31 marzo 1937)* (Madrid: CSIC-Escuela Española de Historia y Arqueología en Roma, 1981), 169.
40 ASMAE, US, b2.
41 Silvio Leoni's diary in Ranzato, Zadra, and Zendri, *'In Spagna per l'idea fascista'*, 70.
42 *El Legionario*, no. 1, 19 March 1937, 1–2. It would later be called *Il Legionario* and change its motto to 'Daily of the Italian Volunteers Fighting in Spain'.
43 *Opera Omnia*, vol. XXVIII, 198–201.
44 ASMAE, US, b38.
45 AMAE, AB, L1459, C9.
46 ASMAE, Us, b10.
47 AGMAV, C2604, 15.
48 ASMAE, US, b2.
49 USSME, F18, b9.

100 *Fascist Italy at war, 1937*

50 AMAE, AB, L1459, C9.

51 USSME, F18, b9.

52 ASMAE, US b38.

53 Or the de facto organisation: there are documents that refer to the creation of the CTV in February, and others in March. ASMAE, US, b5.

54 Including 2,000 artillery units, 700 drivers, 1,000 technicians, 500 Carabinieri, 2,232 officers, 3,359 NCOs, 30,241 troops.

55 USSME, F6, b335.

56 Renzo Lodoli, *Domani posso morire: storie di arditi e fanti legionari* (Rome: Roma Fascista, 1939); the later edition cited here has a different title, *I Legionari: Spagna 1936–1939* (Rome: Ciarrapico Editore, 1989), 131.

57 *Opera Omnia*, vol. XXVIII, 213 for Mussolini's article of 26 June 1937 in *Il Popolo d'Italia*. There was no place for the defeat, but there would be for lying, when he asserted that the existence of an Italo-German bloc was false: 'false', like the landing of 15,000 Italian soldiers '*a Malaga o a Cadice* [Cádiz]. *Falso.*'

58 Ibid. for Mussolini's article in *Il Popolo d'Italia* of 24 September 1937.

59 For an overall view, embellished with personal opinions and a substantial and dubious collection of photos (in some photos it is obvious that the watermark has been removed digitally), see José Luis García Ruiz, *La participación italiana en el Frente Norte. La batalla de Santander (abril-agosto 1937)* (Torrelavega: Librucos, 2015).

60 USSME, F18, 4.

61 USSME, H9, 1; USSME, F6, b328.

62 '*Guernica non esiste più*', quoted in Renzo Segàla, *Trincee di Spagna: con i legionari alla defesa della civiltà* (Milan: Treves, 1939), 172. Segàla was nevertheless of the opinion that the houses had been dynamited from inside, as the insurgent propaganda contended. There is an extensive literature on the bombing, well summarised by Stefanie Schüler-Springorum, *La guerra como aventura: la Légion Cóndor en la Guerra Civil española, 1936–1939* (Madrid: Alianza Editorial, 2014).

63 ASMAE, US, b54 on the bombardments from the sea.

64 USSME, F6, b334.

65 USSME, F6, b15.

66 USSME, F18, b45.

67 ASMAE, US, b160.

68 José Luis Alcofar Nassaes [José Luis Infiesta], *CTV: los legionarios italianos en la Guerra Civil Española 1936–1939* (Barcelona: Dopesa, 1972), 120.

69 *Opera Omnia*, vol. XXVIII, 273.

70 ASMAE, US, b160.

71 USSME, F18, 4 (in facsimile).

72 *Opera Omnia*, vol. XXVIII, 273.

73 USSME, F18, 4.

74 ASMAE, US, b2.

75 USSME, F18, 4.

76 AGMAV. C2605, 86.

77 ACS, MI, PolPol, SPD, CR, f5.

78 AGMAV, C2604, 37. For the order of the CTV's operations against Santander, see AGMAV, C2605, 85.

79 Lajolo, *Il 'voltagabbana'*, 66–67.

80 Something which was in fact not achieved, according to Renzo De Felice, *Mussolini il duce. II. Lo Stato totalitario (1936–1940)* (Turin: Einaudi, 1996), 140.

81 AMAE, AB, L1459/9, C 28.

82 USSME, F18, 4.

83 *Opera Omnia*, vol. XXVIII, 274.

84 USSME, F6, 19.

Fascist Italy at war, 1937   101

85 USSME, F18, 4 (in facsimile).
86 For the quotations and all the Italian documentation consulted on the Basque Army's surrender, see USSME, F6, b280. See also the first-hand testimony of Alberto de Onaindia, *El 'Pacto' de Santoña: Antecedentes y desenlace* (Bilbao: Laiz, 1983); as well as the abundant bibliography on this highly polemical aspect of the war in the Basque Country: José María Garmendia, 'El pacto de Santoña', in *La Guerra Civil en el País Vasco: 50 años después*, eds. Carmelo Garitaonandía and José Luis de la Granja (Bilbao: Universidad del País Vasco, 1986), 157–190; José Luis de la Granja, *República y Guerra Civil en Euzkadi: del Pacto de San Sebastián al de Santoña* (Oñati: Instituto Vasco de Administración Pública, 1990); Fernando de Meer, *El Partido Nacionalista Vasco ante la guerra de España (1936–1937)* (Pamplona: Ediciones de la Universidad de Navarra, 1992); most recently, Carlos María Olazábal, *Negociaciones del PNV con Franco durante la Guerra Civil* (Bilbao: Fundación Popular de Estudios Vascos, 2014); and, most polemical of all, Xuan Cándano, *El Pacto de Santoña (1937). La rendición del nacionalismo vasco al fascismo* (Madrid: La Esfera de los Libros, 2006), which does not make use of the Italian archives. For two summaries of the Italian role in the affair, see John Coverdale, *La intervención fascista en la Guerra Civil Española* (Madrid: Alianza Editorial, 1979), 284ff.; and Ángel Viñas, *El honor de la República: entre el acoso fascista, la hostilidad britannica y la política de Stalin* (Barcelona: Crítica, 2009), 133–139.
87 ASMAE, AP, b20.
88 Ibid.
89 USSME, F18, b12.
90 AGMAV, Zona Nacional, Ejército del Norte, A15, L32, C46bis. On this subject, see my book *Cautivos. Campos de concentración en la España franquista, 1936–1947* (Barcelona: Crítica, 2005).
91 USSME, F18, b12.
92 AMAE, AB, L1459/9, C28.
93 AGMAV, C2604, 22.
94 ASMAE, US, 2.
95 AMAE, AB, L1459/9, C28.
96 Ibid.
97 Ibid.

3 Italy, the CTV, and politics on the *National* side

Viso al sole con la camicia nuova
che tu bordasti in rosso ier
mi avrà la morte se mi trova
il Duce è il mio pensiero.

[Face to the sun with the new shirt
which you edged in red yesterday
death will have me if it finds me
The Duce is my thought.]

'*Viso al Sole*' ['Facing the Sun']
Loose Spanish to Italian translation by Franco Orgara of the Falangist anthem '*Cara al Sol*'.[1]

'But Mussolini, has he perhaps taken us for imbeciles?'
Manuel Hedilla, national head of the Falange, in 1937

In December 1942, Franco gave a speech at the opening of the Third National Council of the Falange. It was possibly one of the most theoretical and doctrinaire speeches given by the Caudillo (and, for that precise reason, it made people suspect that the by then former minister Ramón Serrano Suñer was still collaborating with his brother-in-law). Francesco Lecquio, ambassador and the highest representative of Italian Fascism in Spain, saw in the speech elements of 'eternity and immortality' a 'unity of sentiment and purpose'. Eternity, immortality, and unity of unitary sentiments shared by the European totalitarianisms were at war with democracy and liberalism. The same ambassador would allude to these ideas again later that same year at the ceremony to mark the start of building the *Sacrario Militare* at Zaragoza. He recalled that Spain's dead were the greatest incentive and clearest guarantee of success for European fascism's new and unitary projects. According to Lecquio, the 'National Revolution' begun in 1936 was connected to this union of social aspirations and to the cult of the nation, which was the great 'synthesis of the Fascist Revolution'.[2]

That the Fascist ambassador to Spain expressed such an opinion in 1942 could not simply be the result of excitement about Franco's reference to his country's achievements and the Duce's political stature. Following Italy's intervention in the coup d'état, in the creation of the *FET y de las JONS* (as will be seen further on), in the consolidation of Franco's power, and following the bet on Serrano Suñer and his fall after his journey to Livorno to meet Ciano,[3] the fact that Lecquio saw in the Caudillo's speech that same faith brought from Italy by fascism's evangelists connected, in a symbolic but solid way, a year of severe internal and international crisis like 1942 with a no less critical year like 1936. Alternatively, it might be better to say 1937, because of the political effects and the importance that year had in the relationship between Italian Fascism and *National* Spain. Italy became involved in the Spanish war that year as an additional participant for several reasons. There is no doubt that, among the different economic, geostrategic, and diplomatic motives, one that stood out was political and ideological.

It is interesting to note that some of the bulkiest files in the Italian archives containing documents on the Fascist intervention in Spain are those which deal with political, cultural, and identitarian issues and those of the institutions and administrative bodies which dealt with this type of activity. But more striking still is the polyphony of voices talking about the Spanish war emanating from Fascist Italy or from the Fascist mission. Indeed, going by their own words and documents, Italian political influence on the nascent New Spain was all-encompassing and decisive. If we believe the italian sources, the single state party was a project of the CTV's head of propaganda, Guglielmo Danzi; the union of the Falangists and the *Requetés* was Roberto Farinacci's idea; corporatism and the *Fuero del Trabajo* (Labour Charter) were the answer to Ciano's demands; Franco's first government was Mussolini's idea; and Pedro Sáinz Rodríguez's educational reforms were a copy of Giovanni Gentile's reform. Italian intervention in Spain was much more than military participation in the war.[4] It was also a fight against its own enemies. And the explicit and determined intention was to fascisticise the war. Of course, this is a matter of debate which I in no way pretend to settle. It may even be one of the great contemporary debates in the historiography of modern Spain. Here I will try to contribute some additional elements, in order to consider the question, using sources as privileged as Mussolini himself, the leader of fascism and of the Italy fighting in Spain, and his political representatives.

Fascistisation

What fascistisation was, however, was not always clear and defined. Until 1937 at least, Italian Fascism's political influence appeared to be less the coordinated work of political, diplomatic, and economic spheres in order to become an involved party in the political process of constructing the New Spain than a succession of approximate moves and the acquisition of little pockets of influence, very much determined by the growing importance of the military intervention. Nevertheless, both Mussolini and the different Italian agents in Spain began to develop their own agendas. An example occurred

104 *Italy, the CTV, and politics*

in Barcelona, where, as Ciano wrote to Anfuso in November 1936, the consul general had been approached by the lawyer Maspons Anglasell with a view to the Italian government mediating in negotiations between the insurgents' government and 'Catalan politicians'. According to the documentation, Maspons was acting on behalf of *Estat Català, Juventut Nacionalista La Falç, Unió Democràtica* and important sections of *Esquerra Republicana de Catalunya*, which were seeking to avoid war on their territory and achieve an autonomy similar to the charters (*fueros*) accorded to the Basque people. Everybody would benefit, because Catalan political forces would be able to combat the anarchists and Franco would thereby avoid 'a resistance to the death on the part of the Catalans', meaning the Catalan nationalists. Franco's reply put paid to such a phantasmagorical proposal by indicating that 'his government intend[ed] to grant administrative autonomy to those regions that desire it' but that he could not 'accept separatism'.[5]

As with the analysis of Fascist involvement in the coup d'état, such reports should be treated with a great deal of caution. There was political opinion from early on, even before the coup in 1936 (about which Rome had a considerable amount of information, as we have seen). And, although the earliest political news did not carry Mussolini's signature, the Duce soon began to express his opinion and shape the political debate about Spain. As his collected works (*Opera Omnia*) reveal, Mussolini's first reference to the war was on 30 December in *Il Popolo d'Italia*, when he commented on the article by Niceto Alcalá Zamora that had appeared in various French publications, in which the former President of the Republic asked for help for his children, who were victims of the Bolsheviks in Spain. It is interesting because this piece provided Mussolini with a platform from which to malign Alcalá's role as an ultra-democrat, hence ultra-anti-fascist, who had opened the Republic's doors to the Moscow-style *desperados* (using the Spanish word), thus initiating the suffering, disasters, and catastrophes which had marked the years of the Second Republic. It was all bound, surely, to result in a civil war, 'piling up endless death and ruin'. This was the sweet, gentle, innocent, humanitarian Republic desired by Zamora, a coldly calculating goddess who demanded human sacrifices. According to the Duce, blind terror had accompanied the republic and democracy since '89—since 1789, to be exact.[6]

In any event, whatever importance is attached to the Duce's opinions, the fact is that his government was in the midst of an intervention that, from the beginning, had a strong political component that was not merely implicit. There is no other way of interpreting the agreement of all the sources on the strong anti-communist direction of the final decision-making process in July 1936. Hegemonic control of the Mediterranean also implied strengthening the totalitarian state, easier access for fascist adventures in Africa, and the gradual but unstoppable establishment of a great axis of dictatorships united in what appeared to be their fundamental aim—the eradication of socialism and territorial expansion at the expense of undeveloped countries, even if it meant entering into conflict not only with European countries but also with the rules of international politics and foreign relations. Indeed, anti-communism is the narrative that suffuses almost all the literature, including the historiography, dealing with the Italian presence in the Spanish war. Ciano himself would declare as much at Munich on 25 October 1936, without referring explicitly to communism (there was absolutely no need to):

> We have examined the situation in Spain and we have agreed to recognise that General Franco's National Government is strongly supported by the wishes of the Spanish people in the greater part of the national territory, where this government has managed to re-establish civil order and discipline, as opposed to the anarchic situation that prevailed before in those areas . . . with respect to the grave dangers that threatened Europe's social structure, the Führer and Baron von Neurath, on the one hand, and I, on the other, have confirmed the free decision of the Italian and German peoples to defend with all our strength the sacred heritage of European civilisation in its great institutions based on the family and the nation, institutions on which our civilisation is founded.[7]

Thus, there were a lot of opinions, but above all explicit political action, providing the basis for the drive to transform the institutional architecture of Franco's Spain, which in fact took place from 1937 onwards—that is to say, beginning with the massive Fascist intervention. The exception was Mallorca. There, Bonaccorsi tried to import the most visible elements of *squadrismo* without taking into account the need to give it political, cultural, and identitarian substance. He seemingly failed. Thanks to his organisational capabilities on the island, Bonaccorsi earned a possibly deserved reputation as a political agitator, which he used to spread an aggressive, modernising, and radical image of fascism. However, as we know today, this image was representative of only one of the cultural-identitarian tendencies within the movement. Supposedly, and according to his own calculations, Bonaccorsi organised a parade through Palma of 15,000 fascists in *Balilla* uniforms; created cooperative stores and workers' confederations with no legal framework, in order to abolish the class struggle and strikes; intervened in the labour market; and founded a Falangist militia that was compulsory for those aged between 17 and 60, plus two youth sections, *Balilla* (8–12 years) and *Avanguardia* (13–19 years). Everything was operational by the middle of September 1936. Everything failed, again according to Bonaccorsi, as a result of Spanish inefficiency, the military intrigues within his circle of advisers, and the lack of fascist faith and energy. 'This revolution in Spain is made up of military leaders. . . . It will be bad, but that is how it is and it cannot be changed in a day.'[8] His liaison with Rome, Carlo Margottini, shared the same exact thoughts. For the latter, Italy was backing the July movement 'because it was fascist', and for this reason it was 'essential to encourage the Falange's moves and fight those of the other elements in the nationalist movement', because the Army was good for nothing but

106 *Italy, the CTV, and politics*

'maintaining the military caste's hegemony in Spain'.[9] It would not be an exclusively Spanish failing, however.

Bonaccorsi was critical of the course of events in the Iberian Peninsula and of the difficulties he had encountered in Mallorca when carrying out his revolutionary work. The intensity of his fascist mission and his continual complaints certainly did not make the handling of his presence in Spain easy. Indeed, it was not long before the clash with the Spanish authorities came. In February 1937, when he was already Inspector General of the Voluntary Militias, but referring to his work in the summer of the previous year, he told his 'dearest' Duce that, after seven months of his mission in Spain, he been able to confirm that the Blackshirts' supreme, heroic task of war and love had not only freed Spanish territory of communist tyranny but also succeeded in winning the esteem, confidence, and sympathy of the entire people, who were tired of the atrocities, months of suffering, and widespread shedding of blood. Nevertheless, Bonaccorsi was of the opinion that the work of the Italians would only be taken into consideration by the Spanish government while armed intervention was necessary; once the Red danger had disappeared, it would do everything possible to remove them. He stated, 'We should not expect gratitude nor recognition from a government which does not measure up to the situation and exhibits only unwarranted pride.'

Not even the Falange, the only movement identified by Bonaccorsi with fascism, had a defined social programme, and it 'undoubtedly prefers Hitler's movement to Mussolini's. Germany is its model of courage, capability, organisation, and strength'. Because of this, and in a way corresponding with Italy's sacrifices to save Spain, he considered that Italy must remain in Spain as the '*Nazione Dominatrice*',[10] the dominant nation, above all economically. Spanish backwardness in nearly every aspect of infrastructure and the economy made it necessary to struggle and fight against Germany to secure a good slice of the Spanish economic cake. The agricultural and livestock industries, poultry farming, the intensive cultivation of fruit, and the development of water resources (irrigation, artificial lakes, canals between rivers, etc.) barely existed and were barely mechanised. Electricity generation depended on foreign capital, which also controlled the mining industry. Although the destruction caused by the Reds offered the opportunity of a productive period of reconstruction, there were no property companies. Trade was in the red, with a commercial balance calculated at 32 million gold-pesetas in imports and 29 million in exports. Transportation routes left a lot to be desired. The same was true of the media; radio had to be introduced across the board. And in all these areas, the influence and profit margins for a strong and imperial-wide economy such as Italy's had to be enormous. So great was the responsibility that Bonaccorsi attributed to himself that, according to some studies, he would go so far as to call himself the 'Generalissimo of Mallorca'.[11]

Whether Italian penetration of Spain was a success or a failure depended on what was meant by fascistisation. I believe that, for the Italians, this idea meant not implanting but rather influencing and transforming. It was clearly not about importing Fascism's model of national organisation in Italy. Nor was it a matter of supporting the party closest to fascist ideas, the Falange, although that was the conclusion of a considerable number of agents in Spain. Rather, it was a matter of influencing the configuration of a government born in a specific context, a civil war, using arms and the force of political influence to support a leader who was to foster national unity, victory, and empire, bringing together and melding the different counter-revolutionary, anti-communist, and anti-democratic tendencies fighting on his side. Mussolini's bet was always on the *National* side and on Franco, the 'only fascist in Spain' as the holder of power and authority, as Anfuso said in November 1936. Danzi, Farinacci, Roatta, and the ambassador to Spain—Cantalupo, and later, Viola—cluttered the desks in Mussolini and Ciano's offices with political reports about Spain and Franco. The first reports were probably from Filippo Anfuso, for whom it was obvious that the best bet was the future 'Generalissimo'. These reports on the political situation spoke of the need to properly convince Franco and persuade him to 'domesticate' the Falange—as I understand it, to control the Falange for his benefit and avoid its hostility—if, following the 'cruel conflict', Italy wanted to prevent Spain from falling into a rigidly feudal and clerical state that would eventually lead to more bloodshed.[12]

The question of domestication is, of course, open to many readings. The theory is well known that the Civil War's result behind the lines was, to put it briefly, the denaturing of the Falange, seen in turn as fascism's sole depositary in Spain. This conclusion normally leads to questioning whether Franco's Spain was in fact fascistised, even in the period between 1937 and 1941. The Italian reports, however, point in different directions. Fascistisation would also occur through the creation of a national party by taking control of the 'healthy' political forces. As Danzi wrote after interviewing General José Millán Astray, they both agreed that the Falange was the 'refuge for sinners who had escaped the firing squad' and that the *Requeté* was Spain's 'truly healthy' force 'which adheres spiritually to fascism and longs intensely to assimilate its principles'. That, too, could be meaning domestication. In any case, what is unchanging and beyond any interpretation to the contrary is that everybody saw Franco as the guarantor of authority. Franco's central importance as the leader and national unifying figure is more than evident in all the reports, except those from Cantalupo, who hated him, calling him a 'feudal' general, a representative of the 'past', who would bring only 'ephemeral peace' at the price of an enormous amount of bloodshed.[13]

The Duce, for whom Franco's cause was not a military *pronunciamiento* but a 'sacred, national, and legitimate uprising like the one for independence of 1808', did much more than merely comment on the Spanish politics of the day. He was quick to authorise his agent Guglielmo Danzi, head of the *Ufficio Stampa e Propaganda* (Press and Propaganda Office) of the fledgling MMIS and a personal friend of Ciano's, to work close to the 'Generalissimo' in order to influence the political structure of the New Spain. The mission

108 *Italy, the CTV, and politics*

was Mussolini's, because Danzi was allegedly forbidden by Ciano to involve himself in internal Spanish politics, partly because of his bad relations with Roatta and Cantalupo. Mussolini clearly expected substantial and sincere receptiveness on the part of the emerging State. As early as December 1936, the insurgents' government, known as the *Junta Técnica del Estado* (State Technical Committee)—depicted by Serrano Suñer as a military field camp and somewhat devoid of political content—appealed to Italy via the embassy for all kinds of propaganda material, both academic material for high-level scientific and technical studies and material suitable for wider circulation. The subjects to be covered included corporations, *dopolavoro* (leisure), social assistance, and the judiciary. Also requested were large lithographs and medium-sized photos of the Duce, photos of fascist leaders, and films from the *Instituto Luce*, which by the following March amounted to 51 different titles, plus four created specifically and dubbed into Spanish: *Assistenza fascista ai lavoratori* (Fascist Help for Workers), *Come il popolo ama il suo Duce* (How the People Love Their Duce), *Protezione maternità e infanzia* (Protecting Motherhood and Childhood), and *Bonifica morale e materiale* (Moral and Material Recovery). The cost totalled 150,000 lire.[14] That same December, Nicolás Franco also asked the Italian embassy to send to Salamanca, as soon as possible, 'an expert authority on the subject of corporatist trade unions in order to assess the Spanish situation and to lay the basis of corporatism'.[15] The old corporatism of the Primo de Rivera dictatorship (1923–1930) was no longer an adequate benchmark. The model in the new Europe that Spain aspired to join was Mussolini's Italy.

It is certainly the case that Fascist political influence and propaganda were not lacking in the insurgents' rearguard. In January 1937, Danzi himself spoke with Franco, head of a so-called encampment state, to suggest that, with regard to defining the political character of the New Spain, he consider organising a vast propaganda programme, anti-Bolshevik talks and radio sections on *Radio Salamanca*, and powerful film propaganda. The overall purpose would be to create an 'atmosphere of understanding and sympathy with fascism among the Spanish working masses', for whom it was 'synonymous with slavery, terror, and injustice'.[16] He even suggested Franco's Spain host a World Anti-Bolshevik Congress. Behind this whole assembling of propaganda stood the *Comitati D'Azione per la Universalità di Roma* (CAUR, Action Committees for the Universality of Rome). In Spain, they had an associate close to Franco in the person of Ernesto Giménez Caballero. The CAUR would infuse Italian Fascism's intervention in Spain with a propagandistic narrative.[17] Thus, Fascist Italy's direct and institutional influence on *National* Spain started very early. Furthermore, at the beginning of 1937, the political spadework entrusted by Mussolini to the head of the *Ufficio Stampa* began to bear fruit, if we accept his account as accurate. 'Sticking to my proposal, General Franco has decided to establish a political association of which he will be the official head', wrote Danzi to Ciano on 9 January 1937.[18]

Italy, the CTV, and politics 109

The fact is that Italy had been working along these same lines since the start of the 'National Revolution' of July 1936, as they would call it. Along these lines, Bonaccorsi, the consul sent personally by the Duce for the Mallorcan political laboratory, had acted and apparently failed. Already in December 1936, Bonaccorsi's friend and liaison, Margottini, said of him that, if he left the island, he could dedicate his work to encouraging the merging of the Falange and the *Requetés*. Regardless of the importance given to Count Rossi's experiment, the fact is that the identification, from the very beginning, of the forces that would come together some months later in the *FET y de las JONS* is symptomatic. As early as August 1936, Major Giuseppe Luccardi warned of the antagonism between the Falangists and the *Requetés* and between the former and conservative military elements, who believed there were reforms intended to go against their interests and 'ancient privileges' in the Falangist programme. For that reason, Luccardi said, Italy had to advise the Spanish leaders who were 'completely disorientated'.[19] The Italians would take it upon themselves to guide the Spaniards towards a convergence of forces in a context, as Cantalupo indicated to Ciano in December 1936, in which the differences between the *Requetés* and the Falangists were growing increasingly deeper. According to the ambassador, the former brought together closely knit aristocrats and capitalists with a large military organisation, with means of propaganda and combatants on the front lines. They were combative and were perplexed by the attitude of the Vatican, which had failed to side clearly with the insurgents. As for the Falange, it was without clear leadership following the death of José Antonio Primo de Rivera, but it was a big force in terms of its membership numbers, the modern spirit of its social programme, and its popularity among workers. Furthermore, its leaders had told him that, until there was a state that emanated from its ranks, there was a risk of grave danger. If the Falange's positions were not taken into account, and if what he called a 'kind of persecution' continued, they would take decisions which might not secure victory for the *National* side.

In the future, however, the Falange would be the best organisation to rally militant workers from the 'Red side'. Moreover, once the armed conflict was over, a middle class could emerge from the party to put a brake on political extremism, the cause (the ambassador said) of the war's excesses. In the ambassador's opinion, Franco relied a great deal on the *Requetés* but was openly in sympathy with the Falange, though the party was excluded from power because of its internal crisis. Franco was considered an '*ottimo condottiero*', a great military leader (even if Cantalupo did not share this view). Such was the panorama when, as early as December, the need was posited for a single leader, who, according to the same Falange, had to be Franco. It was a single party and a single militia that the head of state should ratify and give legal form to 'in an unappealable decision'. In this way, Franco would unify the state, 'which in external appearance would consist of [the] red beret of the *Requetés*; [the] blue shirt of the Falange; [the] Roman salute; [the] Yoke and Arrows as symbol; a single national flag'. Inwardly, it would consist of 'God

110 *Italy, the CTV, and politics*

and Catholicism (without discord); united Fatherland; Regime: a Head or Regent; social question: national syndicalism or corporative system'.[20]

It is important to look again at the date of these reports. They are not from April 1937 but from four months earlier, in the case of the unification of party and militia, and three months earlier, in the case of Franco's apparent acceptance of Danzi's political plan. And they originated with Cantalupo, the least keen on Franco of all the Fascist agents deployed in Spain. Thus, in January, according to the MMIS's head of propaganda, the initiative began to take shape thanks to which General Franco would become the 'originator of vast reforms and will seek to accomplish the merging of the parties into a political organism along the lines of the fascist party'. Originator of reforms and unifier of parties in order to create a new one: it was a track, according to Nicolás Franco, of a 'fascist or fascistoid' tendency, which his brother was pondering with an eye to creating a 'government and a State Party called Falange'.[21] The name chosen three months before the decree of unification undoubtedly reveals it was the most relevant political force in the rebel rearguard—or, at least, which was perceived as such—contrary to the insignificance to which it tends to be relegated in the context of the 'encampment state'. It was the force which, thanks to the 'special conditions', went on to become a 'subject of mobilisation' and military organisation and, therefore, an agent for conquering power.[22] It was revealing with regard to the idea of the need to create a state party, consistent with the history of the growth of the Italian *Partito Nazionale Fascista* (PNF, National Fascist Party). In the words of Giuseppe Bottai, whether they provided arms or not, but 'they cannot not provide ideas to the peoples who are fighting'.[23] And, apparently, the first immediate effect of Fascist political intervention in Spain was to provide those ideas, as well as to serve as custodians of a successful path to fascistisation and, therefore (through ideological influence, diplomatic assistance, and military weight), as guarantors to ensure the conditions of fascism's establishment in Spain—an establishment which, furthermore, ought to be beneficial for an Italy which had become something more than mere observer.

It was not a simple matter—at least, not in appearance—particularly given the context of the internal war within which this process of fascistisation had to be carried out. Danzi himself, despite his political determination, had a dreadful image of *National* Spain and, accordingly, a harsh judgement of the potential success of its manoeuvrings. In his opinion, Franco was not in favour of 'the masses' but rather the leader of a military reaction which had paralysed them using terror, as hundreds of people a day continued to be shot without distinction of age or sex. Consequently, they harboured hostility towards the *National* Movement, as there were very few among the working class who had not had a relative shot on the Nationalists' orders. Franco had not connected with his people and had renounced defending the sacred right to work and initiating the task of social renewal, apart from vague declarations to foreign newspapers. For the Nationalist authorities, the Falange was a party full of card-carrying communists waiting on events. As for the

Requetés, they were commanded by the big Spanish landowners, the uprising's financiers, who aimed to protect their privileges and feudal autonomy and undermined aspirations to social justice. And, lastly, the Army was not united but rather an ensemble of contingents with independent leaders opposed to Franco's supremacy.

Danzi was in agreement with Ambassador Cantalupo about all this (although he might have been the only one). Following the Italian occupation of Málaga, the tensions among the rebel generals had worsened noticeably, particularly the tacit and latent conflict between Franco, Mola, and Queipo. Franco directed operations and public life, while the Army of the North, with several tens of thousands of men of little fighting value, was under the command of Mola—Franco's intellectual superior—and the Army of the South was under Queipo, about whose cultural sophistication, he said, there was reason to have the greatest reservations. According to the Italian consulate in Sevilla, Queipo aimed 'to carry out the political cleansing of the province . . . materially eliminating the members of the vast centres of subversion' (some 20 a day in May 1937).[24] Franco had the best army under his command, some 50,000 Moroccans and 15,000 legionnaires who felt love, respect, and obedience towards him. For Cantalupo, the initial equilibrium was leaning in Franco's favour following the meetings with Goering in Rome and the capture of Málaga. Together with his growing prestige in public opinion and among the troops, Franco had obtained his greatest legitimacy by winning Italy and Germany's recognition and, above all, because of Italy's substantial military, diplomatic, and moral assistance—assistance given, it was stressed, 'to him personally'.[25] The personalisation of the assistance, gestating since 1936, had become completely clear by February 1937, to the extent of being a problem, because, as Farinacci (by then on a political mission in Spain), opined from Zaragoza, this dominance could nonetheless adversely affect Franco's prestige.

Nevertheless, according to Danzi, Fascist Italy had to make the most of this dominance for its own benefit. Mola and Queipo were intriguers, politically and militarily undisciplined, and highly ambitious, with kaleidoscopic pasts and great *amour propre*. Moreover, Queipo, who in his radio chats presented himself as the friend and representative of the Andalusian people, was working in Sevilla to build his own political court. The MMIS's head of propaganda said that the leading circles were generally driven by obscurantism, ignorance, lack of understanding, and naivety. 'These people's brains are made of gunpowder', he concluded.[26] In these circumstances, the only hope lay with a Franco who was indoctrinated and evangelised by fascism, the recipient of military assistance, and thereby in debt to the fascist powers. In short, Danzi confirms the argument put forward by Paul Preston as the major factor making for the *Generalísimo*'s supremacy over the rest of the insurgent generals—they were helping him because he was, in Mussolini's words, the only fascist in Spain.

The proposal was clear—consolidate Franco's power through a powerful patriotic front, following the PNF's example and absorbing the national

112 *Italy, the CTV, and politics*

parties, offering guarantees of a social policy like the abolition of privileges and the redistribution of uncultivated land, laws to protect artisans, guaranteed minimum wages, the creation of Institutes for Social Provision and Occupational Hygiene, the creation of institutes for leisure and recreation ('*dopolavoristici*'), and the obligation to work. Vicente Gay and Danzi had set to work in January 1937 to draw up this programme but were told by Ciano in March to stop,[27] not because the doctrinal line was not the correct one, but because it encroached on Spanish areas of competence and on the mission assigned by Mussolini to Cantalupo, namely to contribute to the creation of a 'unitary politico-spiritual-corporative bloc'[28] to serve as the basis of the future totalitarian state. Thus, it is not entirely true that the ambassador was removed from political matters, although his authority was undermined by Farinacci's arrival in Spain only 15 days after he had taken up his post. In fact, there were two parallel political missions, and the ambassador did not want one being allowed preference over the other. Cantalupo would undoubtedly have much less capacity to act. But his capacity to influence and give his opinion remained intact, and he would, in fact, have a notable influence on Italian decisions with regard to internal policy.

For now, his was a line of fascist interpretation of Spain's political reality closely followed by his co-religionists, an interpretation according to which, in addition to Franco's ineptitude to leading the process, it was clear both that the 'traditionalist opportunists' represented exactly that which Mussolini had carried out his fascist revolution against and that the solution could not lie with the Falange's Manuel Hedilla, a leader of 'unmitigated unculturedness'.[29] Alas, the only option was to trust in Franco, who had generally shown himself to be a 'well-liked man, but a poor fellow, lacking ideas, hugely short of feelings, not well-read, with barely family ambitions . . . a stranger to modern Europe—the least fascist imaginable'. Moreover, his 'virility and loyalty' could not be trusted. Indeed, Cantalupo referred on more than one occasion to the Caudillo's femininity and considered him to be easily influenced and of little political stature. According to the ambassador, when he presented his credentials on 1 March 1937, Franco's eyes were moist with tears as he said to him in Italian, '*Grazie al Duce*'. Yet, shortly afterwards, he was incapable of making a speech to the people, reverting to being 'cold, glasslike, and feminine'.[30]

All the members of Mussolini's diplomatic and political network in Spain tried to put into practice the 'Fascist government's dominant thinking, which can be summarised thusly: fascisticising Spain'.[31] This fascistisation would be accomplished, according to the political reports of early 1937, via diplomatic control over Franco, the joint military command of the three fascist powers, and political influence, although Cantalupo believed the human raw materials were lacking. Therefore, the ambassador thought that Franco had to make 'the Falange his own party', in order to prevent it from developing into a revolutionary force in the future. Accordingly, although the Falangists felt themselves to be 'on the Left, close to the enemies in the opposite trench,

Italy, the CTV, and politics   113

far removed from the bourgeoisie, the military, and the clergy', they would accept 'a provisional Franco government and not a merger but an absorption, as Mussolini had done with the Italian nationalists'. That was the reason why, in February, Hedilla had mentioned the need to restore the figure of the charismatic leader in Spain, embodied in 'Generalissimo Franco's young, strong, and typically Spanish spirit', to whom maximum loyalty was guaranteed. The Carlists also regarded the influence exercised by the Italian embassy as being positive, which is why Javier de Borbón did not hesitate to send a letter to Mussolini, declaring his admiration. According to Cantalupo, the Carlists were afraid that the 'Fascist government had the intention of supporting the old monarchy' of Alfonso XIII.[32]

In this situation, the Duce's stance was not to support any single tendency indiscriminately, a stance which could 'lead Franco to . . . the merger of the parties . . . which, candidly speaking, would conclusively lay the basis for the fascistisation of Spain'. Moreover, it would secure 'Italy's future operation in the Iberian Peninsula on an extensive, solid, and enduring basis', established by the regime of the New Spain's itself, 'loyal to us and obedient from its very innermost spiritual and legislative formation'. Fascist Spain would thus become a regime dependent in large measure on Italy, by virtue of the latter's political influence and, above all, its military involvement and blood, even with the 'most scandalous international publicity possible'.[33] From this perspective, fascistisation would not be a process as imagined by Farinacci— that is to say, the result of persuading Franco to adopt institutions copied from Italian Fascism. Rather, it would be the management of a joint response mechanism supervised by Mussolini—in concrete terms, controlling politics, public opinion through the media, and the secret services. It is therefore important to underline this point—for the Italians, at least in their reports about their plans, Spain's fascistisation depended on not explicitly taking the side of any political faction, despite their clear preference for the Falange as the party-militia of action and of the state. In this way, Franco would move forward in creating the single party. And, through this party, the basis of the corporative state would be established, as Commander Ernesto Marchiandi pointed out. He was another of the political envoys sent to Spain, in this instance on behalf of Tullio Cianetti, president of the *Confederazione Nazionale dei Sindacati Fascisti dell'Industria* (National Confederation of Fascist Syndicates of Industry). According to Marchiandi, Spain currently lacked the 'capacity to make internal alliances required for the most basic institutions of a totalitarian character'. And this disunity made things difficult for 'our purposeful and interventionist action in the field of internal politics'.[34]

Nevertheless, here too, the result was a process of trial and error. According to Ismael Saz and Javier Tusell, Farinacci's isolated mission between 3 and 9 March produced sparse results and could certainly be considered a failure, but there was little isolated about it. A distinguished fascist, former general secretary of the PNF, and current member of the Fascist Grand Council, Farinacci was sent by the Duce to mediate between Danzi and Cantalupo's

114 *Italy, the CTV, and politics*

positions and, above all, to support the building of a fascist party along the lines of what he himself had helped to create in Italy. According to the note introducing him to Franco, he was a pioneer of fascism, a born fighter, and a brave pilot officer in the African war, and he was coming to Spain to present his ideas for the future. However, the work he carried out in Salamanca, meeting Roatta, Franco, Hedilla, Cantalupo, Giménez Caballero, Nicolás Franco, the Count of Rodezno, Eugenio Montes, and Agustín de Foxá, was undoubtedly problematic. He looked down his nose at the embassy and confronted Hedilla, who is said to have blurted out to Cantalupo, 'But Mussolini, has he perhaps taken us for imbeciles?' And, according to the ambassador (who saw Farinacci as encroaching on responsibilities which he considered to be his alone), he also caused a fair number of people to question Mussolini's motives. For some, as Cantalupo remarked, referring to his military contacts in Franco's general headquarters, the Duce had sent Farinacci to pit the Falange against Franco, to create a Falangist tendency in opposition to the Caudillo. For others, his objective was to convince the traditionalists of the advisability of drawing closer to the French reactionary Right. Rather than unite, he managed to fragment the Italian political agencies in Spain, even though everybody more or less shared a dreadful opinion of him. As Danzi would take care to report, the jealousy of Cantalupo, who was a 'systematic opponent' of any Italian sent to Spain on a job of a political nature and saw their arrival as 'a political error and an affront to his dignity', rendered sterile the work of fascistisation. Farinacci was a fake, disabled serviceman, having lost his hand fishing with grenades in Africa, as Danzi would remind Nicolás Franco's personal secretary, in an obvious attempt to discredit him in the eyes of the *Generalísimo*. Farinacci, who had put himself forward to be ambassador to Spain and who stirred up some of the most notorious confrontations in the Italian rearguard, was the only matter about which Danzi and Cantalupo were in agreement: he was 'a cretin and an illiterate'.[35]

Cretin or not, Farinacci was the organiser of several political meetings at the highest level in a Spain that seemed to him to be in 'total chaos'. According to his reports, on 4 March he was able to see Franco, who looked timid, politically a kid, not like a leader, and who if he were 'younger and less ugly would look like [Umberto] Puppini, our Minister of Communications'. In his estimation, Franco had no firm idea of what the Spain of tomorrow would be like beyond winning the war, establishing an authoritarian government to 'cleanse Spain' of all those who had had direct or indirect contact or sympathies with the Reds, and implementing a corporatist programme like those 'in Italy, Germany, Austria, and Portugal'.[36] Farinacci thought that the first priority was to 'create the nation', a task that could not be entrusted to the Falangists or the *Requetés* because they lacked leaders of any worth. The next step would be to lay the doctrinal foundation of a Spanish National Party that would unite all political forces and be oriented 'toward the working classes', something in which Franco had shown interest. In any case, the New Spain's political inexperience became clear to Farinacci in his conversations with Hedilla, who was open, in his opinion, to meeting the *Requetés* with a view to creating a 'new national movement that Franco should appreciate and use', and with Nicolás Franco, the government's factotum, who had 'treasured many of my suggestions'—to the point of asking for them in writing—about 'authoritarian and totalitarian' policies of reconstruction, social security, maternity and child protection, and assistance and improvement of the material and moral conditions of the working classes through wage increases, a 40-hour workweek, boosting the military industry and public employment, and a new agrarian policy. However, it was crystal clear to Farinacci that what was needed in Spain would be achieved by a political coup de main.

As Cantalupo would write soon afterwards, the generalised political disaster, Franco's antipathy towards the Falange and its leader, and Hedilla's incompetence and obstinacy regarding integration into a large national movement more favourable towards the traditionalists could only be resolved, in his judgement, by Mussolini's decisive intervention. In the ambassador's opinion—and it was only an opinion, as he had received orders not to involve himself in internal politics and military questions and Farinacci's mission had excluded him from everything to do with the merging of parties—the Duce would have called matters to order by imposing a political action plan in parallel with the military assistance given.[37] Whether Cantalupo was right or not, there are sufficient indications to think that Rome intervened to put an end to the state of political uncertainty in the rebels' rearguard. In fact, besides Danzi—whom Franco allegedly met while the unification decree was being written—Giménez Caballero also claimed to be the faithful collaborator and executive arm of the Duce, who, on '22 January at seven o'clock in the evening', had entrusted him with a mission to give concrete form to that decree. Between them, they had considerable influence—although at times it might appear contrived to the point of exaggeration—on the regime's political configuration as it was being gestated in Salamanca. After talking to the Falange's head of propaganda, Tito Menéndez Rubio (who, in turn, asked him to meet Hedilla), Danzi said that the Falangists were becoming more and more 'convinced fascists' of the Italian sort (and less of the German sort), believers in 'Italophile totalitarian politics'. In other words, they were placing themselves under the protection of 'Mussolini's spiritual paternity'.

The Duce's increasing political influence was in keeping with the fact that he had been the founder of the first fascism to take power and, above all, with the amount of military participation decided by him in favour of Franco and the 'National' side in Spain. In Danzi's words, for the Falangists, everything boiled down to the notion that, while Germany had made Hitler, Mussolini had made Italy.[38] And it was from this position of influence that Francesco Cavalletti, Italian consul in Donostia, was able to assert that the 'national movement' had assumed 'in large part the features of the fascist revolution', even despite 'Franco's mistake' of divulging the unification before Sainz Rodríguez had confirmed Javier de Borbón's support.[39] As the CAUR's propaganda indicated, the plan had been designed in advance. Word for word,

116 *Italy, the CTV, and politics*

the plan was perfect. If what united the Reds was anti-fascism, it logically followed that what had to unite the Whites was fascism. The Falange had prepared itself to capture the state. The differences between the Falangists and the *Requetés* were said to not really be differences and to have been fomented from behind the lines. The community-of-arms at the front had united their volunteers, and they all accepted that the Duce exercise was 'a decisive influence on the Falangist movement'.[40]

As an informant said in early April, it was possibly true that Franco 'has never understood anything about politics' and for that reason needed external influence. The Fascists were always looking to support the parties driven by a rhetoric of a 'popular base' (and not those, like José María Gil Robles, who wanted to go back to the 'good old times'). They aimed to impose 'bold social reforms' and a 'unitary and wholly military conduct of the war', in order to escape from a 'serious and uncertain' situation in which Franco appeared increasingly 'powerless in command, obstinately rejecting the Falangists' requests'. The people 'are suffering from hunger . . . and are galvanised neither by a strong personality, nor by military victories, nor by the vision of a better future'.[41] It is not clear whether political unification was intended to put an end to hunger or to the war, but it certainly was intended to put an end to the political mess. The fact is that this political unification, whose shapes and assumptions had begun to be prepared at the beginning of the year, was forged within days.

In his reports, Danzi took much of the credit for himself, but his excessive focus on personal factors casts doubt on the veracity of his account.[42] On 17 April, in the midst of the political convulsions in the capital of the rebels' zone, Hedilla met Danzi to talk about the *Requetés'* reaction to being absorbed by the Falange and their possible revolt. 'It will not be difficult to quell it', he replied. But, faced with Danzi's objections, he purportedly answered back, 'You are right. I will go to the Generalissimo and say to him, "At your orders"'. Later, Nicolás Franco called him and invited him to eat. If what was indicated in another report is true, that same night 'General Franco called me to his headquarters and together we drew up the plan to merge parties into one',[43] from which one might think that the two brothers were together. According to Danzi's account, Nicolás Franco had done nothing more than ask him, 'What would Mussolini do?', to which he replied that the Duce would do nothing, because 'he would already have done everything'. To bring the evening to a close, at three in the morning, he 'began to take notes', which were later fattened up 'like a pig' and would be the basis for the Decree of Unification.[44] For Tulio Rispoli, it was a Spanish copy of the merger of the Italian nationalists who joined the *Partito Nazionale Fascista*—the 'reconstruction of a unitary, social and imperial sentiment'.[45]

We know it was not that easy. According to his account, once the decree had been published and he saw the composition of the national council of the nascent party, the *Falange Española Tradicionalista y de las Juntas de Ofensiva Nacional Sindicalista* (FET y de las JONS), Danzi spoke to Hedilla,

Italy, the CTV, and politics 117

who said that the unification was in fact 'the liquidation of the Falange' and that he would resign because he could not sit on a council with 'counts who get up at eleven in the morning'. Because the Italian's argument that resignation would play into the hands of international anti-fascism did not impress Hedilla, as a last resort Danzi offered him a trip to Italy. Nevertheless, beyond symbolic questions and the balance of influence with regard to the Germans (who openly supported Hedilla), the fact is that, judging by the Italian general staff's reports, in Rome there was no great interest in the Falange's internal problems. According to the MMIS's information office, Queipo de Llano and his wish to put Sancho Dávila at the head of Spanish fascism were behind them. 'Since Rome's intention is to support Franco', whom the Duce thought was the man who could prevent Bolshevism from 'gaining a foothold in Spain or the Mediterranean',[46] what should be done with regard to the unification of the political parties was to 'probe his thinking so as to be able to support his candidate'. And it turned out that Franco's candidate was Franco himself, so there was little to worry about regarding 'resistance to the unification'.[47]

Quite a few informants pointed out that the unification had simply postponed the problems; that the party was weak, badly organised, and even worse prepared; and that Franco, only superficially of fascist inclination, was not the right person to solve internal problems and, at the same time, military and social problems. The unification was little more than a 'scrap of paper' for Danzi, who by now had transferred his office to Donostia and who soon afterwards would be withdrawn from Spain, according to Roatta, for exceeding his authority. Despite representing the Spain for which so many comrades had 'sacrificed their lives', no one (except Nicolás Franco, he said) would understand that the union had to be the 'categorical imperative' that gave Spain a 'clear and genuinely fascist authoritarian government' that would purify the 'soul of the Spanish people'.[48] However, beyond the surfeit of metaphors (the soul, the people, the nation, the spirit, etc.), behind the fascist political agents there was an explicit programme, based on an active influence dictated from the pinnacle of power by Mussolini. And the Duce's vision of the whole affair was very clear—the fascist party in Spain could not be a minority and ideologically pure party but rather had to be the representative of an entire National Movement.

It was almost a logical outcome that the process of creating the *FET y de las JONS* was problematic and that, in the summer of 1937, disunity prevailed in the party. In fact, if the Falange was indeed the 'shadow of a shadow' and unification 'a dream', in Giménez Caballero's words, the situation would remain controllable. No political issue could be allowed to create public disorder. And, except in the recently occupied zones, where the 'strict political task [was] leading to capital punishment sentences', insurgent Spain's internal situation in June was satisfactory, according to an anonymous Italian informant, with the single party temporarily amalgamated, Franco wielding great authority, and a good atmosphere. This was possibly in line with what

118 *Italy, the CTV, and politics*

Ismael Saz refers to as the 'good life' within the limits to fascistisation fixed by Franco.[49] In fact, compared to the enemy's rearguard, the political situation in the fascist equivalent was barely troubled and facilitated the job of exercising influence over the new central elements of the single party and its National Council. In that sense, Mussolini would appreciate Queipo de Llano's phantasmagorical proposal for agrarian reform. Giménez Caballero would take the opportunity to ask the Duce for economic help in publishing an 'Italophile' newspaper aimed at Spanish combatants.[50] Ciano would undertake to persuade Serrano Suñer in person. However, as will be seen further on, there would be two advisers of particularly honourable standing, in both cases of clear symbolic and cultural significance: Pilar Primo de Rivera and Pedro Sainz Rodríguez.

Satisfaction with the final result of the political process of the spring of 1937 was, in any case, total—'Single party, single militia, single trade union, on these three pillars the great Spain of tomorrow will develop'. This was how Mussolini congratulated Franco on his political success on 13 August 1937.[51] It was, in his opinion, the result of his pressure. He could feel proud; even a curious chart illustrating influences on the Caudillo, designed by Ambassador Viola in November 1937, showed it.[52] Only this process in its entirety can explain the authority with which Ciano wrote on 5 May: 'Suggest to General Franco, with regard to his government programme, that now is perhaps the moment to adopt the *Carta del Lavoro*.' This preceded another famous Mussolinian suggestion to Franco, namely to use the first anniversary of the coup d'état to form a government.[53]

The *Fuero del Trabajo* would be delayed for almost another year, but it would have, in the Duce's opinion, an Italian imprint. When the National Council created a committee to study the bases for the corporatist organisation of the Spanish state, the Italians tried to wield their influence by increasing information about the successes of Italian corporatism, so as to direct the council towards adopting 'our system'. The Italian embassy—according to the public broadcaster *Ente Italiano per le Audizioni Radiofoniche* (EIAR)—urgently asked for 250 'Aquila' wall posters about corporatist legislation, 20 copies of the Duce's speech on the topic, and a large number of corporatist propaganda leaflets.[54] The day before the meeting of the Falange's National Council at which the text was discussed and dozens of amendments were made (mainly favouring the traditionalists), Marchiandi met several council members to 'enlighten them' about the Italian *Carta del Lavoro* and to fix some formal principles to develop in the future that would fully justify 'the idea-based reasons for the Italian intervention in Spain'. Although it was the document that established the political character of the New Spain, the final version of the *Fuero del Trabajo* was, in Viola's view, a doctrinal disaster, lacking 'the clarity that is of capital importance in a document intended to pervade Spain's future regime'. It was not the confirmation of a policy of social reform but a compendium of nice words of no practical use. Nobody knew how to define what exactly a vertical union of producers was. Even so, without being as clear as the *Carta del Lavoro*, it included 'its principal foundations'.[55]

That is how it always was. Those who, like Danzi or Farinacci, each in his own way, had aimed to import the same logic, loyalties, and identities found in Mussolini's regime returned to Italy disappointed. This model of an idealistic, vital, avant-garde, soldierly, mobilising fascism, which served to nationalise the masses, would collide constantly with the reality of the insurgent rearguard in the Civil War. A clear example was the figure of Italo Sulliotti, an impassioned fascist in charge of the *Fascio Raffaele Tarantini de Sevilla*, which was part of the *Fasci Italiani all'Estero*'s delegation in southern Spain. His political reports to the minister Dino Alfieri, in keeping with the language of fascism, are riddled with generalisations, metaphors, and judgements which brought together political 'climates', what 'the masses need', and 'perceptions' of Fascist Italy, depending on the treatment that he received. As Sulliotti believed that Italian Fascism represented a 'superior civilisation', fascisticising Spain was, from his perspective, synonymous with civilising it.[56] But beyond his smug habit of indulging in metaphors and revealing a perception not far removed from what may have been the thinking of many other Italian military and political agents in Spain, his words were very mistaken. He was particularly mistaken in saying that the unification had been a betrayal of the Falangism of 'Antonio [*sic*] Primo de Rivera' and the 'Falangist minority that has understood Mussolini' and, therefore, a stab in the Duce's back. Spain, he said, needed a Mussolini, but Franco was to the Duce what 'a quartermaster sergeant was to Napoleon'. However, his beloved Duce gave no indication of being in agreement. As has already been indicated, in October 1937, Mussolini declared openly that European states were on a fascist track, even when they declared the contrary, and that each would have its own fascism, its own 'complex of doctrines, methods, experiments and achievements' adapted to the needs of each people. And, the context and needs of Franco's Spain were very clear.

The Civil War was the setting which facilitated fascistisation, as well as what determined its process and its results. And, at least if we follow the documentary evidence, as has been done here, of what exactly fascistisation meant and how it was understood by its subjects (influence, leadership, armed support, common objectives, common enemies), we can see, as Morten Heiberg rightly reminds us and as Ferran Gallego has evinced in his discussions of the political debates, that the question of fascist political influence in Spain deserves a well-informed re-examination. A re-examination that, rather than treating the question as a simple anecdote, returns it to its rightful sphere, covering not only political conversations in corridors and meetings with consular advisers but also ideological and cultural permeation, the pressure exercised through propaganda, and, above all, everyday experiences. This has been yet another factor used to diminish the success of fascistisation and, hence, smooth the rough edges of the political nature of a regime that did not emerge from but rather was born in the war—a regime and a war that were followed with

120 *Italy, the CTV, and politics*

'fraternal understanding' from Italy, essentially for three reasons: 'affinity of ideals', the complementary nature of Spain and Italy's 'mission' in Europe, and because 'Italy first, and she alone, fought the same danger'.[57]

Thus, the fascist powers' anti-communism in Spain was not mere propaganda, nor did the Italians devote 'very little' to the task of the cultural dissemination of fascism.[58] Instead, as Vito Beltrani would write in 1939 (among many others, whose testimonies are collected in the next chapter), Italy had become, in his view, the bishop in the chess game of defending European civilisation against 'Bolshevik materialism' that, contrary to fascism, had ricocheted off the walls of the Old Word, walls which fascism tore down. 'Mussolini, Hitler, Pilsudski, Salazar, Franco, Mosley', and the other '*eminenti condottieri dei movimenti a sfondo fascista*' (eminent leaders of fascist-based movements) knew perfectly well that they were called upon not only to reconstruct the nation but also to endow their peoples with a common faith that only fascism could offer.[59] As Mussolini himself would say after the fall of Barcelona in January 1939, this

> splendid victory . . . is another chapter in the history of the New Europe that we are creating. Franco's magnificent troops and our intrepid legionnaires have not defeated only Negrín's army. Right now, many of our enemies are biting the dust.[60]

Evangelise by deed

Italian influence was not wielded only in echoing, carpeted rooms and monasteries hung with velvet, nor only by persons in newly pressed uniforms. The experience of following the combatants 'in the fire, under shrapnel fire, in the ice . . . the mud . . . the snow, without food for more than 50 hours' was what the dense network of informants, consular officials, and PNF agents were lacking, and thus they had not learnt what fascism in Spain really was, as Carlo Basile complained in a report for the *Fasci Italiani all'Estero*. Those who failed to understand included Cantalupo, with his 'enlarged' personality and 'attitude of immovable superiority', who had purportedly exclaimed, following the defeat at Guadalajara, that the war was 'not my problem!'[61] Farinacci, too, shared this opinion of the 'harmful', 'clownish', 'jinxed', 'joke-of-a-fascist' Italian ambassador, who lived entrenched in the embassy's provisional seat in Salamanca, hiding in his bed, always afraid for his life, criticising everything and everybody, and openly condemning the Italian intervention and the volunteers being killed on the battlefields.[62] They, however, were the true evangelists, those who carried the Duce's portrait through the villages, marching to the sound of the '*Giovinezza*'—they who truly disseminated fascism in Spain and did so with their blood.

As the CTV's new commander wrote to Lieutenant Colonel Nulli of the Ministry of Foreign Affairs in November 1937, the Spanish war was 'first and foremost political, and politics exerts a predominant influence on it'.[63] These volunteers and soldiers were the ones creating—at least on paper—the true 'climate favouring [Italian] penetration', in which military action, politics, and propaganda journeyed together.

One of these domains of influence was the information and propaganda media, the preferred means of fascist evangelisation in Spain. Starting in October 1936, we can already find public representations of the fascist imaginary such as the showing of films like *Camisas Negras* (Blackshirts), the 'epic of Italian fascism', which could be seen (in the presence of Queipo de Llano) at the San Fernando theatre in Sevilla. As the publicity leaflets noted, although the film was about Italy, it would interest anybody, whether Falangist or not.[64] Indeed, so important was the question of propaganda that the MMIS had a press and propaganda office 'once the volunteer troops began to be sent'[65] in January 1937, based in Salamanca, which was subsequently transferred to Donostia, once Danzi was received by Mussolini following the defeat at Guadalajara and assumed full authority to reorganise it.[66] Its activity was marked from the beginning by the production of a press bulletin on Fascist Italy's progress (published regularly by about 60 newspapers) and the distribution of propaganda photographs and material, but it soon had other tasks. Shortly after being given the job, Danzi met his friend Millán Astray, head of the insurgents' Press and Propaganda Office at the time, to obtain his assent to them producing their own propaganda about Spain both at home and abroad. He also passed on his office's needs: five journalists, a translator, typists, two cinema operators, and a van with photo and cinema equipment.

Unsurprisingly, Danzi's first movements were tentative and largely improvised. While waiting to be able to offer his own material, he suggested organising a weekly in the form of a wall newspaper, 'few words and lots of illustrations' for a country of illiterates, and creating a powerful photo-cinematographic service, which would allow the 'atrocities of Red barbarism' to be shown in insurgent Spain. Only in July 1937 could he be said to have a complete service at his disposal, with 70 staff under him and a monthly expenditure of 185,000 pesetas, allocated basically to the distribution of material to the soldiers and the wounded, the purchase of 40 radio sets for hospitals, the printing of propaganda leaflets, the subsidising of a special issue of *Domingo* devoted to the CTV, and the purchase of film and office equipment.[67] Nevertheless, the largest share of expenditure would go on the publication of the newspaper *El Legionario*, a free weekly paper in Italian. Despite its poor typography, it was particularly costly because it was edited in Salamanca and printed in Valladolid, even though the place of publication was always billed as the '*Fronte di guerra liberatrice*' (liberation war front). It was published between 19 March 1937 and 30 August 1938. Its contents were mainly political, with a selection of articles from the fascist press, although, after the defeat at Guadalajara, it was ordered to improve its propaganda, considered to be insufficiently humorous. As would be said at

122 *Italy, the CTV, and politics*

the time, the soldier preferred 'a joke to a professor's lecture'.[68] Even down to the crosswords, the two aspects were combined in *El Legionario*—a (supposedly) humorous side alongside gigantic contempt for the enemy and the construction of an identity.[69]

As far as material for radio was concerned, all the *National* side's radio stations had propaganda, music records, and news in Spanish, Italian, and French produced by the *Ufficio Stampa e Propaganda*. Later, *Radio Verdad* (Radio Truth) was established with a mail service for more than 12,000 listeners.[70] It also took charge of distributing material from the Ministry of Popular Culture (known as the *MinCulPop*), with 'particular attention to the recently liberated zones'. Publications like *Rusia no es Europa* (*Russia is not Europe*) by Giovanni Selvi, *Habla el Duce* (*The Duce Speaks*), and *Spirito della rivoluzione fascista* (*Spirit of the Fascist Revolution*) by S.S. Spinetti, translated by Eugenio Montes, would serve as the means for first-rate national and political counter-propaganda. In addition to all this, there were the more than 50,000 Italo-Spanish badges, little cards with Mussolini's picture and quotes, the publication of 30,000 copies of a summary of the Duce's speeches, as well as translations of fascist works. This was the origin of a 'vast programme of cultural penetration in Spain', including translations, exchange of scholars, the arrival of the *Mostra del Libro Italiano* (Italian Book Exhibition), musical concerts, film screenings, and lectures. In addition to the helpdesk for Italian journalists in Spain, the *Ufficio* had its own photo and film service, which followed the CTV in order to use its pictures in the printed press and film newsreels, working hand in hand with the *Instituto Luce*.

The 'Red' rearguard boasted one of the most important broadcasting organisations in Europe, which had faced its 'great test in this war, proving to be an information and propaganda medium . . . faster, more effective, and cheaper than the newspaper'. Looking ahead to the collapse of the front, Italian technical teams would be required to take over from the 'Reds'. Also required would be authorisation to intervene economically, in the EIAR's name, in radio stations through the provision of equipment or credits in other sectors, such as the military. Faced with the (false) prospect of Madrid's immediate occupation and the installation of Franco's government in the capital, a report by the *Ufficio Stampa* noted that there would be a reorganisation of the leading political press and Madrid's radio stations. Action would be required before foreign, 'anti-Italian' influences moved in. Participation in the press by contributing capital would be detrimental and ineffective. More useful and substantive, however, would be to seek and secure the friendship and loyalty of 30–40 political journalists. Some were in hiding in the 'Red' zone (including, purportedly, Ramón Gómez de la Serna). To convince these people, 'journalists and writers put at the service of the National Cause'[71] would make it morally impossible for them to adopt a hostile attitude towards Italy and create a 'preventive enclosure' to protect against the inevitable French, English, and German influence in Spain in the future. It would cost less and be of more use than procuring economic shares in publishing organisations.

It should not be forgotten that Mussolini himself also intended fascistisation to be a means of controlling opinion.

The front did not collapse, but everything required to deploy Italian propaganda in Spain using radio was made available. Very early on, in February 1937, Danzi noted that *Radio Milan* was listened to a great deal in the insurgent zone, but that it included practically no news about Spain. He therefore asked for an increase in mentions, with references to the wealth of provisions and the better living conditions in Franco's Spain. Days later, Spanish-language broadcasts from 8.45 to 9 p.m. from Rome, Milan, Florence, and Genoa and Catalan-language broadcasts from midnight to one in the morning from Milan and Florence were added to the news already broadcast in Spanish at 11.15 p.m. from Milan and Florence. Linguistic advice on the new broadcasts was provided by Dr. Giorgi, secretary of the Italian consulate in Barcelona, and by Delfino Escolà, a Spanish fugitive. The new broadcasts were announced as coming from the *Verdad* radio station. The *Ufficio Stampa* sent the same bulletin to all radio stations. The obsession of Danzi and all those who worked in Italian radio was to not let the German mission take the lead on the airwaves with the big radio station at Salamanca, which later became *Radio Nacional*. Nevertheless, it would broadcast news in Italian for the legionnaires plus official communiqués about the military operations—nothing more, although that already was not insubstantial.

In fact, one of the matters that most concerned the MMIS was that the propaganda was directed excessively at the Spanish in the insurgent and enemy rearguards and not enough at its own Italian soldiers. As Danzi would point out, until the defeat at Guadalajara propaganda activity had been aimed solely at demoralising the enemy, but it had forgotten the heroic fascist fighters. The CTV's directives, in anticipation of a great (and conclusive) Italian military campaign, were to increase the production of fliers and manifestos to be dropped over enemy territory, some two million leaflets. However, during the battle, the failure of Fascist propaganda became clear, even prompting Mussolini to send a telegram from Libya asking if Farinacci was still in Spain, as he could be used for these tasks. 'Our propaganda', Danzi would say, did not compare to the activities of the Republicans, because the necessary technical means were not even available. Roatta learnt that, behind the enemy's lines, fliers were being prepared with photos of the first Italian prisoners. Because he was unable to print counter-propaganda in Salamanca, Danzi had to go to Valladolid to print 40,000 copies of a special issue of *El Legionario*, as well as ten million posters and leaflets, emphasising the pointlessness of the struggle by the 'Reds', the wickedness of their leaders, the good life in *National* Spain, and fascism's generosity to whoever surrendered. As is known, the material did not arrive on time and had no effect whatsoever. Furthermore, complaints were later raised that the fact that the leaflets did not touch on the topics that were important to each unit and the same type of content was used on all the fronts significantly diminished their impact—that is, if they had any real impact at all.

124 *Italy, the CTV, and politics*

The propaganda disaster at Guadalajara was so terrible that Cantalupo's well-known jealousy combined with Roatta's and then Bastico's unease and the complaints that his performance had aroused to cost Danzi his job in July. The military, Cantalupo would say, had become 'fed up with the office's autonomy'.[72] His decision to move the office to Donostia, with its 20 different services, had already proved problematic. It was interpreted in a report seen by the Duce as the product of his fickle character and weak political commitment: the seaside resort season was starting, and it was too hot in Salamanca. All the sources point in the same direction. He was living the high life, racking up huge car and hotel expenses. Indeed, a few of his papers are even dated from the Hotel Excelsior of the Gipuzkoan capital. In any case, his political activities took up so much of his time that he barely paid any attention to his work running the *Ufficio Stampa*. As the ambassador would observe, every now and then he went to listen to a speech by an 'illustrious pedant' and he supervised *El Legionario*, a banal and superficial paper, so gloomy and uninteresting that it would first be overhauled and, soon afterwards, closed in August 1938. Nothing was working. As Anfuso was able confirm on a surprise visit to Salamanca when Danzi was not there, the journalist Lamberti Sorrentino, responsible for radio, was living notoriously in houses of prostitution. Finally, his *Radio Verdad* was too tendentious, even for a fascist, and the way in which it exaggerated the Italian successes was over the top, going so far as to talk about the liberation of Castro Urdiales before it was occupied and about that of Bilbao without having received permission to do so. This could even become counter-productive, as it gave the impression that the capture of Bilbao 'had not been carried out by the Spanish but rather by the Italian journalists'.[73]

For reasons like these, Carlo Bossi, the consul general at Barcelona, became the man of authority on the subject of propaganda. Bossi, highly thought of in all the Spanish and Italian agencies, returned the section to Salamanca and managed to undo his predecessor's work, considered erratic and not very effective as a result of having tried to stay independent of the CTV, which nobody, from Mussolini downwards, wanted.[74] Strengthening its institutional dependence meant, furthermore, returning the focus of attention to the soldiers. Bossi proposed boosting the mobile library, a lorry loaded with about 4,000 books (to become nearly 6,000) which visited the fronts and the wounded and sick legionnaires in hospitals, as well as the areas behind the lines. He obtained subscriptions to various Italian publications and newspapers (6,000 copies of *Il Popolo d'Italia*, 1,400 of *Giornale d'Italia*, 1,000 of *Gazzetta dello Sport*, plus some weeklies) for distribution to the troops, particularly after *El Legionario* was closed down and had to be replaced by other reading material for the trenches. And he managed to organise internal propaganda activities, like the *Befana Fascista* for the legionnaires. Befana is the old woman who delivers presents on the Feast of the Epiphany in Italy. In 1938 and 1939, 52,000 and 60,000 Christmas parcels, respectively, were delivered from Italy containing presents of cigarettes, panettone, and nougat.

Similarly, the work of the CTV's cinematographic service was increased. It was a section of the *Instituto Luce* in Spain, which employed seven people and had a monthly expenditure of 45,000 lire, divided between salaries and supplies. Its films, plus those brought from Italy, were shown in about 50 mobile cinemas.

The job of penetrating civil and political life behind the lines remained a priority objective for Bossi. It was a penetration which, after the slight upsurge of the unification had passed, strung together one success after another from 1938 onwards, from the perspective of the reports reaching Rome. In the autumn of 1937, Carlo Basile, inspector of the *Fasci Italiani all'Estero*, went to Spain with the mission to strengthen the political ties between the PNF and the Falange. One of the most striking results would be the establishment of the *Fascio de Zaragoza*, including a mass in the Basilica del Pilar, with General José Moscardó's only daughter as patroness and with representatives of the Falange and all the corps and specialist units of the CTV under Roatta's command. The mass was followed by the military and political authorities parading through the city, from the basilica to the *Fascio*'s headquarters. Never before, he would say, had such respect been seen by the Spanish for the Italians, for 'Fascist Italy and its New Man who recreates the Roman Legionnaire'. Before his mission, there had been only four *fascios*, and now they were on the verge of having 14, all offering Italian language courses.[75] And this last issue was key. It sounds extraordinary, but, as Basile would come to say, Queipo de Llano had declared himself in favour of replacing French with Italian as the foreign language to be taught in Spanish schools. But at a time of new beginning like a civil war, a 'historic time' to organise the teaching of Italian and 'penetration by our culture', everything was possible. For Ciano, 'organic cultural penetration' through the teaching of the language in secondary schools and universities was a fundamental objective.[76] Italo Sulliotti, sent by the *MinCulPop* to organise language and cultural courses in Andalusia, also spoke of university language instructors, schools in Bilbao and Sevilla attached to the *Ufficio Spagna*. But, above all, he saw how, in Málaga, the Italian language courses were to be formally opened amidst an 'impressive demonstration' of popular enthusiasm, applause for the Duce, and explanations of the reasons for the collaboration between Italy and Spain in the 'field of culture and the spirit', something which Professor Fantuzzi in Sevilla interpreted as a 'plebiscitary demonstration', gathering more than 3,000 people interested in learning Italian.[77]

As Viola would indicate, the growing relationship with Italy was encouraged as much by Serrano Suñer's work as by distancing from German influence.[78] The apparent success of cultural penetration in 1937 led, in fact, to a still more ambitious plan from the *Ufficio Spagna*, which would increase its competences to the point of distributing 117,565 books throughout Spain in 1938; suggesting the need to translate the fundamental works on corporative and constitutional law and corporative economics into Spanish for the academic year; and promoting an exchange programme between universities for

126　*Italy, the CTV, and politics*

students and lecturers. Spanish and Italian intellectuals should work together; thus, the journal *Legiones y Falanges*, in Italian and Spanish, was launched. A comprehensive programme was also proposed for 'Spanish personalities' to visit Italy to become familiar with the 'big problems' and their resolution by fascism.[79] As early as 1937, Pilar Primo de Rivera was invited to get to know Italian Fascism's women's organisations. In August of that year, the secretariat of the *FET y de las JONS* sent a request to Ambassador Viola, asking if they could send a group of Falangist women to Italy, headed by the national leader of the party's Women's Section, with the aim of studying the *Fasci Femminili*, as they had done with the German delegation. The 11 women left by ship on 9 December and stayed in Italy until the 23rd of the month. During that time, they visited facilities of the *Opera Maternità e Infanzia*, the *Dopolavoro*, the *Massaie Rurali* and the *Fasci Femminili* in Naples, Rome, Orvieto (where they saw the fascist women's academy of physical education), Florence, Mantua, Milan, and Genoa. As Viola said subsequently, it had been a particularly revealing trip—not only for the Falangists, because for the first time they had encountered a women's fascism in operation, but also for the Italian fascists, because they had been able to learn that the Falange's women's organisation was still in an 'embryonic state'. For the ambassador, Pilar Primo de Rivera was not a 'real authority' but rather, as José Antonio's sister, 'only symbolic'. As for the second-tier leaders, their 'cultural and general level' was 'not very high'. They were bourgeois women or members of the aristocracy and were not very interested in the Falange's activities. However, they were given the highest privilege, as they wished, on their trip to Italy—they met the Duce.[80]

In the terrain of cultural and ideological penetration, the Italian embassy supported and openly facilitated the work of national council member Pedro Sainz Rodríguez, the National Delegate for Culture, whose plan for cultural reforms of schools and culture was inspired, according to Viola, by the Gentile Reform in Mussolini's Italy. In addition to transforming the Spanish College at Bologna into a centre for the study of fascism's political and social statutes, the theoretical corpus of the New Spain was to be constructed.[81] For this purpose, Sainz Rodríguez asked the Italian embassy for books and information on a very wide range of subjects: the administrative structure of the *MinCulPop*; primary, secondary, and university education; physical and pre-military conditioning; and subjects as varied as national theatre, opera, educational theatre, musical conservatories, dance troupes, music bands, national and mobile libraries, radio, ethnography, folklore, cinema, and so on. The Italian ministry understood the complexity of the request but did everything to attend to it, faced with the opportunity to give a 'fascist stamp to the cultural expressions and art of the New Spain'.[82]

In addition to theoretical material, Fascist Italy sent to Spain a diverse group of technical experts from its fascist ministries. In January 1938, Achille Starace received an invitation from the Falange's general secretary, Raimundo Fernández Cuesta, to send a delegation of the PNF to visit Franco's Spain. The invitation was honoured by sending General Tomaso Bottarti, Consul

Ludovico Ferraudi, General Giuseppe Manni, and the honourable Livio Gaetani and Luigi Scarfiotti.[83] Another delegate from the ministries was Franco Angelini, president of the *Confederazione Fascista dei Lavoratori della Terra*, who, at the invitation of the Ministry of Agriculture, visited Spain in July 1938 to assess its agricultural situation, exchange ideas with Falangist exponents, and establish agreements on cooperation. As he told Viola, these visits were more political than technical and fulfilled a fundamental request from the minister and secretary of the *FET y de las JONS*, namely to study 'the work and agrarian arrangements of our National-Syndicalist Revolution' and disseminate 'the directives that fascist doctrine has put into practice in this area of national activity'.[84] Cooperation and training would also increase with the sending of technicians and professionals to Italy, like the 200 Spanish teachers sent to learn Italian methods in November 1938. José María Pemán, Eugenio Montes, and Pilar Primo de Rivera attended the closing session of this special course. Pedro Sainz Rodríguez made use of the trip in order to 'direct the reform of Spanish schools to follow in the footsteps' of the Italian system.

In Rome, they were awaited by the Marquess Alfonso de Zayas, former provincial head of the Falange in the Balearic Islands and, since June of that year, representative of the *FET y de las JONS* before the Fascist government. The previous month, he had been invited to the mass in Rome to commemorate the fifth anniversary of the Falange's founding and honour the Falangists and the legionnaires who had fallen in Spain. Permeation and influence were also exercised through details which were low profile, so to speak, like this mass and other matters that proliferated before the end of the Civil War. Welfare tasks organised by the *Ufficio Spagna*, such as camps for Spanish children in Italy in 1937 and 1938, the convalescence in Italy of wounded Spaniards, and the several boatloads of food despatched to Catalonia and Alacant in the course of their military occupation, demonstrated the importance of these bilateral political relations for both countries and for both political regimes. While not exactly a dominant nation on Spanish soil, as Bonaccorsi claimed, Fascist Italy did become a central reference point for the construction of the New State. Backed by his imprint on the war, and in the belief that establishing a fascism in Spain was not to support a faction but rather to facilitate the creation of a great national party, Mussolini could be satisfied with his work in Spain for many years—that is, at least until 1943.

Fascism showed itself to be a first-rate political culture in Europe, thanks to both the immediate context of geopolitical, economic, employment, and moral (that is to say, narrative) crisis and to the attractiveness of the solutions it could propose for the lives of Italians, Germans, Spaniards, and Croats in the 1920s and the 1930s. Moreover, much of this success was due to cultural transfers in the form of political cultures, common mythologies, and geostrategic relations within the European continent. Italian Fascism built a cultural network dedicated to ensuring its central position in the New European Order, and Mussolini's intervention in the war in Spain reaffirmed it.

128 *Italy, the CTV, and politics*

The copying in Spain of many of the elements identified with the Fascist regime—from the single party to social organisation (women, youth, students, workers); from hierarchy and obedience, rather than consensus, as a form of socialisation to corporatist policies—speaks of the circulation of convergent ideas developed, as seems obvious, at different times and with unequal results. But, in the process, all this demonstrated the importance that fascism attached to two central elements of fascistisation: the myth of violence and war as a favourable context. The Spanish Civil War, as fascism's own war, was a perfect setting for both.

In my opinion, the fascistisation championed by Mussolini consisted of all of these elements. It was neither permeation, nor acceptance, nor imposition, nor adaptation, nor gutting, nor contamination. It was convergence into a Catholic, counter-revolutionary, and hierarchical movement, which grew in the context of a (necessary, desired, glorious, triumphant) civil war to liquidate the anti-Spain. It joined together different cultural, political, geostrategic, and identitarian elements. Its syncretic results were internalised, as seen in the citation which opens this chapter, the Italian version of the Falangist anthem *Cara al Sol* (*Facing the Sun*), in which the person being sung to is, in fact, Mussolini. It was a war to which to send an entire military contingent to fight in a foreign land but for a common purpose. It was a war that shaped experiences and narratives, which, as will be seen in the next chapter, provide first-hand sources for the study of the most important aspect in this and any other historical investigation—not just the *whats*, the *whens*, the *hows*, and the *wheres*, but, above all, the *whys*.

Notes

1 In Francesco Odetti, *Trenta Mesi nel Tercio* (Rome: M. Carra, 1940). My italics.
2 ASMAE, AP, b61. His opinion was the same as that reflected, in turn, in the opinions in published newspapers as different as *La Almudaina* of 13 December 1942 ('This new politics is what Mussolini created in Italy: it is National Socialism in Germany . . . Oliveira Salazar's totalitarianism in Portugal, and in Spain the National Revolution born on 18 July 1936') and *El Luchador* of 12 December ('The forces of communism . . . can read in the speech Spain's unshakeable decision to oppose their malevolent intentions.')
3 For the Italian Embassy's explanations of the repercussions of Serrano's curious journey to Livorno, the real motive for which in fact remained unknown, see ASMAE, AP, b61. The proposed theories were that he had come to raise the issue of the monarchy with the pretender to the throne, Juan de Borbón, said to already have met Ciano; to discuss Spain's entry into the war; or to broach the idea of a peace conference.
4 This point was demonstrated by Javier Tusell in *Franco en la guerra civil: una biografía política* (Barcelona: Tusquets, 1992), as a result of his joint research with Ismael Saz and of his own analysis of the construction of the state and the politics the New Spain. Unfortunately, it has not been followed in later research.
5 ACS, MI, PolPol, b251.
6 Dulio Sumsel and Edoardo Sumsel, eds., *Opera Omnia di Benito Mussolini*, vol. XXVIII (Florence: La Fenice, 1959), 97–98. Subsequently, at the end of February 1937, he commented on the words of the Gregorio Marañón, when the physician deplored the killings in the zone where the coup d'état had not been successful and called for an end to a 'regime of blood, a republic of assassins'. For the Duce, 'the Republic of Caballero, Blum, Avenol,

Eden has produced 35,000 [victims] in six months'. The paradox of Marañón was that as a 'staunch anti-fascist, you have been saved by fascism', 125–127.

7 Quoted in Francisco Virgilio Sevillano Carbajal, *La diplomacia mundial ante la guerra española* (Madrid: Editora Nacional, 1969), 289. This book, with a prologue by Manuel Fraga, summarises like few others the use of Francoist anti-communism as vector of a past clearly projected onto its own present.

8 ASMAE, GAB, b795. The Italian Ministry of Foreign Affairs would in any case acknowledge that, due firstly to Bonaccorsi and then Casalini of the Milan Fascio, the Balearics were the first place where the single party was born. ASMAE, US, b22.

9 AMAE, AB, L1460, C6.

10 Ibid.

11 Rosaria Quartararo, *Politica fascista nelle Baleari (1936–1939)* (N.p.: Cuaderni Fiap, 1977), 29.

12 John Coverdale, *La intervención fascista en la guerra civil española* (Madrid: Alianza Editorial, 1979), 123.

13 USSME, F18m b9.

14 ASMAE, AP, b23. Among the 51 films sent were *Il cammino degli eroi*, in three parts; *Campo Dux*; *Sotto il segno del Littorio*; *Camicia Nera*, in six parts; and *Giornate del Duce a Milano*, in two parts. The majority featured the invasion of Ethiopia. The first film specifically about the Civil War was called *Arriba Espana* [*sic*].

15 ACS, MI, PolPol, b251.

16 USSME, F6, 327.

17 ASMAE, US, b13.

18 ASMAE, US, b27.

19 USSME, F6, 327.

20 ASMAE, AP, b20.

21 ASMAE, US, b20.

22 Ferran Gallego, *El evangelio fascista: la formación de la cultura política del franquismo (1930–1950)* (Barcelona: Crítica, 2014), 412 and 443ff.

23 Giuseppe Bottai, 'Sul piano imperiale', *Crítica Fascista*, 1 September 1936, quoted in Massimiliano Griner, *I ragazzi del '36. L'avventura dei fascisti italiani nella guerra civile spagnola* (Milan: Rizzoli, 2006), 147.

24 ASMAE, AP, b14.

25 USSME, F18, b2.

26 ASMAE, AP, b14.

27 See the developments laid out by Ismael Saz, 'Salamanca 1937: los fundamentos de un régimen', *Revista de Extremadura*, no. 21 (1996): 81–107, reproduced in his *Fascismo y franquismo* (Valencia: PUV, 2004), 150. Saz is one of the few to believe the Italian sources on the process of merging the parties, also noting that the exhaustion of the Danzi-Gay line was (as suggested by Tusell) what led to the approach 'from below' in February, and Franco's knowledge of it the lever for the *modus operandi* of April, 133–134.

28 ASMAE, AP, b14.

29 ASMAE, US, b10.

30 ASMAE, AP, b21.

31 ASMAE, AP, b14.

32 ASMAE, US, b10. On the Carlists in the Civil War and their doctrinal gyrations, see Mercedes Peñalba, *Entre la boina roja y la camisa azul: La integración del carlismo en Falange Tradicionalista y de las JONS (1936–1942)* (Pamplona: Publicaciones del Gobierno Foral de Navarra, 2014).

33 ASMAE, US, b10.

34 ASMAE, US, b29.

35 ASMAE, US, b25, b10; ASMAE, GAB, b461.

36 ASMAE, US, b2, ACS, SPD, CR, b44; USSME, F18, b2. Farinacci's report to the Fascist Grand Council and notes on his meetings with political figures in Spain can be found in

130 *Italy, the CTV, and politics*

ASMAE, US, b1. For an analysis of his opinions and Franco's government's response, see Saz, 'Salamanca 1937', 137ff.

37 ASMAE, US, b10.

38 Ibid.

39 ASMAE, AP, b14.

40 ASMAE, US, b13.

41 USSME, F6, b336.

42 Indeed, it is symptomatic that the authors who have studied the matter the most—regardless of their perspectives—give practically no importance to Danzi's presence (and that of the Italians in general) in the unification's framework. He does not figure in Maximiliano García Venero, *Historia de la unificación (Falange y Requeté en 1937)* (Madrid: Agesa, 1970); nor in Ricardo Chueca, *El Fascismo en los comienzos del régimen de Franco: un estudio sobre FET-JONS* (Madrid: Centro de Investigaciones Sociológicas, 1983). Nor is this influence perceived in any way in the account by José Luis Rodríguez Jiménez, *Historia de Falange Española de las JONS* (Madrid: Alianza Editorial, 2000). Eminently internally focused visions (from within Spain and the Falange—that is to say, discounting any external influence, in this instance Italian) are those of Mercedes Peñalba, *Falange española: historia de un fracaso (1933–1945)* (Pamplona: Ediciones de la Universidad de Navarra, 2009); and Joan Maria Thomàs, *Lo que fue la Falange. La Falange y los falangistas de José Antonio Primo de Rivera. Hedilla y la Unificación. Franco y el fin de Falange Española de las JONS* (Barcelona: Plaza y Janés, 1999); by the same author, *La Falange de Franco. Fascismo y fascistización en el régimen franquista (1937–1945)* (Barcelona: Plaza y Janés, 2001); and *El gran golpe: el 'caso Hedilla' o cómo Franco se quedó con Falange* (Barcelona: Debate, 2004); Ismael Saz, *España contra España: los nacionalismos franquistas* (Madrid: Marcial Pons, 2003), 161ff.

43 USSME, F6, b334. Gallego provides the best conceptual formulation of the construction of the FET-JONS, *El evangelio*, 456–479. This process can be seen in a very condensed form in Morten Heiberg and Manuel Ros Agudo, *La trama oculta de la Guerra Civil: los servicios secretos de Franco, 1936–1945* (Barcelona: Crítica, 2006), 107ff.; and Francisco Morente, 'Hijos de un dios menor: la Falange después de José Antonio', in *Fascismo en España: ensayos sobre los orígenes sociales y culturales del franquismo*, eds. Ferran Gallego and Francisco Morente (Barcelona: El Viejo Topo, 2005), 211–250—particularly to observe the consequences of the process for the Falangists. For a more extensive account, see Paul Preston, *Franco, "Caudillo" de España* (Barcelona: Grijalbo, 1994), 315ff.

44 ASMAE, US, b27.

45 Tullio Rispoli, *La Spagna dei Legionari* (Rome: Cremonese, 1942), 244.

46 *Opera Omnia*, vol. XXVIII, 184.

47 USSME, F6, b334.

48 ASMAE, US, b10; USSME, F6, b336.

49 USSME, F6, b336; Saz, 'Salamanca 1937', 150.

50 1,500 pesetas monthly from January 1938; ASMAE, US, b28.

51 USSME, F6, b334.

52 ASMAE, AP, b14.

53 ASMAE, GAB, b461; USSME, F18, b7.

54 ASMAE, US, b27.

55 ASMAE, AP, b34; USSME, F6, b336.

56 ACS, MinCulPop, Gab, b75.

57 ASMAE, US, b11.

58 However, this is the opinion of Gabriele Ranzato in 'La guerra de España como batalla de la "guerra civil europea"', in *Historia, pasado y memoria en el mundo contemporáneo: VIII Congreso de Historia Local de Aragón, Rubielos de Mora, 2011*, eds. Pilar Salomón et al. (Teruel: Instituto de Estudios Turolenses, 2014), 66.

59 Vito Beltrani, *Antirussia* (Rome: Tupini, 1939), quoted in Luciano Zani, 'Fascismo e comunismo: rivoluzioni antagoniste', in *Modernità totalitaria: il fascismo italiano*, ed.

Italy, the CTV, and politics 131

Emilio Gentile (Rome/Bari: Laterza, 2008), 191–228. On war as fascism's natural space, see Gallego, *El evangelio*; and Matteo Pasetti, *Storia del fascismo in Europa* (Bologna: Arquetipolibri, 2009).
60 *Il Messaggero*, 28 January 1939.
61 ASMAE, US, b25.
62 ACS, MI, DirPolPol, SPD, CR, b44.
63 ASMAE, US, b40.
64 ACS, MinCulPop, Gab, b75.
65 ASMAE, US, b5.
66 USSME, F6, b335. For a good synthesis, see Alejandro Pizarroso, 'Intervención extranjera y propaganda: la propaganda exterior de las dos Españas', *Historia y Comunicación Social*, no. 6 (2001): 63–96. The question is sufficiently well dealt with by the historiography that I will not elaborate further. See Paola Corti and Alejandro Pizarroso, *Giornali contro: "Il Legionario" e "Il Garibaldino": la propaganda degli italiani nella guerra di Spagna* (Turin: Edizioni dell'Orso, 1993). There are some notes on cultural penetration, although the theme deserves more attention, in Rubén Dominguez, *Mussolini y la exportación de la cultura italiana a España* (Madrid: Arco Libros, 2012). On the *Instituto Luce* in Spain, see Magí Crusells, 'L'immagine cinematografica del CTV', *Spagna Contemporanea*, no. 42 (2012): 91–111; and Félix Monguilot, 'El núcleo foto-cinematográfico del Instituto LUCE: un órgano de propaganda fascista en Salamanca durante la Guerra Civil española', *Archivos de la Filmoteca*, no. 56 (2007): 152–171. See also Victoriano Peña, *Intelectuales y fascismo: la cultura italiana del ventennio fascista y su repercusión en España* (Granada: Universidad de Granada, 1995).
67 ASMAE, US, b29.
68 ASMAE, US, b5.
69 *El Legionario*, no. 2, 26 March 1937, 4.
70 Daniel Arasa, *La batalla de las ondas en la Guerra Civil Española* (Maçanet de la Selva: Gregal, 2015).
71 The important journalists and personalities were, according to the descriptions by the Italians: Ernesto Giménez Caballero, 'for years a proven friend of Italy and Fascism', whose only blemish was his book on Azaña; González Ruano, *ABC* (Sevilla) correspondent in Rome; Fermín Yzurdiaga, editor of *Arriba España* of Pamplona; Víctor de la Serna, son of Concha Espina, editor of the 'pro-fascist' *Informaciones*, Hedilla's secretary, and author of a booklet for the 'moderate' Lerroux-Gil Robles government on the communist atrocities in Asturias; Eugenio Montes, member of the *Consejo Superior de Cultura* (High Council for Culture), theorist on fascism and Nazism who established contacts in Berlin between the Falange and the Anti-Komintern and the German Ministry of Propaganda; Luis Antonio Bolín, *ABC* correspondent in London; Ramón Ruiz Alonso of the *Gaceta Regional* of Salamanca, who despite describing himself as a 'typographic worker' was interested in corporatism, sympathised with syndicalism, and was not recommended, since he was suspected of involvement in the murder of García Lorca (according to the report, the poet had recently made friends with the Falangists, but two men sent by Ruiz Alonso had taken him away); '*El Tebib Arrubí*', Vicente Ruiz Albéniz, son of the musical composer, wealthy, March's right-hand man; Juan Pujol, the Austrians' propaganda head in Spain during the Great War, anti-Semite, head of press and propaganda of the Burgos *Junta de Defensa*, founder of the weekly *Domingo* in Donostia; José María Salaverria; Giménez Arnau, the Falange's press director; Sánchez del Arco of *ABC*; the *Requeté* Fernando d'Ors; Andrés de Lorenzo Cáceres y de Torres, of the General Command's press section in the Canaries; Joaquín Arrarás, esteemed editor of *Debate* when Madrid was taken, was the head of the press service in Pamplona; Juan Losada; Francisco Cossío, editor of the *Norte de Castilla*, enthusiastic anti-Bolshevik; Raimundo García García, editor of the *Diario de Navarra*, a great admirer of Mussolini; the Marquess de las Marismas, editor of *Época*, one of the organisers of the *Movimiento*; Jorge Vigón of *Época*, activist in Calvo Sotelo's *Bloque Nacional*; Julio Camba; José María Pemán; the *Requeté* Pablo Merry del Val, Marquess of Quintanares;

132   *Italy, the CTV, and politics*

Father Tusquests, specialist in the struggle against freemasons and Jews; Joaquín Miquelarena; Francisco Luis Manuel Casares; the Marquess Luca de Tena, liberal Anglophile monarchist; Carlo Mengotti, editor of *Imperio* (Toledo); Delgado Barreto, an admirer of Primo de Rivera and an early supporter of Mussolini ('*sansepolcrista*'); and Agustín de Foxá, Falangist poet.

72 ASMAE, US, b25.

73 For this reason, and faced with the imminent taking of Santander—which would nevertheless be described as an Italian operation and for which they would have a free hand— the correspondents dependent on the *Ufficio Spagna* were asked to underline the qualities and bravery of the Spanish troops. ASMAE, US, b27.

74 ASMAE, US, b10.

75 ASMAE, US, b160.

76 USSME, F18, b2; ASMAE, AP, b31, b33.

77 ASMAE, AP, b33.

78 And above all from November 1938, when the assassination of Von Rath in Paris led to what were called 'excesses', namely *Kristallnacht* and the ghettoization of the Jewish minority.eeee USSME, F18, b9.

79 ASMAE, US, b27.

80 ASMAE, AP, b33.

81 Francisco Morente, 'Los fascismos europeos y la política educativa del franquismo', *Historia de la Educación: Revista interuniversitaria*, no. 24 (2005): 179–204.

82 ASMAE, AP, b34.

83 ASMAE, US, b11. A year later, and on the occasion of the 20th anniversary of the founding of the *Fascisti di Combattimento* in 1919, the same Fernández Cuesta replied to the request that *FET y de las JONS* take part in the commemorative events, proposing that the vice-secretary, Fanjul, Gamero del Castillo, Sancho Dávila, and José del Castaño (head of the Falange's overseas organisation), and Rafael Sánchez Mazas be sent as well.

84 ASMAE, US, b27.

4 Identity, combat, rearguard

Al grido dei fratelli di Spagna/Noi siam corsi comparti e serrati /
A Legionari di Camicie Nere/Per defender l'Iberico suol
Or squilli l'adunata dell'assalto/Echeggi il grido di battaglia /
Con forza leonina e furente/Ci scagliamo sul biecco oppressor!
Salve Duce, per Te noi pugniamo/Legionari del fascismo siam /
In alto il pugnale, da forti/Noi vogliamo la Spagna liberar
Mai ci tremi né braccio né core/Messager di nuova Storia noi siam /
In alto le Insegne, da prodi/Noi vogliamo la Civiltà salvar!
Ognor ci sorrega la Fede/Che ci sprona a tutti i cimenti /
Dell'eterna luce di Roma/Noi en siamo i baldi apportator
L'Europa fascista noi vogliamo/Che desti i popoli oppressi /
E torni il sorriso alle genti/Martoriarte dal rosso insidiator.[1]

'*In alto il pugnale.*' Dagger raised, as it features in many photos. The fascist salute with the steel blade was the symbol of the CTV, created, according to the anthem here, to liberate Spain, usher in a new History, make the peoples oppressed by the Reds smile again, and construct a fascist Europe. It was propaganda, of course. Exaggeration, too. But was it always insincere? The extensive material available on Italian intervention in the wars of Africa and Spain is laden with metaphors and hyperbole. But ruling out the narratives these wars produced in the form of official accounts and memoirs is not something that should be done as a matter of course. Literature written in the first person singular about Italian combatants in Spain (of which we have seen examples in the previous chapter) provides many details which help to describe the fighting, the experience of living behind the lines, and personal identities that can, or cannot, be projected onto the rest of the group. Yet they contain many other narratives. The historian, aware that they are but constructs made at the time of writing, is not so much interested in recovering, defending, or discounting memories as in identifying the narratives and interpretations which are superimposed on the past and become part it. Both the official literature and memoirs tend to give self-interested and sugar-coated views of the reality of war. Fear is never present; it never reeks of excrement; there is never cowardice nor disgust; there are never any lice, bedbugs, and

134   *Identity, combat, rearguard*

nits; no cruelty towards the living enemy nor malice towards cadavers; no sexual relations that are not idealised archetypes, rather than with prostitutes in the cities behind the lines.[2] Memoirs are problematic in substance because, although they try to reproduce what is considered to be the truth, they are actually made up as much of forgetfulness and omissions as of the ordering of events. These events, side by side, woven from a story that makes them coherent, appear to be linked by a relationship of cause and effect.[3] This does not disqualify them, so long as we do not consider them as a sort of revealed word. On the contrary, it makes them basic sources for understanding the complexities of the past.

Indeed, the pasts of war and violence tend to be reconstructed, due to their very nature, from perspectives which are more value judgements than analysis. This is especially the case when the individuals who do the recalling were imbued with the practices of total war and of identification with the leader, the nation, and its fascist civilisation. In these cases, which include most Italian memoirs on the Spanish war, on top of the normal varnish of recollection and forgetfulness there lies another longer-lasting layer, which has often served to discount these sources as unreliable and not objective (though no source is)—the layer of pride. In this age of honouring the memory of the victims, the recollections of the executioner, of the proud and conscious fascist, are necessarily problematic. For this reason, fascist literature is confined to small publishers and self-published volumes, to internet forums of dubious character, and to bookshops crammed with ultra-Right-wing memorabilia.[4] Perhaps this is why, when working from this type of source, emphasis is placed on the combatants who were not proud and were not conscious of what they were doing—on the conscripted, the poor southerners, the naïve. A more wide-ranging look, as will be attempted here, yields substantially different results.

Mussolini's regime conceived and constructed the imperial Ethiopian episode according to the rules of melodrama—light and darkness, salvation and condemnation, white and black (literally), with the final liberation of virtue following spectacular action. In Spain there was not all the paraphernalia of Africa, but that does not mean we cannot find similar norms, at least judging by some of the cultural products referring to the war in Spain and created in places close to the centres of power. In the majority of books, whether memoirs, official accounts, or other works about the involvement in Spain published in Italy, the narrative follows the cycle of sin, fall, and redemption, using explicit and repeated stock images that would make famous the General Cause in Spain but can already be found in the first publications of 1936—Calvo Sotelo's murder, the violation of mummies in churches, hatred of the sacred, women raped by militiamen, fall and then resurrection, the triumph of truth, light, good, with its own elements, of course. On the cover of *Legionari di Roma in terra iberica* (*Roman Legions on Iberian Soil*), a commemorative book by different authors published in 1940, the likenesses of a soldier of the CTV and an Imperial Roman legionnaire, *Il Vincitore*, the victor, are superimposed. It is not Franco; it is Mussolini.[5] But there are also shared elements. One was the perception of Spain, above all Republican Spain, as dirty, sick, backward, uncivilised. Another was the mission of fascist evangelisation that would bring cleanliness, light, hope, victory. This chapter analyses both aspects on the basis of a series of common experiences, such as enlistment, fighting, death, discipline, life behind the lines, and responsibility for violent practices, in an attempt to go deeper into what was in fact the fascist experience of a total war, experienced in the first person singular and plural.

He wrote, *Viva il Duce!*, and then he died

Enthusiasm, perfection, beauty, willpower. The most-repeated words used in the Italian sources to describe the volunteers in Spain always belong to the semantic ensemble of heroism, bravery, and courage. And they make their appearance from the very beginning. The first Italian combatants in Spain, if we leave aside the pilots and technicians of the summer of 1936, were those who arrived at Cádiz and Vigo in September and enrolled in the *Tercio de Extranjeros* (Foreign Legion), volunteers who, in Emilio Faldella's words, 'flocked with enthusiasm', with the 'desire to fight', and with the conviction of 'creating as soon as possible on Spanish soil a tradition of victory and glory for the Italian volunteers'.[6] Indeed, these ideas are repeated constantly: enthusiasm, combat, glory, determination. Nevertheless, a large part of the historiography on the subject has discounted this type of narrative as insincere, propagandistic, or outright false. Instead, it has chosen an analytical line based on the compulsory nature of the mobilisation, on the CTV's lack of fascist identity, or on its general political irrelevance. Heroes of civilisation or deluded cowards. There seems to be no middle ground.

The question is important and, as Gabriele Ranzato rightly points out, the volume of personal sources which help to understand it without the filter of propaganda is sparse, at least when compared to the total volume of Italian combatants in Spain[7]—particularly because, beneath the debates as to whether the Italians in Spain were there voluntarily or under compulsion, there are debates of major scope and significance about the political and socio-cultural nature of fascism (mainly, but not exclusively, of the Italian variety); about the weight of culture, mobilisation, and coercion in the relationship between power and its subjects; and, ultimately, about the success or failure of the fascist alternative as a form of society. The result of these debates is never satisfactory; the historian does not have enough sources available to categorically affirm one thing or the opposite. But uncertainty does not sell well in academia.

Clearly, there were as many motives as there were combatants, and as many combatants as realities—from the genuine volunteer to the conscript; from the fascist evangelist to the man who, out of ignorance, did not even know he was going to war. But common features certainly existed. Davide Lajolo, a

136 *Identity, combat, rearguard*

lieutenant in the Fascist army, who had asked to be sent to Africa, received his call-up orders from the Army at the same time as a colleague in the MVSN, whose officers had received a circular offering them enlistment to 'fight Bolshevism' in what was clearly 'a fascist war'[8] and declaring that all Italian forces had to unite against communism. There are further examples.

Although most of the applications were rejected, the letters from the Italians who reported to the Spanish embassy and consulates in Italy in the summer of 1936 to enrol in the Spanish Foreign Legion (more than 2,000 in Palermo alone) reveal complex and contrasting reasons. Those who wrote from Italy usually gave political or ideological reasons, like Rodolfo de Neri, aged 18, who was drawn to 'Spain's War of Reconquest', as he had already demonstrated in his speeches 'in favour of Spain' and of the 'spirit of the fascist revolution', for which he had been subject to harassment by his teachers, old anti-fascists all of them. The priest Leone Pangallo was motivated by the struggle 'against abominable Bolshevism'. Ubaldo Procacci, not being rich, had only his youth to offer.[9] But there were many more, among them Francesco Odetti, who, having recently returned from Africa, met the secretary of the Spanish embassy at the home of mutual friends. The secretary spoke of the Spanish war as the 'real crusade in defence of the Christian religion and of Western and Mediterranean civilisation'. The following day, Odetti went to the embassy (now in the hands of Admiral Antonio Magaz), where he was received by Rafael Villegas and Rafael Estrada, who, in addition to assuring him that enrolment would be into the Legion, put him in contact with Emilio Martínez de Bujanda, head of the committee in Rome set up for that purpose. Having decided to cross France to reach Spain, he arrived at Saint-Jean-de-Luz and from there went to Salamanca, from where he was sent to Talavera de la Reina, location of the Legion's recruitment office and where he moreover joined the Falange. He was and felt himself to be a fascist who had a moral obligation to fight in Spain. According to his estimate, of the just over 100 Italians who joined the Legion like him, more than 90 died.[10]

However, those who applied to enlist from the colonies (their applications were always signed in Addis Ababa) clearly stated and openly acknowledged economic reasons: better pay, upkeep of a little daughter, a disabled wife. Of course, there were volunteers who were half-hearted and mainly motivated by private interests. Italian officers were seemingly especially annoyed by the number of volunteers to serve in Spain. During the period of voluntary enlistment between July 1936 and January 1937, some 3,365 men enlisted, fewer than 5 per cent of the more than 78,000 who came to serve in Spain. Half of them were said to be over 30 years of age.[11]

There were adventurers as well, like Giuseppe Cordedda, who left without any national identification for an 'unknown destination' out of a 'spirit of adventure'. Aged 19, he was interested in neither the political issue nor the double pay; rather, 'he dreamed of new places, of so many battles, so many acts of heroism, and so much glory'.[12] And there were those who left for, and came back from, a 'war of tourism'.[13] As information coming from the

Identity, combat, rearguard 137

Republican zone, supposedly taken from the Italian prisoners captured at Guadalajara, indicated, the directors of Italian prisons and detention centres had received a request to exert influence on their inmates 'to enrol as volunteers in Spain. They were promised that, in the event of them joining the Foreign Legion, their sentences would be lifted.'[14] And lingering in a shadowy zone is the reality of all those who enlisted for exclusively work reasons. As Lajolo was told in Littoria (a city founded by Mussolini and now called Latina) by the adjutant who noted his enrolment in the *Littorio* Division, these were hard times for everybody, when the poor and unemployed, even those whose hair was greying, would have put their signature to any old document. This was particularly true of those who thought they would be sent to Ethiopia as part of voluntary labour battalions.[15] At all events, real volunteers, adventurers, soldiers, and the unemployed filled the ranks of the expeditionary corps with which Mussolini intervened in what was now a civil war. Nor did he have many more options in a country without anything resembling a Foreign Legion and where, in theory, no recruitment mechanisms existed for a war abroad.

In this context, the initial recourse to the *Milizia*, which contributed about 30,000 men, can be explained basically by the short span of time available to the military and political hierarchy in 1936 and early 1937 to organise a complete expeditionary corps. The voluntary nature of those first contingents nevertheless reflected their motives. The Blackshirts had motives of all sorts—economic motives, of course, but political ones as well. It is striking how relatively little attention the historiography of the subject usually devotes to the ideological and identitarian dimension of enlistment, especially when compared to economic reasons and, to a lesser extent, adventure-seeking or anti-social motives. The news about the dangerous character of the first volunteers, among whom there were convicts for robbery, assault, and even murder, is well known and accepted as fact by the historians Massimiliano Griner and Dimas Vaquero. But, despite the image given of a militia corps comprising mercenaries and outlaws, Griner himself acknowledges that the early volunteers with a troubled past did not exceed 25 per cent. What everything, sources and historiography, seems to agree on is that the militia troops had very little military training, at least in comparison with the regular troops, both at the lower ranks and among non-commissioned and senior officers. Indeed, the decision to make military ranks in the MVSN the same as those in the Army, despite the former's lack of skill and lesser experience in the rudiments of warfare, led to heated complaints and internal tensions within the Italian mission in Spain itself.

The first shipments of troops were accelerated and there was no time to vet them, as demonstrated by the 25 'undesirables' and swindlers trying to pass as officers who were identified in Spain and sent back to their country. With raw material like that, it was no wonder that the first Italians to set foot on Spanish soil (apart from the pilots) constituted a complex group, in which the senior officers were well-trained, looking for double pay and promotion,

138 *Identity, combat, rearguard*

whereas for months the recruitment procedures for ordinary troops were more than questionable. Nevertheless, these recruitment procedures have too often led researchers to hasty conclusions, frequently linked to arguments of economic determinism and clichés about poverty (seen as incompatible with political commitment) and crime. Without demonstrable documentary proof, it is risky, to say the least, to generically brand the volunteers, and above all those of the *Milizia*, as a motley crew of criminals, the unemployed, paupers, alcoholics, and scatterbrains who believed they were embarking for Africa. And yet this stereotype crops up again and again in the current historiography, nearly always without even minimal documentary support.

For one thing, it is questionable to stress the possible confusion that the phrase 'destination unknown' on the recruitment forms might have created in the minds of the volunteers, particularly because, with the African campaign over, the words '*destinazione ignota*' could only mean Spain. Of course, enlistment could entail potential benefits and advantages, and there are quite a few accounts that rather honestly underline this point because, as Lajolo remarked, bravery and the risk of dying had to come with rewards as well. Captain Roberto Cassina declared on a number of occasions that enlistments for Spain were due exclusively to economic conditions; anybody who was going through economic difficulties or unemployed became 'meat for Spain'. In Spain, the combatants themselves, as well as their senior officers, were aware that reasons for enlisting, degree of commitment in the fighting, and heroism in death varied significantly between the Army's volunteers and those of the *Milizia*. The latter were often branded as insincere and self-interested political climbers. It is impossible to know from the documents whether that was the exception or the rule, but, among the various reports on public opinion that passed through the hands of Mussolini's private secretariat, many refer to enlistment for Spain. And, most of them contain negative comments about the intervention and enlistment.

The first surprising point is the degree of far-reaching monitoring and interest in public opinion that went as high as the above-mentioned personal secretariat and, therefore, the Duce himself, to the extent of receiving intelligence on private comments—such as one made by Giovannino Palermitano, deputy squad head in the *Milizia* and volunteer for Spain, who in December 1937 told an egg seller in Naples that, given the disadvantageous economic conditions and the danger involved, he would advise against enlistment at the moment. An informant from Agrigento, travelling by train from Palermo in December 1936, reported the conversation between two soldiers volunteering for Africa who were going on leave. They were talking about Spain and how the regiment commander had blurted out to one of them, 'Whoever among you is ready to leave for an unknown destination, raise your hand!' There being no response, he said, 'Well done, because the destination is Spain, and everybody who goes there faces certain death.' Something similar was said to have happened in the *Guide* Regiment of Parma towards the end of the year, when, after reading the ministry's circular encouraging soldiers to enlist for Spain, the commander added, 'Whoever agrees to enlist will show himself to be not a good soldier but a mercenary.' Other files point in the same direction, like the one reporting a speech by Major Presutti to the ranks in which he underlined their status as 'Legionnaires, certainly, but belonging to the glorious Italian Army. Army, powerful and glorious Army . . . and I say Army', ordering them to fall out without ordering them to salute the Duce. No mercenaries but, of course, few in the Royal Army in Rome enlisted as volunteers in November 1936, despite the offer of exemption from ordinary military service, an insurance policy, and pay of 38 lire a day. In a private conversation between an officer and the Count of Turin intercepted by the secret services, the former indicated that, whereas previously soldiers had been asked if they wanted to go to Spain, now there were orders to send them. 'And who wants to go and get himself killed for a country that is not his own?'[16]

In any case, every situation was different, but there were also common patterns, such as the economic opportunity of settlement. It might sound preposterous, but the Italians who enlisted for Spain were offered land to settle. As Viola indicated in May 1939, this offer was confirmed by Franco himself when, following a lunch in honour of the Condor Legion, he spontaneously told him that, on the one hand, regarding labour rights, all Italian combatants would be considered equal to the Spanish. Moreover, 'in about two years there will be a shortage of labour in Spain for reconstruction, as well as for the expansion of agriculture and industry'. Current thinking was to make some two million hectares of arable land available to Italian labour.[17]

This opportunity for agricultural settlement might have been the central reason why quite a few volunteers were married men from rural areas, men with families to support from southern Italy, Sicily, and Sardinia. According to Giulia Medas's analysis of sentences handed down by the CTV's military court in Spain (which shows, incidentally, that the average age of those tried was low, at between 20 and 24), roughly 16 per cent were from northern Italy, 20 per cent from central Italy, 43 per cent from southern Italy, and 21 per cent from the islands. As for casualties, Vaquero has shown that the largest group of those killed were from the South: Catanzaro, 126; Bari, 105; Cagliari, 82; Campobasso, 79; Catania, 74; Aquila, 71; Agrigento, 44.[18] Thus, both sets of data confirm what was indicated in all the CTV's internal reports—most volunteers came from southern Italy and the islands, overwhelmingly agricultural areas with a per capita income much lower than that of the regions of northern Italy. Various accounts, confirmed in part by analyses following the defeat at Guadalajara, state that many volunteers were either very old or too young, and two-thirds had a wife and children, which was said to considerably limit their military commitment and willingness to take risks in battle. This evidence may well be grounds to question the truly voluntary status of part of the Italian contingent, who might have been compelled to enlist because they were unemployed men with poor economic and life prospects. Also important, of course, were pay and family allowances. Officers' pay for

140 *Identity, combat, rearguard*

enlisting ranged from 7,082 lire in two instalments—one before joining and the other four months thereafter—for a divisional general to a single payment of 567 lire for a battalion adjutant.[19]

Economic causative factors may be valid in some cases, but not if they become the sole explanation. Vaquero states that 'the spirit and fervour to go and fight in Spain for a political cause and ideals' was not the main motive. Many were no longer 'a handful of enthusiastic, idealistic young men', and they were older 'in most cases than the young people whose blood was boiling to come to Spain'.[20] But to reach this conclusion, on the basis, moreover, of data as debatable as the average age of the Italians who died in Spain, assumes several unprovable ideas that commonly act as areas of consensus. Such ideas include the idealism of youth and that only older age groups had economic interests. Another such idea is that officers were more interested in pay and promotion than in the 'idea', as Renzo Lodoli calls it—the fascist idea, which 'once again needed men', officers to fight in an unknown destination, officers who knew how to lead their men to victory or death.[21] It was the same idea that required no more than five minutes of reflection to make a decision, and, according to Lajolo, whose 'unknown destination' was known to possibly be Spain; the words '*destinazione ignota*' were sung with a voice full of pride.[22]

Impoverished old men, young adventurers, and self-interested officers. This image of a CTV devoid of fascist identity cannot seem to find corroborating primary sources. That does not mean, of course, that none of these mechanisms of identification work. We can see both a sincere statement and an acknowledgement of weakness on Berti's part in the fact that the *Ufficio Spagna* insisted throughout 1937 that it was not necessary to force combatants in Spain to join the *Fasci Italiani all'Estero*, because the majority were already members of the PNF, which, it was said, would mean paying two membership fees.[23] In my opinion, the important point is not whether it was one or the other but rather that many—the majority, according to the inspector of the *Fasci*, Carlo Basile—were already members, were sympathisers, or felt engaged with the party that was the backbone of the Fascist nation. I have not been able to document any anti-fascist resistance, at most resilience, within the CTV. For Berti, 'the pride of the voluntary combatants was nothing other than to strengthen from the heart the highest ideal of Italianness and fascism'. This and nothing else had been 'their great motivation to take up arms'. This ideal did not have to be underlined by applications to join the party. We know that was not exclusively the case. But we cannot assert that this motivating factor did not exist at all. Take the example of the motivation underlined by Lodoli when he wrote, in 1939, that he had put his 20 years at fascism's disposal with the sole idea of 'sacrifice, mission, crusade'.[24] In various letters, censored and deposited accordingly in the archives, we can read how a captain (cited in Chapter 2) was enthusiastic about this 'hell of twenty days [that] had been of a marvellous beauty', referring to Guadalajara, and how, in his opinion, it was an experience of death, pain, and loneliness that 'every young person of the New Italy' ought to go through.[25] A large part of the *post-mortem* literature points in the same direction. The publication in honour of the Blackshirt Antonio Curzi, awarded the silver medal and killed during the taking of Santander in the 4th *Banderas* Group, is one of many examples which emphasise the willingness, self-denial, and sacrifice for the fascist faith of those who had fallen in Spain.[26]

The archives house very interesting information of a political nature about some of them. As they were, in many cases, among the first to fall in combat, it was they who, so to speak, generated the first documentation comprising the complete life cycle and death of the soldier. In documents and reports, amongst various procedures and administrative requests, some of which are unfiltered by propaganda, the motives for enlistment are usually accounted for. These motives are far-removed from the dispute with France over control of the western Mediterranean and simple economic self-interest. They have to do with the struggle against the 'old enemy, Bolshevism', the glory of the fatherland, and the news about anti-religious violence.[27] Thus, the central question remains, 'Why enlist to fight in Spain?' That is, if enlistment was always a conscious decision. Clearly, there was an enormous difference between what was going on in the Spain of the Republic and what was known about it, even more so given the scarcity of information in general and the high-level political manipulation in Italy in particular.[28] Perhaps, as the Swiss member of the International Brigades Esolo Morenzoli ventured to say, many legionnaires left to fight in Spain with a distorted and manipulated understanding of the reality of the country, in which stereotypes and biased news about anti-clericalism, the murder of priests, and anti-religious violence weighed heavily when it came to motivating the first enlistments. The vast repercussions of the religious persecution in revolutionary Spain may have contributed to multiplying what Giulio Castelli, in his book *La Chiesa e il fascismo* (*The Church and Fascism*, published in 1951, six years after the end of the Fascist regime), described—in an undoubtedly bold interpretation— as the 'generous, heroic participation of the Italian volunteers' in the fight 'against the barbarism and atrocities of international atheistic communism in its extremism and Bolshevik terrorism'. As in the case of the international geostrategic explanation, we are once again faced with an explanation of the Italian intervention in the war—in this case by private individuals—articulated as a sort of reaction a posteriori. When they went into battle, according to Dario Ferri (a fictitious name assigned by the interviewer), they were the 'new legionnaires of Christ'.[29] 'We volunteers', they said, 'are the true crusaders of the fascist idea, which will triumph with our certain victory in the whole of Spain, imposing on the enemies the human and divine truth which it entails'. Italian fascists 'for the Fatherland and for Christ', volunteers fighting in a sacred Crusade against Bolshevik atheistic terrorism and barbarism.[30]

As the Lombard anarchist Camillo Berneri, who was able to consult papers from Carlo Bossi's consulate in Barcelona and thus denounce Mussolini's policies, wrote with impeccable lucidity: 'Just as, during the conquest of Ethiopia' the Fascist press had 'speculated about slavery, in the intended

142 *Identity, combat, rearguard*

conquest of Spain, it speculates about Red barbarism.'[31] Berneri would end his days in Barcelona, executed in the early hours of 5 May 1937 alongside his friend Francesco Berbi. Nevertheless, political motives in the form of anti-communist reaction have in fact been underlined by many of the authors who have discussed the Italian intervention in Spain, whether in the third person or the first person. Edgardo Sogno, in his vision of the war subsequently compiled in a little volume called *Due fronti* (*Two Fronts*), recalled how, in 1938, at the age of 22, he decided to fight for victory in *National* Spain in order to 'expel the communists from inside Europe'.[32] The violent 'revolution' of the war would therefore permit the confrontation between 'Bolshevik material-ism and Latin Catholic spiritualism',[33] and only a bad Italian and a bad fascist would not have followed 'so many, many Italians who spontaneously run to where the Ideal [*sic*] summons them'.[34]

In the part of the book *La Grande Proletaria* (*The Great Proletarian*) attrib-uted to Bonaccorsi, though clearly plagiarised from Agustín de Foxá, there is large-scale replication of the classic images of Red terror and odious identifi-cation of the enemy. Count Rossi paints a portrait of a Spain of 'Azano [*sic* for Azaña] and Quirosa [*sic* for Casares Quiroga]' which has become a 'province of the socialist Fatherland', an 'operating branch' of the Soviet Union in Europe, a 'forward base' where those who triumphed were loveless women with flac-cid bellies and hunchbacked men with rickets, alcoholics who stank of blood, people who had never entered a museum, devilish beings with a cruel smile, driven by diabolical obsession.[35] And, although it was a reconstruction after the fact, based on readings and plagiarisms, it echoes an element present in the literature justifying the Italian intervention, both the official literature of the state and the writings of individual volunteers: the Bolshevisation of Spain.[36] Mussolini himself wrote in the minutes of the Grand Fascist Council that in Spain, for the first time, and who knew if for the last, the Blackshirts had fought the forces of Bolshevism on the international field. It had been the first confrontation between two revolutions, the nineteenth-century reaction-ary revolution and the twentieth-century fascist revolution.[37] And, a poste-riori, the book of homage to the legionnaires would call them 'Civilisation's Volunteers, defenders of human and divine Law, soldiers of the new Europe' and award them the 'supreme and eternal principle' of faith, progress, peace and harmony, exaltation of life, honour to woman and defence of children, in opposition to the 'convulsed hordes', the 'barbarians', the 'unchained human beast', the obsession with death, massacre, savagery.[38]

As in the case of the literature on Red terror (which I have analysed in another work), this narrative pervaded Italian Fascism's entire cultural, liter-ary, scientific, and technical production. In a publication much less tinged with propaganda than normal, General Sandro Piazzoni recalls how, as the notes of the fatherland's anthems were sounding, the volunteers set sail for Spain to face 'sacrifice and death for the triumph of fascism over Bolshe-vism and of social order over crazy and criminal barbarity'.[39] In fact, this was aggressive anti-communism, but it was defensive as well, because it meant defending their own fascist identity. They would not spill that blood in vain under a foreign flag but rather 'for the salvation of the common civilisation' and of fascism, as only the Duce could understand, because all the forces of the enemy were anti-fascist, and it was fascism that 'democratic Bolshevism' wanted to see buried. For this reason there was 'so much Italian blood sacrificed' for the cause, fundamental for Spain, but not always understood as being beneficial to Italy. It was not only generosity in sacrifice. They departed and fought, this brave aristocracy of war, to fulfil the 'political and spiritual objectives of the Italian Nation [*sic*]'.[40] 'It was right', said Eugenio Colseschi, a commandant of the *Nazionale Volontari d'Italia*, in the commemorative volume *Legionari di Roma* (*Legionnaires of Rome*), that in 'Mediterranean Spain the battle was fought and won in Rome's name'. To defend the Mediterranean was to defend 'the tradition and unity of the whole European continent' and prevent the 'Soviet leper', that 'greedy Empire', from corroding its shores.[41]

This same metaphor of corruption, dirtiness, and darkness is present in many other works dedicated to extolling the heroism of the legionnaires. They were bringers of light, evangelisers of the fascist idea, fighters against a Bolshevism that had started the war and those democracies that, in the words of Enrico Martini, had supported the Madrid government well before the first Fascist assistance arrived. For Martini, the essential reason for the fight was centred on faith, the noble ideal of preserving Latin civilisation in Spain. The legionnaires, 'guided by the light of an idea, which is the sunlight of fascism', would be the new crusaders of the 'Italo-Roman' and Aryan stock, bearers of the faith that would renew the world under the symbol of the *Littorio*.[42] This symbol was also underlined by the legionnaire Bruno Salvatore, who died with the rank of lieutenant in the *Frecce Nere* First Regiment in December 1938. In a letter, which he wrote to his family while on board the *Sardegna* in January 1937, 'sailing in our sea' to Spain, he gave thanks that he would be able to demonstrate with victory that, for him, Italy was more than just a word—just as peace and victory were more than words—with peace would come 'the greatness, the freedom, the unity of this country and this people', from which, in turn, the latter would emanate, the 'victory of liberating and civilising fascism over the barbarity of freemasonry and communism'.[43] It was, in short, a symbol of the *Littorio* and of Imperial Rome, common in combatants' accounts as early as 1936. Francesco Belforte, enrolled in the Legion even before the *Ufficio Spagna*'s creation, recounts how the arrival of the first volunteers in Cádiz was a celebration, one of those events which will go down in history. For the first time since the Roman Age, Italian officers and legionnaires crossed the Straits of Gibraltar, bringing with them the standard of Rome to fight, in the tradition of the *Risorgimento*, by Franco's side.[44]

Civilisers versus barbarism, evangelisers versus obscurantism, liberators versus oppression. 'They look at us with contempt', Franco Bonezzi wrote in his diary. 'The Reds depict us as thieves who have come to Spain to pillage its wealth and take its land.' But '*noi ce ne freghiamo*' (we don't care); one day everybody would realise what they had come to do in 'this land martyred

144   *Identity, combat, rearguard*

by Red barbarism'.[45] They knew they would be treated as mercenaries and legionnaires, wrote Renzo Lodoli afterwards: as deluded fools, adventurers, and self-interested or dragooned. 'But they did not see our faces, or perhaps they did not want to see them', the faces of those who, he said, embodied the most beautiful part of the fight—not that of the office nor petrol, but that of the dagger. They were the faces of those for whom obeying and believing were not incompatible, many of whom would receive the pay for their sacrifice in the form of shovelfuls of earth and a wooden cross.[46] Lodoli's book is a glorification of the Italian combatants' fascist spirit in Spain. Since it was written in 1939, it is difficult not to accuse the author of an acritical and passionate presentism. Nevertheless, that does not disqualify him as a source. Of course, it is a partial and subjective source, as are rest of the sources which refer to almost any historical process, all the more so if the process is laden with identification, mobilisation, and personal sacrifice. The majority of memoirs and first-hand accounts speak of the fascist volunteers' daring character, and often of their contempt for the society which they left behind or to which they returned in 1939, because it saw them as mercenaries. They nearly always speak of love for the fatherland, for whose interests, which were those of fascism as the incarnation of society and of that same fatherland, they would fight in distant lands. The volunteers are, almost unanimously, portrayed as heirs to long ancestral traditions, from the 'volunteers of Giovanni of the *Bandas Negras* and of Attendolo Sforza, the sailors of the victorious crews of Venice and Genoa, of Pisa and of Amalfi' to the soldiers of 'the Savoys, the Viscontis, the Gonzagas, the Scaligers'—those who, with Napoleon, 'arrived victorious in the heart of Russia, whereas the Russians have never reached the heart of Italy and never will'.[47]

The new updating of the past propounded by fascism made the CTV yet another link in the long chain of the Italian tradition of volunteering for just causes for the nation and European civilisation. The instruction received was 'to give one's blood unselfishly for the Fatherland', from which '[we] legionnaires of the DUCE [*sic*] draw the reason and the strength' to achieve the victory which would usher in the New Order.[48] Hence, Italy would join fascism's sacred union, the Crusade to defend European civilisation against the scum of Europe[49]—in defence, thus, 'with a proportion of one to four' in relation to the enemy volunteers, of Europe, of fascism, and of Spain and its people, who were 'of a fickle and simplistic character' but were subject to 'persecution, violated as to their most sacred feelings'.[50] Heinous, criminal, ruthless, the Reds were 'the most despicable members of humanity', renegades from 'what is most sacred: the Fatherland' who had sold themselves 'to the foreigner', 'mercenaries of the Soviet, of freemasonry, and of other rotten and sinister international organisations'. They were 'cowards', as Vittorio Ceccherelli told his girlfriend. When 'they are in a ratio of ten to six, they all rush forward' into battle, whereas when they were in a ratio of five to one in favour of the Italians, 'one of ours broke away and fought chivalrously without anybody helping him'.[51] They were dishonourable cowards, then,

Identity, combat, rearguard   145

and within shooting range of the legionnaires, who 'could sweep Spain clean of this putrefaction', 'exterminate' criminals and defectors, 'stabbers of the Fatherland and Civilisation'.[52] In the words of the *Frecce Nere*'s anthem, 'The enemy standing opposite/we will crush his head without mercy'. It was a matter of faith, and reason was on their side.

Religious faith, fascist faith, faith in the Duce. The faith which, as Francesco Odetti candidly stated, had brought him to fight in Tripoli 20 years earlier, to the bloody trenches of the Karst Plateau, to Fiume and then the March on Rome, more recently to Ethiopia and, finally, to 'this extreme fringe of European soil in order to fulfil my duty as an Italian and as a fascist'.[53] The faith which, according to Lodoli, caused the legionnaire to live for months 'only for his crusade. Somebody called him mad and accused him of being an adventurer. *Se ne fregò*' (He didn't care).[54] The faith of Dario Ferri, a proud fascist (despite hiding behind a pseudonym) who saw them all 'motivated by a single faith' that many, like him, kept alive, from Africa and Spain to the Eastern Front in 1941 and the Republic of Salò.[55] The faith of Davide Lajolo, who felt a crucifix between his fingers, the nails of a Christ who suffered to save the world, and saw the Battle of Guadalajara and the fallen Italians as part of the same sacrifice.[56] The faith which, according to Luigi Mosca, was driving a victory, which from Spain was taking flight to cross the Apennines, beat its wings above the Mediterranean, fly above the imperial roads, and reach the ocean; the Duce had 'conceived the new Europe a long time ago and the war in Spain marks the beginning of this inescapable reality', which would bring about the reconstruction of the continent on the basis of justice and equality between peoples.[57]

Faith in the Duce. In the 1920s, despite its key symbolic importance, the cult of Imperial Rome and the Empire was nothing more than a rhetorical feature, used to legitimise Mussolini's power by connecting him to the mythical past. In the 1930s, however, it became the explanation for the escalation of military aggression. The conquest of Ethiopia contributed powerfully to the projection of an image of Fascism as unstoppable, triumphant, colossal, personified in its Duce, who went from being, in the words of Goffredo Coppola, '*tutti noi*' (all of us) in the 1920s to becoming the incarnation of 'the Nation' and, finally, in the words of Titta Madia, 'Everything'—'*Tu sei tutto!*' (You are everything!).[58] He was not 'like' a god; he was 'a god'.[59] The conquest of Libya in 1926 and the Ethiopian campaigns of 1935–1936 were presented in Italy as revitalising and radicalising components of Fascism's national and racial myth.[60] Indeed, the accentuation of Mussolini's religious dimension had its greatest reverberations in the reification of the empire and the fascist war, insofar as to be fascist signified the supreme communion of all with the hero. The modern and ancient empires united, even physically by Rome's roads. This was the fascist faith, the faith of the volunteer in Spain who incarnated Caesar's ancient legionnaires. A leaflet entitled *Volontari dell'Esercito nella guerra di Spagna* (*The Army's Volunteers in the War in Spain*) was published on Army Day in May 1939 with a front page recognisable throughout

146 *Identity, combat, rearguard*

the Christian world—Saint George slaying the dragon. The leaflet exalted the 'heroic tradition of the volunteers, [a] magnificently recurrent flame in our military and political history', which had set alight 'all the battlefields in Europe and overseas, wherever they fought for the triumph of a great idea' and which had once again been consecrated on Spanish soil. They replied with one voice, it was said, 'old and young, citizens of every status, class, and condition', united in the same belief.

It was a faith demonstrated from the very moment of departure from Italian territory. Reviewing four battalions of *Milizia* volunteers on their way to Spain in January 1937, Luca Petromarchi, head of the *Ufficio Spagna*, marvelled at how they were 'perfect, without exaggerating', a 'vision of solidity and perfect union'. The majority were from the South—Taranto, Bari, Sicily. All had served in the Army and many had fought in Africa. Some officers had even fought in the Great War. But, most importantly, they were 'physically magnificent', mostly tall in stature, a point he would highlight shortly thereafter when speaking of the embarkation of the *Littorio* Division from Gaeta, with General Annibale Bergonzoli at its head, on 1 February. They were 'magnificent battalions, well-groomed boys, happy with the adventure ahead'. 'Tough and solid' people with 'hardened and energetic features', the men who made up the expedition—which had been 'prepared and equipped in 50 days'—shared, according to official documents, two characteristics. Firstly, whether soldiers or members of the *Milizia*, they were 'all volunteers'. Secondly, with the same passion and enthusiasm, they all intensely loved the Duce and the Fascist national ideals. In response to General Russo's rallying cry, they had 'abandoned themselves to a real fantasy of rhythm' to the cry of 'Duce, Duce, Duce'.[61]

Of course, and despite Pietromarchi's denial, there was a lot of exaggeration here. The wording is loaded with emotion, pride, and epic, both in the official documents and in the memoirs. Davide Lajolo admitted as much with regard to his 1939 book on the war, *Bocche di donne e di fucili* (*Mouths of Women and of Rifles*), when he wrote in his later memoir, *Il voltagabbana* (*The Turncoat*), that he had felt forced, in the earlier book, 'to falsify reality, to lend an epic and heroic tone to facts that were sad and full of contradictions and fear', that few had a PNF membership card, and that, in his view, few felt and shared the values of that war.[62] In reality, Lajolo was merely underlining an obvious point, which is simply the complexity of individual experiences, in particular in the context of political mobilisation and war, of the projection of the 'I' onto the 'we', the dissolving of the singular into the plural. Fear and contradictions are components intrinsic to identity and did not disappear with the acquisition of a fascist identity, however much it might transform those components into something different, such as boldness, disempathy, and temerity. Nevertheless, not all had the same horizons in terms of life expectations and identity. In 1937, some Blackshirts wrote to the head of the MSVN's general staff—copied to Achille Starace, Roberto Farinacci, and other Blackshirt commanders in Italy—about Army officers'

Identity, combat, rearguard 147

behaviour towards the *Milizia* and attitude to fascism following the defeat at Guadalajara. 'It is better to treat syphilis than the *Milizia*', a certain Captain Ronzoni had been heard to say, whereupon the squad leader Marcello Buttiti had rushed forward in an attempt to kill him, for which he was arrested and sent to the Bilbao front as punishment. There he died, 'as the Blackshirts know how to die'. This was a state of being peculiar to the fascists. They took the symbols, the slogans, the mythology of the nation, and the 'we' seriously, and they defended them to death. Such was, according to Nuto Revelli, the *Littorio* generation.[63]

This is the generation that we encounter in the photos at the fronts and behind the lines. It is the one that wrote graffiti and paraded carrying Mussolini's bust. It was the generation that learned by heart the legionnaire's commandments, which among other things stated that Mussolini was always right; that total obedience was his great virtue, ferocity the guarantee of his victory, and discipline his sun; that fascism's enemies were his enemies; and that above everything stood duty and, even higher still, Italy.[64] It was the generation that, as Alfonso Pellicciari—a legionnaire disabled in the war—said and repeated, not without a certain pride, had such scorn for danger, such decisiveness and speed, that a high percentage of the losses suffered were due to wounds to the lower limbs. Faced with their well-known, rash bravery, he noted, many among the enemy thought the CTV's soldiers fought wearing cuirasses, which was why they accordingly shot low, aiming for the legs.[65] In their own stories, which nobody exemplifies better than Lodoli, the legionnaires are always unconditionally brave. They considered the trench, waiting in defence, the static war of position to be aspects of war alien to their spirit. Indeed, they hated the trench, the hole, which they depicted as a sort of trap for their spirit and their way of fighting. Envisioned as 'battering rams', their tactic was assault. The rifle, the machine gun, and the mortar were lesser weapons for them. Their true weapon was the hand grenade.[66]

There is no shortage of first-hand accounts of the CTV's life of combat, like the ones collected by journalists, observers, nurses, and doctors in the field. They are full of coarseness, boldness, and bravery, although they obviously have strong echoes of propaganda. Bergonzoli wrote that the *Littorio* Division's heroes, modest heroes, went smiling into battle and, when they died, likewise fell smiling into the arms of death, as if they were embracing their sweethearts, proud of the victories achieved.[67] Glory was always united with sacrifice and martyrdom. Bergonzoli himself was an example. The general known as 'Electric Whiskers' always went ahead in advanced positions, split between risk and glory, and there he was injured.[68] Aldo Santamaria, for his part, covers the war's geography through the testaments to boldness of a CTV fated to be the only army capable of annihilating the bloodthirsty enemy of bandits—stories like that of the 'heroic' second lieutenant Frederico Padovani, who fell fighting in the North against the Basque battalions, 'ferocious Reds' who tried to force him to withdraw; that of the commander of the 5th Group of the *XXIII Marzo* Division, who died heroically while opening the way to victory; or that of the tank driver Renato Zanardo, thrown against the enemy in the middle of an 'indescribable hurricane of fire' to try and prevent the Reds from blowing up a bridge and who, only after he had managed to make them retreat, allowed himself to be transferred to the infirmary, where he was treated for the hand he had lost. But, most notably, this book contains testaments to patriotic obedience, heroism, and national greatness, from the story of Private Mario Donda, who in the face of praise replies that he has only done his duty, to that of Giuseppe Lorenzi, the legionnaire from Ferrara who wrote to his mother that she should be proud to be an 'Italian mum, as I am to be here among so many young people fighting for a just and holy cause', and to his father, a war veteran, that it was now his turn to represent 'our great and beautiful Mother Italy'. These would be his last lines.[69]

Heroism, boldness, *arditismo* (daring). Dario Ferri (pseudonym) describes the enormous courage, more yearning than fear, required—in his opinion— for the use of a fighting tactic which only the Italian assault battalions knew how to use: throw grenades from very close to the targeted positions and, immediately afterwards, rush forward to engage in hand-to-hand fighting using pistols and daggers against the bewildered enemy.[70] 'Attack to conquer' was the *Frecce Nere*'s motto, which, according to their commanding general, came from 'our tactical doctrine, derived from our fascist spirit, forged from the hard foundations of the national war and the radiant days of the March on Rome and our renaissance'.[71] 'Attack to conquer' was the expression of a fascist way of conceiving war, born of bravery, of invincibility, of faith and exalted patriotism, of a combat that produced not fear but pride—according to Lodoli—and a strange feeling of happiness, 'drunk with every moment that passed, happy to suffer'[72]—happy to suffer, as Major Luigi Mosca was when his leg was torn off by a shell at Trijueque. After asking to be operated on without anaesthesia, so that he could feel in his body the blade of the saw used for amputations, he complained that his only suffering was 'having had to abandon the battle'.[73]

Equal proof of such temerity was collected by Alma Giola, a voluntary nurse with the Red Cross. Her evidence took the form of letters sent to the families of the wounded admitted to the hospital ships *Gradisca* and *Aquileia*. The accounts contained in the letters, clearly reworked and perhaps altered (and even invented), speak of the 'glorious heroic story' of the legionnaires. They were fascists like Eugenio Pacitto, aged 22, who was proud to have become, at last, a 'real legionnaire' by shedding his blood for Nationalist Spain; his bloodstained machine gun, better 'than any gold', was transformed into a 'universal relic of pure Italian blood'. Lieutenant Cassandra from Rome, injured by an explosive bullet in a clash with a larger number of 'Reds', had his right arm amputated, crying out 'I still have my left one to fight on with'. Ugo Diappi, a 25-year-old from Milan who had volunteered in Africa and Spain, was wounded in both legs, damaged in the flesh but more in spirit, because he was unable to fight the 'criminal Bolshevik hordes'. He could only count the days before returning to the front, because there 'they fight, suffer, fall in the name of God, but they always win'. Further examples were the Sicilians Giovanni Pizzurro, willing to escape from hospital in order to defend the fatherland, and Salvatore Ciluppo, a 'perfect fascist full of enthusiasm for the fight against brutal communism'. The gunner Seleni from Ragusa had lost both legs in an 'act of superhuman heroism', but what hurt him more than being maimed was not being able 'to return to the front to avenge my dead comrades'.[74]

Along with medical staff, those who gave what was called 'spiritual care' to the combatants also provide evidence of the combat experience at the fronts, as well as themselves being subjects of the great mobilisation for the fascist cause beyond the fatherland. Intended to ignite and channel the combatants' religiosity, each divisional command of the *Frece Nere* had to have an Italian priest to bring 'to the liberated peoples with our fraternal embrace the blessing of God'. For this purpose, the CTV's head chaplain, Aristide Baldassi, organised the recruitment of clergymen—above all from the *Milizia*—according to criteria which, as reported by Mimmo Franzinelli, were considerably political—'under the priest's surplice lies the uniform of the fascist soldier'. They included Giovanni Bergamini, known as Pietro da Varzi, Mussolini's handyman for handling the funeral arrangements in honour of those who had fallen in Spain in 'defence of civilisation' and originator of the *Madonna del Legionario*, the votive chapel built at kilometre 105 on the highway to France.[75] The 60 chaplains transferred to Spain served as the basis for organising the insurgent clergy at the fronts and celebrated mass 'in the face of the Church's enemy, God's enemy'. They were also responsible for certifying epiphanies like the one experienced by Lajolo in Zaragoza's Basilica del Pilar, where he believed that 'the Virgin has listened. She experienced the war with them, at their side, inside the hearts of the soldiers and the mothers. She, too, has wanted to feel the horrors of the war.'[76] Moreover, they took on the task of writing and reading the correspondence of illiterate soldiers, which would give their writings a patina of Catholic militarism. The chaplains thus exercised a double primordial function, covering the fallen in heroism, as they accompanied them at the moment of death, and spreading the word of their martyrdom in political and religious terms. As indicated in a report sent to Mussolini, in language reminiscent of the titles of Goya's engravings, a legionnaire, feet frozen and mortally wounded, requested pen and paper to write the words '"*Viva il Duce*"—and then he dies'.[77]

The clean and the dirty

The dirty: the enemy, the Reds, their women. The clean: the fascists, the combatants, the women of Nationalist Spain, the liberated rearguard. War narratives tend to be composed of binaries: good/evil, clean/dirty, light/darkness. The accounts of the Spanish Civil War by Italians fit this pattern. The first-hand memoirs of legionary fighters written during the war or immediately afterwards are, in the main, creations crafted for propaganda purposes, in

150 *Identity, combat, rearguard*

some cases sugar-coated, in others exaggerated. However, this does not mean they are void of interpretative interest. It is true that most of these books were written by authors whom we can identify as convinced fascists and volunteers, men like Lodoli and Lajolo who were frustrated by the Spain that they had liberated and by the Italy to which they returned, which they identified with conformism, the bourgeois, the grey, lacking military and fascist volunteerism. For this reason, there may be a tendency to inflate their number and relative importance, as well as their interpretations, nearly always excessive, laudatory, and self-exonerating, where the 'we' of boldness and bravery is always confronted with the dreadful 'them'—the Red enemy that sang the repugnant *'Bandiera Rossa'* (Red Flag) before the legionnaires in Guadalajara, in Lodoli's account,[78] or the lazy and backward Spaniard. We are brave; they are cowards. We are fascists; they are scum. However, the distinction was not as clear-cut as it seems.

The issue is complex, but it has generally been buried under the image of the Italian interested in hitching up with girls, arrogant behind the lines and cowardly at the front. Indeed, stories abound of Italian cowardice and ineffectiveness in the face of enemy bullets. That same *Littorio* generation, daring and brave, also included, according to the official sources, a mass of 'subjects unfit for the war effort'. Michelangelo Rubino, the *Milizia*'s consul general, referred to most of the soldiers repatriated after the defeat at Guadalajara as a group getting on in years, in bad physical and spiritual shape and, above all, with serious moral shortcomings, even more so in the eyes of a reverend. Many of the men in the El Puerto de Santa María infirmary and the Haro military hospital, married with children, were said to be there because of syphilis and other venereal diseases. The fanatical fascist Capuchin Pietro da Varzi indicated that, in his view, soldiers had enlisted in poor physical shape, with numerous offspring ('this morning I heard confession from one with ten children'), and 'even those not enrolled in the Party, and with criminal records as well. But since the General Staff recruited them, this is one of those truths best left unsaid.'[79] Of course, all these sources point in the same direction. Nevertheless, it is also true that the evidence that there were volunteers who were old, sickly, or alcoholics was there well before Guadalajara. One such example is the petition presented by the 1st *Banderas* Group to the CTV's command in January 1937, demanding that twelve soldiers be withdrawn from service and returned to Italy because they were drunkards, suffered from acute and chronic blennorrhoea, were ill-disciplined, or had criminal records.[80]

Soldiers who were sometimes too old, many with hernias, varicocele, appendicitis, syphilis, missing teeth, gastric problems—many of them had indicated these ailments in order to get out of going to the front, as an internal report grumbled after the defeat at Guadalajara. Others, frankly, had never handled a rifle. Gunners who did not know how to handle a cannon, soldiers who were incapable of inserting a magazine—poor recruitment done in haste, a problem which extended to the inexperience of the officers, resulting in battalions like the *Indomito* (Indomitable) losing 200 of its 600 men, between those killed and wounded, despite the soldiers' ferocity and bravery.[81] Nevertheless, it must be noted that this and many other reports, on the basis of which many historians have echoed the story of Italian cowardice, refer essentially to the defeat at Guadalajara. This defeat thus becomes a stone weighing down on Italian participation in the war as a whole, fuel for the jokes and contempt hatched behind the lines[82] and which survive to this day.

Indeed, the portrayal of the CTV's combat experience in the publications which appeared during and after the war pursued the barely hidden objective of burying under tons of faith and blood the fiasco of the defeat and the weight of cowardice that fell on them from the enemy and also from friendly fire. The work of Dimas Vaquero is noteworthy for his compilation of jibes about the Italians. Some of these jibes entered the everyday language of the war, such as labelling the acronym CTV as '*Cuando Te Vas*' (when you go) or '*Corren Tutto Veloce*' (all run fast). Verses as original as the following, of Republican origin, were concocted: 'Fewer lorries and more balls/shameless Bergonzoli/general of the defeats/to take Trijueque/with the children you're carrying/squads are not enough/you have to come with balls'.[83] The song '*Guadalajara no es Abisinia*' has already been mentioned in Chapter 2. Carlos Gil provides somewhat different versions, the first sung by Santos Martínez, a soldier from La Rioja in the insurgent army ('Guadalajara is not Abyssinia/ you found the roads already built/and you retreat six at a time/soon you're going to lose us the war'), and another sung by Eustaquio Tricio ('The Italians at Guadalajara/gave Miaja the laureate cross/ the Italians are going to screw us/because they're going to lose us the war').[84] All those songs and jibes basically have their origin in the defeat at Guadalajara. The Italians were held to be insincere and cowardly. According to informants, the legionnaires who ran away were dabbed with paint on their backs. They were humiliated, and their attitude was the cause of widespread mockery. Even Italian officers would see signs of hostility following the defeat. Some left it in writing.[85]

The Italians were barely tolerated, poorly regarded, and highly criticised. Tensions with the Italians began to incubate, according to Captain Frederico Garofoli, from the point when the victory at Málaga was magnified as a success allegedly unattainable by the Spanish troops. The Spaniards could not thank them enough, as Sandri Sandro saw when Millán Astray confessed to him that 'the Italians' had come 'with only your great heart as Latins, with your marvellous contempt for danger. The others, and he was alluding to the Germans, came with the notebook of fees.'[86] Nevertheless, the admiration among senior officials did not necessarily extend to all levels of the insurgents' centre of power. Criticism of the CTV from Franco's general headquarters was particularly harsh. Judging by the constant warnings about deficiencies in training by the CTV's general staff from January 1937,[87] the victory in Andalusia had only been a dangerous mirage, a dream from which they had woken in the middle of the nightmare of Guadalajara. They had been equipped with an enormous war machine, even excessively so, and the defeat of March 1937

152 *Identity, combat, rearguard*

was primarily attributed, both by the Republic and by the Spanish insurgent officials, to the soldiers' lack of fighting spirit. Thanks to the capture of some 300 prisoners, Republican propaganda fabricated an image of the legionnaires as having offered no resistance to being taken prisoner and which claimed that most of them were peasants from Italy's agricultural areas. They were very old or very young, most had a wife and children, and none had served in Abyssinia. None belonged to the Army; they were all volunteers in the *Milizia* on service overseas, which they had not always understood at the moment of departure. In general, judging by their, so to speak, Lombrosian appearance, they were of below average intelligence. Finally, many did not have the character of the soldier nor the imperviousness of the fascist, and a large number were susceptible to embracing communism.[88]

That was, broadly speaking, the information that could be extracted from the prisoners. And, however much the news was deliberately slanted, the fact is that it matches the information that we have about some of the troops that Bastico encountered when he assumed command. Following Guadalajara, the general picture was disastrous—little discipline, low morale, organisational deficiencies, and poor training, above all in the *Milizia*.[89] In Garofoli's words, life was generally too comfortable and lacking in discipline, more that of mercenaries with no desire to fight than that of battle-hardened soldiers. They clashed with and were poorly regarded by the Spanish. Indeed, we have already seen how Italian soldiers expressed their complaints in 1937. The CTV was tired, and many wanted to return home, as their own requests indicated. They had come to Spain thinking they would wage a short, quick war and they were faced with a long, hard one, full of mud, blood, and dead bodies. And, moreover, they had the feeling that their presence was not welcomed by the Spanish. They may have been right. Franco's general headquarters stopped wanting more massive despatches of Italian troops and even considered removing them from the fronts—a staggered withdrawal, of course, so as to be able to instruct Spanish pilots, the shortage of whom was recognised as a very serious problem—in exchange, as we know, for the recognition of belligerency rights and, in turn, the withdrawal of Republican volunteers. It was what began to be called the 'legionnaire problem'. The CTV consisted of a limited number of battalions with a large quantity of arms and war materiel. It was a small army far from home which, despite its fascist daring and willpower, had not managed to avoid being thought of as mercenaries by some and cowards by others. Meanwhile, according to a military report, the Spanish infantry battalions, 'as good hidalgos', looked at the Italian weaponry with 'the envious eye of the poor relation'. The report's conclusion was that Franco wanted 'us to go' and leave the materiel behind. And many wanted leave.[90]

There was some truth in these statements. They were not excessive, but nor is there any shortage of clues to suggest that there were internal tensions among Spanish senior officers and military units with regard to the CTV and, of course, within the mixed units. 'The world is witnessing a historic event', the pilot and consul Ettore Muti would write, 'as a duel between communism and fascism. On one side there are legions of foreign communists . . . on our side . . . we are so few and so poorly used by General Franco that it is a pity.' It was a pity because in Spain fascism was 'at stake', international and Italian fascism.[91] There had even been moments of direct confrontation—rare, judging by the documentary traces, but significant—like the case of the legionary sergeant Ettore Spinelli, who killed a man in Tudela and injured two other people in a confrontation after being attacked at night.[92] In Zuera, on 11 September 1937, a Spanish captain purportedly ordered his squad of the *Frecce Nere* Mixed Brigade to stop, and at that moment Captain Roberto Maccagnani of the CTV started shouting and approached him in a threatening manner holding a gun. The problem is that this document does not explain the cause of the confrontation.[93] Nevertheless, it is evidence of a reality, which is that there were tensions among soldiers and occasionally involving civilians. We have already seen the problems of public order in relation to the CTV and the occupation of the Northern front. Following the defeat at Guadalajara, a group of soldiers being transferred by train alighted at Alcuneza station and set about stealing whatever they came across. Faced with the station guards' resistance, they destroyed and set fire to the benches, the counter, and the waiting room.[94] In 1938, a legionnaire anonymously exposed 'the incidents of various kinds occurring increasingly frequently behind the lines between our soldiers, on the one hand, and the civilian population and the Spanish soldiers, on the other'.[95] These incidents could well have been connected with something Lajolo noticed, when talking to a taxi-driver in Zaragoza. The Italians came across well but, far from being seen as liberators by locals, they were foreigners imposing fascism on another country.[96] In fact, in May 1938, the Army of the North's commander, General Fidel Dávila, had to ban CTV soldiers on leave from Zaragoza, following a succession of incidents between Spanish and Italian officers and soldiers for reasons to do with 'braggartism' and 'arguments about each unit's involvement' in the fighting.[97]

This is not the only place where mention is made of the Italians', and above all the *Milizia* members', sensitivity to the scepticism of those around them and to the passivity of the Spanish, as well as that of their fellow Italian citizens. In 1937, a group of them reported the presumed insult to Italian Fascism by caused by street organs in Sevilla playing its anthems, specifically the '*Giovinezza*', 'between a tango and a foxtrot'. This was in contrast to other national anthems, which street performers were forbidden by regulation to play. People either danced to the Fascist anthem or ignored it, continuing what they were doing in the cafés. Such behaviour was something that, 'fascistically', the group of Blackshirts who were signatories to the complaint could no longer 'tolerate without undertaking' to do something about it. It was the '*Giovinezza*' that accompanied the legionnaires wherever they occupied territory on Spanish soil. It was played in Palma de Mallorca, where 'the Italian flag has the position of honour everywhere, and at nearly all the ceremonies and places open to the public the Duce's photo is on display'.[98] It was possibly the most recognisable symbol of the Italian presence behind the lines.

154 *Identity, combat, rearguard*

The '"*Giovinezza*" was sung all afternoon in the streets', said Italo Sulliotti after the celebration in Sevilla on 31 October 1938 of the anniversary of the March on Rome.[99]

Thus, relations were not always straightforward between Italians and Spaniards. In an anonymous report from the CTV's *Ufficio Informazioni* in May 1937, entitled 'Concerning the damage to modesty', Mussolini was enjoined to order a way 'to impose what it is logical to impose'. It was an allusion to the bad relations between Spanish and Italian troops, the latter clearly burdened by claims of cowardice. When a foreign army, it went on, 'has rushed to help another', like the Italian Army had, the 'sin of pride' was commonplace. And perhaps it was time to emulate this attitude in the face of a 'Spanish character deeply and irremediably saturated with triumphal pride and vanity. The Spanish interpret all racial weaknesses as gifts.' After Málaga and before Guadalajara, the Spanish attitude had been one of 'friendly deference', but afterwards there had been a notable change, an attitude of 'cordial superiority', something 'intolerable . . . we have shed, and are shedding, blood and millions for a nation which is wholly second-rate, whereas we, at the cost of enormous sacrifices, have managed to become who we are'. Thus, the Italians ought to follow the German example of providing little aid, incurring hardly any casualties, but reaping lots of prestige, 'admired and feared' for being 'hard, rigid and, arrogant'. One could not expect the Spanish to respond to 'courtesy with courtesy, to generosity with generosity . . . they are honourable and cruel, kind and insincere . . . they make promises but don't keep them'. Faced with 'force, they surrender; faced with arrogance, they bow'.[100]

Despite the clearly supremacist attitude of the author of the report and the extreme stereotyping of his Spanish comrades-in-arms, it contains other elements that are also found in other information taken from the Italian documents and memoirs, which portray the Spanish as poor, backward, proud, noble, and naïve. The first report written by Roberto Farinacci during his political mission in 1937 was very revealing. Despite his doubts about fascism taking root, what was clear to him from the beginning was that the coup d'état and the political cleansing behind the lines were giving the construction of the New Spain a profoundly brutal character. 'Let us not be under any illusions', he said, 'about the efficiency of our political work'. Blood was flowing amid 'general indifference', with everybody talking about 'shootings as if they were cinema'. The Spanish were in agreement about one thing only, 'massacring each other every day'. Thus, perhaps without realising it, Farinacci inaugurated the written embodiment of an entire identitarian tendency that would infuse the reports of a large number of Fascist informants and agents in Spain, of moral superiority, Italian supremacism and disdain, almost a generalised disgust towards the Spanish. While nobody was in a hurry 'to finish with this butchery', the population had become used to the bloodthirsty climate. Many 'dressed in mourning' but 'talk with indifference about how a brother, a son, a husband has been shot'. As he indicated to his friend Mussolini, Farinacci thought that the issue of mass shootings was problematic for the Italians. They had not come to Spain to assuage the Spaniards' thirst for blood, nor to assist with revenge. They had come to defend fascism against communist attack. In this race to massacre amid equivalent acts of violence, barbarity, he said, was now almost a sport. Yet, the Spanish wanted only the comfort of 'food, *siesta*, and rest' (written in Spanish in the original). Cafés were full, bullfights sold out, and nobody was aware of the fighting that was deciding the fate of Mediterranean civilisation. It was the 'old story of Spain'.[101]

It was an old story of violence and backwardness. Dino Alfieri's envoy to Spain complained that, further to the Duce's requests to take a more active part in the war in 1938, the Spaniards' 'incomprehension and ingratitude for the vast and generous help' provided by the Italians were continuously growing. This was despite the fact that the foreign commentators travelling around 'this simultaneously funereal and carnival-like scene called *National Spain*' thought that without the Italian presence 'Franco's arms would have suffered major defeats'. Fascist help was nevertheless useless for a people, who, behind the trenches, were the same on both sides, wanting to embrace each other again under 'the sign of food, idleness, and discussions about coffee and the electoral merry-go-round'. The Spanish were 'men who were too small to bring about a historic event'.[102] In his journeys through southern Spain, giving talks on the Fascist regime, inaugurating Italian language courses, preparing articles for the Falange in Sevilla, and initiating screenings of Italian films, Dino Alfieri himself had been able to ascertain the 'atrocious physical and moral inferiority of the Spanish', a people with a 'mendacious, colourful mentality', a 'lyrical and romantic soul, fundamentally heroic', who followed the doctrine of the single dish but who 'snacked four times a day', who had clocked up a 'delay of at least two centuries behind civilisation', and whom not even the war, which might have been the 'schism of their rebirth', had taught 'how to live before eleven in the morning'.[103] These contemptuous words tally nevertheless with those of Bonezzi, who wrote in his war diary that 'these people are 50 years behind us'. Mud houses, filth, and lack of personal hygiene make up part of the image of the Spanish which many legionnaires recorded as being true of the whole of the 'liberated' rearguard.[104]

In parallel, and according to Ambassador Wilhelm Faupel's report of December 1937, the 'inordinate glorification of the Italian military deeds, the presumptuousness of the Italian military authorities, the behaviour of the troops at the front and, above all, in their living quarters' were setting the Spanish more and more obviously against the CTV.[105] This perception was present in the political sphere as well. As Marchiandi's secret informers in the Falange and Donostia stated, there was a perception of a 'certain incoherence in the Italians' political attitude in Spain'. Whereas the 'Germans have a single position on all aspects . . . nobody corrects anybody else', the Italians 'overuse' theatricality, that 'excess of regalia which some take . . . as the stuff of operetta and others as contempt for the Spaniard'. 'Italians who are commissioners and inspectors of this, that, and the other abound.' The embassy exercised no

156   *Identity, combat, rearguard*

direct control, and this 'desire for display' created an impression of internal rivalry—and not without cause.[106] Vaquero elaborates the point. Although camaraderie prevailed in the mixed brigades,

> the Spanish character [*sic*] took some of their behaviour as a joke and ridiculed the Italian volunteers' theatrical style, their presumptuousness, their boasting, their animated language, their colourful uniforms, their fine equipment, their extended leaves of absence behind the lines.[107]

Irrespective of the stereotypes, it is true that the Italians' situation in Spain was not without problems. On a number of occasions, their leaves of absence behind the lines were the main reason for conflicts with local and regional commands, even more so than their supposed lack of bravery.

The best example to illustrate that image of the Italians in Spain was particularly fraught with political, national, and identitarian connotations—it was no coincidence that it was the largest foreign contingent—is the importance attached to it by Republican counter-propaganda. Written in Italian and directed specifically, in some cases, at the *Littorio* Division, the propaganda was devised to try and persuade the volunteers to question their presence in Spain, looking for a possible angle to create a split in their support for the war. Accordingly, the 'militiamen of the Santander Army' wrote to the 'Italian Soldier', 'You are not an enemy, because you are a worker like us. Our common enemies are the landowners, the bankers, the arms merchants. Don't risk your life for a cause that is not yours.' 'Why are you peasants going against other peasants?' They had been told that they would go to Africa 'to get land to work', but they had been deceived. Mussolini was unable to 'feed the Italian people', and so he had sent them to the war to die. As 'cannon fodder', under German command, they were admonished to return to Italy 'to conquer your liberty' and give their families security. It was a recurring theme in this type of propaganda dropped over the enemy trenches, based on the high percentage of married men with children found among the prisoners taken at Guadalajara. If they deserted, the men of the *Milizia* and their families would find a future in Republican Spain.[108] However, the most frequently recurring theme may have been the national one. 'Why are you fighting, why are you suffering, why do you want to die?', the Italian legionnaires were asked from the air. Their fatherland 'is Italy . . . what have the Spanish people done to you?'

The question of national identities in the war has been studied brilliantly by Xosé Manoel Núñez Seixas. Various conclusions consistent with what is being examined here can be drawn from his analysis of the imaginary of the Italians in Spain in propaganda. There are at least two conclusions. The first concerns the representation of Mussolini himself. If a concrete imaginary was exploited by the propaganda offices, it was that of the Spanish War of Independence of the early nineteenth century. The Duce was depicted on war postcards as a new Napoleon or Metternich who once again was crushing the Spanish people's yearning for freedom, like the Hundred Thousand

Sons of Saint Louis. The second conclusion concerns what Italian observers in Spain flagged as Hispanic 'national pride', which, without going so far as to explicitly refuse to recognise the foreign intervention's importance in support of Franco, limited its scope and circumscribed the Italians' successes to the ensemble of the *Generalísimo*'s triumphs. Republican counter-propaganda was much more explicit (and critical) regarding the Fascist participation than their own comrades-in-arms.

The presence of Italian troops on the insurgents' side, Núñez Seixas points out, 'was hushed up as far as possible, and many publicists mendaciously denied' it or made 'more sophisticated arguments'. For José María Pemán, Germans and Italians were assisting Nationalist Spain and modernising the 'fraternity' between the Habsburgs and Rome 'incarnated in Emperor Charles I'. For Sabino Álvarez-Gendín, rector of the University of Oviedo, the CTV was cementing the friendship between the two countries inherited from Roman Hispania, Naples, and the Two Sicilies, which 'would have its perfect ending in Mussolini and Franco's joint anti-communist commitment to restore Rome as the City of God'.[109] Nevertheless, the Italian presence appears in explicit form in the propaganda of the governments of Valencia and Barcelona. A clear example was the campaign of 1938 entitled 'Spain for the Spanish!'. Hatched in Republican territory, ostensibly to demand the end of external intervention in the war, it was in fact a direct accusation against the Italians and Germans, as can be read in the postcards collected by the Italian embassy in Salamanca:

> We have been fighting fiercely for 28 months, the two sides squandering brotherly blood in vain, stabbing the hearts of our mothers, who live with the same fears and weep the same tears. Let us finish once and for all. . . . Let the brothers talk together, reconciled for the salvation of the Fatherland. . . . The executioners from Italy and Spain want to divide Spain between them like Austria and Czechoslovakia . . . Spain for the Spanish![110]

As can be seen in these images, the objective of the 'Spanish' was reconciliation, the 'shaking of hands', but only after kicking out 'the invaders' and driving bayonets into the guts of both Hitler and Mussolini, who are portrayed in another image as irate guests at a table being served by a tiny Franco offering them Spain on a platter. The theme of this campaign was, 'We're not afraid of losing the war. We're afraid of losing Spain.' This propaganda was undoubtedly Republican, but it was consistent and converged with the news picked up by the CTV's command when it let Mussolini know, in August 1938, that the 'attitude towards the Italians' was not 'ideal. It is not possible to talk about deep causes nor clear and precise features . . . it is an indistinct, collective state of a mind, a feeling of bother.' It amounted to a 'desire to see no more of those whom the formidable Red propaganda deems invaders'. All this had nothing to do with 'the CTV's behaviour'.[111]

158 *Identity, combat, rearguard*

Nevertheless, that behaviour was not always as magnificent as portrayed in accounts of Italian heroic deeds or reflected in their photos of combat and behind the lines. There is usually no explicit mention in the documentary sources, and the memoirs evade the issue or straightforwardly deny it, but it seems that the *Milizia's* volunteers, rather than soldiers from the Royal Army, were involved in most of the tensions with the Spanish and the civilian population. The testimonies collected by Carlos Gil in the Upper Rioja always point in this direction.[112] The Upper Rioja was an area with legionnaires' camps and, therefore, a place suitable for investigating relations between the Italians and the areas behind the lines. Moreover, in June 1938, Ciano ordered General Mario Berti to remove the troops from Zaragoza and send a battalion to the front; they had been on leave for more than 40 days, filling the city's cabarets and brothels. Similarly, many of the legionnaires' books of memoirs about Spain give indications that the main focus of tension was not so much the issue of the fronts as the rearguard, and the defeat at Guadalajara is always the turning point and the point of no return.

Before the defeat, and particularly after the relatively simple taking of Málaga, we find 'little incidents of drunkenness', 'fun of all sorts', and the 'first sweethearts' during the long stay of 20 days in Sevilla. The most explicit story of this kind is by Renzo Lodoli, who, the original edition and in the re-edition, 50 years later, of *Domani posso morire* (*Tomorrow I can die*), would recall his experience in Spain using ridiculous descriptions of Spanish women; pompous recreations of flamenco shows; expressions like '*Olé*', '*Anda, chica*', and '*Vive tu* mare, *guapa*' (all written in Spanish); and a fascination with the smells and flavours of a 'Spain which entered inside me', 'prisoner of a spell/ in the Sevillian night'.[113] After Guadalajara, however, always come 'sad days', 'dead comrades',[114] and some small satisfaction, usually in the form of drunkenness or sex. In short, the cold shower of reality conveyed by the defeat at the fronts was explicitly or implicitly projected behind the lines. The female sexual stereotypes found in the legionnaires' memoirs range from Andalusian sensuality to Castilian shyness and hostile submission and, lastly, Aragonese and Catalan curtness: from *olés* and bewitchment to women's hands wrinkled by soap and work.

In fact, with regard to the legionary troops' contacts behind the lines, the question which takes on a degree of noteworthy importance is their relations with civilians and, in particular, with women and children—and even, specifically, with girls—more so than their contact with non-mobilised men. The two-way memory of the CTV's passage through Spain is marked by those stains. The soldiers recall the adolescent girls and women with whom they flirt, the elderly women from whom they buy goods or whose houses they occupy, and the boys who run errands for them in exchange for chocolate. These same children and other residents of the villages behind the lines where the Italians stayed remember them for their womanising, for their sexual desire, for occupying houses and barns, and for requisitioning property and food.[115] When Cordedda goes out one evening to visit Bergara during a period of rest between fighting in the North, he finds a deserted town, with only old people in the streets and a support centre where some friendly and pretty girls give them woollen gloves and socks.[116] Franco Bonezzi was revolted by the dirty adolescent girls who offered themselves for money, but not by the 'most beautiful and elegant ladies of the city', referring to Sevilla, who were not 'indifferent to our more or less passionate gazes'.[117]

Lajolo speaks in his memoirs about the wine of the 'Rioka [*sic*]', but mainly about the region's women who, 'like the flowers of peach trees', sprouted from the pavements and joined them like protectresses in the cafés. They experienced the war 'with the utmost feeling', they 'cr[ied], pray[ed], move[d] ahead with the soldiers, resist[ed]'. They made them dream of former loves relived during the nights of fighting. If they crossed them on the pavement, they had 'little heads covered with blond and chestnut ringlets . . . red mouths, red like a lasting fire, with fresh breasts, flourishing, like oranges hidden in silk'. With their 'beautiful busts and generous hips', they waited for the return of their brave and handsome legionnaire.[118] Lodoli, too, writes with real emotion about his sexual encounters behind the lines. At a dance in the officers' dining hall, after having 'freed Catalonia from the nightmare of militias', the women's mourning did not matter. The men wanted the saleswoman, the school teacher, the mayor's niece, or the girl from the *Auxilio Social*, in order to 'clasp a woman in their arms', 'feel a female body close and cover their noses with the fragrances of perfume'. The image appears again and again in the book of the young woman who falls into the arms of the soldier or the Italian officer as the sole moment of deserved peace and serenity in the midst of the war. He even goes as far as throwing aside a 'little blond' called Teresa because he remembers that that morning she had washed his underpants with her hands. '*Vete, biondina, el teniente de los de la muerte è un tipo strano*' (Go away, blondie, the lieutenant of those of death is a strange guy). It must have seemed ridiculous to Lodoli as well, because in the 1989 reedition the reprimand is limited to '*Vete, biondina*'.[119]

Unofficial sources also point in this direction. Among the songs mocking the CTV, the ones that stand out are those that combined cowardice and lechery, lack of bravery, and womanising, like one that appears to be from the Francoist zone. Once again sung to the tune of *Faccetta Nera*, it had the following lyrics: 'Spanish girl, don't fall in love/Spanish men will be in charge in Spain/the Italians will go away/and they will leave you a baby as a souvenir.'[120] Italian priests officiated about 250 marriages between Italian soldiers and Spanish women, plus some 500 by proxy, mainly in the zones where the CTV rested or military schools used by the MMIS were located. The MMIS provided training and advanced courses for officers, as well as courses for specialists at its centres in Burgos, Valladolid, and Segovia.[121] I do not have any figures for pregnancies due to Italian soldiers, nor has any investigation tried to hazard a guess, although the small number of legionnaires who ended up settling down in Spain after the war could indicate one of two things. The first is that it all amounted to a self-interestedly mythologised story, which

160 *Identity, combat, rearguard*

the memoirs contributed much to shaping; judging by some books, the war in Spain would appear to have been a tourist jaunt with women freely available. The other interpretation reinforces the extremely negative image of the CTV as a body of thieving, violent, whoring, cowardly, womanising soldiers, the latter group, moreover, leaving behind a trail of unacknowledged babies.

However, when talking about complex situations, peculiar to the Civil War but nonetheless controversial when it comes to the construction of the memory of the CTV, the most important is its rather polemical relation to the violence against Republican soldiers and civilians and to the Spanish insurgents' occupation policies. As has already been indicated, the CTV had neither the power nor the capacity to manage the use of violence in the heat of the moment, judicial investigations, and the treatment of prisoners and civilians in recently occupied and billeting zones. Moreover, the statements by their military and political leaders were nearly always tinged with the rhetoric of integrating the vanquished, which, as they took care to state on numerous occasions, did not fit well with the policies of cleansing and repression implemented by the *National* side. There are several reports that refer to the same reality. As early as 1936, Ettore Muti complained that in Badajoz and Mérida, where the Savoia-81 aircraft played an important role, all the prisoners were shot 'in reprisal for their exhausting and courageous defence'. 'Our beautiful fascism', he said, 'is something different'.[122] On an inspection trip through Spain (from Donostia to Cádiz and Toledo), Sandro Sandri wrote to Ciano that he had the opportunity to speak to many prisoners before they were shot, 'as usual', including the execution of militia women, 'poor creatures . . . who had lost their sense of femininity, they died bravely, saluting the firing squad by raising a clenched fist'. And, he said, while the evidence of 'Red terror' was not reassuring, with accounts of communists hanging civil guards by the testicles, inserting explosives into men's anuses to blow them up, raping women, and dismembering children in the villages which they abandoned—which, by the way, was extremely strange, because there is usually no time for that sort of thing during a retreat—the 'Whites' also had few scruples. Their entry into a village meant the beginning of the 'cleansing'. Nobody was tortured; they were killed right away. 'From the Generalissimo down to the last soldier, they are all ready to exterminate without mercy.' The bodies were burned with petrol, without last respects and without making a note of their names, 'as if they were animal carrion'. 'When the insurrection is over, it is presumed that between 800,000 and a million will have disappeared.' In Sevilla, 50 were shot at dawn each day, and he presumed that the 15,000 members of the parties of the Left in the Andalusian capital would suffer this fate. In Asturias, 30,000 miners would be needed to replace those executed.[123]

In Málaga, in the North, in Alacant, the reports submitted by the Italians speak of horrible acts, of mass shootings. As we have seen, the Italians' contempt for these acts and shootings would spring not from a benevolent and humanitarian view of the defeated so much as from the belief that they were tactical and political mistakes, which would give rise to great difficulties when rebuilding in the future and which were shaped by the Spanish character itself. It should be remembered that Livio Gaetani, Cantalupo's representative in Málaga, saw the violence as necessary, though it was becoming excessive. As the Duce could read in a report in 1937, in contrast to his good heart, 'the Spaniard's bloodthirsty character has been on show in the most violent ways in this war . . . prisoners are tortured, the shooting machine functions without interruption'.[124]

These and other expressions, which have been seen all through the previous chapters, and particularly those of the first Italian fighters writing up their impressions of the insurgents' policy of terror, were consistent with the fascist notion of violence and its use in killings and political repression. The 'effective' violence called for by Mussolini, conceived in ontological and organicistic terms, sacralised, and all-consuming, was the mechanism by which to carry out a permanent struggle, a state of continuous war and, used to the extent required, would serve to protect and unite the healthy part of society by means of cleaning the dirty, integrating through exclusion. After all, the implementation of a notion specific to fascism like that of palingenetic rebirth and the renewed updating of the nation's past could only be done through purging, cleansing, destruction, and ruins.[125] Thus, it is paradoxical, to say the least, to underline the Italian commentators' disregard for the insurgents' violence when, at the same time, the fighters themselves do nothing but constantly praise the proactive and procreative beauty of the largest possible setting for violence, cleansing, and purification—that is to say, war. For them, destruction was a necessary precondition of reconstruction, and the experience of violence and of living with violence the process by which to achieve integration into the fascist national community. Therefore, the many Italian expressions of alienation, disapproval, and rejection of the insurgents' violence belong inside parentheses. Firstly, because these sentiments were exceptional as a rule and purely personal; they did not reflect the official political, military, and juridical position of the Fascist state and its representatives. Secondly, whether officials or private individuals, they do not oppose nor express their revulsion at the violence as a whole, but rather at its excesses. Thus, it is a rejection not of the nature of the violence but rather of its scope. It is basically a question of scale.

Thus, the Italians were repelled by Queipo de Llano telling their legation in November 1937 that, after the war, the Spanish would not change and that, consequently, it was necessary 'to get rid of these people. We have to carry on shooting or set up big concentration camps in the Canaries or in Fernando Po [sic].'[126] They questioned that, in conversation with Danzi, Tito Meléndez justified the Falangists taking part in shootings, despite supposedly being forbidden to do so, as the result of 'totally personal reactions'.[127] They complained about the indiscriminate shooting of prisoners after Málaga and Santoña and asked for them not to be handed over to Spanish soldiers.[128] But all this, like the initial complaints about the bloodbath of 1936—that everybody, from Franco on down, was 'inclined to exterminate'—was done,

162   *Identity, combat, rearguard*

as in Cantalupo's case, in order to avoid such crimes being associated with the presence of the Italians or to avoid the 'Red mass' eventually turning against the occupiers. There was no rejection of violence, but rather a questioning of its indiscriminate use. There could be no rejection of violence by the volunteer pilots who wanted to cleanse Spain; nor by the 'volunteers of death' who arrived in July 1936 and, like Vittorio Ceccherelli, had 'the honour of being among the first to fight' in a duel; nor by Ciano, who was fascinated by the bombing of civilian populations, like the New Year's Day bombing of Barcelona, as will be seen in the next chapter, which left 'buildings pulverised, traffic interrupted, panic turning into frenzy: 500 dead, 1,500 injured. A fine lesson for the future.' Nor was there any rejection of violence by the military administrators of the 155th Battalion of Workers, formed in Miranda del Ebro from 400 Republican prisoners allocated to serve the CTV, whose leaders imposed punishments contrary to the codes of military justice by tethering prisoners' feet and hands to trees or lampposts and 'by keeping them there for several days', as one of them, the head of the concentration camp at San Juan de Mozariffar, complained. Nor, of course, was there any rejection of violence by those in charge of the *Frecce Nere* in which Dario Ferri fought. According to him, they decided on the summary shooting of four civil guards for firing at them from the castle of Girona when they occupied the city.[129]

According to Sandro Attanasio, the Italians never carried out mass executions, behaved in a gentlemanly manner towards prisoners in compliance with international conventions, did not involve themselves in political matters, and were always seen as 'clever and courageous Italians'.[130] The reality was infinitely more complex. In fact, the CTV's own reports, quoted by the same author, admitted that unarmed prisoners had been shot *in situ* in Málaga, but also in Guadalajara, where they could not blame the presence of Spanish troops because, as they took pains to stress, the Spaniards had left them alone.[131] And they feared the effects of the insurgents' violence, over which they had little control, because cleansing the areas behind the lines was not their mission, and because it stiffened resistance and made it more desperate. We do not have enough sources to be able to assert categorically that the CTV was involved in the policy of systematic violence as part of the occupation routine implemented by the Francoist command and troops and their agencies of political and social control. Nor can we affirm that the Italians were entirely disengaged with this policy. In point of fact, we do not have sources, neither in memoirs nor from the archives, enabling us to make categorical statements about practically any aspect of the polyhedral map which I have sought to sketch in this chapter. We cannot identify the combatants as a whole as mercenaries, idealists, or unemployed men in pursuit of earnings. Nor can it be concluded that they were a bunch of sexual predators or saintly Christian soldiers who behaved courteously towards women and children. But, these obvious remarks aside, and if we accept that the Italian intervention in Spain and the experiences of the soldiers and militiamen who took part in were highly complex and cannot be reduced to a handful of stereotypes,

Identity, combat, rearguard 163

there are sources available in the archives and memoirs which point in a more unsettling and disturbing direction—that which pinpoints the CTV as yet another muscle in the insurgents' enforcing arm against the anti-Spain. The air raids carried out against civilian targets under direct orders from Rome, as will be seen in the next chapter, provide the clearest inculpatory evidence.

Notes

1 Antonio V. Savona and Michele L. Straniero, *Canti dell'Italia fascista (1919–1945)* (Milán: Garzanti, 1979), 306–307.
2 Almost the sole exception is Davide Lajolo's second book dealing with his involvement in Spain, *Il 'voltagabbana'* ('The Turncoat') (Milan: Rizzoli, [1963] 1981). On the CTV, there are various highly technical books which are not official—that is to say, not published by state institutions—but which are clearly consistent with the view made standard by the Fascist Ministries of Foreign Affairs, the Army, and Popular Culture: Gaetano Amoroso, *Mortai e Lupi in Catalogna* (Turin: Rattero, 1941); Alberto Angelini, *Altre verghe per il Fascio: un Legionario dodicenne alla guerra di Spagna* (Rome: Cooperativa Il Legionario, 1938); Maurizio Bassi, *Da Cadice ai Pirenei* (Florence: Le Monnier, 1941); Marco Alessi, *La Spagna della monarchia al governo di Franco* (Milan: Istituto per gli studi di politica internazionale, 1937). See also the book by the journalist Curio Mortario, *Con gli insorti in Marocco e in Spagna* (Milan: Treves, 1937); and above all, the four volumes by Francesco Belforte, *La guerra civile in Spagna* (Milan: ISPI, 1938). There are also works of fiction, which have been analysed by Luciano Curreri, *Mariposas de Madrid. Los narradores italianos y la guerra civil española* (Zaragoza: Prensas de la Universidad de Zaragoza, 2009).
3 In this respect, the books written by Italian correspondents in Spain also stand out, such as Sandro Volta, *Spagna a ferro e fuoco* (Florence: Vallecchi, 1937); Renzo Segàla, *Trincee di Spagna: con i legionari alla difesa della civiltà* (Milan: Fratelli Treves, 1938); Italo Sulliotti, *Europa svegliati!: Scene e figure della guerra di Spagna; con illustrazioni fotografiche fuori testo* (Milan/Florence: G. Agnelli, 1938); Lamberti Sorrentino, *Questa Spagna: avventure di una coscienza* (N.p.: Edizioni Roma, 1939)—cause and effect, but with no context.
4 This is, in fact, what Giorgio Bocca wrote in his preface to the book in which Lajolo, director of *L'Unità* (organ of the Italian Communist Part) and partisan in the Italian civil war, explained his past as a fascist: 'our publishers consider fascist memoirs something filthy'. It was easier to avoid mentioning a time when it was normal to 'speak, hope, plan for colonies and empires, mentions in dispatches, and *Mare Nostrum*.' Lajolo, *Il 'voltagabbana'*, 6.
5 *Legionari di Roma in terra iberica* (Milan: Sagdos, 1940), 185.
6 Emilio Faldella, *Venti mesi di guerra in Spagna (luglio 1936-febbraio 1938)* (Florence: F. Le Mannier, 1939), 231.
7 Gabriele Ranzato, 'Volontari italiani in Spagna: identità e motivazioni', in *'In Spagna per l'idea fascista': legionari trentini nella guerra civile spagnola 1936–1939*, eds. Gabriele Ranzato, Camillo Zadra, and Davide Zendri (Rovereto: Museo Storico italiano della Guerra, 2008), 9–28.
8 Lajolo, *Il 'voltagabbana'*, 41ff.
9 AMAE, AB, L1460, E18 and L1464, E26.
10 Francesco Odetti, *Trenta mesi nel Tercio* (Rome: M. Carra, 1940).
11 Tracy H. Koon, *Believe, Obey, Fight: Political Socialization of Youth in Fascist Italy, 1922–1943* (Chapel Hill: University of North Carolina Press, 1985), 239.
12 Giuseppe Cordedda, *Guerra di Spagna. 100/17, alzo zero* (Sassari: Chiarella, 1996), 7ff. On the 'unknown destination', see also Lajolo, *Il 'voltagabbana'*, 40.

164 *Identity, combat, rearguard*

13 Edgardo Sogno uses this phrase to refer to the short time spent at the front. See Nino Isaia and Edgardo Sogno, *Due Fronti: la grande polemica sulla guerra di Spagna* (Florence: Liberal Libri, 1998).

14 AMAE, RE106, C26.

15 Lajolo, *Il 'voltagabbana'*, 43.

16 ACS, MI, DirPolPol. SPD, CR, f1 and f5.

17 ASMAE, AP, b58.

18 Giulia Medas, *¿Quienes fueron los voluntarios? Identità, motivazioni, linguaggi e vissuto quotidiano dei volontari italiani nella guerra civile spagnola* (PhD diss., Universities of Cagliari and Valencia, 2014); Dimas Vaquero, *Credere, Obbedire, Combattere: fascistas italianos en la Guerra Civil Española* (Zaragoza: Mira, 2009), 105.

19 Family could mean a wife and children under 14; parents; orphaned brothers and sisters under 14; or grandparents who had no other male children or grandchildren over 18. Allowances varied according to the beneficiaries' place of residence. ASMAE, US, b1.

20 Vaquero, *Credere, Obbedire, Combattere*, 183–184. Here I share the opinion of Olao Conforti, *Guadalajara: la prima sconfitta del fascismo* (Milan: Mursia, 1967).

21 Renzo Lodoli, *Domani posso morire: storie di arditi e fanti legionari* (Rome: Roma Fascista, 1939); republished as *I Legionari Spagna 1936–1939* (Rome: Ciarrapico Editore, 1989), 3.

22 Davide Lajolo, *Bocche di donne e di fucili* (Osimo: Barulli, 1939), 3.

23 ASMAE, US, b160.

24 Lodoli, *Domani posso morire*, 79.

25 ACS, MI, SPD, CR, b71.

26 Antonio Curzi, *Gioventù italica legionaria e guerriera* (Velletri: G. Zampetti, 1939).

27 AMAE, AB, L1059, C302–315 contains papers of Italian volunteers of 1936 who, having fought, requested economic compensation in the form of grants or pensions. An example was Alberto Mario Amedei, who left Italy with the Bourbon prince, both renouncing any economic benefit. Amedei was enrolled into the *Tercio de Navarra* with the rank of second lieutenant in January 1937. He was wounded and repatriated.

28 Paolo Murialdi, *La stampa del regime fascista* (Rome/Bari: Laterza, 2008); Paul Corner, ed., *Il consenso totalitario. Opinione pubblica e opinione popolare sotto fascismo, nazismo e comunismo* (Rome/Bari: Laterza, 2012).

29 In Massimo De Lorenzi, *Teruel-Malaga 1936–1939. Un antifascista svizzero e un fascista italiano nella guerra civile di Spagna: memorie di lotta, sofferenze, passioni* (Varese: Edizioni Arterigere, 2010), 123.

30 Castelli, quoted in Aldo Albonico, 'Accenti critici di parte fascista e cattolica alla cruzada', in *Italia y la Guerra Civil Española, Simposio en la Escuela de Historia y Arqueología de Roma* (Madrid: CSIC, 1986), 1–8.

31 Camillo Berneri, *Mussolini a la conquista de las Baleares y otros textos* (Madrid: La Malatesta, 2012), 41. This re-edition of the book, originally published in 1937, contains too many additions and a decidedly un-critical spirit.

32 Isaia and Sogno, *Due fronti*, 66. The same motivation is given by Domenico Palladino, an auxiliary major in the *Milizia*. Domenico Palladino, *Terza oferta. Ricordi della guerra civile di Spagna* (Bari: Palladino Editrice, 1967). It is likewise the reason given by the father of 12-year-old Alberto Angelini for leaving for Spain with his son. Angelini, *Altre verghe per il Fascio*, 2.

33 Luigi Incisa, *Spagna nazional-sindicalista* (Bologna: Cappelli, 1941), 6. See also Paola Lo Cascio, 'La retaguardia italiana: el discurso del fascismo italiano en la Guerra Civil Española: el caso de la narrativa y ensayística publicada en Italia entre 1937 y 1942', *Revista Universitaria de Historia Militar*, no. 6 (2014): 87–103.

34 Angelini, *Altre verghe per il Fascio*, 2.

35 Arconovaldo Bonaccorsi et al., *La Grande Proletaria* (Rome: Centro Editoriale Nazionale, 1958), 464.

36 This same element is found in Massimiliano Griner, *I ragazzi del '36. L'avventura dei fascisti italiani nella Guerra Civile Spagnola* (Milan: Rizzoli, 2006); Galli and Lenoci, *Dossier*, and Romeo di Colloredo, *Frecce*. It is thus a view with a long trajectory.

37 Belforte, *La guerra civile in Spagna*, vol. III, 9.

38 *Legionari di Roma in terra iberica* (Milan: Sagdos, 1940), XXI.

39 Sandro Piazzoni, *Le Frecce Nere nella guerra di Spagna (1937–1939)* (Rome: Edizioni della Rivista Nazione Militare, 1939), 13.

40 Luigi Mosca, *Camicie nere a Guadalajara* (Naples: Partenope, 1941), 13ff.

41 *Legionari di Roma*, XXIII.

42 Enrico Martini, *Croce e spade contra falce e martello* (Rome: n.p., 1939), 285–286 and 289ff.

43 Other collections of legionnaires' letters are Gentile Campa, *Lettere familiari della Spagna: di un legionario caduto nella battaglia dell'Ebro* (Florence: Rinasicmento del Libro, 1939); and those of Giacomo Fiori, *Cuore di Legionario: lettere di Giacomo Fiori, caduto in Spagna* (Rome: Vittorio, Ferri, 1939).

44 Belforte, *La guerra civile in Spagna*, vol. III, 83.

45 Alessandro Bonezzi, *Il diario del nonno fascista* (Rome: Robin, 2006), 4. The Italian verb '*Fregarsene*' can be translated as 'to not care', but here the exact expression is important, because one of the most typically fascist cries was precisely '*Me ne frego!*' ('I don't give a damn!').

46 Lodoli, *Domani posso morire*, 14–15.

47 Cited in Odetti, *Trenta mesi nel Tercio*, 205.

48 Mosca, *Camicie nere*, 10. The capital letters appear in the original.

49 Guido Pietro Matthey, *Legionario di Spagna* (Turin: Società Editrice Torinese, 1941), 48; Lodoli, *Domani posso morire*, 70. See also Miguel Alonso, 'Camicie Nere, Camisas Azules: una propuesta interpretativa del fascismo español a través de un estudio comparado con el caso italiano', communication presented to the *XII Congresso Internazionale di studi storici di Spagna contemporanea: le culture politiche in Spagna e in Italia secoli XIX e XX: un approcio comparato*, 2012; and, by the same author, '"Cruzados de la civilización Cristiana": algunos apuntes en torno a la relación entre fascismo y religión', *Rúbrica Contemporánea* 3, no. 5 (2014): 133–154.

50 Licio Gelli, *'Fuoco!' Cronache legionarie della insurrezione antibolchevica di Spagna* (N.p.: Pistoia, 1940), 13 and 32.

51 Enrico Santoni, *Ali di giovinezza, ali di Vittorio: come visse e morì Vittorio Ceccherelli, medaglio d'oro; con prefazione di Giuseppe Valli* (Florence: Vallechi, 1939).

52 *El Legionario*, no. 6, 17 April 1937.

53 Odetti, *Trenta mesi nel Tercio*, 19–20.

54 Lodoli, *Domani posso morire*, 152.

55 De Lorenzi, *Teruel-Malaga*, 159.

56 Lajolo, *Bocche di donne*, 49–50.

57 Mosca, *Camicie nere*, 16.

58 Both articles appeared in 1938 in *Il Popolo d'Italia*, quoted by Luisa Passerini, *Mussolini imaginario. Storia di una biografia 1915–1939* (Rome/Bari: Laterza, 1991), 163.

59 Quoted in Álvaro Lozano, *Mussolini y el fascismo italiano* (Madrid: Marcial Pons, 2012), 347.

60 Alessandra Tarquini, *Storia della cultura fascista* (Bologna: Il Mulino, 2011), 134–135; Gabriele Turi, *Lo Stato educatore. Politica e intellettuali nell'Italia fascista* (Rome/Bari: Laterza, 2002), 216ff. See also Pier Giorgio Zunino, *L'ideologia del fascismo. Miti, credeze i valori nella stabilizzazione del regime* (Bologna: Il Mulino, 1995); and Simonnetta Falasca-Zamponi, *Fascist Spectacle: The Aesthetics of Power in Mussolini's Italy* (Berkeley: University of California Press, 1997).

61 ASMAE, US, b1.

62 Lajolo, *Il 'voltagabbana'*, 150.

166 *Identity, combat, rearguard*

63 Nuto Revelli, *La strada del davai* (Turin: Einaudi, 2010), quoted in David Alegre, '"Scaricare tutta la mia rabbia": codificación, supervivencia y fascismo en el relato de los italianos y españoles en el frente del Este (1941–1943)', communication presented to the *XII Congresso Internazionale di studi storici di Spagna*, 2012.

64 ACS, MI, PolPol, SPD, CR, b71, F4.

65 Alfonso Pellicciari, *Arriba España* (Turin: Studio Editoriale Torinese, 1938), 65.

66 Lodoli, *Domani posso morire*, 90.

67 Annibale Bergonzoli, prologue to Lajolo, *Bocche di donne*, XI-XII.

68 Lodoli, *Domani posso morire*, 107.

69 Aldo Santamaria, *Operazione, 1936–1939* (Rome: G. Volpe, 1965), 79, 85, and 97.

70 De Lorenzi, *Teruel-Malaga*, 131.

71 Piazzoni, *Le Frecce Nere*, 189.

72 Lodoli, *Domani posso morire*, 23.

73 Mosca, *Camicie nere*, 92.

74 Alma Giola, *Voci di legionari feriti. Documento storico della crociata fascista in terra di Spagna* (Como: Cavalleri, 1941), passim.

75 Odetti, *Trenta mesi nel Tercio*, 202.

76 Lajolo, *Bocche di donne*, 201.

77 Mimmo Franzinelli, *Stellete, croce e fascio littorio: l'assistenza religiosa a militari, balilla e camicie nere 1919–1939* (Milan: Franco Angeli, 1995), 263ff.

78 Lodoli, *Domani posso morire*, 38.

79 Franzinelli, *Stellette, croce e fascio littorio*, 266.

80 AGMAV, CGG, A36, L1, C1.

81 ASMAE, US, b2.

82 Behind the lines, in the plural—as Paola Lo Cascio reminds us, the Italian rearguard was a far-off one, in which mobilisation for and opinion about the Spanish war were part of everyday political life. Lo Cascio, 'La retaguardia italiana'. As she rightly points out, no good study exists on the justification of Italian military and political commitment in Spain directed at public opinion. The only exceptions are Alberto Acquarone, 'La guerra di Spagna e l'opinione pubblica italiana', *Il cannochiale*, nos. 4–6 (1966); and Luciano Casali, *L'opinione pubblica italiana e la guerra civile spagnola* (Madrid: Taravilla, 1984).

83 Vaquero, *Credere, Obbedire, Combattere*, 124ff.

84 Carlos Gil Andrés, *Lejos del frente: la guerra civil en la Rioja Alta* (Barcelona: Crítica, 2006), 337ff.

85 Silvano Bernardis, *Fino a Madrid. Diario della guerra di Spagna* (Gorizia: L. Luchesi, 1941), cited in Xosé Manoel Núñez Seixas, *¡Fuera el invasor! Nacionalismos y movilización bélica durante la guerra civil española (1936–1939)* (Madrid: Marcial Pons, 2006).

86 ASMAE, GAB, b472.

87 USSME, F7, b1.

88 Quoted in James W. Cortada, ed., *La guerra moderna en España: informes del ejército de Estados Unidos sobre la Guerra Civil, 1936–1939* (Barcelona: RBA, 2014), 191–192. On the other hand, regarding prisoners captured by the CTV and held at the base at Almazán, see AGMAV, C2604, 24.

89 Giorgio Rochat, *Le guerre italiane 1935–1943; dall'impero d'Etiopia alla disfatta* (Turin: Einaudi, 2005), 115.

90 USSME, F8, 336.

91 ASMAE, GAB, f792.

92 AGMAV, CGG, A2, L145, C65.

93 AMAE, AB, L1459, E9.

94 AGMAV, CGG, A2, L147, C68.

95 USSME, F18, b2.

96 Lajolo, *Il 'voltagabbana'*, 102.

97 AGMAV, CGG, A 16, L35, C14.

98 ASMAE, US, b10.
99 ACS, MinCulPop, Gab, b75. Queipo de Llano purportedly explained to him that day why he felt more admiration for Mussolini than for Hitler: 'because I understand him more'.
100 USSME, F6, b335.
101 ASMAE, US, b2, ACS, SPD, b44; USSME, F18, b2. For Farinacci's report to the Fascist Grand Council and notes of his meetings with political figures in Spain, see ASMAE, US, b1.
102 ACS, MinCulPop, GAB, b75.
103 Ibid.
104 Bonezzi, *Il diario del nonno fascista*, 9.
105 José Luis Alcofar Nassaes [José Luis Infiesta], *CTV: los legionarios italianos en la Guerra Civil Española 1936–1939* (Barcelona: Dopesa, 1972), 186.
106 ASMAE, US, b29.
107 Vaquero, *Credere, Obbedire, Combattere*, 122.
108 For a selection of these leaflets, see Nicola della Volpe, *Esercito e propaganda fra le due guerre (1919–1939)* (Rome: Stato Maggiore dell'Esercito, 1992).
109 Núñez Seixas, *¡Fuera el invasor!*, 267ff., with reference to José María Pemán, *Poesía de la bestia y el angel* (Madrid: Ediciones Españolas, 1939) and the homage to Italy of 27 May 1938 in Oviedo.
110 ASMAE, US, b25.
111 ASMAE, US, b51.
112 Gil Andrés, *Lejos del frente*, 336ff.
113 Renzo Lodoli, *I Legionari: Spagna 1936–1939* (Rome: Ciarrapico Editore, 1989), 221–224.
114 Silvio Leoni's diary in Ranzato, Zadra, and Zendri, *In Spagna*, 67–71.
115 For general context, see Barbara Spackman, *Fascist Virilities: Rhetoric, Ideology, and Social Fantasy in Italy* (Minneapolis: University of Minnesota Press, 1996). For the opposite side, see Victoria De Grazia, *How Fascism Ruled Women: Italy, 1920–1945* (Berkeley: University of California Press, 1992).
116 Cordedda, *Guerra di Spagna*, 44.
117 Bonezzi, *Il diario del nonno fascista*, 5.
118 Lajolo, *Bocche di donne*, 18, 66, 144.
119 Lodoli, *Domani posso morire*, 208 and 215; republished as *I Legionari*, 190.
120 Vaquero, *Credere, Obbedire, Combattere*, 124ff.
121 ASMAE, US, b5. In 1937 there were 13 active courses, in which some 1,000 Spanish officers were trained: 'it was about asserting and disseminating Italian military thinking, making [the Spanish] appreciate the war materiel and disseminating it', according to the director Colonel Emilio Bartisti. ASMAE, US, b67.
122 ASMAE, GAB, f792.
123 ASMAE, GAB, b472.
124 ASMAE, US, b10.
125 I have written on this subject in 'Violencia y fascistización en España sublevada', in *España en la crisis de entreguerras: república, fascismo y guerra civil*, ed. Francisco Morente (Madrid: Los Libros de la Catarata, 2012), 79–95; and in 'A este lado del bisturí: guerra, fascistización y cultura falangista', in *Falange: las culturas políticas del fascismo en la España de Franco (1936–1975)*, ed. Miguel Ángel Ruiz Carnicer (Zaragoza: Institución Fernando el Católico, 2013), 143–167. See the literature cited in both. For bibliography on this subject for cases such as those of Italy, Germany, Romania, and Croatia, see Daniel Woodley, *Fascism and Political Theory: Critical Perspectives on Fascist Ideology* (London: Routledge, 2009). Since then, the key study which has tackled the dimension of discourse and violent praxis in fascism has been Ferran Gallego, *El Evangelio fascista: la formación de la cultura política del franquismo (1930–1950)* (Barcelona: Crítica, 2014), in particular

168 *Identity, combat, rearguard*

443ff. I have tried to provide further ideas in *Políticas de la violencia: Europa siglo XX*, ed. Javier Rodrigo (Zaragoza: Prensas Universitarias de Zaragoza, 2014).

126 ACS, MinCulPop, GAB, b75. 'Fernando Poo' was the name given to the island of Bioko in Equatorial Guinea during the Spanish colonial period.

127 ASMAE, US, b10.

128 USSME, F18, 4.

129 De Lorenzi, *Teruel-Málaga*, 133.

130 Sandro Attanasio, *Gli Italiani e la guerra di Spagna* (Milan: Mursia, 1974), 257.

131 Ibid., 129, for Attanasio's account of the shooting of snipers at Trijuerque.

5 A European war in Spain, 1938–1939

'It means that we will make war against France on the soil of Spain.'

Galeazzo Ciano, 5 January 1939, referring to the news of a possible French intervention across the Pyrenees

The Italian troops' honour, their bravery, their spirit of sacrifice, and all their virtues had been handed over to the incompetence of the Spanish command. That was how Ettore Muti, pilot and consul general of the *Milizia*, summarised the CTV's activity to Ciano in 1937. Muti was the 'typical exponent of the fierce *squadrismo*' of Romagna and of the 'heroic volunteerism' of those who could not miss the fight in Spain 'for the anti-Bolshevik crusade'. Commander of the aerial patrol that arrived in Spain on 28 July 1936 to help the insurgent army deal with the crisis, his voice was of good repute and prestigious. He had fought in the air and on land from the start of the conflict. He was responsible for the attack on the Republican cruiser *Miguel de Cervantes*, which was blocking access to Sevilla via the river Guadalquivir. He put pressure on the enemy in the battle of Oviedo in October 1936 using the *National* side's sole aerial formation, under his command, and similarly at Córdoba, Badajoz, Mérida, and Madrid, 'achieving the *Aviazione Legionaria*'s mastery over Spain's skies'. He was subsequently in action at Talavera de la Reina, Maqueda, Toledo, and Valverde before arriving at the gates of Madrid, where he fought as a soldier in the *Tercio de Extranjeros*. Then, as an aviator, he flew over Málaga, Guadalajara, Brunete, Santander, Bilbao, Gijón, Belchite, Teruel, the Ebro, Tortosa, the Valencian coast, Catalonia, and Madrid. More than 1,000 flying hours in hundreds of military operations and his work liaising between the air force and the CTV made Muti one of the most valued non-diplomatic advisers to Ciano and Mussolini.[1]

And Muti was not one to bite his tongue. 'Wherever our men have fought, we have always advanced', he said, referring to Guadalajara, Bilbao, Santander, Málaga, and rectifying the front at Zuera. Where they had not, there had been losses, at Belchite, Brunete, Jaca, and Teruel. Detached from reality, Franco, 'the writer, the politician, the strategist, the statesman, the Christ-like figure (*ecce homo*)', did not realise that 'if he breathes, he owes it

170   *A European war in Spain, 1938–1939*

exclusively to the oxygen given to him by the Duce'. 'He promises, he promises . . . and does what he likes. And I don't think that Berti, with a relatively small force, will be able to assert his authority.' In those circumstances, he went on, it was necessary to intervene to either reinforce the CTV or to create a mixed command, or else the best thing was to leave Spain, 'abandoning the materiel and . . . with happy memories'.[2] But they did not leave Spain, nor did they impose a mixed command. And whether they left with happy memories is debateable. The CTV did not go home from Spain until the very end of the Civil War. Too many things forced them to stay, one of which was the international situation.

That the conflict was a European war on Spanish soil was said as early as December 1936 by Commander Carlo Margottini, one of Bonaccorsi's defenders in the Balearic Islands.[3] The presence of not only interests but vessels and crew from France, Italy, and Great Britain in the Balearics could certainly have led any well-informed observer to that conclusion. Nevertheless, this dimension became clearer still following Mussolini and Ciano's meeting with Ribbentrop in November 1937 and, above all, during the course of 1938. From that year until the end of the war, the CTV underwent a major readjustment, in large measure prompted by the climate of tension in Europe which would end up being the prologue to the Second World War. It was a changing situation that evolved with Anthony Eden's resignation as British foreign minister on 20 February, replaced by Lord Halifax, which, in the Duce's opinion, created an atmosphere which would favour a victory by the *National* side. As he telegrammed General Mario Berti, fortune 'was once again on Franco's side'. The increasingly blatant policy of appeasement and non-intervention in the face of German expansionism in Austria and Czechoslovakia provided the context for the open and unabashed maintenance of voluntary troops in Spain, fighting de facto as representatives of foreign belligerent countries. Ultimately, the Anschluss, the occupation of the Sudetenland, and the Munich Pact completed the foreshadowing of the conditions for large-scale war in September of the following year. Mussolini's Italy, fervently determined to help Franco, was not absent from the preparation of the European war. In such circumstances, it was fundamental to keep up the impression that Italian force wanted to project in Europe. Therefore, it was 'necessary to accelerate the pace of the war and not to believe in winning solely by diplomatic recognition'.[4]

One of principal theatres of this continent on the edge of conflagration was not only the Spanish war per se but, above all, its dimension as a European war between the de facto belligerent fascist powers and the anti-fascist powers. No longer paying lip service to the Non-Intervention Agreement, and with Fascist Italy out of the League of Nations from December 1937, participation in Spain in 1938 and 1939 was open and uninhibited. It was a time when Mussolini was able to continue pressurising Franco with the stipulation that 'we fight or we go home' and the extremely fraught international situation prevented further international efforts, which, consequently, made the existing Italian assistance even more decisive. Franco would continue to reject large-scale offensives while he waited to carry out the 'cleansing of the environment, under the strange illusion he could make all those who might be his enemies after his success disappear'. But, following the battle of Teruel, according to the Duce, 'withdrawing the Italian flag' was no longer an option. That would be like losing everything, all the efforts exerted in a year and a half of intense fighting at the side of the true Spain.[5]

Without inhibitions

The CTV went through a new phase of changes following the campaign in the North. After Santander, due to casualties, the three Italian divisions were reduced to two, the *Littorio* and the *XXX Marzo*, joined in the winter by the *Frecce* Mixed Division. The latter was made up of the *Frecce Azzurre* brigades, which had basically remained at the Extremadura front, and the *Frecce Nere*, which had fought at Madrid and in the North (Bilbao and Santander). The *Frecce Nere* stayed and fought at the Zuera line, but a little more that year. Franco decided to use the Italians fundamentally as a reserve force, and the CTV spent the rest of 1937 in that position. In September, the Italian military command presented a proposal to Franco's general headquarters to undertake operations against Aragon, now that the Asturian front was coming to a close. The Italians were ready to intervene there, but the front fell on 22 October without the CTV taking part. On 10 December, Berti, in command of the CTV since October, announced imminent action against Guadalajara, which was eventually scrapped because of the Republican attack on Teruel, where a substantial role was played by the Italian artillery. It was surely the urgency arising from the demoralised state of the troops that led Mussolini to authorise him to announce that it would be the last action involving the CTV, apart from the air arm based in the Balearics.[6] As we know, it was far from the last Italian battle in Spain.

As stated in an internal CTV report, probably written by its commander, time favoured an enemy of equal strength, against whom Franco proposed an 'oriental' model of war, which lacked the haste and the military concepts that were familiar to the Italians (mass, economy of forces, reserves, etc.).[7] In fact, Berti saw a long war ahead, which could only be clearly decided, thanks to the Italian contribution of Alpine forces specialised in winter fighting. In any case, there were already many who thought that providing unconditional material support and exiting the war were perhaps preferable, despite the fact that now (during the battle of Teruel) was not the best time. It was Mussolini who was not in agreement with this thinking.

Once the 'Italian lions' in Santander had finally erased the disgrace of Guadalajara, many thought that they had earned the right to return to Italy as heroes. The Italians had been temporarily placed in the reserve in Miranda del Ebro (*Fiamme Nere*), Haro (*XXIII Marzo*), Logroño (*Littorio*), and Zaragoza (*Frecce*), and the officers and many soldiers believed the Corps would be

172 *A European war in Spain, 1938–1939*

withdrawn.[8] They had been fighting for a year and a half, and the majority for at least eight months. Many had thought that they were enlisting for a short and straightforward campaign lasting three months, without much danger and with economic advantages. Some were older men and they had families, as the commander-in-chief pointed out. And they had been told that, following a major victory, those who wanted to would return home.

Thus, many combatants believed that the end of their Spanish adventure was in sight, even in spite of the command's threats. To Mussolini's offer to repatriate part of the CTV because of tiredness, General Enrico Francisci purportedly replied that none of his legionnaires wanted to return to Italy. He is said to have subsequently approached them, one by one, to ask them, at the same time threatening them that anyone who went back to Italy would never again be able to hold his head high, would have his PNF membership card ordered taken away, and would never again find work. However, his attitude was an isolated one. In fact, the Duce had been asked by the party that, in order to honour the heroes and the fallen, the war in Spain be considered an official campaign that would grant combatants access to military and civil rights and advantages once it was over. Furthermore, commemorative medals should be struck; fighters should earn the right to join the PNF; participation should entail a specific distinction, like that held by the volunteers of the Great War; combatants should be given war crosses; and officers should be able to earn merits for promotion for military merit. These were requests which precede a withdrawal, in every sense. In this situation, which many interpreted as being final, Spain's request for the despatch of a reserve reinforcement of 4,500 soldiers was 'like a cold shower'. For Mussolini, it did not make sense to send forces while repatriation was being discussed, but he decided both matters in parallel. Accordingly, he supported the plan to create two divisions made up entirely of legionnaires (*Littorio* and *Fiamme Nere-XXIII Marzo*), plus the *Frecce* as a mixed division, leaving the artillery, engineers, and vehicles at the orders of Franco's armies. The divisions would be reinforced by a newly assembled contingent, and all who put in a request would be repatriated. A smaller but stronger army was preferable to one that was bigger but demoralised, uninterested in fighting, and reluctant to follow orders.

Indeed, the command spoke of 4,500 men as reinforcements, but what was actually approved at the end of August 1937 was greater: 2,000 soldiers, 1,000 artillerymen, and 1,000 engineers from the Army with 100 officers, plus 6,000 soldiers of the MSVN with 200 officers. They were mobilised to depart on 8 September. However, the despatch was delayed for political reasons linked to threats against Italy for sending new volunteers, following the apparent rapprochement with the French government in Nyon Pact of 14 September to curb attacks on shipping in the Mediterranean.[9] The British Intelligence Service had detected Italian engineers and reserves being sent to Spain at the end of September and beginning of October. It was the time of the first British and French plan for the withdrawal of volunteers. It did

A European war in Spain, 1938–1939   173

not come to fruition because the Italian government always made it a condition that the Soviets leave Spain and belligerency rights be conceded to the two parties to the conflict, rights that were not recognised by the insurgents. Franco made it known that he would accept a withdrawal of volunteers, on condition that it be proportional on both sides in quantity and quality, that it not include the Moroccans, that volunteers not be identified by language or passport (easy to falsify), and that the Pyrenees be closed off. The Italian government put forward the same conditions, as it was practically the Spanish rebels' unofficial spokesman in the field of international policy.

Mussolini, Ciano, and Ribbentrop discussed these issues at their meeting on 6 November 1937. There, Mussolini declared that he had no intention of sending fresh troops to Spain 'except in unexpected circumstances', given that Franco already had victory in hand, thanks to the effective naval blockade and the demoralisation of the Republican rearguard, among other factors, and therefore would not need them. As he would demonstrate some years later, Mussolini was a dreadful analyst of the immediate future of the wars that he embarked on, and he almost always saw victory around the corner. For that reason, he wrongly contended that there would be no more troop despatches. Moreover, in this instance, his way of thinking made him suspicious about British diplomacy's rapprochement with Franco's circle. It was essential that Spain, now that it had been 'saved' thanks to German and Italian help, stay 'closely bound to our game . . . only if Spain remains in our system will we be able to count on getting all of our money back'. 'We want to be and must be paid', he declared. Hence, collaboration between Germany and Italy had to lead to Franco always following 'our policy' and

> our political system, because, in the first place, our joint pressure will prevent him from distancing himself, and also because, despite his ideology being close to ours, he has taken a path that he will not be allowed to step back from.[10]

As Berti wrote to Lieutenant Colonel Nulli of the Ministry of Foreign Affairs, it did not make much sense for Franco to ask for the repatriation of 5,000 volunteers for 'political' reasons, given how directly dependent he was on the Axis's political, diplomatic, and military support. In his opinion, it was inevitably something to do with a détente in relations with the United Kingdom. Nevertheless, in his opinion, if 'the three of us, Italy, Spain, and Germany, make the war, the three of us also ought to make Spanish foreign policy'. Thus, in the CTV commander's opinion, Franco's decisions ought to pass through a political filter that was consistent with the fascist powers' involvement on his side, in the same way Mussolini was constantly demanding a single military command of the three powers. As the Italian ambassador in Berlin, Bernardo Attolico, indicated after talking to Field Marshal Werner von Blomberg, Goering agreed to follow a common line marked by the Duce and Ciano of respecting the *Generalísimo*'s supreme command but

174 *A European war in Spain, 1938–1939*

strengthening the weight of the two military representatives in Spain, Berti and General Hellmuth Volkmann, whose words—it would have to be made clear to Franco—would be 'those of the Duce and Hitler'.[11]

All in all, these points underline the European dimension of the Spanish war at a time when no combatant was ready to retreat from its military undertaking, nor from the projection of its military power. In particular, to ask for the return to Italy of such a large group of soldiers would mean, in Berti's opinion, the de facto reduction of Italy's intervention to insignificance. The *real* Italian combatants would have been reduced to some 10,000, he calculated, with the artillery and the air force, which would, to a large extent, make maintaining assistance to Nationalist Spain difficult. 'Great things cannot be done this way', he said. Berti had doubts about the effectiveness of a reduced CTV, and he was worried that the winter would force operations to be suspended. He therefore asked for the training of the Italian troops to be accelerated. Their obligation, he stated, was 'to maintain or enhance' the Italian nation 'in terms of success and reputation'.[12]

The situation had, in fact, varied notably since early 1937, when the Italians arrived in Spain 'to increase the prestige of our arms' and 'for an ideal objective: the defeat of communism'. At that time, communism could 'consider itself weakened', and it would be more so, because in 'most Spanish people in Red Spain' it had 'the fiercest enemies of communism; they have been able to gauge all its horrors'. In November 1937, when 'the enemy army [had been] virtually defeated', the CTV's intervention was considered 'not indispensable and perhaps not even desired'. Given the problem that the Italians taking cities like Lleida and Barcelona might pose for the reconstruction of post-war Spain by the 'paladin of independent and imperialist Spain', the question had to be asked, according to Berti, 'whether the Spanish problem' ought to be returned to its political origins and, in sum, whether Italy ought not to act more greedily given its material and human sacrifices, in order 'to gain priority rights which the *Nationals* apparently want to deny us'.[13]

The truth of the matter is that there was an important political cause for the repatriations and the CTV's restructuring in 1938, an attempt to fulfil the requirements of Italian grandeur and, at the same time, respond to the complaints reaching Rome from the lips of soldiers, militiamen, and all manner of envoys on Spanish soil. It might be said that there was a double political motive. Firstly, it would serve as a bargaining chip in the international arena, always maintaining a complex balance, which made a withdrawal unthinkable; as Ciano pointed out, it would be a serious problem to give credit, before friends and enemies, to those who thought that Italy's military power had been exhausted. Secondly, it would serve as a mechanism for rearranging the internal balance between the Army and the Blackshirts, as with the first repatriation in April and May of 1937. We have the CTV's surveys from several months in 1938, and if we compare them to the figures for October 1937 (1,489 officers and 19,787 soldiers from the Army and 878 officers and 16,806 soldiers from the *Milizia*, making a total of 38,960 men including

A European war in Spain, 1938–1939 175

Table 5.1 Italian Army and *Milizia* troops in Spain, October 1937–October 1938

Month	Army	Difference	Milizia	Difference	TOTAL	Difference
Oct. 1937	21,276			17,684	38,960	
Jan. 1938	17,810	–3,466	14,655	–3,029	39,069	109
Apr. 1938	16,269	–1,541	12,963	–1,692	35,608	–3,461
May 1938	16,303	34	12,228	–735	34,837	–771
Sept. 1938	19,674	3,371	12,009	–219	39,250	4,413
Oct. 1938	15,161	–4,513	7,277	–4,732	28,687	–10,563

Source: Author's calculations, based on AMAE, US, b40.

service corps, air force, and so on) or, even more so, to the figures from January 1938 (17,810 men in the Army and 14,655 in the *Milizia*, making a total of 39,069), we can see that the adjustment was made principally to the Blackshirts—their numbers were reduced in a year by 10,407, while the soldiers of the Royal Army were reduced by 6,115 men in total. However, they would go on to increase in number in September 1938 within the context of the withdrawal of volunteers, which was clearly not an obstacle to maintaining the total of Italian forces in the war in Spain (see Table 5.1).

This information allows us to venture several ideas about the CTV's composition. The Blackshirts' initial contribution was enormous, because it was the contingent that was easiest to mobilise, despite its poor training in military tactics. This would be the principal reason why the majority were repatriated in 1938, and not the reason that was officially given, which was that the volunteers were being repatriated in compliance with international rules. Indeed, on paper at least, both the men of the *Milizia* and the soldiers of the regular Army were volunteers. However, whereas the former were withdrawn, the latter were replaced. The new restructuring of the CTV and the repatriation of soldiers led, accordingly, to the merger of the Blackshirts' divisions and to the greater weight given to the regular Army, in line with Franco's wishes. Despite these changes, the Italian troops' task was far from inconsequential. Nobody thought of it as a step backwards in terms of military and political importance. For instance, on 9 January 1938 and in the heat of the battle for Teruel, Mussolini insisted impatiently on quick and decisive Italian intervention by Berti. The CTV's operations, he said, must not be confined to minor objectives; rather, they must have a big impact and be coordinated with the different powers helping Franco. If the CTV was being restructured, it was not in order to train behind the lines but to bring greater glory to the nation.

In January, Brigadier General Gastone Gambara, the CTV's chief of staff and future commander-in-chief, presented a plan for rapid action by integrated units, in parallel with Ambassador Viola's report to Ciano, in which, among other matters, he summarised a conversation with Franco. The latter had explained that, since Santander, little use had been made of the CTV because the war had not required it; that he would understand the partial

176 *A European war in Spain, 1938–1939*

withdrawal of volunteers; that, although he foresaw an increase in his forces by calling up new conscription contingents who were undergoing training—about 40,000 men—they would not replace the brave volunteers; that he only wanted to use the CTV in operations guaranteed to succeed and satisfy Italian military prestige; that the death of Italians would pose a serious international problem, as well as being a waste if they were killed in operations of no distinction; that, in any case, they had been of major importance at Teruel because of their artillery; and that he held them in high regard as representing Fascist Italy's tangible support and solidarity. They were a precious reserve, of organic perfection and great firepower, which filled the rearguard with security and tranquillity. They were an unknown quantity for the enemy, a permanent cause of anxiety and bewilderment.[14]

But, despite these words, Franco wanted to keep the CTV for selective operations, so as to maintain pressure on the enemy and prevent them from achieving further successes like Teruel—which, in Mussolini's opinion, might have positive consequences to a certain extent, by putting an end to dangerous optimism and demonstrating that it was possible to fight in winter.[15] Therefore, the Duce ordered Berti, in a somewhat surly manner, to ask Franco to decide what he needed, and then they would consider what to do.[16] The last verb chosen by Mussolini was not by chance. The idea was exactly that, 'to do'. What Mussolini was seeking had a central objective—a Republican capital. It would be tactically difficult to take Barcelona because of its distance from the front, its fortifications, and the hostility of the local population. Valencia would not be so difficult, and Madrid, despite bringing with it considerable complications, was worth the effort because of its great moral significance for the Francoists, Republicans, and internationally. In early 1938, Mussolini wanted the war to end within a period of four months by means of an operation that would destroy the enemy. But Franco, as he said, always preferred smaller operations. Therefore, Mussolini wrote to Franco at the beginning of February, 'if it is your plan', meaning a large operation and the rapid destruction of the enemy, 'ask me for whatever I can do. If that is not the case, it is clear that the Italian legionnaires' presence must end, because it would have no further purpose.' To a message from Franco telling him of the arrival in Rome of his brother Nicolás to negotiate the purchase of the naval cruiser *Trento* and two destroyers, Mussolini replied on 2 February with another message 'from a friend who has given you and will continue to give you concrete proof of his friendship'. In his opinion, Franco should not count on a Republican collapse, because despondency had not spread behind the enemy's lines following the re-conquest of the Aragonese city and the fifth column would not emerge decisively before a big Francoist victory.[17] In this same period, Mussolini sent a telegram about Franco's good fortune which included the famous, concise phrase 'they either fight or come back'.

They did not come back, and then they fought. They had less of a footprint, but they stayed at the side of the *Nazionali*. Franco replied to Mussolini two weeks after receiving his message, thanking him for his concern about the war's long duration and stating that Teruel had confirmed his suspicion that he had to proceed firmly. A minor, local, and momentary victory on the periphery of the front would be enough to reduce faith in the final victory. Wars were won not only by conquests but also by avoiding unsuccessful offensives. Franco sought only to annihilate the enemy, destroying its army with a crushing victory. Accordingly, while he requested help in the form of armaments to boost the fire-power of his large units, he explicitly called for Mussolini to proceed cautiously with regard to using volunteers because of the complicated international situation. There could be no flaunting for the time being. In the future, it might be possible to highlight the international volunteers' importance, but now was the time to be 'very discreet'.[18]

Mussolini, as always, agreed with Franco and his perspective as a great soldier and politician and was convinced by his arguments. As Ciano had indicated, 'we have to win this war in Spain' and, he added, 'we have to do so quickly'.[19] This last remark was a personal opinion, but the first was what really counted. It was to support Franco unfailingly. Thus, after returning from Italy, Berti confirmed to Franco that the troops would stay in Spain and would fight if necessary. In March, a plan called 'Plan V' was ruled out. It would have meant supporting the occupation of Valencia by means of a massive seaborne landing—which would have been a major strategic innovation—and thus taking a major Republican city. Although he agreed to the Italian plan, Franco gave no orders for reconnaissance and did not seem inclined to consider the CTV's participation as urgent. Nevertheless, and despite all this, the Italians did fight, and not only in the rearguard nor as reserve troops. These were the months of the aerial bombings of Barcelona and the advance by land on Aragon and Catalonia. In March and April 1938, the CTV in its entirety took part in taking Aragon, occupying around 200 kilometres. In the words of Colonel Amilcare Farina, they were called on to fight and then keep quiet.

At the end of March, the commander of the *Frecce* wrote some heartfelt and revealing lines, in which he told his troops:

> Thank you! You are fulfilling your duty . . . your pride is to fight and die in silence, always on the path of glory . . . my four hundred and seven *Flechas Negras*. All sons of Spain and Italy, together.[20]

It does not appear to have been the best moment in internal relations, which brought about numerous complaints about how the Italian troops were treated and, more specifically, the treatment of those who belonged to the *Frecce*. Some of the replies were haughty and scornful towards the Spanish, as seen in the previous chapter. As Berti would acknowledge, most of the soldiers had asked to be repatriated. However, in his view, they had to understand that their action was necessary and that they were not mere attendants to the Spanish troops, who were 'slow, distrustful, haughty, ignorant of the ways of war, their leaders jealous of one other, and with no sense of cooperation'.[21]

178 *A European war in Spain, 1938–1939*

And, above all, they were suspicious of the Italian command. With 'good arms, indispensable for bringing the war to a quick end' and low morale 'from the company commander on down', any impatience was, nevertheless, useless. To prove the point, Berti gave the example of the capture of Alcañiz. The Aragonese town was bombed on 3 March by 15 Savoia aircraft of the *Aviazione Legionaria*, and then three fighters followed to strafe the population.[22] It was occupied by the CTV on 14 March. Following the appropriate military parades and accolades, the CTV was ready to continue forward on 16 March but had to wait for the Spanish until the 26th.

Indeed, this is one of the key issues to understanding Italian participation in the Spanish war, as well as the notable differences in approach and warfare between the Spanish and their Fascist allies. The question of bombing villages, towns, and civilians, as well as submarine warfare in the Mediterranean—11 vessels were sunk and four seized in August and September 1937 alone—undoubtedly influenced the evolution of Italian foreign policy. In fact, the bombings did not stop with the end of the war in the North. In late September 1937, the Italians had 476 aircraft in Spain, compared to the Spanish insurgents' 42 aircraft. Up to that date, they had sent 5,580 tons of bombs, including 47,000 bombs of 50 kilograms, 94,000 incendiary bombs, and 260,000 splinter bombs ('*spezzoni*').[23] Because of their proximity to the air base on the Balearics and even Italy (from where numerous attacks on Barcelona were launched), Italian planes prepared and accompanied the Francoists' territorial advances in Aragon and Catalonia with greater intensity—if that was even possible. The Italian bombing of Lleida on 2 November 1937 (which produced dozens of civilian victims, among them secondary school pupils), of Barbastro on 4 November, and of Aragonese towns like Bujaraloz, Caspe, and Alcañiz marked the end of a year of intense destruction launched from the air, leading to another, 1938, during which the *Aviazione* carried out the largest number of attacks, increasingly centred on the non-combatant population. Its mission consisted of 'terrorizing the Red rear guards, and especially urban centres'.[24]

Practically all the major cities on the Catalonian and Valencian coast were bombed constantly and repeatedly by combined formations of the Italian air force and the German Condor Legion during these months. For instance, Tarragona and Reus were bombed more than 15 times, as were cities like Gavà, Badalona, and Mataró. Likewise, the *Aviazione* was fully engaged, from its base at Logroño, in the preparation of the campaigns to occupy Aragon (Alcañiz, Sariñena, Fraga, Monzón) and Catalonia's interior. At all events, few had as many repercussions as the air strikes on Barcelona.[25] Barcelona was subjected to a terror campaign from the air, beginning with the bombing on New Year's Day carried out by General Giuseppe Valle himself. The general's mission, ordered by Mussolini and which Ciano was not informed about in advance, had a double objective, as he himself would write—firstly, to provide tangible evidence that Italian planes could carry out missions of more than 1,000 kilometres carrying a bombload of a ton, and secondly, to 'deliver New Year's greetings to all the Reds gathered in Barcelona to meditate on the defeat at Teruel'.[26] With his S-79 aircraft loaded with 850 kilograms of bombs and with total radio silence, the dropping of the bombs from 3,000 metres (5,000 when the searchlights were turned on) took the city's defences by surprise. In his opinion, the anti-aircraft gunners must 'have been celebrating New Year's Eve'. In the epilogue of his revolting report, Valle felt obliged to thank the Duce for the 'great honour' of having been chosen for the mission and having shown 'with genuine pride' that, 19 years after his last bombing, his physical efficiency and experience acquired in war were still intact and now in the hands of Fascist Italy's fate.

This terror campaign reached its apex with the raids of 30 January and, above all, of 16–18 March. For up to eight days in January, Italian planes dropped their bombs on the port and city centre, destroying air raid shelters like the church of St. Philip Neri. Ciano confessed in his diary that he had never read such a terrifying document as the report on the bombings in January, despite them being carried out, he said, by only nine S-79s and each raid lasting one and a half minutes. It is worth repeating his impressions: '500 dead, 1,500 injured. A good lesson for the future', because it provided proof of the uselessness of anti-aircraft forces and air-raid shelters. The 'only way of escaping the aerial attacks was to evacuate the cities'. On 16 March, the *Aviazione* received a direct order from Mussolini 'to begin, starting tonight' a 'violent action over Barcelona' in the form of a 'hammering staggered in time'—up to 13 flights organised in such a way that, in the time that they were in progress, there would be no interruption in bombs falling on the city centre nor in sirens sounding. The bombings of Barcelona were a practical demonstration of the degree of autonomy from the Francoist command enjoyed by the *Aviazione Legionaria*. In the judgement of the scholars who have analysed these bombings, they were deliberate attacks on the civilian population. Air strikes were also carried out throughout 1938 on munitions and weapons factories, ports, airfields, and fuel depots, but none of these types of facilities were located in the centre of the Catalan capital.

The British ambassador in Rome even suggested to Ciano that, if Italian planes were proved to have taken part in the bombings of Barcelona, both the French and the British would intervene to defend the city and its port. Ciano's reply oozed arrant hypocrisy, in my view. He claimed that the conduct of the war was Franco's responsibility alone.[27] It should be remembered that the *Aviazione Legionaria*'s command was directly responsible to the government in Rome; the decision-making chain did not even go through the CTV's command. The air raids on Barcelona, like those on Alcañiz, Granollers, and Alacant, and later Sitges and Torrevieja, did not discriminate between military and civilian objectives and were intended to terrorise the non-combatant population and, by their random nature, diminish the will to resist. This is not only my conclusion. It was that of the committee to investigate the bombings, which was set up in Toulouse at the request of the Republican government. It investigated at least six raids on Alacant, the raids on Barcelona

180   *A European war in Spain, 1938–1939*

in August 1938, and several others along the eastern Mediterranean coast in 1939. In the committee's reports, the retired RAF Captain R. Smyth-Piggott and Commander F. B. Lejeune analysed the distance between the explosions and the supposed targets (ports, railway stations) and the non-existence of large armaments or war materiel factories in any of the places investigated.[28] They were deliberate attacks on civilian areas. The committee did not have access to the reports of the Francoist authorities nor to the orders received by the pilots for any of its investigations.

Moreover, the attacks aimed to prepare the ground for the subsequent land occupation, in support, precisely, of the CTV's troops. I have not found any specific order in this regard, but it seems a reasonable conclusion, judging by the places which suffered the severest bombings. It was not by chance that the *Aviazione Legionaria*'s operations focused on the areas where the *Frecce Nere* were in action. In fact, while the *Azzurre*, reinforced by the Corps' artillery, remained in the area of the lower Ebro, the *Nere* were in action between the Maestrazgo and the Mediterranean. It would be the reinforced and active Italo-Spanish troops who occupied Tortosa on 19 April, dividing the Republican territory into two. And it was their advance that was made easier by the bombings carried out from the air bases in Logrõno and the Balearics. The intense bombing of Tortosa, for example, broke defensive communications and the Republican Army's escape lines, which expedited the town's capture four days later. It was the *Aviazione*, under orders from Rome, which cleared the path for the *Frecce* to be the conquering troops, the troops that achieved great successes in battle, the troops that would not repeat the disaster of Guadalajara. 'We are peering out at the Mediterranean, liberated, at this part of the shore, from the barbarism of those who are anti-Christ and anti-Fatherland', as Piazzoni wrote in his order of the day. A symbolic cycle was ending, a cycle which had opened in the Bay of Biscay and was coming to a close on the coasts of the common sea, a symbol of brotherhood, he said, like the symbol of black arrows itself—Falangist arrows, black like the Fascist shirts.[29]

The possible withdrawal of the Italian volunteers was not without problems, planned as it was at a time when Mussolini was making a constant show of force against Republican Spain, thus forcing the favourable conditions which led to the Anglo-Italian agreements of 16 April 1938. Among the questions dealt with in the so-called Easter Pact (*Patti di Pasqua*), as part of the British policy of appeasing the fascist powers (and purportedly neutralising the relations between these powers), tactic recognition was given to the Italian Empire in East Africa, and it was agreed that the peace would be kept in the Mediterranean and that the volunteers would be withdrawn from Spain. The latter point would be effective as of October, once the USSR accepted the British plan.[30] In any case, these agreements did not signify the immediate end of hostilities, even if the British government appeared to believe it was very imminent. This belief was based on the Republic's weakness, as demonstrated at Teruel and augmented by the constant, pounding bombing of its territory, which continued throughout the year, primarily targeting cities which had

A European war in Spain, 1938–1939 181

already been struck repeatedly: Barcelona, Tarragona, Reus, Castelló, Valencia, Sagunt, Alacant. The marketplace in Alacant was bombed on 25 May, causing more than 300 deaths. Only a few days later, Savoia-Marchetti aircraft attacked Granollers, a city that was ill-prepared against bombing, leaving more than 220 victims on the ground.[31]

Thus, despite the threats and pacts, Italian troops were in action during the first half of July to the south of Teruel. And, far from being withdrawn, new reserves arrived in May (2,000 men), June (4,000), and July, when the previously planned 2,500 reservists landed in Cádiz, along with 1,500 new reservists. Although Ciano noted in his diary that they had been sent on the Duce's orders and had to be sent in small contingents wearing civilian clothes, some had been ready since December, when the Republican offensive at Teruel had forced the insurgents to request urgent military help from Italy and Mussolini had approved the creation of ten infantry reserve battalions and one Blackshirt battalion with 53 officers.[32] Between 13 and 24 July, they participated in their entirety in the attack on Valencia, which was suspended on the 25th because Republican troops crossed the Ebro, in the battle of which the whole of the Italian artillery and the tank section took part. While the *Littorio* Division was held in reserve in Castile, the *XXIII Marzo* remained initially in reserve and then, in September, was used in the counter-offensive in the Javalambre sector.

In any case, the fact that the troops remained in Spain and fought with more or less good fortune did not always serve as a counterweight to Fascist aspirations to attain great victories. With Italy out of the League of Nations and the international community fully assuming the country's de facto belligerence in Spain at its natural ally's side, such victories would bring international prestige on the battlefield to Italy, now largely dependent on its allegiance to German foreign policy. Mussolini accordingly exploited the moments that attracted the most attention to make his more or less veiled threats to withdraw his troops, as we have already seen in the context of Teruel. He did so again in the context of the Battle of the Ebro. First, in July, he warned that, given the complicated international situation, only small groups of specialists and reserves could be sent. Italian pressure on Franco only increased in August. On the 20th, Berti met Franco and laid out the three real options regarding the CTV's future, according to Mussolini. The CTV needed officers in order to 'carry out the decisive action' and soldiers for divisions not amounting to more than 5,000 men each—that is to say, half of those found in the Spanish divisions. The first option would be to send three divisions; the second to send 10,000 reservists (in other words, two to three complete divisions) to maintain their efficiency; and the third to withdraw the infantry, leaving tanks, the air force, and engineering, while increasing their quantity and quality. This last option was in fact the solution which the Duce considered preferable and 'more total' ('*totalitario*'), given the CTV troops' tiredness, as ascertained by Berti, and the complex international situation. Thus, at the same time as the Italian government confirmed its intention to give

182 *A European war in Spain, 1938–1939*

Franco unconditional support until total victory was achieved, it reproachfully told him that, in order to do so, it needed to know his concrete plans. As Ciano said, if Franco was decided on giving up foreign troops, he would have to send them off with full honours and not allow their withdrawal to be attributed to the Non-Intervention Committee's 'humiliating formalities'. In Berti's words, the news of a possible withdrawal made a 'deep impression' on Franco. When he found out, Mussolini wrote to his CTV commander that he was not trying to give Franco the impression that they were abandoning him at a time when things were not going well for him. 'My style is to stay by my comrade's side to the end.'[33]

For this reason, he proposed a reorganisation that would allow the *Littorio* and *XXIII Marzo* Divisions to be merged and part of the *Corpo*—the approximately 10,000 men who had been in Spain for more than a year and a half—to be repatriated.[34] Captain Agostino Uberti wrote very optimistically that, 'based on meetings with officers, it is clear that the mass of volunteers are motivated by the highest spirit', but that, 'nevertheless, some would like to return to Italy, believing their work to be finished'.[35] However, Ciano did not hide his concern about the situation of constant complaints by Italian legionnaires. According to Ettore Muti, they were people who 'have been fighting abroad for more than 22 months' without any encouragement 'from a country that only makes use of them, does not see their families and does not look after their own interests'. It was therefore 'humanly understandable that they felt the desire to return home'. This was all the more the case in circumstances such as the Ebro, in which the infantry did not take part in the fighting—in his view, because of past grudges—and aircraft and artillery were not put to full use, suffering from 'the ineptitude of the *Nationals* in conducing the war'. At Gandesa, Muti said, they wasted their resources for no tactical gain. And, in these conditions, 'the use of our units would represent a useless sacrifice of legionnaires and, what's more, the danger of having them involved in unsuccessful operations', to the point that Gambara asked for the resignation of the CTV's general staff during the Battle of the Ebro. 'The commander [Berti] is going through a period of little peace', Viola said, 'obsessed by a morbid sort of persecution that makes him see enemies everywhere, in Spain and in Rome'. He was 'icy and lugubrious', in Muti's words, and the soldiers no longer had confidence in him. The man to lead the CTV had to be Gambara.[36] However, none of this provided a real solution. In his opinion, the Spanish were waiting 'longingly for the nightmare of the Italian legionnaires' presence to end'.

Either Muti was a visionary or his opinion was very much taken into account in Ciano's ministry, because his proposals were implemented almost in their entirety. Or, more obviously, the European political context compelled decisive positions to be taken to enable support for Franco to be maintained. It was a changing context, in which the Axis's participation in the Spanish war represented an element of tension, perhaps not at the level of German territorial claims on Czechoslovakia but nonetheless of great importance, especially for bilateral relations. In view of the tenor of events in the summer of 1938, the British and French governments' threats to intervene on Spanish soil and, more specifically, the threat of a French invasion of Catalonia and Spanish Morocco were in fact real and verifiable. They were made immediately before the Munich Agreement and led to the request that Italy urgently send 50,000 rifles and 20 million cartridges to defend Spain's African colonial territory.

However, it was obvious, at least to Franco's Minister of Foreign Affairs, Francisco Gómez Jordana, that his side would be unable to withstand a French attack.[37] Therefore, to ward off such threats, he had to confirm that Spain might remain neutral in the event of a large-scale European conflict. However, the Spanish minister later maintained that this had been a malicious interpretation, a distortion by a French journalist. This possible neutrality greatly annoyed Germans and Italians. Ciano even wrote in this regard, 'How disgusting!' It was not surprising. For the Axis, confidence in future Spanish belligerence was not only a general political question but also a vital problem. Ciano wanted to have the most favourable strategic and military conditions in Spain 'with the maximum urgency', with an eye to a future global conflict. This was one of the reasons why Italian blood was being shed in Spain. When Jordana was finally able to speak to Ciano on 22 September, the latter told him that the possibility of a European war no longer existed and that the 'only solid alliance in Europe' was the Axis. Yet, following the 'incident of the declaration of neutrality', Franco's government sought much closer collaboration with Italian Fascism, made more attractive in comparison by Germany's expansionist behaviour and by the negative impact of *Kristallnacht*. The solution to the crisis thereby had the result of strengthening Italy's position relative to Germany's. This was the background to the Spanish missions to Italy—including the one led by Pilar Primo de Rivera—the Ministry of the Interior's request for collaboration to establish a national film industry, and, generally, the expectation of greater and more intense cultural exchange with Italy.[38] There was nothing like a crisis and the threat of a split to strengthen bilateral ties in the short term. In the long term, it is more difficult to locate this solidarity. It should not be forgotten that, when Fascist Italy was really in a tight spot in the Balkans, in Greece, and in Africa during the Second World War, it never had a single Spanish combatant at its side to return the loyalty demonstrated in the Civil War.

Nonetheless, the context of greater international pressure produced a clear response from the Italian government, in the form of the decision to withdraw some 10,000 volunteers from Spain. In preparation for the withdrawal, Jordana wrote a letter to Mussolini in which he praised his 'great talent and political experience'; underlined the dangers to Italy of Nationalist Spain being defeated in a potential war against France; requested the despatch of more arms because, had they had them, they could have won the war by then; and, lastly, portrayed the volunteers' withdrawal as 'a further victory to be added to the many that he achieved'. In fact, the French threats were key to the maintenance of Fascist support for Franco. The thinking was that, if it were lost, Spain would fall into 'Red' hands, creating another enemy for Mussolini's Italy.[39] Jordana had a different perspective from his government,

184 *A European war in Spain, 1938–1939*

however. In his assessment, it was crucial to present the volunteers' withdrawal as the outcome of an express Spanish desire and not as part of Italy's negotiations in Europe, so that the 'sacrifice not be exploited exclusively by Italy'.[40] This amounted to using the withdrawal as a bargaining chip for recognition as a belligerent and, with regard to their Italian allies, to exert moral pressure in order to avoid them keeping their weapons for a possible European conflict. Judging by the insistence evident in the military and political documents, this view was almost a dogma of faith. Nationalist Spain had the human resources to organise 25 divisions, to win the war, and to support Italy in the event of an international conflict, but it did not have anything with which to arm them. As we will see, and as is very well known, Spain's inadequacy in terms of armaments, the economy, and military infrastructure would be the reason given again and again to demand more and more assistance and to refuse to give assistance when demanded in return.

On 2 October, Mussolini and Ciano decided to inform the British ambassador, Lord Perth, of the withdrawal of the 10,000 Italian volunteers from Spain, although they reserved the option of increasing the contingent in the future. In his telegram of the same day—in which he explicitly mentioned, in the home for disabled veterans in Rome, the Casa Madre, the more than 1,000 men disabled in Africa and Spain[41]—the Duce ordered the CTV's command to proceed to return to the 10,000 legionnaires to Italy in four ships, according to the criterion of 'length of service in Spain'. It was evidently news known in advance, given that 2 October was the date chosen for the reciprocal celebration in Spain of Italo-Spanish solidarity, following the same event held in Italy on 29 May, with Millán Astray present as the highest-ranking Spanish official.[42] It was not a coincidence that, this time, the celebration consisted of awarding decorations to Spanish units and the CTV. In Franco's words, 'We present you with the love of a people and pay *National* Spain's homage to that Great Italy, to the Imperial Italy that preserves the purity of Immortal Rome's spiritual treasures.' Berti replied by saying that the honour given by Franco to the volunteers 'moves us and arouses feelings of the most intense recognition'. It was the day of brotherhood in arms between Italians and Spaniards in this 'war of Spanish independence', in which the legionnaires hurried to 'serve Spain and defend civilisation against barbarism', a 'great and holy' work for the triumph of 'peace with justice', of the family, the Fatherland, and God. In the CTV commander's concluding words, the struggle for an ideal 'does not require compensation'. The only thing they would take away with them would be the sincere affection of the Spanish.[43] Millán Astray referred to the 'admiration for our beloved Caudillo, Spain's saviour and the benefactor of Humanity, together with Mussolini and Hitler'. And, as a reminder for anyone who understood, the Legion's founder declared in his delirious speech that

> your dead remain here with ours forever, and the arms of the crippled, glorious Italian legionnaires shake hands with the Spanish forever. This

A European war in Spain, 1938–1939 185

glorious legacy of the ashes of your dead and the limbs of your men is the most precious root of the friendship of our peoples.

'They return to their Fatherland', according to the newspaper *Amanecer* of 15 October, 'those who came to fight for the unity, the greatness, and the liberty of ours', with the promise to 'preserve in the lands of the Mediterranean the eternal and immutable spirit of the fascist and national-syndicalist revolution. Italian volunteers fallen for the new civilisation, Present and Correct!' The embarkation of the 10,151 men (including 4,676 of the Army and 5,076 of the *Milizia*) took place from Cádiz on 16 October. Franco, who wanted to give the ceremony the 'greatest splendour',[44] asked Queipo de Llano by telegram to organise at least two music bands and between 10,500 and 11,000 baskets of ham, sweets, cakes, and wine. On the 18th, Franco wrote to Mussolini in gratitude for his help in freeing Spain from the communist invasion. The latter replied that Fascist Italy remained and would remain in the future always by his side until the victory of the new, strong, and heroic Spain, with which the new ties of shed blood united them.[45] On the 20th, the 'King-Emperor' Vittorio Emanuele III reviewed the repatriated men in Naples. On the 26th, 300 repatriated officers of the *Littorio* and *XXIII Marzo* divisions visited Mussolini at the Palazzo Venezia, and the Duce praised their courage in defending Franco's cause and European civilisation.[46] On the 29th, they were finally demobilised.

However, the war was not over. To deal with what remained of it, a reorganisation took place on 24 October 1938, by which the CTV's command was handed over to General Gastone Gambara. The basis of the Italian force would be the new Littorio Legionary Assault Division, but the operational bulk would lie with the Mixed *Frecce* Divisions (*Nere, Azzurre, Verdi*). To these would be added the groups of tankers, engineers, and training centres (central school and centre for further training). As Mussolini telegraphed Franco, the Fascist government remained 'firm in its intention to give him unconditional support until total victory is achieved'. And, once again, precisely for that reason, he wanted 'to know the plans so as to be able to take his own decisions accordingly. [Mussolini] also considers indispensable the creation of a mass of forces that can prevent possible Red initiatives which might paralyse current operations.'[47]

As is well known, the attrition entailed by the offensive and counter-offensive at the Ebro took a big toll on the Republic's People's Army, which, once it thought the battle finished, practically took the war to be lost. With the *Aviazione* and the Condor Legion clearing the path ahead and after receiving Mussolini's direct orders, the CTV played a very important role in occupying Catalonia. The powerful attack, with no protection on its flanks, lasted eight days, breaking the Lleida-Tarragona artery and surrounding Lieutenant Colonel Enrique Líster's defences as far as Igualada (a kind of new *guerra celere*), and might have made possible the fall of Barcelona and involved a drive that forced the Francoist command to take on more risks. It resulted in the taking

186   *A European war in Spain, 1938–1939*

of 16,500 of the 40,000 prisoners captured by the Army of the North. Entering Les Borges Blanques and Igualada on 23 January, the CTV was also in action at Terrassa and Sabadell and reached the north of Barcelona and Badalona on 25 January. According to its own estimate, the legionnaires occupied 151 towns and six cities apart from Barcelona and Tarragona, marching over 258 kilometres over terrain that was 'atrociously difficult' due to the enemy's destruction. Of the Army of the North's total casualties, 39 of the 70 officers who were killed, 200 of the 350 officers who were wounded, 316 of the 620 soldiers of the mixed brigades who were killed, and 2,000 of the 4,000 who were wounded were Italian.[48] Thus, it was not a minor campaign, despite the scant importance given to it by the historiography, in comparison with the treatment of Italy's entry into the war, Guadalajara, and Santander.

'Tell Franco that I am pleased by the brilliant carrying out of his Army's operations and I appreciate his decision that forces representing the CTV will enter Barcelona together with the *Nationals*', Mussolini wrote to Gambara on the 23rd.[49] Nevertheless, even before the CTV and the Francoist troops entered the city in a motorised column from Sant Andreu, Carlo Basile, inspector of the *Fasci Italiani all'Estero* (Italian Fascists Abroad), had already done so, according to his own account (of doubtful reliability) at three o'clock in the afternoon on 26 January. He had arrived from the north of the city, by car, along the deserted roads of the outskirts, accompanied by an Italian chauffeur and a Spanish lieutenant. People were fearful at first, said Basile, but soon began to shout Franco's name in a frenzy and, on recognising the Italian by his uniform, the Duce's. Hugged, swept along by the crowd, he made his way to the Casa de Italia, of which he took possession. He recorded the scene as a kind of collective delirium, greater even than that of Málaga and Bilbao, with women crying and men's eyes out of their sockets.[50] The 'liberation' of Barcelona marked a new chapter in the 'history of the New Europe that we are creating', Mussolini declared from his balcony of the Palazzo Venezia on the 26th, at about a quarter to eight in the evening. 'Franco's magnificent troops and our intrepid legionnaires have not only defeated Negrín's government. Many others among our enemies are biting the dust at this moment.' And he concluded, 'we have passed, and I tell you that we shall pass', in clear allusion to the anti-fascist slogan, 'They shall not pass.'[51]

Sacred testament

A clean uniform, with no dust or stains and particular attention to the buttons. Boots inked, helmets as well, no straps hanging down, socks of the same colour, black ties, no scarves, no decorations around the neck. Shaved, well-groomed, with leathers, pockets, and belts straight and at the waist level, the buckle on the left, and the bayonet at the hip, never on the stomach or the shoulder. In a formation of 28 lines of 18 men of uniform height, including officers, all in step. No equipment. The battalion commander, the only man marching outside the line. The most important thing was to give an

A European war in Spain, 1938–1939   187

impression of uniformity. The parade in Barcelona on 21 February, for which the above instructions were given, had 'to constitute a show of force, order, and beauty. The reasons that will spur numerous observers to fix their gaze on our formations are evident.'[52]

A military parade, above all one celebrating victory and liberation, is order, tidiness, and cleanliness, just the opposite of war. But it is a good representation of the concept that is intended to be shown of war: power, obedience, uniformity, beauty. And, indeed, there was no lack of reasons to look at the Italian soldiers with special attention in February 1939, and particularly in Barcelona. After all, they were part of the contingent responsible for the bombings suffered by the city, and practically the whole surrounding area, for months on end; which had just occupied Girona against the last Republican resistance in Catalonia; and which, since the withdrawal of volunteers in October, had been used in international political and diplomatic negotiations. Gambara asked the soldiers, used to marching under the sun, under fire from the air, and with the smell of sweat and excrement, to parade clean and tidy. Those who could not stay in step were not to parade, the straps over the chin were to be cut, and they were not to raise their arms too high when presenting their weapons to the authorities. In short, they were not to look ridiculous and were to project the pride of being fascists.

A few weeks earlier, the CTV had taken part in the last major operation in Catalonia, the occupation of the city of Girona, whose gates Gambara's troops reached at nine in the morning on 4 February, according to the account by the correspondent of *Il Popolo d'Italia*.[53] Having increased their speed with night operations the previous day, at 10.30 a.m. the order was given to enter the city centre. And at twenty to twelve, the legionary flag was waving above the town hall of a city full of 'buildings in flames, set alight by the Reds before fleeing', the smoke making a lovely umbrella, while the crowds 'applauded the liberating division'—a 'tremendous shout by thousands of voices salutes General Gambara' and the heroism of his troops. However, this did not appear to tally with the Spanish command's opinion, which was unsparing in its criticisms. According to an unsigned report (but perhaps in line with Dávila's opinion), the main features of the CTV's operation were carelessness and disengagement; the command's disobedience; the lowering of tone since Berti's departure; Gambara's immaturity, 'all heart and impulse'; and excessive casualties in proportion to the objectives achieved, despite some 'extremely favourable circumstances' which had prevented their 'lamentable incompetence' being revealed. The CTV, the report said, believed it was 'fighting its own battle when the battle was that of the Army of the North'.[54] Dávila and the Army of the North's command were said to be extremely dissatisfied with the performance, which the Italians sought to portray as heroic, victorious, unstoppable, and decisive for the fate of the war and of Spain. Even so, the way the war evolved would leave the question hanging as to who was right.

The Italian divisions, already small, were incorporated into the Army of the Centre before the final Francoist offensive after the occupation of Catalonia.

188   *A European war in Spain, 1938–1939*

Towards the end of the war the CTV represented a very small percentage of an army which, in April 1939 (the moment of its best military organisation, according to Gambara), comprised 14 call-up classes and three large armies (*Levante*, Centre, South) divided among 15 army corps, 54 infantry divisions, two cavalry, and five reserves, amounting, it was said, to a total of about a million men. However, as such, the Italian contingent remained relatively stable. The 28,362 men of January 1939 grew to the 29,882 of March and 33,772 when the war was drawing to a close, an increase of nearly 4,000 troops, placed exclusively in the Royal Army. The disproportion in relation to the *Milizia Volontaria* became increasingly obvious as the months passed, with the final result, in the war's last month, being 20,579 soldiers to just 6,145 Blackshirts, slightly over a third of the total.[55]

Even so, its qualitative importance did not diminish. During the so-called victory offensive, the Italians covered the distance from Toledo to Alacant via Madrid, Guadalajara, and Albacete, in four days. As for the *Aviazone Legionaria*, after the occupation of Catalonia, it basically covered the southeastern Mediterranean coast, from Valencia to Cartagena via Alacant and Gandia—which had the sad honour of being the last place to be bombed by Italian aircraft on 28 March 1939—and central Spain, flying over Madrid, Guadalajara, and Álcala de Henares. Beforehand, it had pounced on one of the few objectives that had resisted the insurgent army, the island of Menorca. The bombing of the island, which would take place on 8 February, began with the dropping of propaganda leaflets announcing a window of four days to surrender before being attacked. During those days, and without the CTV's command being notified, the Spanish air force commander Sartorious was entrusted with starting negotiations with 'the Reds of Mahón'. Faced with the possibility of being bombed, a rebellion at Ciutadella put it on the side of the Francoists on 7 February. But, even then, faced with the choice of attacking the island or not, the Italians decided to do so. Not only did they strafe the columns heading towards the insurrectionists in a kind of civil war within the island, but they also bombed Maó, contrary to the decision of the Francoist commander, Admiral Francisco Moreno, not to bomb the island, because the 'Reds' would surrender the following day. During the night, in fact, the 'Red criminals' retreated, and their commanders boarded the British naval vessel *HMS Devonshire*. In the minds of the Italian command, the island's surrender had been the result of its air force's intimidating action.

The war was reaching its end. Once again, as in the case of Barcelona, the fall of Madrid into the hands of the Francoist army came with a demonstration below the Duce's balcony. On 28 March, before the cheering coming from the square below, Mussolini hailed the defeat of Bolshevism. This was how the enemies of Italy and of fascism met their end, he said.[56] 'From the great and bloody effort will rise the Spain of tomorrow, free, united, strong', he declared in a telegram to Franco the following day.[57] For Ciano, it was a 'new and formidable victory for fascism, possibly the greatest so far'. As Gambara told his soldiers once Alacant was taken, 'It's finished. We have won, totally, definitively. . . . Legionnaires, embrace one another', because theirs was 'the embrace of two peoples, their union cemented by the blood spilt in common. Your embrace is an oath of indissoluble brotherhood.'[58] Once again, there was a military parade, firstly through Spain's capital, once the enemy had been definitively defeated—a defeat which, as Ciano would write in his diary, bore the name of Mussolini. Another parade was held on 11 May in a Logroño adorned for the occasion, with a mass celebrated on the Avenue of Espolón and Serrano Suñer's speech extolling the 'duty, performed in perpetuity, to maintain the dignity, the freedom' of Spain, of which the legionnaires were the bearers.

The decision to definitively withdraw the CTV on 31 May brought an end to the bulk of the military operations in Spain. The orders received by Gambara were to bring together all the Italians in the Littorio Division, after the parade in Madrid, with a view to carrying out their repatriation from Cádiz, while the few Italians remaining in the *Frecce* divisions would embark for Italy at Alacant.[59] Some 20,000 men (1,010 officers and 19,410 soldiers) were gathered in Cádiz and left for Naples on 1 June. In his farewell speech, Giménez Caballero (hated by Ambassador Viola, but who had given various talks for the CAUR and at the *Instituto Luce*'s film screenings, always behind the lines, of course) recalled, in an exposition very similar to Serrano Suñer's, that

> they came at the end of 1936, having heard Spain's cry of horror and desperation, its neck gripped by the slimy, murderous hands of the Marxist democracies. They went to Spain like a mother attends to the cry of a daughter in danger. This is how Rome has always been—and will be—in Spain's history: a *Mother*. Franco made the 'fourth filial call to Mother Rome', who came and 'gave her blood and brought us her standards . . . without asking anything of us. Without demanding anything of us. Leaving only to our gratitude as sons . . . the payment of so much love and unselfishness.[60]

On their arrival in Italy, they were received by the monarch, accompanied by Ciano. Mussolini was waiting in Rome, like a year before. His were the first words of welcome, which spoke of the victorious war against the democracies and Bolshevism, of the union sealed by blood between Italy and Spain, of the Italian sacrifices above which Franco's Spain was rising again, united, great, and free. And, he added, as a way of summarising their importance in the international arena, 'For 30 months you have been the pluto-democracies' nightmare—literally—and that should make you proud.'[61]

Travelling with them was Ramón Serrano Suñer, who was received by the Duce in the Palazzo Venezia on 7 June, in a kind of final closing of the Fascist intervention in Spain. In response to the toasts, Mussolini underlined the 'fraternal solidarity' between the two countries. They had felt from the beginning that there was a decisive test for Europe's destiny and its civilisation in the Spanish struggle. For that reason, they had not hesitated in giving their

190   *A European war in Spain, 1938–1939*

open support from the first day until the final victory, creating a brotherhood of blood, of arms, of spirits, and of willpowers. Serrano replied, as a way of delivering and closing the Italian adventure, 'we came to this great Nation which your genius has reincarnated as an Empire. Now all Italy's legionnaires are here.' However, they were not all in fact all there; nearly 4,000 'remain there together with many thousands of Spanish soldiers . . . their bodies buried, but not so their names, their spirit, and their memory, because you know well, Duce, that there is not enough soil on earth to cover them'. And it is worth pausing to consider the overarching explanation given by the minister, inasmuch as, according to him, and contrary to what historians have shown, the Italian intervention had been reactive and followed the arrival of volunteers to defend the Republic. When, one day, there 'descended in droves across the Pyrenees into Spain men of all races and countries' to fight against the true Spain, 'only then did the founding nation of Italy', one of the 'most decent and most humanitarian nations', alert to the sufferings caused by the Reds in their *Chekas* and in the streets, 'come to fulfil its duty to defend its own spiritual heritage and in generous solidarity with its sister nation on the other side of the Latin sea'.[62] We well know, and it has been demonstrated here, that, once again, Serrano was lying.

That friendship, unity, brotherhood of blood and the trenches, that trial by fire to which the Fascist leader and the no less fascist Spanish minister referred were to be what guaranteed Spain room to be strong in the new Europe being born. In a continent of armed peace, the victory by Francoist arms would guarantee the peace 'that allows us to be strong, not a peace that turns us into slaves'. It was a peace based on fascist friendship which, in General Alfredo Kindelán's words, would be confirmed at the fronts of a future European conflagration, with Spanish and Italian wings united in the continental skies.[63] (Kindelán also travelled to Italy, accompanying the legionary aviators, although there is much less information available about this trip.) It was, ultimately, a friendship which was also a political alignment from the moment when Spain announced its adherence to the Agreement against the Communist International of the protocol of 25 November 1936, or Anti-Comintern Pact. The announcement came on 8 April 1939, although the invitation and the Spanish government's decision dated from February; indeed, as early as November 1937, Franco, speaking for himself, had expressed his wish to Ambassador Viola to join soon.

For Jordana, it was a question of entry 'into the natural order of things'. Prior to the pact, Franco's Spain was engaged, it would seem, in the struggle against communism, a struggle 'of ideologies and moral concepts of universal value', with the commitment of the 'most valuable blood of its youth called to arms by Franco'. Stalin's butchers 'had invaded Spain's sacred soil via Democracy's frontiers, filling it with furrows of blood'. And faced with 'that friendship between democracy's paladins and the Kremlin's hordes', Spaniards, Germans, and Italians 'sealed with blood . . . a brotherhood of heroes'.[64] As Franco told Mussolini, Spain would always be 'the firmest bulwark against communism'.[65] This closeness would be confirmed by Ciano's visit to Spain in July. Judging by a note from the Spanish embassy in Rome dated 17 July, the visit had had an 'unprecedented reception' and had signified a 'genuine national plebiscite', reflecting how the masses 'take part in the programme of Hispano-Italian friendship'.[66] The newspapers published those days were indeed full of hyperbole and exaggeration, but they also offered very interesting explanatory details as to the nature of the 'Nationalist' victory and of its European allies. They were, it would be reported, much to Mussolini's liking.

A few examples can convey an idea of the importance given to the Duce's son-in-law's tour of Spain. 'May Count Ciano be welcome. His badges of blood are also those of intelligence, fearlessness, and sensitivity' (*Madrid*, 14 July); 'He deserves the gratitude of the whole of Spain rising to its feet as a man passes by who, day and night, . . . never lost sight of our enemies' movements . . . as a result of his intelligence, his youth, and his love of Spain, who, with virility, guarded our backs against the foreign stab' (*Arriba España*, Pamplona, 14 July); 'The whole of Seville will thrill today with the warmth of sacred brotherhood and union with Fascist Italy . . . in passionate homage to Italy, to the Duce, and to his minister Ciano' (*Fe*, Seville, 16 July); 'We do not know of any visit of such deep significance during the course of recent centuries . . . the most trusted and capable interpreter of the brilliant ideas conceived by Mussolini's titanic mind . . . arrives in Spain preceded by incorruptible heralds: the dead legionnaires' (*El Correo Español*, Bilbao, 11 July); 'A perfect Roman' (*Sur*, Málaga, 11 July); 'Remembrance . . . for the Italians who fell in our Fatherland, to which they had come of their own free will to fight for our freedom and join in our land the battle against the threat of the Soviet' (*Unidad*, Donostia, 12 July); 'If the deviant Barcelona of Catalanism could direct its spurious cultural gaze towards a Latinism of Lyceum, the Barcelona of Spain, the Barcelona of Franco, lifts its gaze intuitively and with dignity towards the living Latinity of the Mediterranean' (*El Correo Español-El Pueblo Vasco*, Bilbao, 12 July); 'He is not coming to seal a pact but to join his heart with the Spanish heart in an embrace of friendship' (*El Norte de Castilla*, Vallodolid, 7 July); 'Two peoples who, after long years of separation and oblivion, meet again on the glorious rough path of service to civilisation under threat' (*Libertad*, Valladolid, 7 July); 'He recalls the best examples of the Renaissance for his human complexity. Action and thought seemed to become divorced in the modern world until fascism came to reunite them' (*El Correo Español-El Diario Vasco*, 27 June); 'Politician and fighter, statesman and writer, representative example of an Italy resurgent, young, impetuous, ambitious for power, replete with the great virtues which will enable the offering to history of the grand spectacle of a nation raised from a deep abyss to the shining heights of glory in the short space of a couple of decades' (*Heraldo de Aragón*, Zaragoza, 9 July).

In Ciano's words as much as in Serrano's—and certainly in those of Mussolini and Franco as well—there was not a modicum of enmity, self-interest, disloyalty, or envy, only gratitude and recognition. According to Ciano, in

192   A European war in Spain, 1938–1939

statements collected by Giménez Arnau for the news agency EFE while they were travelling to Spain, the Italians had shared 'for three years . . . day by day, their heroic struggle with the Spanish people, in a communion of arms'. They had 'shared the yearning of the war and the victories', shed 'the blood of our youth in common'. The 'Caudillo's glorious flags' had 'been our flags'. All Italy had 'taken part in your war, with the conviction and the enthusiasm of a cause which we felt to be our own' and which they had 'served and defended with the tenacity and vigour with which Fascist Italy knows how to defend its ideals'. He concluded that at the beginning of the

> National Revolution, the Italians promised Spain that it would not abandon her in her struggle until the day when victory was achieved. The 4,000 legionnaires who sleep the eternal dream of glory in the lands of Spain are sacred testament of our loyalty.[67]

It was sacred testament which, moreover, had also to be a lever for the future of Spain, Italy, and Europe. 'Spain, having regained, after the recent struggle' its 'rank of great power', was being called upon 'to intervene dynamically in European politics', according to *L'Osservatore Romano*. In fact, Ciano's visit should be the lever for Spain's entry into not just the Anti-Comintern Pact but also the Pact of Steel, based on a solidarity of 'blood spilt in common during the struggle', on the 'affinity of interests of the two nations', and on the 'spirit of the Fascist Revolution, which is power for renewal at home and recognition of indisputable rights abroad'. Hence, it was 'useless for the democracies to take the trouble of looking for a document that specifies the trip's political results. The history of great relations between peoples is not made of documents; it is built on spirits.' There being no documents, the trip had pursued one aim, Spain's collaboration with Fascist Italy in the 'policy of European reconstruction' in a 'communion of sentiments and identity of purposes', according to *Il Regime Fascista*. Bound by the indissoluble ties of blood, the two nations were marching 'united towards a common destiny', the 'path of European revolution that bases its triumphal stages on the action of Fascism, Nazism, and Falangism', wrote *Il Corriere della Sera*.[68]

Beyond the figures of speech and declarations, Ciano's visit to Spain fulfilled a double objective: firstly, to strengthen (at least, from his perspective) the importance of fascism as represented principally by the figure of Serrano Suñer, and, secondly, to carry Mussolini's message to Franco, in which he said plainly, directly, and with no frills that he considered the return of the monarchy 'exceedingly dangerous for the regime' founded by Franco with 'so many blood sacrifices'. Franco could not expect much from France or England, 'by definition irreconcilable enemies of YOUR [*sic*] Spain'. And he must get closer to what was the 'great force of the Nation': the 'people'. At a time when, according to all the reports, the plots to restore the monarchy were serious—to the extent that Rome's police took note and reported on the movements of monarchist personalities (like General Kindelán himself) visiting Alfonso

A European war in Spain, 1938–1939 193

XIII—Mussolini reverted, as in 1937, to taking sides in Spanish internal politics. As is well known, his and Ciano's big bet was Serrano, the closest to an Italy whose 'fascist soul' Franco would be able to feel very soon, the Duce wrote, when he finally travelled to Rome.[69]

In the long report written by Ciano for the Duce after his meeting with Franco, the latter appeared as a confused person, with a simple manner and way of thinking—which is, incidentally, how Cantalupo had portrayed him—who would retain his enormous gratitude for Mussolini's essential collaboration in the war and expect nothing other than to be guided by him on matters of social and domestic policy, while foreign policy would be 'clearly directed'. Therefore, he was saying nothing new. While he would require about five years of peace before undertaking any adventure, his stance appeared to be close to the Axis and, above all, to Italy and his intention was not to remain in a position of 'moral inferiority' in Europe. On the issue of internal policy, he seemed to be opposed (as was Falange, in Ciano's opinion) to the return of decadent systems like the monarchy in a Spain breathing 'new air'. According to Mussolini's son-in-law, Franco was ready to develop a policy of large-scale social reforms, even though for the moment more effort was being devoted—in a very Fascist metaphor—to rebuilding temples than to reactivating railway traffic.[70] Indeed, Franco was 'completely dominated by Mussolini's personality' and would thus feel that in order to 'deal with the peace he would need him as he needed him to win the war'. Ciano ended his report by adding that, with a journey to Madrid that would conclude the work of the 'victorious legionnaires', Mussolini would assuredly unite Spain's fate with that of the Roman Empire.

To ensure this peace and influence, a military mission stayed behind in Spain, consisting of about 8,000 men (1,000 officers and 7,000 soldiers), intended to serve Italy's government both as a diplomatic link providing geostrategic information about an allied country, Spain, and also as a means to influence political decision-making. Once the issues of materiel and supplies relating to the repatriation and the end of the military presence in Spain had been resolved, the mission was reduced very quickly to 60 officers, 90 non-commissioned officers and troops, and 55 civilians, with an annual budget of 12 million for management and personnel expenses. In October of the following year, there were 37 officers, 53 non-commissioned officers, 19 soldiers, four attached postal workers, 10 civilians, three officers, and four non-commissioned officers of the company responsible for maintaining the graves of the fallen—excessive personnel for the work they actually accomplished. For Gambara, head of this new Italian military mission, the central objective was 'to continue and develop the military collaboration in Spain begun by the CTV',[71] with specific sections for cultural collaboration, topographic mapmaking, and information. The idea was to 'ensure a unity of doctrine and military organisation, Italian and Spanish . . . on equal terms', thanks to which Italy would contribute in the military sphere to the country's reconstruction, in what Gambara considered a 'period of transition', through which 'Spain

194 *A European war in Spain, 1938–1939*

will certainly achieve the autarchy which corresponds to her great national pride and her imperial mission resurgent today in the national consciousness'.[72] However, its main function was to send information regarding Spain's possible entry into the World War; the fortifications in the Pyrenees; France, Portugal, and Gibraltar; and the political situation in Spain and the military's hatred of Serrano Suñer.[73] Moreover, the mission would have a specific section, headed by the military chaplain Pietro de Varzi, for the repatriation or collective burial of the bodies of the legionnaires who had died in Spain. In fact, this new mission would take on the task of building and running the Italian Military Sacrarium (*Sacrario Militare Italiano*) at Zaragoza, the tall tower that, even today, serves as a cemetery, housing the bodies of 2,889 Italian soldiers, of whom only 22 are from the antifascist Garibaldi Brigade.[74]

As Gambara announced in April, the *Ufficio Stampa* would remain in Spain as well as in Donostia. He was convinced that it could be of use, as it had already been, not only as moral assistance to the troops, but also, more importantly, for the 'spiritual, Italian, and fascist' penetration 'of the complex Spanish environment', thus orienting the New Spain towards Italian interests and, furthermore, neutralising the influence of competitors.[75] On taking charge of the *Ufficio* in March 1939, Vittorio Foschini had described it as a sort of hotchpotch: a 'tourism, translation and press cuttings office'.[76] But it was of no use whatsoever to the CTV. Now, in a time of peace, its mission would also be to supply military information about the war's evolution near the Iberian Peninsula. For that purpose, in addition to its headquarters in Madrid, with four officers and four non-commissioned officers, it would have a centre in Barcelona (one officer and one non-commissioned officer), a northern centre in Donostia (one officer and one non-commissioned officer), an African centre in Tétouan (an officer with radio), and a centre in the Canary Islands (one non-commissioned officer). Group heads also collaborated in border areas and sensitive military zones like Seville (for Gibraltar and southern Portugal), Majorca, and Ceuta, totalling 11 staff, from secretaries to agents scattered throughout Spain. Lastly, Italy would have four maritime observers to check sea traffic in Gibraltar and the Straits, the Bay of Biscay, and the Catalan coast, the information about which would go directly by radio to Rome. They worked in collaboration with the German secret services: they had 25 permanent maritime observers and ten mobile observers.

After the fall of France, the information centres in Barcelona and Irun were discontinued, as information about the other side of the Pyrenees was of more interest than about Catalonia or the Basque Country. At the same time, the centres near Portugal were strengthened (Vigo, Badajoz, and Huelva) and a secret centre was opened in Lisbon, with consular and commercial agents and the *Fasci all'Estero* as a front.[77] Thus, there were many metaphors and much rhetoric about the communion of interests, alliances of blood and trenches, and the fraternal union of peoples. The fact is, however, is that behind this rhetoric, two political ambitions in international matters coexisted for the Spanish. The first was to decisively align with the Axis, in order to be part of

A European war in Spain, 1938–1939   195

the new fascist Europe, no holds barred—or, at least, to make Spain's national interests converge with those of the allies to whom an 'indelible' debt of sacrifice was owed. The other was to do so without forgetting that it was the New Spain which had truly made the great sacrifices. A memorandum of 1938 on Spanish international policy in the future, possibly by Jordana, indicated how, once 'the war ended with our glorious and most gruelling victory', and without the demographic pressure of Germany and Italy, Spanish aspirations had to be the absolute integrity and sovereignty of its national and colonial territory, the security of its coasts, friendship with Portugal, and the strengthening of the Spanish spirit in Latin America and the Philippines. Mention was also made of the 'friendship with Italy', above all for 'geographic reasons' and for 'reasons of gratitude about which it would not be fair to haggle'. But neither was it possible to 'ignore the enormous service that we have provided them by preventing the creation of a Bolshevik state at the gates of the Mediterranean, which would have endangered their current political regimes'.[78]

This would have meant not taking into account the international context of Franco's recently initiated peace nor the Caudillo's intention to make Spain and himself important actors in a European arena that was about to shatter into a thousand pieces. Only from this perspective is it possible to understand both Ciano's declaration that, in the event of a peace conference, Italy would make Spain's participation a sine qua non condition and Franco's offers to act as a peacemaker.[79] Twice the Caudillo put himself forward as the one who could warn of the 'absurdity of a terrible conflict'—first, in a telegram to Mussolini and again, at the end of August 1939, at the request of the French Minister of Foreign Affairs, Georges Bonnet. On this latter occasion, he put himself forward to Ciano and Mussolini as a mediator with Hitler, with a view to preventing the outbreak of war, or at least to postponing it. However, the proposal was rejected by Italy with the argument that it was a ploy to undermine Franco's prestige in the Führer's eyes, because it was bound to fail, and to delay Hitler's move until the start of the rainy season in Poland.[80] The desire to have an international presence at the side of its natural allies even led to a study, paid for by the Spanish, on the possible division between Italy and Spain of territorial areas of influence in the Mediterranean. Also in August 1939, with the international war imminent, Gambara (now Italy's ambassador in Madrid) wrote to Ciano that he had received Juan Luis Beigbeder's invitation to study, confidentially and personally, a partition of North Africa in broad terms, bearing in mind Italian interests in the Suez Canal and Spanish interests in the Straits of Gibraltar. The senior Italian military figure in Spain said that he did not know whether or not the minister had spoken on his own initiative. But, just in case, he was asking him not for his opinion on the matter but rather which meridian should be used, approximately, as the reference point for such a partition.[81]

The new Spanish government, more 'totalitarian' and with a 'determined orientation towards a totalitarian state and the centralisation of all powers in Franco's hands', together with the growth of the figure of Serrano, suggested

196 *A European war in Spain, 1938–1939*

a greater 'possibility of action' by Italy, which became a common policy at the start of the Second World War (in the shape of a neutrality made more significant by the German-Soviet Pact) to try and prevent an extension of the conflict.[82] It was also the moment of non-belligerence, which only fell apart after Germany attacked the Western Front in May 1940 and Mussolini and Italy subsequently entered into the conflict. It was a 'Formula for a new, pragmatic international Law which signifies greater flexibility', moving away from the 'cold and indifferent posture of a strictly neutral country'.[83] Spain's was an 'armed neutrality' and 'benevolent to the Axis', which would contribute to its victory by blocking 12 French divisions in the Pyrenees and eight in Morocco.[84] In this situation, the issue rapidly became one of further strengthening bilateral relations. The mere possibility of the Caudillo's plan to visit the Duce in Rome, anticipated for September 1939, but finally made unfeasible by the European situation, led *Il Popolo di Roma* to write of a meeting of the 'Caudillos of two Revolutions. The world awaits.' For *Il Giornale d'Italia*, Franco's visit was the reflection of 'a common destiny', 'an identical history, an identical ideal . . . an identical civilisation, the new one', a 'common Mediterranean mission'. For *Il Lavoro Fascista*, Rome was waiting for Franco as it knew how to 'for the greatest'. The brotherhood between the two countries, wrote Farinacci in *Il Regime Fascista*, did not need treaties, because it was dynamic and living.[85] For Luigi Mosca, only in 1940 was it possible to confirm the importance that Franco's victory had had, supported by Italy; Spain had been a 'prelude, a necessary premise for this greater struggle, *then* in a potential state, *now* underway'.[86]

'Fascist Italy follows with immutable sympathy the rising path of the new Spain, which under your guidance as victorious head, goes forward towards a glorious future',[87] Mussolini wrote to Franco on 4 April 1940. But, despite the increase of contacts in preparation for the bilateral meeting, which finally took place at Bordighera, the Duce soon stopped paying him so much attention. Only four days later, he told him of the difficulties that he faced in maintaining a neutral position; his decision was that Italy would enter the war. And 32 days later, he declared war on France and England on the side of Germany—which, had he not done so, likely would have occupied his country, three years before the eventual occupation. From that moment onwards, whether or not to enter the war on the side of Italy and the Axis was the question that guided Spain's foreign policy and a large part of its internal policy. At his meeting with Mussolini and Ciano on 1 October 1940, Serrano avowed a position that was, right from the start, 'spiritually' on the side of the Axis. He did not hide that the internal difficulties were great, particularly regarding politics and supplies, but he believed that entering the war would serve to unite all Spanish forces and that Franco wished to do so. He was right. Entering the war, especially once the outcome was already decided, would bring the desired political, territorial, and military advantages at little expense. Mussolini was convinced that 'Francoist Spain could not miss the great struggle that must decide the fate of peoples', following its own 'vital

A European war in Spain, 1938–1939   197

needs', recognised by the Axis. Entry into the war would be the answer to those vital needs, and the insistence that Spain's fight would be against the United Kingdom suggested, fundamentally, that Spain's vital need par excellence was the question of Gibraltar. For this reason, according to the Duce, Spain ought to speed up its military preparations with the help of the Axis.[88] As General Juan Yagüe told Gambara, 'we will be with Italy', either 'in poverty . . . or sailing in gold, if everything goes as we want it to'.[89]

The relations begun in July 1936 with the Italian intervention in support of the coup d'état, intensified from 1937 onwards with the despatch of an army to Spanish soil—as a belligerent country but without belligerency rights— would have its epilogue on 12 February 1941, the day of the meeting between the 'Head of the Fascist Revolution' and the head of the 'Spanish National Revolution', with regard to which the Italian newspapers spoke in terms of an 'identity of viewpoints' and 'analogies between Fascism, National Socialism, and Falangism', pointing to the 'common principles and ideals of these three ideologies, drawing the conclusion therefrom that the three countries have identical enemies'.[90] At a time when, as Mussolini indicated, 'all European countries are either occupied countries, are within [Germany's] orbit, are her friends, or are her allies', Russia was 'out of the game',[91] and the victory of the Axis was so certain as to push Spain to join the war, Franco and Serrano declared their willingness to do so—but in return for guarantees which, in fact, depended on German willingness and assistance.[92] Italian help would not be much more than to act as an intermediary with the Führer, passing on the Spanish chief of staff's report which laid out the provisions and raw materials needed by the military and the civilian population. Indeed, as a result of the meeting, the Duce informed Ribbentrop that, rather than forcing Spain's entry into the war, they had to keep the country 'in our political camp', giving it time to 'overcome the crisis of famine and that of an almost complete lack of military preparation'. This personal opinion was, however, not included in the notification made to Serrano of the telegram to the Nazi minister.[93]

Soon the reality became visible. Only then, no longer in the terrain of declarations, telegrams, and propaganda, but rather, once again, in that of war, did the reality of Italian Fascism emerge in all its coarseness. Its evangelising influence on the Civil War may have been intense and the 'Giovinezza' may have been sung, as mentioned in the soldiers' diaries, in every place captured by CTV as a sort of symbolic occupation. But the economic, military, and human expenditure incurred first in Africa and later in Spain would be key to understanding the disastrous unfolding of the Second World War for Fascist Italy. As Giorgio Rochat points out, Spain was a war in which no plans were made in advance for the intervention, nor were definite objectives set, nor were costs forecast.[94] The costs incurred by Italy have not been investigated thoroughly, but it has been calculated that, between the Ministry of War's estimates and the actual costs, there was an increase in 1935–1936 of 201 per cent and in 1936–1937 of 309 per cent. Italian assistance appears to have totalled $355 million in the currency of the day, repayable over 15

198 *A European war in Spain, 1938–1939*

years without interest, although at the end of the war Mussolini reduced the debt by 33 per cent. The real cost remains in the shadows, although John Coverdale espouses Felix Guarneri's figure of '*otto miliardi e mezzo*', eight and a half billion lire, which is clearly too low because it does not include expenditure such as personnel, indemnities, and medical care. As of 30 June 1938, it appears that the expenditure in Spain of the Ministries of War, the Navy, and the Air Force together reached 4,035,821,648.70 lire. The despatch of materiel rose to a total value of 6,086,003,680 lire. Thus, by mid-1938, total expenditure was over 10 billion lire.[95] And, most importantly, counting the dead, the wounded, prisoners, and the missing, Italy lost 16,655 men, the equivalent of an army corps and a half.

Italy was to pay dearly for the reduced investment in the quantitative and qualitative development of Italian armaments, the abandonment of much materiel, and the excessive confidence stemming from military successes in Spain from 1940 onwards, when these factors became obstacles in the preparation for the European conflict. There are interpretations that differ from this view, such as that of General Carlo Montanari, for whom the problem in Spain was not the abundance of modern means but the shortage of them. But even those who are least critical of the conduct of the Italian campaigns before the Second World War acknowledge the high cost in relation to the scant reward obtained—and an even higher price, the 'illusion of easy war'. In Ethiopia and Spain, triumphalist assessments and the rhetoric of fascist security confidence transformed concepts like 'decisive, dynamic war of movement' into 'easy war'.[96] This calculated blurring of what was certain with what was desirable would cost Italy from 1940 onwards. Mussolini won the Spanish war, but in Spain he may have lost the world war.

Notes

1 ASMAE, US, b38.
2 ASMAE, US, b40.
3 ASMAE, US, b23.
4 ASMAE, UC, b46.
5 ASMAE, US, b22.
6 USSME, F18, b9.
7 USSME, F6, b336.
8 Emilio Faldella, *Venti mesi di guerra di Spagna (luglio 1936-febbraio 1938)* (Florence: F. Le Mannier, 1939), 429.
9 USSME, F18, b9.
10 ASMAE, UC, b46.
11 Ibid.
12 ASMAE, UC, b40.
13 Ibid.
14 USSME, F18, b7.
15 Telegram from Mussolini to Berti, 15 January 1938, USSME, F18, b9.
16 USSME, F18, b9.
17 ASMAE, US, b2.
18 AMAE, AB, L833, C27.

A European war in Spain, 1938–1939   199

19 ASMAE, UC, b46.
20 AGMAV, C2604, E 41bis.
21 USSME, F18, b9.
22 José María Maldonado, *Alcañiz, 1938: el bombardeo olividado* (Zaragoza: Institución Fernando el Católico, 2003); by the same author, *Aragón bajo las bombas* (Zaragoza: Gobierno de Aragón, 2010). For a general and up-to-date analysis, see Edoardo Grassia, '"Aviazione Legionaria": il commando strategico-politico e tecnico-militare delle forze aeree italiane impiegate nel conflitto civile spagnolo', *Diacronie*, no. 7 (2001), https://doi.org/10.4000/diacronie.3411. For an overall view, see José Luis Alcofar Nassaes [José Luis Infiesta], *La aviación legionaria en la guerra española* (Barcelona: Euros, 1976).
23 ASMAE, UC, b46. The *Aviazione* also took part in reconnaissance flights and military intelligence. Diego Navarro and Guillermo Vicente, 'Photographic air reconnaissance in the Spanish Civil War 1936–1939: doctrine and operations', *War in History*, no. 20/3 (2013): 345–380.
24 USSME, F18, b9.
25 Likewise, there is a greater amount of literature devoted to the bombings of Barcelona. See, among others, Joan Villarroya, *Els bombardeigs de Barcelona durant la Guerra Civil: 1936–1939* (Barcelona: Publicacions de l'Abadia de Montserrat, 1999); Santiago Alberti and Elisenda Alberti, *Perill de bombardeig! Barcelona sota les bombes (1936–1939)* (Barcelona: Alberti, 2004); Paola Lo Cascio and Susanna Oliveira, *Imatges 1936–1939: bombes sobre Barcelona* (Girona: El Punt, 2008); and Edoardo Grassia, 'Barcellona, 17 e 18 marzo 1938', *Diacronie*, no. 7 (2011), https://doi.org/10.4000/diacronie.3237.
26 ASMAE, UC, b46.
27 USSME, F18, b9.
28 AMAE, L833, E28.
29 Sandro Piazzoni, *Le Frecce Nere nella la guerra di Spagna (1937–1939)* (Rome: Edizioni della Rivista Nazione Militare, 1939), 124 and 189.
30 'Great Britain and Northern Ireland and Italy—Agreement regarding Questions of Mutual Concern consisting of a Protocol and Annexes, signed at Rome, April 16th, 1938 . . .', *League of Nations Treaty Series*, 1939, consulted 1 August 2015, www.worldlii.org/int/other/LNTSer/1939/42.html.
31 As Villarroya and Solé note, in April, May, and June the largest cities in Tarragona province were again bombed, as were some places in Girona province—including the city of Girona, Roses, and Portbou—and, of course, Barcelona, Badalona, and Sant Adrià de Besòs. Also subject to bombings were the Valencian cities of Castelló, Sagunt, Valencia, Benicarló, and Alacant, among many others. See Josep Maria Solé i Sabaté and Joan Villarroya, *España en llamas: la guerra civil desde el aire* (Madrid: Temas de Hoy, 2003). For the complete list for 1938–1939, see Alcofar, *La aviación legionaria*, 375–382.
32 USSME, F18, b5.
33 ASMAE, GAB, b468.
34 ASMAE, US, b2, b5.
35 USSME, F18, b5.
36 ASMAE, US, b40.
37 USSME, F18, b9 and AMAE, AB, L833, C25.
38 ASMAE, US, b10 and b51.
39 Ibid.
40 AMAE, AB, E834, Cc17–22.
41 Duilio Sumsel and Edoardo Sumsel, eds., *Opera Omnia di Benito Mussolini*, vol. XXIX (Florence: La Fenice, 1959), 167.
42 ASMAE, US, b11. On 19 May it was requested that speakers be sent to Italy, in particular José Millán Astray. The Spaniards who went to Italy (and their political affiliations, according to the Italian documents) were Millán Astray, Esteban Bilbao (FET-JONS national councillor, traditionalist), Pemán (FET-JONS National Council member, monarchist), Lequerica, Giménez Arnau (FET-JONS national councillor), José Final (Count

200 *A European war in Spain, 1938–1939*

of Mayalde), Jesús Muro (Falange head in Zaragoza), Javier Martínez de Bedoya (national councillor), Manuel Falcón (national councillor, director of *Vértice*), Jesús Suevos (national councillor, provincial head in Galicia), Jaime Soler de Murillo, Santiago Sangro y Torres, García Morato. and Manuel Aznar. At the last minute, Soler de Murillo withdrew from the group and was replaced by Julián Pemartin. They toured Italy from 27 May to 6 June and were received by Starace, Mussolini, and Ciano. They visited the Forums, the *bonifiche*, the *Mostra della Romanità* (an archaeological exhibition celebrating the anniversary of the birth of Augustus), the *Mostra del Dopolavoro* (recreational exhibition), Ostia, Venice, Milan, and Genoa, where they embarked. Previously, on 29 May, the group had split up, travelling to different cities across the Italian peninsula to celebrate the day of solidarity. In Rome, the speakers were Pemán and Millán Astray. See also *Opera Omnia*, vol. XXIX, 110, for the reception given on 30 May at the Palazzo Venezia to the representatives of 'Franco's New Spain'.

43 USSME, F18, b9. *Hoja Oficial del Lunes* and *Lunes: Hoja Oficial de Navarra*, 2 October 1938.
44 AGMAV, C2604, 47.
45 *Opera Omnia*, vol. XXIX, 463–464.
46 *Il Messagero*, 27 October 1938.
47 ASMAE, US, b40 and b2.
48 ASMAE, US, b2.
49 AGMAV, C2605, E99.
50 ASMAE, US, b160.
51 *Opera Omnia*, vol. XXIX, 228–229.
52 USSME, F6, b256.
53 Ibid.
54 AGMAV, C2605, 102.
55 ASMAE, US, b40.
56 *Opera Omnia*, vol. XXIX, 254.
57 Ibid., 474.
58 Adelchi Albanese, *Nella bufera spagnola con le Camicie Nere della 'Divisione d'assalto Littorio'* (Florence: Bandettini, 1940), p. 207.
59 ASMAE, US, b25. Among other works about the province of Alacant, see José Ramón García Gandía, 'Nella bufera spagnola: los italianos y el final de la guerra civil en Aspe', *La Serranica*, no. 52 (2016): 109–116, https://aspe.es/wp-content/uploads/2018/07/Aspe-La-Serranica-2016.pdf.
60 ASMAE, GAB, b70.
61 *Opera Omnia*, vol. XXIX, 483–484.
62 ASMAE, GAB, b469 and AMAE, AB, L1188, E57.
63 ASMAE, AP, b53.
64 AMAE, AB, L1188, E57.
65 Quoted in *Opera Omnia*, vol. XXIX, 475.
66 AMAE, AB, E1065/13.
67 Ciano would write, on Ambassador Viola's comments on a speech delivered in November 1938 by Giménez Arnau—a law graduate of the University of Bologna, inclined to support a Francoist Falange, previously pro-Nazi but now increasingly turning to the Italian position that José Antonio must not be a paralysing factor paralysing history—that '*Giménez Arnau farà strada*' ('Giménez Arnau will get on in life'). USSME, F18, b9.
68 AMAE, AB, E1065/13.
69 ASMAE, UC, b47.
70 Ibid. As is well known, the issue of the shootings had made a very negative impression on him, although the Spanish population maintained a spirit of 'serene coldness' in the face of the regime of terror.
71 USSME, H3, 24.
72 AGMAV, C2604, E52.

73 The reports of interviews with Lieutenant Rafael García Valiño, General Antonio Aranda, and Lieutenant General Carlos Asensio can be found in ASMAE, US, b26.
74 In turn, a Spanish military mission in Italy was established, made up of 'about 50 officers of the different armed services' and headed by the displaced Queipo de Llano, an 'incorrigible traitor', according to Serrano Suñer, who requested that he be kept under surveillance in Italy. USSME, H3, b24 and ASMAE, UC, b47.
75 ASMAE, US, b27.
76 Ibid.
77 ASMAE, US, b10.
78 AMAE, AB, L1065, E9.
79 ASMAE, UC, b47.
80 AMAE, AB, L1460, C3.
81 ASMAE, GAB, b468.
82 Javier Tusell and Genoveva Queipo de Llano, *Franco y Mussolini. La política española durante la segunda guerra mundial* (Barcelona: Planeta, 1985); Massimiliano Guderzo, *Madrid e l'arte della diplomazia. L'incognita spagnola nella seconda guerra mondiale* (Florence: Manent, 1995).
83 AMAE, AB, L1188, E57.
84 ASMAE, GAB, b467.
85 AMAE, AB, L1462, E32.
86 Luigi Mosca, *Camicie Nere a Guadalajara* (Naples: Partenope, 1941), 17 (italics in the original).
87 *Opera Omnia*, vol. XXIX, 479.
88 ASMAE, UC, b21. For the question of supplies, see ASMAE, UC, b24.
89 ASMAE, UC, b47.
90 AMAE, AB, L1462, E32.
91 ASMAE, UC, b24.
92 As Anfuso notes, Mussolini wanted to meet Franco in order to fulfil the promise made to Hitler to try and persuade him to collaborate militarily with the Axis. 'I will tell Franco whatever is necessary, but I am under no illusions: he will have decided before I even open my mouth', the Duce purportedly declared. Filippo Anfuso, *Da Palazzo Venezia al lago di Garda. 1936–1945* (Bologna: Cappelli, 1957), 153.
93 ASMAE, UC, b24. Serrano was removed from office shortly after his last ministerial visit to Italy, where he met Ciano at Livorno. ASMAE, AP, b61.
94 Giorgio Rochat, *Le guerre italiane 1935–1943. Dall'impero d'Etiopia alla disfatta* (Turin: Einaudi, 2005), 141.
95 ASMAE, US, b5.
96 Giuseppe Santoro, *L'aeronautica italiana nella seconda guerra mondiale* (Milan/Rome: Esse, 1950–1957), 69. Both quotations are taken from Ferruccio Borti and Virgilio Ilari, *Il pensiero militare*, 245ff. Also highly critical is the assessment in *L'Esercito italiano tra la 1a e la 2a Guerra Mondiale. Novembre 1918-Giugno 1940* (Rome: Stato Maggiore dell'Esercito, 1954), 154; and Oreste Bovio, *Storia dell'Esercito italiano (1861–2000)* (Rome: Stato Maggiore dell'Esercito, 2010), 310.

Conclusion

> *Victorio Emmanuele III Regnante Dum*
> *Roma Contra Eversores Juris et Fidei Pugnat*
> *Italiae. Duce Auspice Concorde Hispaniae*
> *Moderatore. Romano Pontifice Pio XII Be-*
> *nedicente. Hoc Pacis Opus. More Patrum.*
> *Ad Majus Pietatis Incrementum Italiaeque*
> *Militum Memoria. Romana Virtute. Extolli-*
> *tur Mense Martio A.D. MCMXLII. A Fasci-*
> *bus Restitutis XX.*

Inscription on the foundation stone of the Italian Military Sacrarium at Zaragoza, laid 3 May 1942.

Fascism, as a project to generate a new future, experienced not gold-fever but stone-fever, an unconcealed eagerness to absorb the symbols of the past and make a monument of the present, with its eyes fixed firmly on posterity.[1] Under these precepts, the memory of the Italian intervention in the Spanish Civil War depended on the management of the memory and the cult of its fallen, of its dead as generators of life, of their heroism and fascist faith. The death of Pietro Barresi, the first legionnaire to fall in battle at Esquivias (in the province of Toledo) on 29 October 1936, ushered in a particular manifestation in Spain and Italy of the cult of the Italians who had died for fascist civilisation but, in turn, were naturalised as fighters 'in defence of the Holy Cause of Franco's Spain [who] have given their lives for God and Our Fatherland'—the dead watched over by the fatherland, who 'with love and gratitude constitute indissoluble ties of the fraternal and ever-lasting relations between Italy and Spain'.[2] As they said in a letter to the Spanish ambassador in Rome, for the widow, the orphaned daughter, and the mother of the hero Giuseppe Luciano Mele, who died in 1938 at Javalambre and was a member of the editorial team at *Il Giornale d'Italia*, only their pride was comparable to the bitter pain that they felt for their loss. 'These feelings unite us forever to the great Spain of Franco', they wrote.[3] These were three women united in their sadness at the death of their son, husband, father. Their pride was sincere, difficult as it is to accept this. Sincere pride and real pain.

Every legionnaire's tomb was placed under the care of a Spanish godmother. In the homage at Zaragoza on 12 June 1941, Pilar Primo de Rivera herself took on the responsibility of caring for the tomb of the first Italian to fall in Spain. Every tomb had a godmother, and all the tombs were in the care of the sister nation, represented by the capital of Aragon. It was there, in fact, that a large part of the events to remember the legionnaires were concentrated. The first was on 7 November 1940, when the area created for the Italian airmen in the Torrero cemetery was inaugurated. In Zaragoza, Italian and German authorities convened, and Ambassador Francesco Lecquio visited some of the city's anti-liberal and anti-French locations, like the Puerta del Carmen, symbol of the early nineteenth-century War of Independence. And there in Zaragoza, as a perennial reminder of Italy's gesture in Spain and at the suggestion of Pietro da Varzi, Mussolini decreed the creation of a sacrarium to gather together 'the remains of four thousand Italian soldiers who died fighting for the cause of *National* Spain'. The idea was quickly accepted by the Spanish government, which ceded land free of charge in the city's Torrero neighbourhood. The *Banca Nazionale del Lavoro* bought the adjacent 8,000 square metres for the convent attached to the tower. The project by the Carlist architect Víctor Eusa was for a tower 83 metres high, which would make it the highest point in the city. The first stone of the future military sacrarium was laid on 3 May 1942. It was a solemn ceremony. First, Ambassador Lecquio was received by Generals José Monasterio and Álvaro Sueiro, the mayor, the head of the Falange, and Zaragoza's local authorities. Then, His Holiness's Nuncio Monsignor Cicognani, the Bishop of Huesca, and the Minister General Fidel Dávila, representing the Caudillo, took part in the event.

At 11 o'clock, a cordon of Italian and Spanish flags encircled an altar at the place where the tower was to be erected. There, said Lecquio, it 'was right to bring together these bloody remains in order to preserve them religiously as relics of martyrs', as it was right to build the monument in 'Zaragoza, which bears in its name that of its Imperial Roman founder' and which was the sanctuary of the 'Hispanic Race, spiritual centre of the Nation', ever since the Blessed Virgin had set her Pillar there. There, all the dead would remain as a perennial reminder of the 'new, common trial by fire', experienced by Spain and Italy and alluded to in the speech by Felipe Ximénez de Sandoval, as an incentive for the present and for a future of 'new and common sacrifices of blood'.[4] Amid the 'struggle being waged against the false plutocratic democracies'—a barely veiled allusion to the battles of the Second World War—the 'heroes of the Spanish Crusade' signified the 'best guarantee of final victory'. The mothers and wives of the fallen would be, at last, 'rest assured when they know that the venerated ashes of their sons and husbands have been entrusted to the courage and nobility of the Aragonese'.[5]

Those dead sons and husbands—between 3,400 and 3,800–4,300 according to the *Ufficio Spagna*—were part of the largest foreign army that fought in the Spanish Civil War, the army of Fascist Italy, 78,846 strong: 43,189 were from the Royal Army, 29,646 from the MVSN, and 5,699 belonged to the

204 *Conclusion*

aeronautical arm, plus 312 civilian workers, again according to the *Ufficio*. It was a fascist army for a total war, whose intervention had its origins in diplomatic and political positioning, but which ended up making Italy, to all intents and purposes, a third belligerent in Spain. The year 1936 was a time of radicalisation and success, two processes which were perceived as cause and effect, respectively. Mario Roatta—head of the Military Information Service (SIM) and future commander-in-chief of the Italian forces in the Civil War— and Ciano, who were the two other top decision-makers regarding intervention in Spain, shared with the Duce the idea that success in Spain would also mean success in fascist cooperation in Europe. In short, the Spanish Civil War was the process that really transformed relations between the fascist powers in Europe, giving them, for the first time, a feeling of universality.[6]

As has been shown—and leaving aside the trivialisations and underestimations in use—there is a strong consensus that Mussolini's decision to intervene in Spain gravitated around the core issue of controlling the Mediterranean. The fundamental piece on the playing board of the *Mare Nostrum* was, precisely because of its importance, the object of complex policies and decision-making that affected the governance of Europe.[7] And that might be true, although I disagree with the undiscussed primacy of the geostrategic question. As a matter of fact, I am inclined to think that the reasons for the Italian intervention in Spain were neither monolithic nor unequivocal. Rather, they included a variety of dimensions. And they changed during the months that the war lasted, based on the changing contexts of Spain, Italy, and Europe. Mussolini's aspirations in Spain were far from being modest. As Heiberg has said, 'it was not simply circumstances that led the Duce and his aspirations to the Spanish quicksands'.[8] Rather, it was a struggle for imperial supremacy, at the heart of which was the desire to fascisticise Spain, to contribute with military intervention to the triumph of the political option which was the most advantageous for Italy or for identarian, political, and economic colonisation; for the expansion of influence in the institutional and geostrategic framework; and for the development of a converging system and a system of friendship in a common identity.

These three possibilities—to differing degrees, depending on the immediate interests or the context in which they arose—are present in the various political, military, economic, social, and legislative reports sent from Spain by the constellation of leaders of the PNF; the Army; the *Milizia*; private enterprise; the Ministries of Industry, Foreign Affairs, and Popular Culture; and the SIM. In the pursuit of any one of these three options, the SIM was already in contact with the rebels from June 1936, or even earlier. Clearly, much more was known in Rome about what was going to happen in Spain than was said afterwards. Only in this way is it possible to explain the fact that, on 18 July itself, the Fascist ambassador sent a detailed plan of action drawn up by the rebels and that the rebels were rapidly supported by Mussolini. There was more to it than geostrategic calculation. After overcoming some initial hesitation, Italy became the largest non-Spanish power involved in the internecine conflict. And, as Ciano said, Mussolini had decided that, after Spain, he would concoct something else—the character of the Italians had to be forged in combat.[9]

Italy's participation and help expanded to all fronts: military, political, weapons, diplomatic, and propaganda. The predominantly political and diplomatic historiography has contributed strongly to the knowledge of some of the geostrategic and international motives and derivatives of an extremely complex intervention in the field of foreign policy. But, at the same time, it has tended to disregard the actual development of the intervention and, above all, its military and war-related dimension, generally leaving these aspects in the hands of military historians. Nevertheless, the Fascist participation in the Spanish Civil War, from the end of 1936 to the withdrawal of the last troops, was de facto much more important in the military field than in other areas. The Italians in Spain amounted to a contingent of soldiers numerically greater than the International Brigades as a whole (as much as double their total, according to the lower estimates that mention 35,000 international brigadiers, or 20,000 more, according to others). Furthermore, they had radio, newspapers, the CIAUS (training centres), field hospitals (at Zaragoza and Valladolid, with 1,000 and 1,500 beds, respectively), and a battalion of workers, as well as programmes of political action, economic penetration, and cultural permeation, represented by the constellation of leaders stationed in Spain of the PNF; the Army; the *Milizia*; private enterprise; the Ministries of Industry, Foreign Affairs, and Popular Culture; and the SIM. The war allowed them to explore war techniques such as the bombing of civilian populations, as seen in Aragon, Valencia, and Catalonia. And, despite what Roberto Cantalupo wrote, it was an intervention with a strong political component. It began as help with weapons for geopolitical and diplomatic reasons to a friendly nation against a common enemy—real or imaginary—but, following the failure of the initial plan to stage a coup and rapidly take the capital, the war quickly became a conducive setting for fascisticising Spain. In this context, the political missions by figures such as Cantalupo, Gulglielmo Danzi, and Roberto Farinacci were used as much to establish a link between Franco and Mussolini as to transmit the idea of fascistisation—understood as convergence within the European sphere of counter-revolution. Fascistised Spain would have a single political party headed by Franco, a totalitarian system in the historical sense of the term, a palingenetic culture, and a legislative framework in which the most noteworthy element would be, for obvious reasons, the Labour Charter—the *Fuero del Trabajo*, a copy of the Italian *Carta del Lavoro*.

Integrated and under Franco's orders—but with enough of its own characteristics to underline its specific nature—was the Army. Given its double status, military and fascist, it best transmitted the idea of fascistisation in practice and by means of war. However, its internal organisation was not simple to manage. The post of commander of the Italians in Spain was of great importance within the organisational structure of Fascist military power. The

206 Conclusion

first head of the CTV, General Mario Roatta, was replaced after the fiasco of Guadalajara by Ettore Bastico (from March to September 1937). Coming from Ethiopia, Bastico commanded the CTV in campaigns that were perceived as overtly successful, such as those of Biscay and Santander, but had to leave the post because of his disagreements with Franco. The latter's favourite was Mario Berti (October 1937–October 1938). He was succeeded by Gastone Gambara (previously chief of staff to Bastico and Berti and then promoted general), who remained in charge until the end of the war. Gambara stayed in Spain in the immediate post-war period as head of a reduced military mission, intended for training, assistance, and cultural influence.

The first CTV under Roatta had, as has been seen, four divisions, each under the command of an Italian general (*Dio Lo Vuole*, Edmondo Rossi; *Fiamme Nere*, Amerigo Coppi; *Penne Nere*, Luigi Nuvoloni; *Littorio*, Annibale Bergonzoli), plus a fifth group under the command of Enrico Francisci, which brought together the 4th and 5th groups of the *Banderas XXIII Marzo*. In April 1937, the remaining units were the *Fiamme Nere*, under the command of Luigi Frusci; the *Littorio*, under Bergonzoli; and the Francisci group, to which the *Frecce Nere* mixed brigades, under Sandro Piazzoni, and the *Frecce Azzurre*, under Mario Grussardo were added. Following the post-Guadalajara purge, the *XXIII Marzo* Division re-emerged after absorbing the *Banderas* of the Francisci group, while the rest of the divisions and mixed brigades remained the same. Once Santander had been captured, the divisions were reduced to three, *Fiamme Nere-XXIII Marzo* (Frusci), *Frecce* (Roatta), and *Littorio* (Bergonzoli). And, after the return to Italy in June 1938 of the *Fiamme Nere-XXIII Marzo* and the dividing of the mixed brigades for operational reasons, the CTV comprised, until the end of the war, a *Littorio* division under the command of Gervasio Bitossi, always made up of soldiers of the Royal Army, and three mixed brigades under the command of three Italian colonels: *Frecce Verdi* (Emilio Battisti), *Frecce Nere* (Valentino Babini), and *Frecce Azzurre* (Salvatore La Ferla).

The air force was independent, first as the *Tercio de Extranjeros*' air force and then as the Legionary Air Force (*Aviazione Legionaria*), which organisationally reported to General Alfredo Kindelán, but which received direct orders from Rome. Between July 1936 and April 1939, Italy sent 414 fighter aircraft, 44 attack aircraft, 68 reconnaissance planes, 213 bombers, and 20 seaplanes to Spain. It lost 216 and left the rest to the insurgent air force, modern aircraft in good condition, although, by 1939, they had been overtaken in terms of speed, manoeuvrability, and weaponry by the Russian and German fighters. There were 5,699 air force personnel in Spain, including pilots (862 officers and 573 non-commissioned officers) and other staff (203 officers, 1,196 NCOs, 2,865 soldiers), and some 200 died. No less important was the participation of the *Regia Marina* (Royal Navy). According to José Miguel Campo's calculations, 89 Italian surface ships and 58 submarines completed 677 and 91 missions, respectively. The surface units undertook at least two bombardments, firing 195 shots and launching 12 torpedoes, which sunk three steamers and damaged one other. The submarines fired 245 shots and launched 71 torpedoes, sinking six steamers and damaging another nine. Furthermore, the Italian navy made 258 sea voyages transporting supplies and transferring troops and the wounded.

On war materiel in Spain alone, Italy spent 4,171,565,771 lire on the army, 150 million on the navy, and 1,764,437,909 on the air force. The final debt, calculated at the time of the CTV's withdrawal in May 1939 at 8,300 million lire and fixed at 5,000 million, was finally repaid in 1967. The most aberrant legacy was, however, the hundreds of victims left behind in Spain, both the fallen in battle and the civilians bombed by the Legionary Air Force—many of them children. The bombings using lower explosive charges destroyed the limbs of adults. The orthopaedic treatment of these victims made Dr. Josep Trueta famous in Barcelona. The same bombs hit children's vital organs.

The CTV's story was, ultimately, the result of a changing situation, in which military and diplomatic support for the insurgency turned to participation as a belligerent country fighting on foreign soil. The Italians were responsible for successes for the rebel army, such as the occupations of Málaga, Bermeo, and Santander; the stabilisation and breaking of the Aragon fronts; the joint occupation of Barcelona and Girona; and the end of the campaign on the Valencian coast (known as the *Levante* in Spanish). They were, moreover, responsible for the no less successful terror campaigns in the Republican rearguard, bombings of Valencia, Alacant, and Barcelona. But they were also responsible for notorious failures, like Guadalajara, the name and symbolic place of memory forever associated with the CTV and with Italian Fascism. The factors which determined the defeat are far-reaching, and the explanations complex. And to reduce everything to the motely and cowardly conduct of the Italian fascists would be a *reductio ad absurdum*. To project what can be called *Guadalajara syndrome* onto the whole of the Italian participation in the war would be problematic, to say the least: firstly, because Italian Fascism's participation in the war was much more far-reaching, extensive, and intense than that of those days of 1937; secondly, because the defeat at Guadalajara was the result of a series of problems which cannot be blamed solely on Italian incompetence in battle; and, thirdly, because when there was incompetence—and there was, as we have seen—we do not have enough reliable sources to attribute it exclusively to the combatants' cowardice.

And, in the end, who were the Italians, and what did they do in Spain? In my opinion, as I have said from the very beginning of this book, they were first and foremost fascists. Whether they came enlisted in the Royal Army or in the *Milizia*, whether they were fervent believers in the Mussolinian faith or doubted the war's ability to evangelise, for all of them, combat and sacrifice in Spain were combat and sacrifice for Italy, for the nation, identified with fascism, which was much more than a mere political faction—it was Italy. That is why it seems to me a little artificial to assert that the CTV hardly had a fascist identity by using the arguments that there were internal differences between the Royal Army and the *Milizia*, that their willingness to fight stemmed largely from economic and employment issues, and that fascism—embodied above all in the *Milizia*—had a secondary role in the war. Such arguments amount to making a rule of the exception. In the first place, because they mean assuming that a regime's institutions can never be in conflict with one other (which nevertheless occurred in Italy, Germany, and Spain) or that these conflicts were so unacceptable as to discredit the institutions' adherence to the same cause. Secondly, because the role of fascism, if identified exclusively with the Blackshirts of the *Milizia* (a view I do not share), is far from being irrelevant. For instance, the *Milizia* provided the bulk of the victims at Guadalajara (417 compared to 161 in the Royal Army) and at Santander, because it made up most of the infantry until mid-1937. The number of officers and non-commissioned officers was less than in the Army, but in terms of the total of infantry soldiers the proportions were largely similar, if not to the credit of the Blackshirts. Among other reasons, it was because practically the whole artillery arm belonged to the Army, as did the auxiliary services in the main.

But the third and overriding reason to reject this line of argument is that, although there were as many reasons to fight as there were combatants, such economic and political determinism, based on an extensive repertoire of stereotypes, rules out all those who fought 'for the fascist idea', those who were not unemployed, poor, or from the South—and even those who were, because it was possible to be poor, unemployed, and from the South and yet believe fervently in fascism, regardless of the logical argument that the work and the salary could hardly outweigh the risk of dying on the field of battle. Three thousand lire on enlisting, a daily allowance of 20 (increased by five lire for those who had completed 18 months of service in 1938), plus the supplement from Franco of 5.4 pesetas a day, reduced in reality to two, was the pay for killing and dying for Italy, Spain, the Duce, and the supremacy of the fatherland. In the meanwhile, as Davide Lajolo would say bitterly, other people continued with their lives in that same fatherland, looking after their businesses and holding their arm high in salute. Furthermore, the evolution of the war's dynamics ended up repositioning the longings and the fearlessness of some and the cowardice and economic interests of others. Life in wartime Spain was a factor that radicalised some legionnaires. By experiencing battle, they lived the ultimate reality and the most perfect form of fascism—war.

Thus, fascism was far from being irrelevant or insignificant, much as its discourse and its culture have been ascribed to the terrain of empty rhetoric (no doctrinal framework, no theoretical texts, no essayistic foundation, no ecumenical vocation, no political strategy—pure chit-chat), and much as this has flattened the poles of its historical significance, filed down its horns as a major phenomenon of its age, and taken the focus off of its capacity for aesthetic, political, ideological, and identarian appeal. There is no need to underline the well-known fact that no fascism ever matched up to its own national myths—neither Nazi Germany and its racial and hierarchical stratification of Europe, whose brutal epilogue was the war of racial resettlement in the east, nor Francoist Spain and its myth of *Hispanidad*. Thus, it is right to downplay the reach of the Mussolinian imperial myth, the ultra-nationalist effervescence of which was promoted by the Fascist regime, even retroactively, starting in the 1930s. Nevertheless, this should not lead us to the mistake of thinking that, because they did not turn out to be successful, European fascisms' plans of national unification and homogenisation are not important to understanding the nature of their power. Despite their superficial contradictions, these fascist myths shared a nucleus of palingenetic ultra-nationalism. The fact that they failed does not mean that the methods used by the fascist dictatorships to bring them to fruition were irrelevant. The imperial dimension of the inter-war fascist dictatorships tried to live up to their loftiest social and political plans. It gave them their categorically definitive form and was part of their very essence and nature.

It is not possible to understand the political nature of the Italian regime, which gave its name to perhaps the most successful of the European political forms peculiar to the twentieth century, without analysing its imperial nature. It was a nature that undoubtedly had a strong figurative and rhetorical content, but it was also firmly moored to what Enzo Collotti called a politics of 'strength' ('*potenza*'), which substantially contributes to recognising both the Italian operations in Africa in pursuit of Empire and Fascism's diplomatic, military, and cultural actions in the western and eastern Mediterranean as consistent with each other and with Mussolini's regime.[10] The sources concur in identifying an uninterrupted continuity between Fascist foreign policy and the broad outlines of Italy's earlier unitary history and in acknowledging that the image as a great power that Fascism projected did not correspond with diplomatic, military, and geostrategic reality. However, the study of fascist politics and culture reveals a landscape of profoundly violent and aggressive radicalisation, particularly in the 1930s, with logical and recognisable results. The last among the great powers or the first among the lesser powers, Fascist Italy was a potential enemy of all the countries of the Mediterranean in this period—Yugoslavia, because of Dalmatia; Greece, because of Corfu; Turkey, because of the Anatolian coast; France, because of Corsica and Tunisia; and England, because of Malta and the Suez Canal. It was the African campaigns which showed most clearly what Fascism considered to be its rights as a power and what the means were to defend them. Nevertheless, the real turning point was the Spanish war. The campaigns in Libya and Ethiopia thus marked the start of an extremist policy that led Italy from the sweetest of hopes to the bitterest of defeats in the Second World War. The link between those hopes and defeats was the Spanish Civil War.

War. Features specific to fascism—such as mass ritual, violence, ultra-nationalist xenophobia, the sense of a new beginning, and the patriotic desire for the palingenetic rebirth of the nation and the building of a homogeneous and strong national community, a community threatened by the internal and external enemy and perceived by ex-combatants as a community of suffering and pain—are incomprehensible without putting war in the equation.[11]

210   *Conclusion*

Italian Fascism proclaimed itself as the only authentic movement of the 'new Italians'.[12] Regenerated by war, the fascists considered themselves prophets, apostles, evangelists, soldiers of the religion of the fatherland purified by the fire of war, and citizen-soldiers.[13] Thus, war became the last and most important of the revolutionary stages. Speaking from the perspective of 1940, Renato Farnea wrote, 'this [war] is the third age of the Revolution. It is the Revolution that has become war'.[14]

Through war, proletarian and Fascist Italy would claim its 'place in the sun' in a world occupied, as would be said, by the demo-plutocratic powers.[15] For fascism, war would be the fundamental tool for achieving maximum expansion, the framework conducive to the fascistisation of Europe. There is no other way to interpret what was indicated in the article 'Europe and Fascism', almost certainly written by Mussolini, published in *Il Popolo d'Italia* on 6 October 1937. In a wartime context like that of that autumn, and referring to his own declaration in Berlin that the Europe of tomorrow would be fascist, he stressed that this was, in fact, not a matter of propaganda but of facts, of the logical progression of events. The new countries already were and, above all, many European states were marching 'along the road of Fascism, even when they assert the opposite . . . every nation will have its fascism; that is to say, a fascism adapted to the particular situation of each specific people'. There would not be 'a fascism exportable in standardised forms, but a complex of doctrines, methods, experiences, and achievements . . . which is gradually penetrating all the States of the European community'. The doctrine and atmosphere of the twentieth century would, in consequence, be fascist.

Fascism would be, in a word, a product, in the style of San Sepolcro (the square in Milan where Mussolini's *fasci di combattimento* met for the first time in 1919), of the political, institutional, and value crisis of the liberal system of the 1920s and of the birth of the socialist alternative—but not only that. It would be the response to the Great Depression and to the growth of revolutionary alternatives in the Europe of the 1930s, in the style of Nuremberg (the National Socialist city-party, which gave its name to the racial laws of 1935), in the shape of mobilisation, ultra-nationalism, palingenesis, and violence (sometimes preventive)—but not only that. It would also be the product of the internal conflicts, open and hidden, of territorial occupation and expansion by the consolidated fascist regimes, in the style of Auschwitz (the most perfect of the Nazi camps because it combined internment, slavery, and extermination), in the Europe of the 1940s—but not only that. In fact, fascism was the result of all these elements: San Sepolcro, Nuremberg, Auschwitz. And also, Madrid, Málaga, Guadalajara—places of fascist war. It would be the result of the mechanisms of integration and well-being united with violence, expulsion, cleansing, and war. It would be the result of fascistisation—precisely what the Italians wanted to do in Spain.

The Italians' behaviour in Spain was not far removed from how the Fascist troops conducted themselves in other contexts of military intervention and occupation. Fascist Italy assaulted Ethiopia in 1935 and intervened in the

Spanish war against the Republic in 1936, but in 1939 it occupied Albania, in 1940 it attacked Greece and attempted a miserable offensive against France, and in 1941 it joined Germany in the invasion of Yugoslavia and the Soviet Union. And in all these instances, although principally in the wars of occupation, the result was immense violence. War was, as in Spain and later on Italian soil itself, the favourable context, the natural and desired space, the perfect place for the development of fascisms' true political and social designs, already aimed at in peacetime but radicalised in the period of the Italian wars from 1935 to 1945.[16] Three years of war were nevertheless enough to show that the means did not exist to fulfil imperial aspirations against real and well-armed enemies. In the end, Mussolini's wars concluded with a civil war. Perhaps, it could not have been otherwise.

The Civil War in Spain was the real point of no return in the radicalisation of Fascist expansionist policies, whether justified or not by an Italian demographic problem, articulated by Mussolini and with obvious similarities to the programmes of resettlement and racial and economic hierarchical restructuring in the Europe of the Third Reich. Of course, there were obvious differences, in that the Italian mission in Spain was not one of territorial conquest and control and management of the occupation and violence. Rather, it was one of assistance, alignment, and identitarian twinning. This does not diminish its importance; on the contrary, it magnifies it. It is enough to recall that the Italian occupation army in Ethiopia, initially composed of 110,000 soldiers, comprised 330,000 by the end of the campaign, to whom nearly 90,000 native soldiers (the Ascari) and about 100,000 conscripted workers must be added.[17] In Spain, which was not a war of sovereignty and occupation intended to incorporate territory, the figure reached was 78,000. For the *sole* purpose of assistance to a friendly faction at war, Mussolini sent a quarter of the total military personnel used to conquer the Fascist Empire to Spain. The case that followed Spain, the attack on Albania in 1939, was different. Only a few months after it began, Mussolini had already engaged 30 military divisions, with more than 20,000 officers and nearly half a million non-commissioned officers and soldiers. The context was different. And, in fact, Albania marked the beginning of a series of military campaigns which, within the framework of a total and unrestrained war like the Second World War, sealed Fascist Italy's military, geostrategic, and political decline. As Rochat rightly points out, viewed in perspective these Fascist military campaigns can be seen as milestones leading to catastrophe, particularly if we consider that the fall of fascism had much to do with international politics and its almost total and exclusive transformation into a politics of war. However, in 1939, it still appeared that all the Duce's decisions on foreign affairs, including the intervention in Spain, were but an unstoppable succession of incomparable successes.

Thus, the Spanish war was not like the disastrous missions in Yugoslavia and Greece in the Second World War. But it was their immediate precedent in more than one sense. Indeed, the key names in Italian expansionism during

212   Conclusion

the world conflict are linked to Spain. Roatta had command of the Army in Croatia and was responsible for Slovenia's Italianisation and de-Balkanisation and for setting up the system of internment camps in order to, as he put it, substitute the Slovenian population with Italian nationals in the recently created province of Lubiana. Bastico, appointed governor of the Peloponnese, was the commander-in-chief of the Italian islands of the Aegean. Berti commanded the XV Army Corps on the French front and then the artillery in Italian North Africa, where Bergonzoli was taken prisoner. Gambara, who like Roatta would take refuge in Franco's Spain after the war, fought against France after leaving his post as ambassador in Spain, commanded the VIII Army Corps in Albania in the war against Greece, and took part in the war in Libya. He was subsequently the head of the XI Army Corps in Slovenia and then became Chief of the General Staff of the Italian Social Republic (*Repubblica Sociale Italiana*, RSI), the Republic of Salò, forever loyal to his Duce. Talking of loyalty, nobody compares to General Enrico Francisci. Having fought on the Eastern Front in Russia, he died in 1943 defending Sicily against the Allied occupation.

This fascist faith remained very much alive with many other veterans of the Spanish war. Ettore Muti, who died in the summer of 1943 while in detention after Mussolini's fall and had become Starace's replacement as head of the PNF, was decisive in the occupation of Albania. Junio Valerio Borghese had been the commander of the submarine *Iride* when it mistakenly attacked the *Havock*, flying the British ensign, and had come close to provoking a large-scale international conflict. Under the Italian Social Republic, he commanded the tenth MAS flotilla (torpedo-armed motorboats), the Italian Navy's famous assault group involved in the fight against the partisans on the Gothic Line. In post-war Italy, he was appointed honorary president of the *Movimento Sociale Italiano*, which he left to establish the *Fronte Nazionale*. He was, moreover, responsible for the failed extreme Right-wing coup d'état in 1970. As for Arconovaldo Bonaccorsi, he was made a prisoner of war in Africa in the Second World War. In 1950, he founded the *Associazione Nazionale Combattenti di Spagna*, guardian of the memory of fascist fighters on Spanish soil and organiser of commemorative trips to Guadalajara, Bermeo, Santander, and Zaragoza. Many of the CTV's big names are linked with the expansionist violence immediately following the Civil War, and others with managing the memory of a fascist war like the Italian war in Spain.

***

'You are the first Italians to come and ask; Italians often come, but to remember.'[18] Leonardo Sciascia heard this, or something very similar (we must always be wary of the exact wording of oral accounts), from the mouth of a local man 50 years after the Battle of Guadalajara, when he visited Brihuega, Trijueque, and Ibarra Palace with the photographer Ferdinando Scianna. It was one of the trips he made through Spain in the 1980s, visiting the sites of a Civil War which a young Sciascia must have discovered at the age of

Conclusion 213

16 through the filter of fascist propaganda. The elderly native of La Alcarria summarised in a single sentence half a century of sediment deposited by time on the Italian intervention in Spain. Little history, much memory; few questions, many mementoes—the majority are confined within the walls of the military sacrarium at Zaragoza, the remains of that Fascist Era which was to have lasted the whole century but which perished, in the case of Italy, devoured in a war both civil and of double occupation between 1943 and 1945. Of the tower's originally planned height of 83 metres, only 42.65 were built, because the budget ran out while Italy was sinking. When it was inaugurated, on 25 July 1945, it was already a problem. Stranded in time, it became an anachronism—and, finally, a historical falsehood, when in 1987 22 Italians of the International Brigades were buried next to the graves of the legionnaires.

The fascist war in Spain: 8,300 million lire; two million hand grenades; 135,000 flight hours; 105,000 rifles; 78,846 soldiers; 11,500 tons of bombs dropped from the air; 5,328 aerial attacks; 4,000 vehicles; 3,400 bodies; hundreds of widows and mothers with no sons; hundreds of victims as well, dozens of boys and girls destroyed by the 'marvellous' Legionary Air Force; 87 tons of gunpowder; 72 ships; four leaders; two nations made brothers by the blood of their fallen; a tower.

For the rest, silence.

Notes

1 For the Roman case, see the study by Emilio Gentile, *Fascismo di pietra* (Rome/Bari: Laterza, 2010).
2 The quotations from the speech by the mayor of Soria are taken from Dimas Vaquero, *Credere, Obbedire, Combattere: fascistas italianos en la Guerra Civil Española* (Zaragoza: Mira, 2009).
3 Archivo del Ministerio de Asuntos Exteriores, AB, L1059, C301–315 (hereafter AMAE).
4 Archivio Storico Ministero degli Affari Esteri, AP, b61 (hereafter ASMAE).
5 ASMAE, AP, b61.
6 Aristotle Kallis, *Fascist Ideology: Territory and Expansionism in Italy and Germany, 1922–1945* (London/New York: Routledge, 2000), 76ff., 96, and 146.
7 In 1932, Paolo Giudici pointed out that in respect of foreign policy fascism reaffirmed assumptions about expansion in the Mediterranean. See Paolo Giudici, *Storia d'Italia narrata al Popolo* (Florence: Nerbini, 1932), 841–845, quoted in Antonella Randazzo, *L'Africa del Duce: I crimini fascisti in Africa* (Varese: Arterigere, 2008).
8 Morten Heiberg, *Emperadores del Mediterráneo: Franco, Mussolini y la guerra civil española* (Barcelona: Crítica, 2004).
9 For an overall view, see MacGregor Knox, *Common Destiny: Dictatorship, Foreign Policy and War in Fascist Italy and Germany* (Cambridge: Cambridge University Press, 2009).
10 Enzo Collotti, Nicola Labanca, and Teodoro Sala, *Fascismo e politica di potenza: politica estera 1922–1939* (Milan: La Nuova Italia, 2000).
11 War, violence, and cultural analysis, which Roger Griffin calls the 'new consensus' on fascism, come from his books *The Nature of Fascism* (London: Routledge, 1993) and *Modernism and Fascism: The Sense of a New Beginning under Mussolini and Hitler* (London: Palgrave Macmillan, 2007), both useful despite some misunderstandings of the Spanish case. Pointing in the same direction but with different objectives is Aristotle Kallis with

214 *Conclusion*

his chapter 'Fascism, violence and terror', in *Terror: from Tyrannicide to Terrorism*, eds. Brett Bowden and Michael T. Davis (Brisbane: University of Queensland Press, 2008), 190–204; and, principally, his book *Genocide and Fascism: The Eliminationist Drive in Fascist Europe* (New York: Routledge, 2009).

12 This idea is taken from Ferran Gallego's prologue to the Spanish-language edition of this book, *La guerra fascista: Italia en la Guerra Civil española, 1936–1939* (Madrid: Alianza Editorial, 2016).

13 Emilio Gentile, 'The Myth of the National Regeneration in Italy: From Modernism Avant-Garde to Fascism', in *Fascist Visions: Art and Ideology in France and Italy*, eds. Matthew Affron and Mark Antliff (Princeton: Princeton University Press, 1997), 25–45.

14 Renato Farnea, 'Dalla "questione sociale" alla guerra-rivoluzione fascista', *Gerarchia*, September 1940, quoted in Emilio Gentile, *La Grande Italia: Ascesa e decline del mito della Nazione nel ventesimo secolo* (Milan: Mondadori, 1997).

15 Quoted in Salvatore Lupo, *Il Fascismo: la politica in un regime totalitario* (Rome: Donzelli, 2005), 426.

16 Kallis, *Genocide and Fascism*; Eric Goberti, *Alleati del nemico: l'occupazione in Jugoslavia (1941–1943)* (Roma/Bari: Laterza, 2013).

17 Nicola Labanca, *Oltremare: storia dell'espansione coloniale italiana* (Bologna: Il Mulino), 2002), 189.

18 Ignacio Martínez de Pisón, *Las palabras justas* (Zaragoza: Xordica, 2007), 35–39. His novel is entitled *Dientes de leche* (Barcelona: Seix Barral, 2008).

Bibliography

Archives, Libraries, and Documentary Collections

Archivio Centrale dello Stato (Rome)
Archivio Storico, Ministero degli Affari Esteri (Rome)
Archivo General Militar (Ávila)
Archivo General de la Administración (Álcala de Henares)
Archivo del Ministerio de Asuntos Exteriores (Madrid)
Archivo Municipal (Zaragoza)
Biblioteca di Storia Moderna e Contemporanea (Rome)
Biblioteca Nacional (Madrid)
Biblioteca Nazionale (Florence)
Biblioteca Nazionale Braidense (Milan)
Library of the European University Institute (Florence)
Ufficio Storico, Stato Maggiore dell'Esercito (Rome)

Published sources

Documents on German Foreign Policy 1918–1945, Series D (1937–1945), volume III. London: His Majesty's Stationery Office, 1951.
Ministero degli Affari Esteri. *I Documenti Diplomatici Italiani, Ottava serie 1935–1939*. Rome: Istituto Poligrafico e Zecca dello Stato, 2001.
Sumsel, Duilio, and Edoardo Sumsel, eds. *Opera Omnia di Benito Mussolini*, 44 volumes. Florence/Rome: La Fenice, 1951–1963, 1978–1981.

Newspapers and periodicals

Critica Fascista
El Legionario
Excelsior
Gerarchia
Il Messagero
Il Popolo d'Italia
La Domenica del Corriere

Memoirs

Albanese, Adelchi. *Nella bufera spagnola con le Camicie Nere della 'Divisione d'assalto Littorio'*. Florence: Bandettini, 1940.

216 Bibliography

Alessi, Marco. *La Spagna dalla monarchia al governo di Franco*. Milan: Istituto per gli studi di politica internazionale, 1937.

Amoroso, Gaetano. *Mortai e Lupi in Catalogna*. Turin: Rattero, 1941.

Anfuso, Filippo. *Da Palazzo Venezia al lago di Garda 1936–1945*. Bologna: Cappelli, 1957.

Angelini, Alberto. *Altre verghe per il Fascio: Un Legionario dodicenne alla guerra di Spagna*. Rome: Cooperativa Il Legionario, 1938.

Attanasio, Sandro. *Gli Italiani e la guerra di Spagna*. Milan: Mursia, 1974.

Bassi, Maurizio. *Da Cadice ai Pirenei*. Florence: Le Monnier, 1941.

Belforte, Francesco. *La guerra civile in Spagna*. Milan: ISPI, 1938.

Beltrani, Vito. *Antirussia*. Rome: Tupini, 1939.

Bernardis, Silvano. *Fino a Madrid: Diario della guerra di Spagna*. Gorizia: L. Lucchesi, 1941.

Berneri, Camillo. *Mussolini a la conquista de las Baleares y otros textos*. Madrid: La Malatesta, [1937] 2012.

Bolín, Luis. *España: los años vitales* (Madrid: Espasa Calpe, 1967). Published in English as *Spain: The Vital Years* (London: Cassell, 1967).

Bonaccorsi, Arconovaldo. 'La guerra civile spagnola'. In *La Grande Proletaria*. Rome: Centro Editoriale Nazionale, 1958.

Bonnezzi, Alessandro. *Il diario del nonno fascista*. Rome: Robin, 2006.

Campa, Gentile. *Lettere familiari dalla Spagna: di un legionario caduto nella battaglia dell'Ebro*. Florence: Rinascimento del Libro, 1939.

Cantalupo, Roberto. *Fu la Spagna. Ambasciata presso Franco. Febbraio-Aprile 1937*. Milan: Mondadori, 1948.

Ciano, Galeazzo. *Diario 1937–1943*. Edited by Renzo de Felice. Milan: Rizzoli, 2004.

Conforti, Olao. *Guadalajara: la prima sconfitta del fascismo*. Milan: Mursia, 1967.

Cordedda, Giuseppe. *Guerra di Spagna: 100/107, alzo zero*. Sassari: Chiarella, [1983] 1996.

Cursi, Antonio. *Gioventù italica legionaria e guerriera*. Velletri: G. Zampetti, 1939.

De Lorenzi, Massimo. *Teruel-Malaga 1936–1939. Un antifascista svizzero e un fascista italiano nella guerra civile di Spagna. Memorie di lotta, sofferenze, passioni*. Varese: Edizioni Arterigere, 2010.

Faldella, Emilio. *Venti mesi di guerra in Spagna (luglio 1936-febbraio 1938)*. Florence: F. Le Mannier, 1939.

Fiori, Giacomo. *Cuore di Legionario: lettere di Giacomo Fiori, caduto in Spagna*. Rome: Vittorio Ferri, 1939.

Gabrielli, Manlio. *Una guerra civile per la libertà. La Spagna degli anni 30 alla luce degli anni 60*. Rome: Volpe, 1966.

Gelli, Licio. *'Fuoco!': Cronache legionarie della insurrezione antibolscevica di Spagna*. Pistoia: Tipografia Commerciale, 1940.

Giola, Alma. *Voci di legionari feriti: Documento storico della crociata fascista in terra di Spagna*. Como: Cavelleri, 1941.

Giudici, Paolo. *Storia d'Italia narrata al popolo*. Florence: Nerbini, 1932.

Incisa, Luigi. *Spagna nazional-sindicalista*. Bologna: Cappelli, 1941.

Lajolo, Davide. *Bocche di donne e di fucili*. Osimo: Barulli, 1939.

———. *Il 'voltagabbana'*. Milan: Rizzoli, [1963] 1981.

Legionari di Roma in terra iberica. Milan: Sagdos, 1940.

Lodoli, Renzo. *Domani posso morire: Storie di arditi e fanti legionari*. Rome: Roma Fascista, 1939. New edition: *I Legionari: Spagna 1936–1939*. Rome: Ciarrapico Editore, 1989.

Martini, Enrico. *Croce e spade contro falce e martello*. Rome: n.p., 1939.

Matthey, Guido Pietro. *Legionario di Spagna*. Turin: Società Editrice Torinese, 1941.

Mortari, Curio. *Con gli insorti in Morocco e in Spagna*. Milan: Treves, 1937.

Mosca, Luigi. *Camicie nere a Guadalajara*. Naples: Partenope, 1941.

Bibliography 217

Mussolini, Benito. *La mia vita*. Milan: Biblioteca Universale Rizzoli, [1928–1930] 1999.
Odetti, Francesco. *Trenta mesi nel Tercio*. Rome: M. Carra, 1940.
Palladino, Domenico. *Terza offerta: Ricordi della guerra civile di Spagna*. Bari: Palladino Editrice, 1967.
Pelliciari, Alfonso. *Arriba España*. Turin: Studio Editoriale Torinese, 1938.
Piazzoni, Sandro. *Le Frecce Nere nella guerra di Spagna (1937–1939)*. Rome: Edizioni della Rivista Nazione Militare, 1939.
Revelli, Nuto. *La strada del davai*. Turin: Einaudi, [1966] 2010.
Rispoli, Tullio. *La Spagna dei Legionari*. Rome: Cremonese, 1942.
Santamaria, Aldo. *Operazione Spagna 1936–1939*. Rome: G. Volpe, 1965.
Santoni, Enrico. *Ali di giovinezza, ali di Vittoria: Come visse e morì Vittorio Cecherelli, medaglio d'oro: Con prefazione di Giuseppe Valle*. Florence: Vallecchi, 1939.
Segàla, Renzo. *Trincee di Spagna: Con i legionari alla difesa della civiltà*. Milan: Treves, 1939.
Serrano Suñer, Ramón. *Entre Hendaya y Gibraltar*. Barcelona: Planeta, [1947] 2011.
Sorrentino, Lamberti. *Questa Spagna: avventure di una coscienza*. N.p.: Edizoni Roma, 1939.
Sulliotti, Italo. *Europa svegliati! Scene e figure della guerra di Spagna; con illustrazioni fotografiche fuori testo*. Milan/Florence: G. Agnelli, 1938.
Volta, Sandro. *Spagna a ferro e fuoco*. Florence: Vallecchi, 1937.

Secondary sources

Acquarone, Alberto. 'La guerra di Spagna e l'opinione pubblica italiana'. *Il Cannochiale*, nos. 4–6 (April–June 1966): 3–36.
Aga Rossi, Elena. 'La politica estera e l'Impero'. In *Storia d'Italia, vol. 4, Guerre e Fascismo 1914–1943*, edited by Giovanni Sabatucci and Vittorio Vidotto, 245–303. Rome/Bari: Laterza, 1997.
Albanese, Giulia. *La marcia su Roma*. Rome/Bari: Laterza, 2006.
———. 'Comparare i fascismi: una riflessione storiografica'. *Storica* 15, nos. 43–45 (2009): 313–343.
Alberti, Santiago, and Elisenda Alberti. *Perill de bombardeig! Barcelona sota les bombes (1936–1939)*. Barcelona: Albertí, 2004.
Albonico, Aldo. 'Accenti critici di parte fascista e cattolica alla cruzada'. In *Italia y la Guerra Civil Española: Simposio celebrado en la Escuela Española de Historia y Arqueología de Roma*, 1–8. Madrid: Consejo Superior de Investigaciones Científicas (CSIC), 1986.
Alcofar Nassaes, José Luis [Infiesta, José Luis]. *CTV: Los legionarios italianos en la Guerra Civil Española 1936–1939*. Barcelona: Dopesa, 1972.
———. *La marina italiana en la guerra de España*. Barcelona: Euros, 1975.
———. *La aviación italiana en la guerra española*. Barcelona: Euros, 1976.
Alcalde, Ángel. *Los excombatientes franquistas: La cultura de guerra del fascismo español y la Delegación Nacional de Excombatientes (1936–1965)*. Zaragoza: Prensas Universitarias de Zaragoza, 2014.
Alegre, David. '"Scaricare tutta la mia rabbia": Codificación, supervivencia y fascismo en el relato de los italianos y españoles en el frente del Este (1941–1943)'. Paper presented at the *XII Congresso Internazionale di studi storici di Spagna contemporanea: Le culture politiche in Spagna e Italia secoli XIX e XX: un approccio comparato*, University of Modena and Reggio Emilia, 2012.
Alonso, Miguel. 'Camicie Nere, Camisas Azules: Una propuesta interpretativa del fascismo español a través de un estudio comparado con el caso italiano'. Paper presented at the *XII Congresso Internazionale di studi storici di Spagna contemporanea: Le culture politiche in*

218 Bibliography

Spagna e Italia secoli XIX e XX: un approccio comparato, University of Modena and Reggio Emilia, 2012.

———. "Cruzados de la civilización cristiana": algunos apuntes en torno a la relación entre fascismo y religión'. *Rúbrica Contemporánea* 3, no. 5 (2014): 133–154.

Alpert, Michael. *Aguas peligrosas: Nueva historia internacional de la Guerra Civil Española 1936–1939*. Madrid: Akal, 1998. Originally published in English as *A New International History of the Spanish Civil War*. London: Macmillan, 1994.

Arasa, Daniel. *La batalla de las ondas en la Guerra Civil Española*. Maçanet de la Selva: Gregal, 2015.

Baldissara, Luca, and Paolo Pezzino, *Il massacro: guerra ai civili a Monte Sole*. Bologna: Il Mulino, 2009.

Battini, Michele, and Paolo Pezzino. *Guerra ai civili: occupazione tedesca e politica del massacro, Toscana 1944*. Venice: Marsilio, 1997.

Bidussa, David. 'Il mito del bravo italiano'. In *Crimini di guerra: il mito del bravo italiano tra repressione del ribellismo e guerra ai civili nei territori occupati*, edited by Luigi Borgomaneri, 113–132. Milan: Guerini e Associati, 2006.

Botti, Ferruccio, and Virgilio Ilari. *Il pensiero militare italiano dal primo al secondo dopoguerra (1919–1949)*. Rome: Stato Maggiore dell'Esercito, 1985.

Bovio, Oreste. *Storia dell'Esercito Italiano (1861–2000)*. Rome: Stato Maggiore dell'Esercito, 2010.

Campo Rizo, José Miguel. 'El Mediterráneo, campo de batalla de la guerra civil española: la intervención naval italiana: una primera aproximación documental'. *Cuadernos de Historia Contemporánea*, no. 19 (1997): 55–88.

———. *La Ayuda de Mussolini a Franco en la Guerra Civil Española*. Madrid: Arco Libros, 2009.

Campos, Miguel I. 'La historiografía en torno a la internacionalización de la guerra civil española (1936–1939): el caso italiano'. *Ab Initio*, no. 3 (2011): 119–141.

Cándano, Xuan. *El Pacto de Santoña (1937): la rendición del nacionalismo vasco al fascismo*. Madrid: La Esfera de los Libros, 2006.

Carotenuto, Gennaro. *Franco e Mussolini: la guerra mondiale vista dal Mediterraneo: i diversi destini dei due dittatori*. Milan: Sperling & Kupfer, 2005.

Carrubba, Marco. 'La memoria del Cuerpo de Tropas Voluntarias en las publicaciones del régimen fascista y en las biografías de los volutarios'. In *I Encuentro de Jóvenes Investigadores en Historia Contemporánea de la Asociación de Historia Contemporánea*, edited by Óscar Aldunate León and Iván Heredia Urzáiz. Zaragoza: Prensas Universitarias de Zaragoza, 2008. Electronic resource.

Casali, Luciano. *L'opinione pubblica italiana e la guerra civile spagnola*. Madrid: Taravilla, 1984.

Casanova, Marina. 'El inicio de la guerra civil y sus repercusiones en los diplomáticos españoles acreditados ante el Quirinal y el Vaticano'. *Espacio, Tiempo y Forma*, Serie V, *Historia Contemporánea* IV (1991): 31–40.

Chueca, Ricardo. *El Fascismo en los comienzos del régimen de Franco: un estudio sobre FET-JONS*. Madrid: Centro de Investigaciones Sociológicas, 1983.

Collotti, Enzo. *Fascismo, fascismi*. Florence: Sansoni, 1989.

———, Nicola Labanca, and Teodoro Sala. *Fascismo e politica di potenza: politica estera 1922–1939*. Milan: La Nuova Italia, 2000.

Corner, Paul, ed. *Il consenso totalitario: opnione pubblica e opinone popolare sotto fascismo, nazismo e comunismo*. Rome/Bari: Lateraz, 2012.

Cortada, James W., ed. *La guerra moderna en España: informes del ejército de Estados Unidos sobre la guerra civil 1936–1939*. Barcelona: RBA, 2014.

Bibliography 219

Corti, Paola, and Alejandro Pizarroso. *Giornali contro: 'Il Legionario' e 'Il Garibaldini': la propaganda degli italiani nella guerra di Spagna.* Turin: Edizioni dell'Orso, 1993.

Coverdale, John. *La intervención fascista en la guerra civil española.* Madrid: Alianza Editorial, 1979. Originally published in English as *Italian Intervention in the Spanish Civil War.* Princeton: Princeton University Press, 1975.

Crusells, Magí. 'L'immagine cinematografica del CTV'. *Spagna Contemporanea,* no. 42 (2012): 91–111.

Cruz, Rafael. 'iLuzbel vuelve al mundo! Las imágenes de la Rusia Soviética y la acción colectiva en España'. In *Cultura y movilización en la España contemporánea,* edited by Rafael Cruz and Manuel Pérez Ledesma, 273–304. Madrid: Alianza Editorial, 1997.

Curreri, Luciano. *Mariposas de Madrid: los narradores italianos y la guerra civil española.* Zaragoza: Prensas Universitarias de Zaragoza, 2009.

De Felice, Renzo. *Mussolini il duce, vol. II, Lo stato totalitario (1936–1940).* Turin: Einaudi, 1996.

De Grazia, Victoria. *How Fascism Ruled Women: Italy 1920–1945.* Berkeley: University of California Press, 1992.

De la Granja, José Luis. *República y Guerra Civil en Euzkadi: del Pacto de San Sebastián al de Santoña.* Oñati: Instituto Vasco de Administración Pública, 1990.

De Meer, Fernando. *El Partido Nacionalista Vasco ante la guerra de España (1936–1937).* Pamplona: Ediciones de la Universidad de Navarra, 1992.

De Onaindía, Alberto. *El 'Pacto' de Santoña: antecendentes y desenlace.* Bilbao: Laiz, 1983.

Del Arco Blanco, Miguel Ángel. 'El secreto del consenso en el régimen franquista: cultura de victoria, represión y hambre'. *Ayer,* no. 76 (2009): 245–268.

Del Boca, Angelo. *Gli Italiani in Libia: dal fascismo a Gheddafi.* Rome/Bari: Laterza, 1988.

———. *I gas di Mussolini: il fascismo e la guerra di Etiopia.* Rome: Editori riuniti, 1996.

———, ed. *Le guerre coloniali del fascismo.* Rome/Bari: Laterza, 1991.

Della Volpe, Nicola. *Esercito e propaganda fra le due guerre (1919–1939).* Rome: Stato Maggiore dell'Esercito, 1992.

Di Feo, Gianluca. *Veleni di Stato.* Milan: BUR, 2009.

Di Nolfo, Ennio. *Mussolini e la politica estera italiana (1919–1933).* Padua: CEDAM, 1960.

Domínguez, Rubén. *Mussolini y la exportación de la cultura italiana a España.* Madrid: Arco Libros, 2012.

Ebner, Michael R. *Ordinary Violence in Mussolini's Italy.* Cambridge: Cambridge University Press, 2011.

Falasca-Zamponi, Simonetta. *Fascist Spectacle: The Aesthetics of Power in Mussolini's Italy.* Berkeley: University of California Press, 1997.

Fogu, Claudio. *The Historic Imaginary: Politics of History in Fascist Italy.* Toronto: University of Toronto Press, 2003.

Francone: la mirada de Mussolini en la guerra de España. Zaragoza: Gobierno de Aragón, Departamento de Educación, Cultura y Deporte, 2009.

Franzinelli, Mimmo. *Stellette, croce e fascio littorio: l'assistenza religiosa e militari, balilla e camicie nere 1919–1939.* Milan: Franco Angeli, 1995.

Fulvetti, Gianluca, and Francesca Pelini, eds. *La politica del massacro: per un atlante delle stragi naziste in Toscana.* Naples: L'ancora del Mediterraneo, 2006.

Gallego, Ferran. 'Ángeles con espadas: algunas observaciones sobre la estrategia falangista entre la Revolución de Octubre y el triunfo del Frente Popular'. In *Fascismo en España: ensayos sobre los orígenes sociales y culturales del franquismo,* edited by Ferran Gallego and Francisco Morente, 179–209. Barcelona: El Viejo Topo, 2005.

———. 'La realidad y el deseo: Ramiro Ledesma en la genealogía del franquismo'. In *Fascismo en España,* edited by Gallego and Morente, 253–447.

220 Bibliography

———. *Ramiro Ledesma Ramos y el fascismo español*. Madrid: Síntesis, 2005.

———. 'Fascismo, antifascismo y fascistización: la crisis de 1934 y la definición política del periodo de entreguerras'. In *De un Octubre a otro: revolución y fascismo en el periodo de entreguerras 1917–1934*, edited by José Luis Martín Ramos and Alejandro Andreassi, 281–354. Barcelona: El Viejo Topo, 2010.

———. *El Evangelio fascista: la formación de la cultura política del franquismo (1930–1950)*. Barcelona: Crítica, 2014.

García, Hugo. 'Historia de un mito politico: el *peligro comunista* en el discurso de las derechas españolas (1918–1936)'. *Historia Social*, no. 51 (2005): 3–20.

García Gandía, José Ramón. 'Nella bufera spagnola: los italianos y el final de la guerra civil en Aspe'. *La Serranica*, no. 52 (2016): 109–116. https://aspe.es/wp-content/uploads/2018/07/Aspe-La-Serranica-2016.pdf.

García Ruiz, José Luis. *La participación italiana en el Frente Norte: la batalla de Santander (abril-agosto 1937)*. Torrelavega: Librucos, 2015.

García Venero, Maximiliano. *Historia de la unificación (Falange y Requeté en 1937)*. Madrid: Agesa, 1970.

Garmendia, José María. 'El pacto de Santoña'. In *La Guerra Civil en el País Vasco: 50 años después*, edited by Carmelo Garitaonandía and José Luis de la Granja, 157–190. Bilbao: Universidad del País Vasco, 1986.

Gelli, Licio, and Antonio Lenoci. *Dossier Spagna: gli Italiani nella guerra civile (1936–1939)*. Bari: Giuseppe Laterza, 1995.

Gentile, Emilio. *Il culto del Littorio: la sacralizzazione della politica nell'Italia fascista*. Rome/Bari: Laterza, 1993.

———. *La Grande Italia: Ascesa e declino del mito della nazione nel ventesimo secolo*. Milan: Mondadori, 1997.

———. 'The myth of the national regeneration in Italy: From modernism avant-garde to fascism'. In *Fascist Visions: Art and Ideology in France and Italy*, edited by Matthew Affron and Mark Antliff, 25–45. Princeton: Princeton University Press, 1997.

———. *Fascismo di pietra*. Rome/Bari: Laterza, 2010.

Gibelli, Antonio. *L'ufficina della guerra: La Grande Guerra e le trasformazioni del mondo mentale*. Turin: Bollati Boringhieri, 1991.

———. *La Grande Guerra degli Italiani 1915–1918*. Milan: Sansoni, 1999.

Gil Andrés, Carlos. *Lejos del frente: La guerra civil en la Rioja Alta*. Barcelona: Crítica, 2006.

Gobetti, Eric. *Alleati del nemico: l'occupazione italiana in Jugoslavia (1941–1943)*. Rome/Bari: Laterza, 2013.

González Calleja, Eduardo. 'La violencia y sus discursos: los límites de la "fascistización" de la derecha española durante el régimen de la Segunda República'. *Ayer*, no. 71 (2008): 85–116.

Grassia, Edoardo. '"Aviazione Legionaria": il commando strategico-politico e tecnico-militare delle forze aeree italiane impiegate nel conflitto civile spagnolo'. *Diacronie*, no. 7 (2011). https://doi.org/10.4000/diacronie.3411.

———. 'Barcellona 17 e 18 marzo 1938'. *Diacronie*, no. 7 (2011). https://doi.org/10.4000/diacronie.3237.

Griffin, Roger. *The Nature of Fascism*. London: Routledge, 1993.

———. *Modernismo y fascismo: la sensación de comienzo bajo Mussolini y Hitler*. Madrid: Akal, 2010. Originally published in English as *Modernism and Fascism: The Sense of a Beginning under Mussolini and Hitler*. London: Palgrave Macmillan, 2007.

Griner, Massimiliano. *I ragazzi del '36: l'avventura dei fascisti italiani nella guerra civile spagnola*. Milan: Rizzoli, 2006.

Guderzo, Massimiliano. *Madrid e l'arte della diplomazia: l'incognita spagnola nella seconda guerra mondiale*. Florence: Manent, 1995.

Bibliography 221

Heiberg, Morten. *Emperadores* del *Mediterráneo: Franco, Mussolini y la guerra civil española.* Barcelona: Crítica, 2004.

———, and Manuel Ros Agudo. *La trama oculta de la guerra civil: los servicios secretos de Franco 1936–1945.* Barcelona: Crítica, 2006.

Howson, Gerald. *Arms for Spain: The Untold Story of the Spanish Civil War.* London: John Murray, 1998.

Isaia, Nino, and Edgardo Sogno. *Due fronti: la grande polemica sulla guerra di Spagna.* Florence: Liberal Libri, 1998.

Kallis, Aristotle. *Fascist Ideology: Territory and Expansionism in Italy and Germany 1922–1945.* London/New York: Routledge, 2000.

———. '"Fascism", "parafascism" and "fascistization": on the similarities of three conceptual categories'. *European History Quarterly* 33, no. 2 (2003): 219–249.

———. 'Fascism, violence and terror'. In *Terror: From Tyrannicide to Terrorism*, edited by Brett Bowden and Michael T. Davis, 190–204. Brisbane: University of Queensland Press, 2008).

———. *Genocide and Fascism: The Eliminationist Drive in Fascist Europe.* New York: Routledge, 2009.

Keene, Judith. *Luchando por Franco: voluntarios europeos al servicio de la España fascista, 1936–1939.* Barcelona: Salvat, 2002.

Klinkhammer, Lutz. *Stragi naziste in Italia 1943–1944.* Rome: Donzelli, 2006.

Knox, MacGregor. *Common Destiny: Dictatorship, Foreign Policy and War in Fascist Italy and Germany.* Cambridge: Cambridge University Press, 2009.

Koon, Tracy H. *Believe, Obey, Fight: Political Socialisation of Youth in Fascist Italy, 1922–1943.* Chapel Hill: Univesity of North Carolina Press, 1985.

Kramer, Alan. *Dynamic of Destruction: Culture and Mass Killing in the First World War.* Oxford: Oxford University Press, 2007.

Labanca, Nicola. 'L'internamento coloniale italiano'. In *I campi di concentramento in Italia: dall'internamento alla deportazione (1940–1945)*, edited by Constantino Di Sante, 40–67. Milan: Franco Angeli, 2001.

———. *Oltremare: Storia dell'espansione coloniale italiana.* Bologna: Il Mulino, 2002.

———. *Una guerra per l'impero: memorie della campagna d'Etiopia 1935–1936.* Bologna: Il Mulino, 2005.

———. *La guerra italiana per la Libia 1911–1931.* Bologna: Il Mulino, 2012.

Lanzardo, Liliana. *Immagine del fascismo: fotografie, storia, memorie.* Milan: Franco Angeli, 1991.

Lichtner, Giacomo. 'Italian cinema and the fascist past: tracing memory amnesia'. *Fascism*, no. 4 (2015): 25–47.

Lo Cascio, Paola. *La guerra civile spagnola: una storia del novecento.* Rome: Carocci, 2013.

———. 'La retaguardia italiana: el discurso del fascismo italiano en la guerra civil española: el caso de la narrativa y ensayística publicada en Italia entre 1937 y 1942'. *Revista Universitaria de Historia Militar*, no. 6 (2014): 87–103.

———, and Susanna Oliveira. *Imatges 1936–1939: bombes sobre Barcelona.* Girona: El Punt, 2008.

Lozano, Álvaro. *Mussolini y el fascismo italiano.* Madrid: Marcial Pons, 2012.

Lupo, Salvatore. *Il fascismo: la politica in un regime totalitario.* Rome: Donzelli, 2000.

Lyttelton, Adrian. *La conquista del potere: il fascismo dal 1919 al 1929.* Rome/Bari: Laterza, 1974. Originally published in English as *The Seizure of Power: Fascism in Italy, 1919–1929.* London: Weidenfeld & Nicolson, 1973.

———. 'The "crisis of bourgeois society" and the origins of fascism'. In *Fascist Italy and Nazi Germany: Comparisons and Contrasts*, edited by Richard Bessel, 12–22. Cambridge: Cambridge University Press, 1996.

Maldonado, José María. *Alcañiz 1938: el bombardeo olvidado.* Zaragoza: Institución Fernando El Católico, 2003.

222 *Bibliography*

———. *Aragón bajo las bombas*. Zaragoza: Gobierno de Aragón, 2020.

Mallet, Robert. *Mussolini in Ethiopia 1919–1935: The Origins of Fascist Italy's African War*. Cambridge: Cambridge University Press, 2015.

Martínez de Pisón, Ignacio. *Las palabras justas*. Zaragoza: Xordica, 2007.

———. *Dientes de leche*. Barcelona: Seix Barral, 2008.

Massot i Muntaner, Josep. *Vida i miracles del 'Conde Rossi'*. Barcelona: Publicacions de l'Abadia de Montserrat, 1988.

———. *El primer franquisme a Mallorca*. Barcelona: Publicacions de l'Abadia de Montserrat, 1996.

———. *Guerra civil i repressió a Mallorca*. Barcelona: Publicacions de l'Abadia de Montserrat, 1997.

———. *'El comte Rossi*: un fantasma a la guerra civil'. In *De la guerra i de l'exili: Mallorca, Montserrat, França, Mexic (1936–1975)*, 71–92. Barcelona: Publicacions de l'Abadia de Montserrat, 2000.

Mazzetti, Massimo. 'I contatti del governo italiano con i cospiratori militari spagnoli'. *Storia Contemporanea*, no. 6 (1979): 1181–1193.

Medas, Giulia. '*¿Quiénes fueron los voluntarios?* Identità, motivazioni, linguaggi e vissuto quotidiano dei volontari italiani nella guerra civile spagnola'. PhD. diss., Universities of Cagliari and Valencia, 2014.

Monguilot, Félix. 'El núcleo foto-cinematográfico del Istituto LUCE: un órgano de propaganda fascista en Salamanca durante la guerra civil española'. *Archivos de la Filmoteca*, no. 56 (2007): 152–171.

Monticone, Alberto. *Gli Italiani in uniforme 1915–1918: intellettuali, borghesi e disertori*. Roma/Bari: Laterza, 1972.

Moradiellos, Enrique. *El reñidero de Europa: las dimensiones internacionales de la guerra civil española*. Barcelona: Península, 2001.

———. *La guerra de España (1936–1939): estudios y controversias*. Barcelona: RBA, 2012.

Morente, Francisco. 'Hijos de un dios menor: la Falange después de José Antonio'. In *Fascismo en España*, edited by Gallego and Morente, 211–250.

———. 'Los fascismos europeos y la política educativa del franquismo'. *Historia de la Educación, Revista Universitaria*, no. 24 (2005): 179–204.

Murias, Carlos, Carlos Castañon, and José María Manrique. *Militares italianos en la guerra civil española: Italia, el fascismo y los voluntarios en el conflicto español*. Madrid: La Esfera de los Libros, 2010.

Murialdi, Paolo. *La stampa del regime fascista*. Rome/Bari: Laterza, 2008.

Navarro, Diego, and Guillermo Vicente. 'Photograpic air reconnaissance during the Spanish Civil War 1936–1939: doctrine and operations'. *War in History*, no. 20/3 (2013): 345–380.

Núñez Seixas, Xosé Manoel. *¡Fuera el invasor! Nacionalismos y movilización bélica durante la guerra civil española (1936–1939)*. Madrid: Marcial Pons, 2006.

Olaya, Francisco. *La intervención extranjera en la guerra civil*. Madrid: Madre Tierra, 1990.

Olazábal, Carlos María. *Negociaciones del PNV con Franco durante la guerra civil*. Bilbao: Fundación Popular de Estudios Vascos, 2014.

Othen, Christopher. *Franco's International Brigades: Adventurers, Fascists and Christian Crusaders in the Spanish Civil War*. London: Hurst, 2013.

Panebianco, Angelo. *La politica estera italiana: un modello interpretativo*. Bologna: Il Mulino, 1977.

Pasetti, Matteo. *Storia dei fascismi in Europa*. Bologna: Arquetipolibri, 2009.

Passerini, Luisa. *Mussolini immaginario: storia di una biografia 1915–1939*. Rome/Bari: Laterza, 1991.

Bibliography 223

Pastorelli, Pietro. 'La politica estera fascista dalla fine del conflitto etiopico alla seconda guerra mondiale'. In *L'Italia fra tedeschi e alleatti: la politica estera fascista e la seconda guerra mondiale*, edited by in Renzo de Felice, 103–114. Bologna: Il Mulino, 1973.

Pavone, Claudio. *Una guerra civile: saggio storico sull moralità nella Resistenza*. Turin: Bollari Boringhieri, 1991. Published in English as *A Civil War: A History of the Italian Resistance*. London/New York: Verso, 2013.

Payne, Stanley G. *Historia del fascismo*. Barcelona: Planeta, 1995. Published in English as *A History of Fascism 1914–1945*. Madison: University of Wisconsin Press, 1995.

Peli, Piero. *L'Italia nella Prima Guerra Mondiale 1915–1918*. Turin: Einaudi, 1968.

Peñalba-Sotorrío, Mercedes. *Falange española: historia de un fracaso (1933–1945)*. Pamplona: Ediciones de le Universidad de Navarra, 2009.

———. *Entre la boina roja y la camisa azul: la integración del carlismo en Falange Española Tradicionalista y de las JONS (1936–1942)*. Pamplona: Publicaciones del Gobierno Foral de Navarra, 2014.

Pezzino, Paolo. *Anatomia di un massacro: controversia sopra una strage nazista*. Bologna: Il Mulino, 2007.

Pizarroso, Alejandro. 'Intervención extranjera y propaganda: la propaganda exterior de las dos Españas'. *Historia y Comunicación Social*, no. 6 (2001): 63–96.

Podestà, Gian Luca. *Il mito dell'impero: economia, politica e lavoro nelle colonie italiane dell'Africa orientale 1898–1941*. Turin: Giappichelli, 2004.

———. 'Il colonialismo corporativo: politiche economiche e amministrazione coloniale nell'Africa italiana'. In *Governare l'oltremare: istituzioni, funzionari e società nel colonialismo italiano*, edited by Gianni Dore, Chiara Giorgi, Antonio M. Morone, and Massimo Zacarria, 59–70. Rome: Carocci, 2013.

Poesio, Camilla. *Reprimere le idee, abusare del potere: la Milizia e l'instaurazione del regime fascista*. Rome: Quaderni della Fondazione Luigi Salvatorelli, 2010.

———. 'La violencia en la Italia fascista: un instrumento de transformación política'. In *Políticas de la violencia: Europa siglo XX*, edited by Javier Rodrigo, 81–115. Zaragoza: Prensas Universitarias de Zaragoza, 2014.

Preston, Paul. *Franco, 'Caudillo de España'*. Barcelona: Grijalbo, 1994. Originally published in English as *Franco: A Biography*. London: HarperCollins, 1993.

———. 'La aventura española de Mussolini: del riesgo limitado a la guerra abierta'. In *La República asediada: hostilidad internacional y conflictos internos durante la guerra civil*, edited by Paul Preston, 41–70. Barcelona: Península, 1999. Originally published in English as Paul Preston and Ann L. Mackenzie, eds. *The Republic Besieged: Civil War in Spain, 1936–1939*. Edinburgh: Edinburgh University Press, 1996.

———. *La guerra civil española*. Barcelona: Debate, 2006. Originally published in English as *A Concise History of the Spanish Civil War*. London: Fontana Press, 1996.

Puppini, Marco. 'Gli italiani alla guerra civile spagnola'. In *Congreso Internacional sobre la Batalla del Ebro, vol. 1, Ponencias*, edited by Josep Sánchez Cervelló and Sebastián J. Agudo Blanco, 171–187. Tarragona: Arola, 2011.

———. 'Las difíciles cuentas con el pasado: bibliografía italiana reciente sobre la guerra civil española'. *Studia Storica. Historia Contemporanea*, no. 32 (2014): 385–399.

Quartararo, Rosaria. *Politica fascista nelle Baleari (1936–1939)*. N.p.: Cuaderni Fiap, 1977.

Randazzo, Antonella. *L'Africa del Duce: i crimini fascisti in Africa*. Varese: Arterigere, 2008.

Ranzato, Gabriele. 'La guerra de España como batalla de la 'guerra civil europea'. In *Historia, pasado y memoria en el mundo contemporáneo: VIII Congreso de Historia Local de Aragón*, edited by Pilar Salomón and Pedro Rújula. Teruel: Instituto de Estudios Turolenses, 2014.

224 Bibliography

————, Camillo Zadra, and Davide Zendri. *"In Spagna per l'idea fascista": legionari trentini nella guerra civile spagnola 1936–1939*. Rovereto: Museo Storico Italiano della Guerra, 2008.

Recalde Canals, Ignacio. *Los submarinos italianos de Mallorca y el bloqueo clandestino a la República (1936–1938)*. Mallorca: Objecto Perdido, 2011.

Rochat, Giorgio. 'La repressione della resistenza cirenaica (1922–1931)'. In Enzo Santarelli, Giorgio Rochat, Rainero Romain, and Luigi Goglia. *Omar Al-Mukhtar e la reconquista fascista della Libia*. Milan: Marzorati, 1981.

————. *Guerre italiane in Libia e in Etiopia: studi militari 1921–1939*. Paese: Pagus, 1991.

————. *Le guerre italiane 1935–2943: dall'impero d'Etiopia alla disfatta*. Turin: Einaudi, 2005.

Rodogno, Davide. *Fascism's European Empire: Italian Occupation during the Second World War*. Cambridge: Cambridge University Press, 2006.

Rodrigo, Javier. *Cautivos: campos de concentración en la España franquista 1936–1947*. Barcelona: Crítica, 2005.

————. 'Violencia y fascistización en la España sublevada'. In *España en la crisis de entreguerras: república, fascismo y guerra civil*, edited by Francisco Morente, 77–95. Madrid: Los Libros de la Catarata, 2012.

————. *Cruzada: paz, memoria: la guerra civil en sus relatos*. Granada: Comares, 2013.

————. '"A este lado de la bisturí": guerra, fascistización y cultura falangista'. In *Falange: las culturas políticas del fascismo en la España de Franco (1936–1975)*, edited by Miguel Ángel Ruiz Carnicer, 143–167. Zaragoza: Institución Fernando El Católico, 2013.

————. '"Su Majestad la Guerra": debates sobre la primera guerra mundial en el siglo XX'. *Historia y Política*, no. 32 (2014): 17–45.

————. *Políticas de violencia: Europa siglo XX*. Zaragoza: Prensas Universitarias de Zaragoza, 2014.

Rodríguez Jiménez, José Luis. *Historia de la Falange Española de las JONS*. Madrid: Alianza Editorial, 2000.

Romeo di Colloredo, Pierluigi. *Frecce Nere! Le camicie nere in Spagna 1936–1939*. Genoa: Clio, 2012.

Ropa, Rossella. 'L'Italia fascista nel conflitto spagnolo'. In *Immagini nemiche: la guerra civile spagnola e le sue rappresentazioni 1936–1939*, edited by Luca Alessandrini, 243–272. Bologna: Editrice Compositori, 1999.

Rovatti, Toni. *Leoni vegetariani: la violenza fascista durante la RSI*. Bologna: CLUEB, 2011.

Rovighi, Alberto, and Filippo Stefani. *La partecipazione italiana alla guerra civile spagnola*. Rome: Ufficio Storico dello Stato Maggiore dell'Esercito, 1992.

Santoro, Carlo Maria. *L'Italia e il Mediterraneo: questioni di politica estera*. Milan: Centro Studi e Ricerche di Politica Comparata, Università 'L. Bocconi' Angeli, 1988.

Savona, Antonio V., and Michele L. Stranieri. *Canti dell'Italia fascista (1919–1945)*. Milan: Garzanti, 1979.

Saz, Ismael. 'Antecedentes y primera ayuda material de la Italia fascista a los sublevados en España en julio de 1936'. In *Italia y la Guerra Civil Española*, 155–169.

————. *Mussolini contra la Segunda República: hostilidad, conspiraciones, intervención*. Valencia: Alfons el Magnànim, 1986.

————. 'El franquismo: ¿régimen autoritario o dictadura fascista?'. In *El Régimen de Franco (1936–1975): política y relaciones exteriores*, edited by Javier Tusell, Susana Sueiro, José Mª Marin, and Marina Casanova, vol. I, 189–201. Madrid: UNED, 1993.

————. 'Salamanca 1937: los fundamentos de un régimen'. *Revista de Extremadura*, no. 21 (1996): 81–107.

————. 'Fascism and empire: fascist Italy against republican Spain'. *Mediterranean Historical Review* 13, nos. 1–2 (1998): 116–134.

————. *España contra España: los nacionalismos franquistas*. Madrid: Marcial Pons, 2003.

Bibliography 225

———. *Fascismo y franquismo.* Valencia: PUV, 2004.

———. 'El fascismo y la guerra civil española'. In *Las caras del franquismo.* Granada: Comares, 2013.

———, and Javier Tusell. *Fascistas en España: la intervención italiana en la guerra civil a través de los telegramas de la 'Missione Militare Italiana in Spagna' (15 diciembre 1936–31 marzo 1937.* Madrid: CSIC-Escuela Española de Historia y Arqueología en Roma, 1981.

Schüler-Springorum, Stefanie. *La guerra como aventura: la Legión Condor en la guerra civil española 1936–1939.* Madrid: Alianza Editorial, 2014.

Schwartz, Fernando. *La internacionalización de la guerra civil española: julio de 1936—marzo de 1937.* Barcelona: Ariel, 1971.

Sevillano, Francisco Virgilio. *La diplomacia mundial ante la guerra española.* Madrid: Editora Nacional, 1969.

SME-Ufficio Storico. *L'esercito italiano tra la prima e la seconda guerra mondiale: novembre 1918—giugno 1940.* Rome: Stato Maggiore dell'Esercito, 1954.

———. *L'esercito italiano: dal primo tricolore al primo centenario.* Rome: Stato Maggiore dell'Esercito, 1961.

Smyth, Denis. 'Duce Diplomatico'. *The Historical Journal,* no. 21/4 (1978): 981–1000.

Solé i Sabaté, Josep Maria, and Joan Villarroya. *España en llamas: la guerra civil desde el aire.* Madrid: Temas de Hoy, 2003.

Spackman, Barbara. *Fascist Virilities: Rhetoric, Ideology and Social Fantasy in Italy.* Minneapolis: University of Minnesota Press, 1996.

Sullivan, Brian. 'Fascist Italy's involvement in the Spanish Civil War'. *Journal of Military History,* no. 59 (1995): 697–727.

Tarquini, Alessandra. *Storia della cultura fascista.* Bologna: Il Mulino, 2011.

Thomàs, Joan Maria. *Lo que fue la Falange: la Falange y los falangistas de José Antonio, Hedilla y la unificación, Franco y el fin de la Falange Española de la JONS.* Barcelona: Plaza y Janés, 1999.

———. *La Falange de Franco: fascismo y fascistización en el régimen franquista (1937–1945).* Barcelona: Plaza y Janés, 2001.

———. *El gran golpe: el 'caso Hedilla' o cómo Franco se quedó con Falange.* Barcelona: Debate, 2014.

Thompson, Doug. *State Control in Fascist Italy: Culture and Conformity, 1925–1943.* Manchester: Manchester University Press, 1991.

Torcellan, Nadia. *Gli italiani in Spagna: bibliografia della guerra civile spagnola.* Milan: Franco Angeli, 1988.

Turi, Gabriele. *Lo stato educatore: politica e intellettuali nell'Italia fascista.* Rome/Bari: Laterza, 2002.

Tusell, Javier. *Franco en la guerra civil: una biografía política.* Barcelona: Tusquets, 1991.

———, and Genoveva Queipo de Llano. *Franco y Mussolini: la política española durante la segunda guerra mundial.* Barcelona: Planeta, 1985.

Urteaga, Luis, Francesc Nadal, and José Ignacio Muro. 'La cartografía del Corpo di Truppe Volontarie, 1937–1939'. *Hispania,* LXII/1, no. 210 (2002): 283–298. https://doi.org/10.3989/hispania.2002.v62.i210.273.

Vaquero, Dimas. *Credere, Obbdeire, Combattere: fascistas italianos en la Guerra Civil Española 1936–1939.* Zaragoza: Mira, 2009.

Villarroya, Joan. *Els bombardeigs de Barcelona durant la guerra civil 1936–1939.* Barcelona: Publicacions de l'Abadia de Montserrat, 1999.

Viñas, Ángel. *La soledad de la República: el abandono de las democracias y el viraje hacia la política de Stalin.* Barcelona: Crítica, 2006.

———. *El honor de la República: entre el acoso fascista, la hostilidad británica y la política de Stalin.* Barcelona: Crítica, 2009.

226 *Bibliography*

————. 'La connivencia fascista con la sublevación y otros éxitos de la trama civil'. In *Los mitos del 18 de julio*, edited by Francisco Sánchez Pérez, 79–181. Barcelona: Crítica, 2013.

Woodley, Daniel. *Fascism and Political Theory: Critical Perspectives on Fascist Ideology*. London: Routledge, 2009.

Zani, Luciano. 'Fascismo e comunismo: rivoluzioni antagoniste'. In *Modernità totalitaria: il fascismo italiano*, edited by in Emilio Gentile, 191–228. Rome/Bari: Laterza, 2008.

Zunino, Pier Giorgio. *L'ideologia del fascismo: miti, credeze e valori nella stabilizzazione del regime*. Bologna: Il Mulino, 1995.

Websites

Academia, www.academia.edu

Archivio Luce, www.archivioluce.com/archivio

Archivo de Zaragoza, www.zaragoza.es/ciudad/usic/

Bundesarchiv, www.bundesarchiv.de/index.html.de

Museo Storico Italiano della Guerra, www.museodellaguerra.it

Index

1st *Banderas* Group 150
4th *Banderas* Group 141
4th Navarre Brigade 87
XXIII *Marzo* Division 80, 147, 182, 185, 206
XXX *Marzo* Division 80, 147, 171–172, 181–182, 185, 206

ABC 28, 131
Adrover, Father 40
Aguinaga, José María 34–35
Aguirre de Cárcer, Manuel 34
Aguirre, José Antonio 90–92
Ajuriaguerra, Juan de 92–94
Alcalá Zamora, Niceto 104
Alfieri, Dino 64, 119, 155
Alfonso XIII 28, 113
Altiso, Capuchin father 90
Álvarez del Vayo, Julio 37
Álvarez-Gendín, Sabino 157
Amba Aradam, Battle of 18
Anfuso, Filippo 28, 47, 61, 104, 107, 124, 201
Angelini, Franco 127
Ansaldo, José Antonio 22
Anschluss 170
anti-clericalism 141–142
anti-communism/anti-communist 5, 6, 17, 20, 31–32, 38, 104, 107, 120, 129, 142, 157
anti-fascism/anti-fascist 6, 19–21, 29, 52, 68, 72, 78, 104, 116–117, 129, 136, 140, 143, 170, 186
Anti-Komintern Pact 131
Aranda, Antonio 201
Army of Africa 23, 31, 33, 46
Army of the North 111, 186–187
Artetxe, Lucio de 94
Asensio, Carlos 201

Associazione Nazionale Combattenti di Spagna 212
Attanasio, Sandro 58, 162
Attolico, Bernardo 173
Augustus (Roman emperor) 19, 200
Avenol, Joseph 128
Aviazione Legionaria 2, 38–39, 62, 82, 87, 169, 178–180, 206
Axis powers 31, 47, 52, 61, 173, 182–183, 193–197
Aznar, Manuel 200

Babini, Valentino 206
Badoglio, Marshal Pietro 20
Balbo, Italo 22, 67
Baldassi, Aristide 149
Banca Commerciale 52
Banca d'Italia 52
Banca Nazionale del Lavoro 203
Barrera, General Emilio 28
Barresi, Pietro 202
Barreto, Delgado 132
Barroso, Colonel Antonio 93
Barzini, Luigi 63
Basile, Carlo 84, 120, 125, 140, 186
Basque Nationalist Party 89–94
Bastico, General Ettore 79–81, 85–96, 152, 206, 212
Battisti, Emilio 206
Beigbeder, Juan Luis 195
Belforte, Francesco 21, 143
Beltrani, Vito 120
Bergamini, Giovanni 149–150, 194, 203
Bergonzoli, General Annibale 62, 71, 74, 77–78, 83, 88, 146–147, 151, 206, 212
Berti, General Mario 79–82, 93–98, 140, 158, 170–178, 181–184, 206, 212
Biancheri, Admiral Luigi 61
Bianchi, Tranquillo 5, 64–66

228   *Index*

Bilbao, Esteban 199
Bitossi, Gervasio 206
Blackshirts *see Milizia Volontaria per la Sicurezza Nazionale*
Blomberg, General Field Marshal Werner von 173
Blum, Léon 30, 128
Bolín, Luis Antonio 27–30, 131
Bonaccorsi, Arconovaldo 4, 39–40, 48–49, 66, 99, 109, 142
Bonardi, Vittorio 42
Bonezzi, Franco 73, 143, 155, 159
Bonnet, Georges 195
Bono, Emilio de 17
Bonomi, Ruggero 33
Bordighera, meeting of Franco and Mussolini at 196
Borghese, Junio Valerio 212
Bossi, Carlo 32, 90–91, 124–125
Botella, Captain Ángel 87
Bottai, Giuseppe 19, 110
Bottarti, Tommaso 126

Calvo Sotelo, José 24, 44, 134
Camba, Julio 131
Canaris, Admiral Wilhelm 37–38, 47
Cantalupo, Roberto 6, 33–34, 51, 62–69, 77–79, 96, 107–115, 120, 124, 161–162, 193, 205
Cara al Sol 102, 128
Carabinieri 79, 100
Carlists 23, 24, 28, 113, 129, 203
Carpi, Ernesto 22
Carta del Lavoro 118–119, 205
Casares, Francisco Luis Manuel 132
Casares Quiroga, Santiago 44, 142
Cassandra, Lieutenant 148
Cassina, Roberto 138
Castaño, José del 132
CAUR *see Comitati d'Azione per la Universalità di Roma*
Cavalletti, Francesco 90–91, 115
Ceccherelli, Vittorio 144, 162
CEDA *see Confederación Española de Derechas Autónomas*
Cianetti, Tullio 113
Ciano, Galeazzo 10, 19–20, 25–29, 32–53, 61–65, 70, 76, 78, 83–89, 96–98, 103–109, 112, 118, 125, 158–160, 169, 173–184, 188–196, 200, 204–205
Ciaurriz, Doroteo 90–91
CIAUS *see Corso Italiani Adestramento Ufficiali Spagnoli*
Cicognani, Monsignor Amleto Giovanni 203
Ciluppo, Salvatore 149

Cini, Vittorio 67
Colloredo, Pierluigi Romeo 6
Comitati d'Azione per la Universalità di Roma (CAUR) 108, 189
Comunión Tradicionalista 22
Condor Legion 82, 139, 178, 185
Confederación Española de Derechas Autónomas (CEDA) 39
Confederazione Fascista dei Lavoratori della Terra 127
Conforti, Olao 68–69
Coppi, General Amerigo 71, 79, 206
Cordedda, Giuseppe 136, 158
corporatism/corporatist 26, 103, 108, 114, 118, 128, 131
Corso Italiani Adestramento Ufficiali Spagnoli (CIAUS) 83, 205
Cossío, Francisco 26, 131
Crispi, Francesco 17
Curzi, Antonio 141

Da Cunto, Major 90–92
Danzi, Guglielmo 103, 107–124, 161, 205
Dávila, Fidel 93, 153, 187, 203
Dávila, Sancho 117, 132
De Blasio, Major 50
Delgado, Francisco 87
De Peppo, Ottavio 20, 42
De Pretis, Agustino 17
De Rossi del Lion Nero, Pier Filippo 27–33, 38
Devoto, Nanni 73
Diappi, Ugo 148
Dio lo Vuole Division 62, 71–74, 79, 99, 206
Donda, Mario 148
Doria, General (codename) *see* Bastico, General Ettore

Easter Pact 180
Ebro, the Battle of the 10, 59, 169, 180–185
Eden, Anthony 39, 48, 129, 170
Egilleor, Sabin de 92
EIAR *see Ente per le Audizioni Radiophoniche*
Ente per le Audizioni Radiophoniche (EIAR) 118, 122
Errico, Marshal Francesco 42
Escolà, Delfino 123
Escudo Pass 86–88, 94
Estrada, Rafael 34–36, 44, 136
Eusa, Víctor 203

'Facetta Nera' 75
Falange 22, 29, 39, 46, 102, 105–118, 125–130, 136, 155, 193, 203; *see also FET y de las JONS*

Falange Española Tradicionalista y de las Juntas de Ofensiva Nacional Sindicalista see FET y de las JONS
Falcón, Manuel 200
Fal Conde, Manuel 23
Falconi, Lieutenant-Colonel Enzo 84
Faldella, Emilio 27, 37, 42, 50, 58–59, 62, 67–69, 74, 79, 135
Fanjul, Juan Manuel 132
Farina, Colonel Amilcare 93, 177
Farinacci, Roberto 76–77, 103, 107, 111–115, 119–123, 146, 154, 167, 196, 205
Farnea, Renato 210
fasci di combattimento see National Fascist Party (PNF)
Fasci Femminili 126
Fasci Italiani all'Estero 84, 119–120, 125, 140, 186
Fascist Foreign Movements *see Movimenti Fascisti Esteri*
Fascist Grand Council 19, 76, 113
Faupel, Wilhelm 43, 155
Favagrossa, General Carlo 79
Fedele, Sergeant Michelangelo 42
Fernández Cuesta, Raimundo 126, 132
Ferraudi, Ludovico 127
Ferretti, Admiral Giovanni 42
FET y de las JONS 103, 109, 116–117, 126–127, 132; *see also* Falange
Fiamme Nere Division 62, 71–73, 80, 171–172, 206
Final, José, Count of Mayalde 199
Flechas Mixed (Italian-Spanish) Divisions 97, 177
Fontanelli, Luigi 67
Foreign Legion (Spain) *see Tercio de Extranjeros*
Foschini, Vittorio 194
Foxá, Agustín de 114, 132, 142
Francisci Blackshirts Group (Francisci Infantry Group, Blackshirts' Francisci group) 62, 72, 80, 84, 206
Francisci, General Enrico 88, 172, 206, 212
Franco, Nicolás 49, 108–110, 114–117, 176
Frecce Azzurre Brigade 171, 206
Frecce Nere Brigade 62, 80–83, 87–89, 93, 143–145, 148, 153, 162, 171, 180, 206
Frecce Verdi Brigade 206
Frusci, General Luigi 80, 88, 206
Fuero del Trabajo 103, 118, 205
Führer *see* Hitler, Adolf

Gabrielli, Lieutenant Colonel Manlio 25
Gaetani, Livio 65, 127, 161

Gambara, General Gastone 87–88, 175, 182, 185–189, 193–197, 206, 212
Gamero del Castillo, Pedro 132
García Conde, Pedro 76
García García, Raimundo 131
García Morato, Joaquín 200
Garibaldi Brigade/*Garibaldini* 72, 194
Garibaldi, General Ezio 41–42
Garofoli, Federico 80, 151–152
Gay, Vicente 112, 129
Gelich, Ferdinando 91
Geneva Disarmament Conference 15
Gentile, Giovanni 103, 126
German-Soviet Pact (aka Molotov–Ribbentrop Pact) 196
Gernika, bombing of 12, 82–83
Gil Robles, José María 23, 116, 131
Giménez Arnau, José Antonio 131, 192, 199–200
Giménez Caballero, Ernesto 108, 114–118, 131, 189
Giola, Alma 148
'*Giovinezza*' 120, 153–154, 197
Goering, Hermann 48, 52, 61, 111, 173
Goicoechea, Antonio 22, 27–30
Gómez de la Serna, Ramón 122
Gómez Jordana, Francisco, Count of Jordana 32, 183, 190, 195
González Ruano, César 131
Grandi, Dino 17, 20
Grazzi, Umberto 24
Grillo, Consul 70
Guadalajara, the Battle of 2, 6, 16, 34, 51, 53, 59, 68–81, 84–88, 94, 98, 120–124, 137–140, 145–147, 150–158, 162, 169, 171, 180, 186–188, 206–208, 210, 212
Guarini, Filippo 42
Guassardo, General Mario 84

Halifax, Viscount 170
Hedilla, Manuel 102, 112–117
Hitler, Adolf 4, 8, 19, 32–33, 46–48, 105–106, 115, 120, 157, 167, 174, 184, 195, 197, 201
Horn, José 90

Imperial Rome *see* Roman Empire
Instituto Luce 108, 122, 125, 189
International Brigades 12, 44, 50, 69–70, 75–77, 141, 205, 213
Italian Army *see Regio Esercito*
Italian Empire (twentieth century) 15, 84, 180
Italian Military Mission in Spain *see Missione Militare Italiana in Spagna*

230 *Index*

Italian Military Sacrarium *see Sacrario Militare Italiano*
Italian Naval Mission *see Missione Navale Italiana*
Italian Navy *see Regia Marina*

Jarama, the Battle of 34, 69–70, 74
Jordana, Count of *see* Gómez Jordana, Francisco, Count of Jordana
Junta Técnica del Estado 32, 108

Kindelán, General Alfredo 190–192, 206
Kleinwort Sons & Company (London) 32

Labour Charter *see Carta del Lavoro*; *Fuero del Trabajo*
La Ferla, General Salvatore 206
Lajolo, Davide 73, 88, 135, 137–138, 140, 145–146, 149–150, 153, 159, 208
Landeta, Eduardo de 90
Lasarte, José María 90–92
Laval, Pierre 18
League of Nations 7, 18–19, 37–38, 45–46, 52, 170, 181
Lecquio, Francesco 102–103, 203
Legionary Air Force *see Aviazione Legionaria*
Leizaola, Jesús María de 90, 94
Lejeune, Commander F. B. 180
Leoni, Silvio 74
Lequerica, José Félix 199
Líster, Lieutenant-Colonel Enrique 74, 185
Littorio Division 62, 71–74, 80, 84, 87, 137, 143, 146–147, 150, 156, 171–172, 181–182, 185, 189, 206
Liuzzi, Consul General Alberto 73
Lizarza, Antonio 28
Lodoli, Renzo 140, 144–150, 158–159
Longo, Luigi 72
Lorenzo Cáceres y de Torres, Andrés de 131
Losada, Juan 131
Luca de Tena, Marquess of 28, 132
Luccardi, Giuseppe 27–30, 37, 109

Maccagnani, Roberto 153
Magaz, Admiral Antonio 35–36, 42, 47, 136
Málaga, the Battle of 2, 5, 10, 23, 27, 34, 38, 41, 45–53, 59, 62–73, 78, 84, 88–89, 111, 125, 151, 154, 158, 160–162, 169, 186, 191, 207, 210
Mancini (codename) *see* Roatta, General Mario
Manni, General Giuseppe 127

March, Juan 32, 39
Marchiandi, Ernesto 113, 118
Margottini, Carlo 39–40, 105, 109, 170
Martínez Barrio, Diego 26
Martínez de Bedoya, Javier 200
Martínez de Bujanda, Emilio 136
Martini, Enrico 143
Martini, Giuseppe 78
MAS *see Motoscafo Armato Silurante*
Maspons Anglasell, Francesc 104
Mazo, Colonel 71
Mele, Giuseppe Luciano 202
Menéndez Rubio, Tito 115
Mengotti, Carlo 132
Merry del Val, Pablo, Marquess of Quintanares 131
Miaja, General José 151
Military Information Service *see Servizio Informazioni Militare* (SIM)
Milizia see Milizia Volontaria per la Sicurezza Nazionale (MVSN)
Milizia Volontaria per la Sicurezza Nazionale (MVSN) 2, 39, 44, 48, 50–51, 62, 79–80, 84, 96, 136–138, 146–147, 149–150, 152–153, 156, 158, 169, 174–175, 185, 188, 203–208
Millán Astray, General José 107, 121, 151, 184, 199
Miquelarena, Joaquín 132
Missione Militare Italiana in Spagna (MMIS) 2, 37–39, 49, 51, 63, 66–69, 77, 107, 121–123, 159
Missione Navale Italiana (MNIE) 41
MMIS *see Missione Militare Italiana in Spagna*
Mola, General Emilio 23, 28, 30, 43, 46, 83, 111
Molinari, General Luca 73
Monasterio, General José 203
Montanari, General Carlo 198
Montaner, Francisco 36
Montes, Eugenio, Count of Rodezno 114, 122, 127, 131
Monzón, Telesforo de 90
Moreno, Admiral Francisco 188
Morenzoli, Eolo 141
Morocco 23, 27, 33, 183, 196
Mosca, Luigi 145, 148, 196
Moscardó, General José 71, 125
Motoscafo Armato Silurante (MAS) 41, 212
Movimenti Fascisti Esteri 20
Movimento Sociale Italiano 212
Munich Pact 105, 170, 183
Muro, Jesús 200

Muti, Ettore 33, 46, 152, 160, 169, 182, 212
MVSN *see Milizia Volontaria per la Sicurezza Nazionale*

Napoleon 119, 144, 156
National Association of Combatants of Spain *see Associazione Nazionale Combattenti di Spagna*
National Council of the Falange 102, 116–118, 126, 199–200
National Fascist Party (PNF) 76, 110–113, 120, 125–126, 140, 146, 172, 204–205, 212
Negrín, Juan 120, 186
Neri, Rodolfo de 136
Neurath, Baron von 46, 105
Non-Intervention Committee 37, 44, 61, 67, 182
Nulli, Lieutenant Colonel 120, 173
Nuvoloni, General Luigi 71, 206
Nyon Pact 172

Odetti, Francesco 136, 145
Olazábal, Rafael 28, 45
Onaindía, Alberto de 90–91
Orgaz, General Luis 34, 69, 78
Ortiz, Captain Palmiro 87
Ortueta, Anacleto 90

Pact of Santoña 92–94, 161
Padovani, Federico 147
Pangallo, Leone 136
Pariani, General Alberto Tancredo 97
Parlade, Jaime 29
Partido Nacionalista Vasco see Basque Nationalist Party
Partito Nazionale Fascista see National Fascist Party (PNF)
Pedrazzi, Orazio 22–27, 32
Pellicciari, Alfonso 147
Pemán, José María 127, 131, 157, 199, 200
Pemartín, Julián 200
Penne Nere Division 62, 71–73, 79, 206
Pereda, Jesuit priest 90
Perth, Lord 184
Piazzoni, Colonel Sandro 5, 81–83, 142, 180, 206
Pietromarchi, Count Luca 146
Pizzurro, Giovanni 149
PNF *see* National Fascist Party
Presutti, Major 139
Primo de Rivera, Carmen 45
Primo de Rivera, José Antonio 28, 45, 109, 119

Primo de Rivera, Miguel 45
Primo de Rivera, Pilar 118, 126–127, 183, 203
Puerto del Escudo *see* Escudo Pass
Puxana, Raimundo de 92

Quai d'Orsay 32
Queipo de Llano, General Gonzalo 43, 65, 117, 121, 125, 161, 185

Radio Milan 123
Radio Salamanca 108
Radio Verdad 122–124
Ramírez de Olano, Pantaleón 91
Regia Marina 206
Regio Esercito 2, 51
Republic of Salò 7, 145, 212
Requeté/Requetés 24, 43, 103, 107, 109, 111, 114–116; *see also* Carlists; *Comunión Tradicionalista*
Revelli, Nuto 147
Ribbentrop, Joachim von 39, 170, 173, 197
Rispoli, Tulio 116
Roatta, General Mario 25, 27, 34, 37–38, 42–50, 62–64, 66–71, 73–79, 85, 89, 91–92, 95–97, 107–108, 114, 117, 123, 204–206, 212
Roman Empire 19, 193
Rossi, Count Aldo *see* Bonaccorsi, Arconovaldo
Rossi, General Edmondo 71, 74, 79, 206
Royal Army (Italy) *see Regio Esercito*
Rubino, Michelangelo 150
Ruiz Albéniz, Vicente 131
Ruiz Alonso, Ramón 131
Russo, General 146

Sacrario Militare Italiano 8, 102, 194
Saint-Jean-de-Luz 23, 136
Sainz Rodríguez, Pedro 28, 31, 39, 103, 115, 118, 126–127
Salaverria, José María 131
Salò *see* Republic of Salò
Salvatore, Bruno 143
Sánchez del Arco, Manuel 131
Sánchez Mazas, Rafael 132
Sandri, Sandro 74, 151, 160
Sanjurjo, General José 22–23
Santamaria, Aldo 147
Santander, the Battle of 2, 78, 85–97, 141, 156, 169, 171, 175, 186, 206–208, 212
Sartriarca, Vicente 38
Savoia-Marchetti aircraft 31–33, 38, 82, 181

232 Index

Scarfiotti, Luigi 127
Sciascia, Leonardo 212
Second Republic, the 7, 16, 18–22, 30,
 104
Selassie, Emperor Haile 18
Selvi, Giovanni 122
Serna, Víctor de la 131
Serra, vice-consul 36
Serrano Suñer, Ramón 7, 31, 102–103, 108,
 118, 189, 192–194
Servizio Informazioni Militare (SIM) 15, 23,
 25–27, 42–45, 204–205
Sezione S (section of the SIM) 42
Sirombo, Carlo 42
Smyth-Piggott, Captain R. 180
Società Idrovolanti Alta Italia (SIAI) 31
Sogno, Edgardo 142
Soler de Murillo, Jaime 200
Sorrentino, Lamberti 124
Soviet Union/Soviets 20, 29–32, 37, 142–144,
 173, 191, 196, 211
Spinelli, Ettore 153
Spinetti, S. S. 122
squadrismo 105, 169
Starace, Achille 126, 146, 200
State Technical Committee *see Junta Técnica
 del Estado*
Stefani, Filippo 51
Straits of Gibraltar 20–21, 39, 143,
 194–197
Sudetenland, the (Czechoslovakia), German
 occupation of 170
Sueiro, General Álvaro 203
Suevos, Jesús 200
Suez Canal 195, 209
Sulliotti, Italo 64, 119, 125, 154

Tercio de Extranjeros 135, 169, 206
Teruzzi, General Attilio 88
Torre, Heliodoro de la 90
training courses for Spanish officers *see Corso
 Italiani Adestramento Ufficiali Spagnoli*
 (CIAUS)
Tricio, Eustaquio 151
Troncoso, Major 94
Trueta, Josep 203

Turrini, Captain Donato 97
Two Sicilies 157

Uberti, Agostino 182
Ufficio Spagna 44, 48–50, 74, 97, 125, 127,
 140, 143, 146, 203
Ufficio Stampa e Propaganda see Danzi,
 Guglielmo; *Missione Militare Italiana in
 Spagna* (MMIS)
unification decree *see FET y de las JONS*
United Kingdom 35, 173, 197

Valiño, Rafael García 201
Valle, General Giuseppe 61, 178–179
Varela, General José Enrique 46, 78
Varzi, Pietro da *see* Bergamini, Giovanni
Versailles, Treaty of 8, 17
Viana, Marquess of 28
Vigón, Jorge 209, 131
Villegas, Rafael 35–36, 96, 136
Viola di Campalto, Count 96
Vittorio Emanuele, 'King-Emperor' 18, 185
Volkman, Air Commander Hellmuth 174
Volta, Sandro 163

Wal-Wal (incident) 18
Warlimont, Lieutenant-Colonel Walter 42
War of Independence (Spain, nineteenth
 century) 156, 203
Western civilisation 61, 88
withdrawal of foreign volunteers and troops
 152, 173–176, 180–184
women's fascism *see Fasci Femminili*
Women's Section of the Falange 126

Ximénez de Sandoval, Felipe 203

Yagüe, Lieutenant Colonel and General Juan
 197
Yugoslavia 6, 20, 209, 211
Yzurdiaga, Fermín 131

Zanardo, Renato 148
Zayas, Alfonso 127
Zulueta, Luis de 36
Zunzunegui, Luis María 28